LEONHARD EMMERLING is a German art historian, curator and writer who has worked across museums and art institutions in Germany and New Zealand and taught at art academies in Auckland, Düsseldorf and Munich. He has worked with the Goethe-Institut since 2010 and has served as director of the Goethe-Institut Chicago since 2021. His recent books include *Aesthetics: What For?* and *The Art of Diremption*.

PARNAL CHIRMULEY is an associate professor at the Centre of German Studies, School of Language, Literature and Culture Studies, Jawaharlal Nehru University, New Delhi. Working between German and English, she has translated Leonhard Emmerling's *The Art of Diremption* as well as Hermann Kulke's *History of Precolonial India: Issues and Debates*.

THE GERMAN LIST

LEONHARD
EMMERLING

# Idiots

The History of the Homo Nullus

FOREWORD BY W. J. T. MITCHELL

TRANSLATED BY PARNAL CHIRMULEY

Seagull Books

LONDON NEW YORK CALCUTTA

**Seagull Books, 2026**

First published in German as *Idioten*



First published in volume form by Seagull Books, 2026

Paper ISBN 978 1 80309 655 1

Cloth ISBN 978 1 80309 626 1

**British Library Cataloguing-in-Publication Data**

A catalogue record for this book is available from the British Library

Typeset by Seagull Books, Calcutta, India

# Contents

FOREWORD

# Useful Idiocy

How can an academic, scholarly monograph be simultaneously timeless and timely? An answer is provided by this book, which traces a history of the evolution of the figure of 'the idiot' in the West, from the Greek polis to Christian Europe to psychiatric discourse to modern art to contemporary political culture. *Idiots* features a cast of thousands: heretics who become saints, outsiders who become insiders, nobles turned beggars, mad geniuses, professional fools and their gullible audiences, transgressors who become models, mountebanks who pose as shamans, avant gardes that become canonical and obsolete, perversions normalized, and liars who create new realities.

The ambitions of Leonhard Emmerling's book are correspondingly grand and modest at the same time. 'The figure of the idiot', the author notes, 'is far from playing a driving or decisive role' in human history. Until, perhaps, the present moment, when a certifiable idiot is the most powerful man on the planet. For Emmerling, however, this polemic is secondary to a treatment of the idiot as a metaphor, 'a figure of projection or reflection' that makes changes in the relations of individual and society 'legible'. The idiot (up until now) is not 'the central agent of social change' nor can he be universalized beyond Western culture. Emmerling's idiots are not funny themselves, even though they provide endless material for comedy and satire. And the author admits that writing about idiots is 'risky' because it implies that the author himself is *not* an idiot, which is patently impossible, since everyone (except the idiot) has to admit to behaving like an idiot at certain moments: 'only an idiot believes that it is always only the others who are idiots'.

Clearly, the reader of this book will have to be prepared to engage in a complex dance featuring paradoxes, contradictions, and (the philosopher's magical stone) 'dialectics'. William Blake put this doctrine even more concisely than Hegel or Marx: 'Without Contraries is No Progression'.

Emmerling's idiot as a character (as opposed to 'idiocy' as a condition) nullifies dialectical reasoning; he is a figure of pure negation, *Homo nullus*. In French psychiatric literature he is declared 'une nullité', beyond the reach of medical science.

But to say this is already getting ahead of ourselves. Emmerling does not just want to produce a timeless taxonomy of the idiot and his difference from the fool, the jester, and the mental patient. He offers a history that traces the word, the idea, and the phenomenon from the *idiōtēs* of Athenian democracy to the *idiota* of Christianity to the idiots of modern times. The Attic character is the closest Emmerling comes to a positive image of the political outsider. He 'steps onto the political podium' (p. 242) as an amateur, not a professional politician, who 'claims authenticity and the virtue of honesty of the non-professional actor', the outsider's perspective on the political scene. He is linked with Cynics like Diogenes of Sinope, who is homeless, lives in a barrel, and stands outside society to criticize it as absurd and corrupt. He may be idiosyncratic in his indifference to politics, but he understands that he exists within the political, where his withdrawal from society counts as a political statement. 'In the ideal case the *idiōtēs* was still able to oversee the totality of matters affecting the polis' (p. 243). 'Today', however, 'this is no longer possible', even as contemporary political idiocy has taken power. The useful outsider has become the destructive tyrant.

The next stage is the *idiota*, Saint Francis of Assisi serving as the canonical example. Characterized by renunciation of the world, withdrawal into contemplation, abstinence, and self-mortification, this version of the idiot appeals to a transcendence and access to another world. These 'fools for Christ' are a thorn in the side of established religion, but are assimilated within the embrace of a universal Catholic Church that finds a way to put these useless pains in the ass to work. Sebastian Brant's *Ship of Fools* and Erasmus's *Praise of Folly* perform an ironic inversion of the idiot into a necessary figure for the elaboration of social criticism.

Emmerling's history traces the way idiocy began to be medicalized as an incurable condition. With its ever-growing taxonomy of mental disorders, psychiatry banishes idiocy to the outer darkness, contrasting it with the numerous kinds of treatable madnesses, with mania, depression, and (above all) schizophrenia serving as the favoured subjects of psychiatric power. Medical science prepares the way for the modern denigration of the idiot as a personality disorder, with the psychopathic narcissist as its figurehead. At the same time, a certain idiocy is normalized, according to Emmerling, in

> the politician who ruthlessly pursues his own interests, the provincial, small-minded know-it-all to whom education means nothing, but having an opinion means everything, and who, with his smartphone in front of his nose, blurts out his views masquerading as news into the digital world incessantly.

As should be clear, the triumph of idiocy in our time demands a polemic against the triumph of fascism and authoritarianism, which deploys Lenin's famous doctrine of the 'useful idiot', who is easily influenced by propaganda, gaslighting, and disinformation. I would point here to an interesting contrast provided by the mythic practice known as 'brainwashing', which puts psychiatry to work in the form of drugs and torture to operate directly on the sensorium.

Paradoxically, then, Emmerling's massively learned treatise finds a way to put idiocy to work, to make it 'useful' in the way that Erasmus deployed the figure of the Fool, as an instrument of social criticism. It is when he turns to art criticism (my own field) that I begin to feel the sharpest pain in my own side, as I watch him deploy the figure of the idiot in a critique of a certain tradition in modern art that traces a path from Duchamp to Warhol, from Dubuffet to Beuys, gathering Dadaism, surrealism, actionism, performance art, Fluxus, and punk into a constellation of highly creative idiocy. The repetition of certain tropes springs quickly into focus: shamanism, nakedness, absurdity, nonsense, obscenity, ugliness, violence, scandal. There is regular absorption of transgressive, negative artistic gestures into a vanguard that is rewarded by the capitalist demand for novelty, with the result that the outsider artist is rapidly absorbed and commodified as an insider. Artist Maurizio Cattelan's *Comedian*, taping a banana to the gallery wall and pronouncing it a work of art that sold at auction for $5.2 million, is perhaps the latest example of the recuperation of idiotic negation by the transcendent value of money.[1] Just as Saint

---

1 This price was fetched at a Sotheby's auction in November 2024. Tim Jonze, '$5.2m for a duct-taped banana: Has the buyer of Maurizio Cattelan's artwork slipped up?', *The Guardian* (21 November 2024).

Francis's nakedness could be put to work by the Church, so Warhol's indifference to all distinctions of value could become a kind of aesthetic catharsis for the secular religion of Capital.

Despite Emmerling's insistence that his 'narrative has [ . . . ] become extremely unfunny' in our time, then, it will be very difficult for his readers to fully accept his 'painful decision' to renounce 'an in-depth study of absurd humour' in favour of a serious investigation of idiocy as an 'absolute negation' that resists all 'catharsis', much less comedy. Taken at face value, this is a very dark book. But this is a preface, or perhaps a post-face, that insists on looking behind the mask of darkness to contemplate the irrepressible humour that underlies the whole project. Is it unfair of me to reveal, for instance, that the author may well be a recovering punk rocker, whose encyclopaedic knowledge of idiotic performance goes well beyond saints and shamans to embrace a detailed account of Pussy Riot, the Sex Pistols, Lou Reed and the Velvet Underground, Iggy Pop, and the stage-diving Jim Morrison, whose band was named 'the Doors', after William Blake's proverb, 'If the Doors of perception were cleansed, everything would appear to man as it is, Infinite'. Blake's absurdly mixed metaphor (doors becoming windows to be 'cleansed') leads him directly to the fusion of vision and imprisonment in Plato's Cave: 'For man has closed himself up, till he sees all things thro' narrow chinks of his cavern'. As we know, when the philosopher returns from his vision of the world outside the cave to enlighten the prisoners he will immediately be denounced as an idiot and madman.

So I refuse to accept the mask of humourless solemnity that is betrayed by the trenchant irony, caustic satire, and dialectical gymnastics that make this book a delightful feast of learning and reasoning. Perhaps Emmerling's multilingual virtuosity is, in part, the mask of the *idiot savant* that conceals the face of a critical humanist in the tradition of Erasmus. He gets the joke, but like any skilled comedian, he knows better than to laugh at it, maintaining the deadpan countenance that shifts the catharsis of laughter and critical insight to his audience. In deadly serious times like this, comedy (along with art, science, history, and literature) is more necessary than ever.

*W. J. T. Mitchell*

# Preface to the English Translation

When the German version of this book was published in 2022, there was but a brief moment when one could hope that the figure of the idiot had lost its unsightly topicality: after four years in which vulgarity, ignorance, shameless self-centredness, and unbelievable hubris had become the norm of political performance, the world seemed to have returned to a mode that broadly corresponded to what had once been called rules-based, sensible politics. But then came Russia's war of aggression on Ukraine, the massacre in Israel on 7 October 2023 by Hamas terrorists, and finally the return to the global political stage of a criminal with a strange fondness for tanning creams. The Idiot was back, and suddenly it was once again time to pay attention, and present what follows in English translation: a history of the Idiot, from the Greek ἰδιώτης (*idiōtēs*) through the early Christian and high-medieval *idiota* to its current, obscenely evil manifestation, stripped of all religious and salvific consolation.

As a figure that necessarily led to inversion, the figure of the *idiota* was embedded in the process of a revaluation of all values under the sign of redemption: a god would be born as a child and crucified as a criminal; what degraded itself would be exalted, and what exalted itself would be degraded; the last would be first, and the first would be last; those who had been considered social scum would prove to be blessed by divine benevolence; it was the wisdom of the street that surpassed the wisdom of the libraries, and the *simplex* knew more than the *literatus*. All the inversions of ugliness into beauty, of ignorance into knowledge, of spiritual simplicity into wisdom, made sense in view of the redemption through which the ills of an ailing world would finally be corrected—through the inversion of this inversion. Secularization, however, deprived this logic of inversion of its foundation; what we observe today is the practice of a permanent inversion and revolution without a system of basic and shared convictions that is considered valid in principle and in agreement: that truth, truthfulness, and rightness should be normatively valid communicative categories that guide action and discourse. There should be agreement also on the idea that lies should be regarded as lies and criminals as criminals, that expertise is not elitist nonsense, that the selfishness of the few is incompatible with the freedom of the many, that the law should apply to all, and so on. The lack of an eschatological perspective lends the purely innerworldly process of inversion and revaluation the character of a malicious farce. While the *idiota de mente*, the spoon carver of Nicholas of Cusa, was able to attribute his talent and his ability to create out of nothingness to divine inspiration and his knowledge of the 'infinite arts', today the claim to possess the natural abilities of a genius, even though one has de facto no idea about anything, is nothing but a tasteless, undignified parody of actual expertise.[1] With the salos of early Christianity, it was not possible to decide whether the display of one's own idiocy was the spectacle of an idiot who is able to mime a wise man who is an idiot but knows how to behave like a wise man who wants to appear to be an idiot. Today, these camouflages play a decisive role in the assertion of evil as a principle of the political. For instance, if the reference to Shylock from Shakespeare's *The Merchant of Venice* (1600) is excused by the fact that one does not know that this reference is an anti-Semitic stereotype,[2] then the perfidy of the idiot—who tries to evade the accountability that this role demands of him by doubling his idiocy through its performance—is hidden behind ostensible cluelessness, which is scandalously inappropriate to the office itself: the idiot as an actor of himself. A name has now been found for such strategies: the madman strategy.[3] And even if one would do well to mistrust such classifications because their invention owes a great deal to their ease of use and their predictable media success, one cannot escape the impression that unpredictability is too harmless a characterization of

1 David Nakamura, '"Maybe I have a natural ability": Trump plays medical expert on coronavirus by second-guessing the professionals', *The Washington Post* (6 March 2020).

2 Rebecca Schneid, 'Trump Speaks Out After Using Term Widely Considered to Be Antisemitic: "Never Heard That"', *TIME* (5 July 2025). Natasha Bertrand and Zachary Cohen, 'Hegseth did not inform the White House before he authorized pause on weapon shipments to Ukraine, sources say', *CNN Politics* (8 July 2025).

3 Allan Little, 'How Trump is using the "Madman Theory" to try to change the world (and it's working)', *BBC News* (6 July 2025).

what pervades global politics. The third way beyond dialectics, which the *idiota* once hoped to be able to follow, now runs as an errant trail in the gloom of a reason doomed to destruction, which refuses any *sensus communis*, even though it perfidiously invokes 'common sense'. The obduracy of the *salos* and *idiota*, who are closed to intersubjectivity and whose opacity is softened by the light of a divine benevolence, mutates in the presence of the idiot into choleric autism, the tyranny of unpredictable whims, a ruthlessness and fickleness that owes itself to a profound narcissistic disorder: the sociopath in action.

The fact that this text confines itself to following the idiot almost exclusively in the context of the Western (more precisely, the formerly Christian) world has to do with the aforementioned fact that his story (also) turned out to be a story of secularization. The figure characterized by tipping and inversion is itself tipping, it is tipping from the light of divine grace into the darkness of unreason. However, the accompanying restriction to political figures in Washington, London, or Budapest, Brasília, Belgrade, or Bratislava does not mean that only they should be regarded as representatives of the culture of open lies, shameless self-enrichment and taking advantage, and the disregard for moral, legal, and political standards that have long been considered internationally valid. It is not only the clowns in Washington, London, and Budapest who are guilty of violating human rights and oppressing minorities, of intolerance, and of disregarding legal norms. Rulers in Riyadh, Jerusalem, and Beijing, in Pyongyang, Ankara, and New Delhi—and this alone is the difference—cannot be associated with the figure of inversion and the revaluation of values. The *idiota* and its contemporary incarnations only make sense against the backdrop of the Christian revolution and its secular end. Secularization is a phenomenon of the Western world. We cannot speak of secularization with regard to either the Indian subcontinent or the People's Republic of China, to name just two examples. There may be a dictatorial regime of injustice and a proto-fascist, populist electoral democracy; but just as little as the figure of the *idiota* has a home there, the tradition of publicly manifesting reason, ideally shared by all, accessible to all, and ideally encompassing all equally, is not to be found there. It is this specifically European form of reason whose decline we are currently observing. The figure of the ἰδιώτης and the *idiota* cannot be generalized transculturally. The semantic scope and meaningfulness of this narrative must therefore be seen as clearly limited from the outset, even if the actions of the protagonists of this narrative have global consequences.

In the introduction to the German edition, I wrote that, although all the personifications of absurd humour and laconic slapstick had come into consideration, I had not succeeded in writing a funny book, and that the figure of the idiot—unlike the clown, the comedian, or the buffoon—gave little cause for laughter, not even the opportunity to smile. That is because the idiot is deadly serious. His capers are disguises in which—under the sign of faith—the irrefutable truth of salvation, albeit in the post-religious, secularized world an unambiguous evil, is concealed. And unfortunately, there is little hope that things will get any funnier from hereafter.

*Leonhard Emmerling*

INTRODUCTION

# A History of Nullities

## I.

The following story is about a volatile and unsightly, repulsive, obdurate, and two-faced, tricky and terribly humourless character: the idiot. His story, from the *idiōtēs* of the Greek polis to the *idiota* of Christianity to the idiots of modern times, is embedded in a larger story that deals with the relationship between the individual and the masses, with the outsider and his relationship to society. In this story, as in any good drama, secondary characters such as the Fool and the Madman, the Priest and the King, appear and, like any good story, it deals with shifting fortunes, broken promises, unfulfilled ambitions, along with hope and failure.

The figure of the idiot—and his brothers, the *idiōtēs* and the *idiota*—occasionally appears when the relationships between the individual and society undergo a process of reorganization. Far from playing a decisive role in these processes of transformation, the idiot seems to run through the history of these changes as a figure of projection or reflection that makes legible the aims and intentions of those who make use of it. Thus, the *idiota*, whom we encounter in the Acts of the Apostles, in the writings of Saint Francis and Nicholas of Cusa, represents a form of social outsider who, equipped with a knowledge of the third kind, attempts to evade the social dialectic of inclusion and exclusion, affirmation and protest, and is actually able to do so, often at the cost of great abjurations. The *idiota* insists that he knows and can do something that can be learned neither from books nor from tradition, that neither the ancients nor nature teach, but of which he is aware rather by way of intuition, a flash of insight, a realization out of nothing.

This figure of the outsider, endowed with a knowledge of which traces can be found neither in libraries nor in traditions, has, since the dawn of the modern age, been increasingly framed by a medical taxonomy, which is of course also one of power.

If the locus[1] of the relationship between outsider and society is to be described with the help of the distinction between profane and sacred, between mundanity and transcendence, it falls victim to a dialectic in the course of secularization. A world that becomes completely this-worldly can no longer tolerate a third to its own dialectics. The *idiota* thus disappears behind the walls of the institution; it becomes the object of social hygiene as a social nullity, and in the twentieth century experiences phases of reactivation only in short-lived explosions as an erratic, convulsive phenomenon of antisocial revolt. Paradoxically, however, its final demise consists of its widespread renaissance as the political and social idiot who has conquered the scene since the 1980s: the politician who ruthlessly pursues his own interests, the provincial, small-minded know-it-all to whom education means nothing, but having an opinion means everything, and who, with his smartphone in front of his nose, blurts out his views, masquerading as news, into the digital world incessantly.[2] This includes the followers of influencers, hypnotized by the paradoxically intertwined mechanism of an individualized, singularized mass taste (they are themselves simultaneously protagonists and victims of a politics of the self, of fake authenticity and authentic fictionality, a cult of subjectivity that obsessively denies its origins in the attention economy). Part of the same scene is the mass of narrow-minded protesters fixated entirely on their own concerns, who trample upon the boundary between private and public, between particularity and universality,[3] by recourse to an outsider and minority status claimed at all

---

1 I borrow the term *Systempunkt* from Hans Blumenberg, *Die Legitimität der Neuzeit: Säkularisierung* (Frankfurt am Main: Suhrkamp, 2017 [1966]), p. 74 and *passim*.

2 Joseph Vogl calls this 'indifference zone' between advertising, entertainment and news *infopinion*. Joseph Vogl, *Kapital und Ressentiment: Eine kurze Theorie der Gegenwart* (Munich: C. H. Beck, 2021), pp. 143–44; Joseph Vogl, *Capital and Ressentiment: A Short Theory of the Present* (Neil Solomon trans.) (Cambridge: Polity, 2023).

3 See Hans-Georg Gadamer, *Wahrheit und Methode: Grundzüge einer philosophischen Hermeneutik* (Tübingen: Mohr Siebeck, 1999 [1960]), pp. 18–19: 'It is the general essence of human education to make oneself an all-embracing spiritual being. Whoever abandons himself to particularity is uneducated [ . . . ]. Hegel shows that such a person basically lacks the power of abstraction: he cannot look away from himself and look towards a general [ . . . ]. The sense of self of the working consciousness contains all the moments of what constitutes practical education: detachment from the immeasurable

times, no different from the supposedly marginalized victims of ubiquitous micro-aggressions who choose universities and lecture halls to perform their ever more proliferating designs of a transitory self and its assertion of rights. Each of these represents the renaissance of the *idiōtēs*, the private individual in the Greek polis who concentrates solely on his own concerns and interests, and who precedes both the *idiota* and the idiot. His return can be described as the culmination of the transformation that the systemic relationship between outsider and majority is undergoing.

The present narrative is not an encyclopaedia of the manifestations of the *idiota* and his brothers; it is not about stylizing him as the central agent of social change or as a figure of universal significance. The *idiota* does not play a role in every episode of social change, and many of the battles that the individual fights with the masses are fought without recourse to him. Nor is the relationship between the individual and society in non-Western contexts determined by parameters that differ from those of European culture, within which the figure of the idiot appears. The story told here is closely linked to phenomena that are part of the development of the Greek polis, the foundation of Christianity before and after its elevation to a state religion, and the emergence of Western human sciences, among others. In other words, this story unfolds within certain boundaries and limitations; it cannot be universalized without forcibly distorting other cultural contexts so that the *idiota* could be situated within them.[4]

---

of desire, personal need and private interest and the imposition of a general. [ . . . ] For to behave theoretically is as such already alienation, namely the imposition "to occupy oneself with something that cannot be communicated, with something alien, with something belonging to memory, remembrance and thinking". Theoretical education thus goes beyond what people know and experience directly' (translated by LE).

4 For a transcultural survey of the fool, see Beatrice K. Otto, *Fools Are Everywhere: The Court Jester around the World* (Chicago, IL: University of Chicago Press, 2001). It might be fruitful to link certain characteristics of the *idiota* (preference for a practical culture of action over written knowledge, resistance of the broad 'common' population to the dominance of an educated upper class) with the Lokayata, a school of thought in Indian philosophy known only through the writings of its opponents. See Debiprasad Chattopadhyaya, *Lokayata: A Study in Ancient Indian Materialism* (Mumbai: People's Publishing House, 1959). See also Wendy Doniger, *Against Dharma: Dissent in the Ancient Indian Sciences of Sex and Politics* (New Haven and London: Yale University Press, 2018), pp. 123–24.

Unfortunately, this narrative has also become extremely unfunny. What could have been more obvious than to give as much space as possible to slapstick, to jackassery, to the whole production of supposedly pointless brainteasers? Doesn't a genre named after the fool's clapper call for extensive treatment in this context, especially since recourse to slapstick can be found in many works of contemporary art?[5] And wouldn't an in-depth treatment of absurd humour be in order?

The reasons for the painful decision to deny the corny, the nonsensical, the staged madness, the laughter and the absurd in this story the place that these phenomena have in real life are as follows:

Firstly, the practice of the *idiota*, in contrast to that of the jester, the comedian, and the jackass performer, is not one of catharsis. The *idiota* is not concerned with temporary excess or the depiction of an inverted world, the truth of which is shown in its mimetically distorting reflection, but with the permanent, final, irrevocable reversal of everything that has been established before, an irreversible revaluation of values. Nevertheless, when telling the story of the *idiota*, tribute must be paid to the fool because of the role he plays as an intermediary figure between the *idiota* and the idiot at the beginning of the modern era in the texts of Sebastian Brant and Erasmus of Rotterdam.

Secondly, the absurdity of the *idiota's* life practice does not stem from the absence of transcendental consolation, but from the trust in a sphere

5 This is how Steve McQueen (b. 1969) re-staged the scene from Buster Keaton's 1928 silent film *Steamboat Bill, Jr.* in his short video *Deadpan* from 1997. The scene consists of the collapse of a wooden house facade in front of which the hero is standing. As the facade crashes to the ground, Keaton's and/or Steve McQueen's figure rises up unharmed at the exact spot where the opening of a window is located. Clemens von Wedemeyer (b. 1974) refers to *Big Business* by Stan Laurel and Oliver Hardy (1929) in his video of the same title, in which prison inmates from the Waldheim correctional facility take over the total destruction of the house, garden and car instead of the hapless Christmas tree sellers and their choleric customer. Artists such as Peter Land (b. 1966), Pipilotti Rist (b. 1962), Fischli & Weiss (b. 1952, resp. 1946–2012), Campbell Patterson (b. 1983), Anna and Bernhard Blume (1936–2020, resp. 1937–2012), Erwin Wurm (b. 1954), Andreas Slominski (b. 1959) or the members of the artist group Gelitin refer to reason that disavows itself in the absurdity of its logic through self-portrayals as tree-climbing Hansel and Gretel, car-whipping Amazons, free-swimmers wallowing in the Venetian cesspool or as irrational cucumbers.

of transcendence from which thinking the world is an absurd undertaking. The stoicism of the salos, the early Christian incarnation of the *idiota* in the Eastern Church who insists on his practice of public scandal, unimpressed by the merely human world, is related to the stoicism of Sisyphus. Indisputable as this may be, the difference between Sisyphus and the salos is nevertheless serious. The salos's view of the world as absurd theatre results from the certainty that he lives in the truth of the hereafter, while Sisyphus's conviction of the absurdity of existence springs from the certainty that there is only one truth of the mundane. For the one, the absurdity of this world is nothing, as it is irrelevant from the perspective of the hereafter and eternal truth; for the other, absurdity is everything, as from the point of view of the loss of transcendence, the world is all that remains. The one is lost to the world; the other embraces it with all the fraternal tenderness of which he is capable.[6] Even when transcendence has faded, the absurd behaviour of the advocates of the idiotic, the Dadaists and their successors, is a revolt of nonsense against the cruelty of rationality and against the absurdity of social madness. While it is an exclusively inner-worldly protest against social perversion, it is not the heroic perseverance in consciousness of the necessity of the absurd or even the joy that his fate once again belongs to man.[7]

## II.

At the end of this story, we find the idiot as we know him. Writing about him is a high-risk undertaking. Anyone writing about idiots claims that it is always the other who is the idiot, never the one who writes. For anyone who writes about idiots claims that he or she is not one: the idiots are always the others. And the idiot cannot know that he is one. His being fully himself blocks his view of the possibility of understanding himself as the What, the object of his own thinking, a mental operation that requires courage, education of the mind, and the realization that diremption is inevitable.

6 See Albert Camus, *Der Fremde* (Hamburg: Rowohlt, 1961 [1940]), p. 94.

7 Albert Camus, *Der Mythos des Sisyphos* (Hamburg: Rowohlt, 2000 [1942]), p. 177.

As long as the idiot is able to avoid the gesture of diremption, he is able to conceive of himself as the centre of the world he inhabits. But perhaps it is also the other way around: since he sees himself as the centre of the world, it is not necessary for him to carry out the operation of diremption. What is the point of a world outside the one that he surveys so completely in its overwhelming positivity? He does not need to recognize anything foreign as his own, his homeland.[8] His is a world that corresponds in its entirety and in all its parts to his needs, longings, and hardships. It is constructed in all its elements in such a way that it corresponds perfectly to his wishes and options at hand. His world and the one that could exist beyond its horizon have no relationship to each other, not even one of mutual exclusion. The will behind his world is his desire, and it is his desire that gives his world its own narrowness and beauty, limitation, density, and inner consistency. It is entirely singular, yet without internal difference.

At the same time, however, only an idiot believes that it is always only the other who is the idiot, as a result falling into the trap of deceitful idiocy. In his attempt at self-exemption, he assumes the attitude of a permanent know-it-all, exhibiting a strained and callow cleverness. Through a torrent of words, a stuttering display of what he knows, he tries to ward off doubts in his own understanding, to ward off the suspicion that he may have the very same feeble intellect as the idiot he tries to ridicule.[9] The goal is to be immunized against the suspicion that the writing subject is ultimately referring only to himself.

There is a difference between writing about idiocy and writing about—let us say—martial arts. While judokas can claim to understand something about judo, the idiot cannot understand anything about himself, as long as he is an idiot. There is a fundamental incompetence of the idiot for himself. He is either not an idiot if he writes, or he tries to hide the fact that he is one by writing. The idiot is always the victim of heteronomy. It is impossible for him to determine the discourse about himself, or else he is

8 Gadamer, *Wahrheit und Methode*, p. 352.

9 See Zoran Terzić, *Idiocracy: Denken und Handeln im Zeitalter des Idioten* (Zurich: Diaphanes, 2020).

denied the insight that, precisely because he believes he can discern what he thinks he is different from, he proves to be what he vehemently denies he is. In both cases, it is the discourse of the other in which he becomes entangled. At the same time, however, no one can deny having behaved like an idiot at some point, even if it was only for a moment. This moment, however brief it may have been, is enough to bring down the wall behind which one tries to hide from idiocy. No matter how hard I try, I cannot avoid the realization that I am implicated in the subject of my writing as an impure subject.

## III.

The recurring motifs of this tale about the idiot and his brothers—inversion of hierarchies, revaluation of values, rejection of written knowledge, eminence of the ordinary, indifference and *apatheia*, the preference for what is natural, the creation out of nothing—are linked to two central thematic complexes: the enigma of the creative and the rejection of the world. It is evident that these two thematic complexes are in turn linked to each other insofar as the necessity of the creative and the rejection of everything created result equally from dissatisfaction with an imperfect world. The Art Brut artist creates an idiosyncratic cosmos in the *bricolage* because the one he encounters, despite its well-orderedness, seems to him to be imperfect. Like Franz Kafka's hunger artist, he is unable to find the 'food that tastes good'.[10] His dissatisfaction with this world results from a subjectivity driven to extremes, which no longer corresponds to anything on the outside, so that all that remains is to replace the existing world with another, new one, the composition of which corresponds entirely to these subjective needs. In contrast to this, the rejection of the world by the apostles and, following them, by Saint Francis, the ascetics of the Eastern Church, and the punks is not motivated by idiosyncrasy, but correlates with a rejection of the self. The individual with his desires, needs, and wants is as irrelevant as the world, which should have come to an end long ago and whose continuation into time represents an inexplicable scandal.

10 Franz Kafka, 'Ein Hungerkünstler' (1924) in *Das Urteil und andere Erzählungen* (Hamburg: Fischer, 1954), p. 201.

If the *idiota* as an artist creates a world out of nothing, the *idiota* who empties himself of himself desires the return of the world to nothingness, the abolition of time, and the restoration of the original indifference of all that exists with regard to God.

## Creation from Nothingness

At number 122, at the end of the fictitious interview that the French painter, collector, and theorist Jean Dubuffet (1901–1985) conducted with himself and which was published shortly after his death under the title *Bâtons rompus*,[11] he mentions that he is fascinated by the idea of a *maieutic of nothingness*.[12] However, Dubuffet adds that this nothing should not be considered a real nothing, but merely a so-called nothing. As with all terms and concepts, he also tends to assume here that 'our distinction between positive and negative is a deception' and that it is therefore not possible to speak of a real nothing.

In his writings, Jean Dubuffet proves himself to be a master of a method of argumentation that he adopted from Nietzsche: he takes a concept—for instance, culture, truth, rightness, illness—and, in the second step, tears it apart as falsely founded. Then, in the third step, he claims that all concepts are only the results of a certain perspective and that thinking is in no way capable of creating concepts appropriate to reality, so that the reader, having followed the 360-degree movement of the argumentation, wonders what goal the whole effort is supposed to have achieved. As it turns out, it achieves the goal of criticizing what Dubuffet sees as a suffocating and toxic culture. Not only does he want to question the validity of certain concepts, he also wants to question the idea of concepts as such; to

---

11 Jean Dubuffet, *Bâtons rompus* (Paris: Les Éditions de Minuit, 1986). See also Jean Dubuffet, *Die Autorität des Vorhandenen: Autobiographisches*, Schriften Band IV (Andreas Franzke ed., Elke Kronjäger trans.) (Bern and Berlin: Gachnang und Springer, 1994).

12 According to Plato, Socrates used the art of maieutics as a technique to produce knowledge in dialogues with the help of questions and answers. See 'Mäeutik' in Christian Schäfer (ed.), *Platon-Lexikon: Begriffswörterbuch zu Platon und der platonischen Tradition* (Darmstadt: Wissenschaftliche Buchgesellschaft, 2013), pp. 226ff.

assert that it is not only necessary to abolish a false concept of culture, but every concept of culture.[13]

Starting from an understanding of culture as the totality of exemplary works that represent certain values of a society,[14] he attacks this concept as both sclerotic and illusory. According to Dubuffet, all terms and ideas, concepts and notions, depend on the perspective and location of the person who develops them; they are bound by perspective and change as soon as the viewer's or speaker's vantage point changes. This view, which Dubuffet also adopted from Nietzsche,[15] leads him to demand reflection on incoherence,[16] on a multiplicity of simultaneous centres,[17] a curvilinear way of thinking,[18] which is capable of operating according to the spherical or three-dimensional shape of things. It is clear that in this context Dubuffet not only focuses on the specific values that constitute the system of culture, but also on the concept of value itself. This concept must itself be abolished and replaced by predilection and momentary fascination, a sudden desire,[19] a quick and possibly temporary but intense pleasure that seeks no legitimation and needs none. Dubuffet understands his cultural critique as a critique of society, since culture and society are created from the same material: stable values, fixed concepts, unchangeable structures. At the same time, he understands society as a subcategory of culture.[20] As a result,

13 Jean Dubuffet, *Prospectus et tous les écrits suivants* (Hubert Damisch ed.), VOLS 1–2 (Paris: Gallimard, 1967), VOLS 3–4 (Paris: Gallimard, 1995).

14 Jean Dubuffet, *Wider eine vergiftende Kultur*, Schriften Band II (Andreas Franzke ed., Elke Kronjäger trans.) (Bern and Berlin: Gachnang und Springer, 1992), p. 30

15 Friedrich Nietzsche, 'Über Wahrheit und Lüge im außermoralischen Sinn' in *Kritische Studienausgabe*, 2nd EDN (KSA) (Giorgio Colli and Mazzino Montinari eds) (Munich: Deutscher Taschenbuch Verlag, 1988), VOL. 1, p. 888. See also Friedrich Nietzsche, *Nachgelassene Fragmente 1887–1889* in *Kritische Studienausgabe*, 2nd EDN (KSA) (Giorgio Colli and Mazzino Montinari eds) (Berlin: De Gruyter, 1988), VOL. 13, p. 334.

16 Jean Dubuffet, *Asphyxiante Culture* (Paris: Les Éditions de Minuit, 1986), p. 55.

17 Dubuffet, *Asphyxiante Culture*, p. 74.

18 Letter to Max Loreau (2 October 1962) in Dubuffet, *Prospectus et tous les écrits suivants*, VOL. 2, p. 368.

19 Dubuffet, *Wider eine vergiftende Kultur*, pp. 37, 68, 70.

20 Dubuffet, *Asphyxiante Culture*, pp. 108–09.

it is not a question of changing society, but rather of changing culture, since it represents the comprehensive totality that encompasses the social as a subcategory within itself. What Dubuffet calls for is work against the grain of culture, its subversion.

To illustrate what he sees as the difference between revolution and subversion, he borrows the metaphor of the hourglass from Max Loreau: revolution means turning the hourglass upside down; subversion means destroying it.[21] Consequently, it is not a matter of correcting a set of circumstances, but of abolishing the culture in which these circumstances occur. The work of art serves as an instrument of subversion. As the result of creative individuality, the work of art smuggles something previously unthinkable into the stable system of values and concepts; it represents a fact whose existence could not have been inferred from what was previously known. It is absolutely new (or it is not art). Since nothing that had ever existed pointed to this newness, since nothing that is known has paved the way for this newness, it juts out into the present as if it originated from nothingness. The 'midwifery', the *maieutic of nothingness*, is synonymous with the sudden visibility, the sudden emergence of something unthinkable, on the basis of whose existence culture will have to admit that it does not reflect the totality of everything that exists. There is something of which it knew nothing. The work of art becomes the paradigmatically new by representing something unforeseen and unforeseeable, the a-cultural, and, as such, is paradigmatically subversive.

But how does this midwifery of nothingness take place? What makes it possible? Dubuffet uses the concept of alienation in his attempt to explain it. The artist is the paradigmatically socially alienated figure, and he is not only antisocial (that would be revolutionary), but also asocial (subversive).[22] He has nothing in common with culture and society; he has no knowledge of it and has no wish to engage with it, he follows no examples or role models, and he does not want to overcome or surpass any. In the void between him and culture, there is complete silence. Intoxication, delirium, and mental illness serve as catalysts in the process of alienation. Dubuffet

21 Dubuffet, *Asphyxiante Culture*, p. 62.

22 Dubuffet, *Asphyxiante Culture*, p. 119.

plays with the double meaning of *aliénation*, which cannot be rendered in English: in French, the word means both alienation and mental illness. What the non-ill artist has to labour for laboriously comes easily to the madman: alienation as a gift, thanks to which the insane person is able to master the midwifery of nothingness without any effort. Since there is no connection whatsoever between the world in which he operates and the world in which culture has established its sclerotic regiment, he succeeds in creating that of which culture can know nothing, the absolutely new.

*Art Brut* is how Dubuffet eventually refers to this art of the absolutely new. In his view, this kind of art—in its themes, in the ways it is realized, in its choice of materials—owes its existence entirely to the intentions of its creator. This excludes two central categories of European art theory, which were used to justify art as imitation and mimesis: the exemplarity of the ancients and the exemplarity of nature. Since the culture against which Dubuffet's indignation is directed is identical to the outmoded system of established values of beauty and decorum, the ancients cannot serve him as role models. Instead, all his efforts are directed towards destroying the values they represent. The paradigm of the mimetic depiction of natural beauty, in turn, is declared null and void, given the idea that the concept of beauty is obsolete. More importantly, it is rejected with the argument that—bearing in mind the perspectival nature of all thought—there is no single world which could serve as a model. Instead, one could just as well speak of a multitude of possible worlds. The reproduction or conception of these worlds could be undertaken with the same justification as the reproduction or conception of this world which, especially under the influence of photography,[23] is mistakenly regarded as the correct one. According to Dubuffet, there is no reason to assume that other realities cannot be conceived just as justifiably as the one that has, for reasons of convention, been agreed to be true.

This in turn echoes Nietzsche, who accuses Christianity in particular of having established the real as equal to the fictitious in a series of inversions: the true turned into the false and the false into the seemingly true world, whereby he considers art as an invention and a lie as an antidote to

23 Dubuffet, *Bâtons rompus*, no. 30.

the debilitating power of nihilism. When the apparent world is claimed to be the true world, it is justified to treat fiction as being equal to truth and to expand the spectrum of possible worlds and realities, without having to specify any limits. If from one point of view the world appears to be ordered in a certain way, then from another point of view the same world proves to be incoherent or incomplete, and there is no point at which an imagining of other possible worlds would necessarily have to come to a standstill.

Related to *aliénation* is the concept of *étrangeté*, which Dubuffet occasionally uses. It denotes an extreme remoteness of the speaker's or the observer's position from all intellectual processes of culture and thus enables lucid insight: in a text on his own works, *Tables paysagées, Paysages du mental, Pierres philosophiques*,[24] he writes: 'J'ai la conviction que la vérité est étrange; c'est tout au bout de l'étrangeté qu'on a chance de trouver les clefs des choses', 'I am convinced that truth is strange; it is at the furthest reaches of strangeness that one has a chance of finding the keys to things'. And in a letter to Marcel Arland:[25] 'La vérité ne se laisse pas circonscrire, embrasser tout entière du regard. On n'en peut qu'attraper des facettes. Et encore: par lueurs. Et pas par le raisonnement, mais par d'obscures inspirations', 'Truth does not allow itself to be circumscribed, to be encompassed in its entirety by the gaze. One can only catch glimpses of facets. And even then only in flashes. Not through reasoning, but through obscure inspirations'. Dubuffet contrasts knowledge acquired by way of laborious study with knowledge comparable to a flash of lightning, knowledge akin to obscure or opaque inspirations. In the context of the critique of knowledge, employing the theory of perspectivity (borrowed from Nietzsche) and the critique of the concept of value, the view that only such sudden revelations would have relevance takes on special meaning. It completes the critique of stable values and concepts and complements the affirmation of the

24 The text was written for the exhibition at the Pierre Matisse Gallery in New York in February 1952 and translated into English in collaboration with Marcel Duchamp. Jean Dubuffet, 'Tables paysagées, paysages du mental, pierres philosophiques' in *Prospectus et tous les écrits suivants*, VOL. 2, pp. 76–82; see also p. 438n70.

25 Letter (25 June 1944) in Dubuffet, *Prospectus et tous les écrits suivants*, VOL. 2, p. 232.

sudden, momentary, incoherent, and incomplete. This view betrays the conviction that access to knowledge can be gained without the detour via learning and the acquisition of skills. Just as there is the possibility of direct creative power, there is also the possibility of direct cognition that comes to us as inspiration. It is not without significance that Dubuffet calls these inspirations, by means of which realization occurs, 'obscure', as he had for a time considered calling the art he collected *art obscure*, a suggestion that came from the painter René Auberjonois.[26] The darkness from which art springs and in which inspiration originates is the darkness that shrouds the reality that is neither visible nor relevant from the point of view of culture: it is nothingness.

Dubuffet's criticism of the way in which culture asserts its own values, concepts, and structures is often accompanied by a critique of the academic and elitist that does not shy away from strong words. For example, he accuses André Malraux of 'shitting the bed'[27] and makes fun of the academic milieu by linking sluggishness of mind with chronic constipation due to predominantly sedentary work. He knows, he says, only one face of the state, that of the police. The intention behind this can be seen, for example, in the title of a collection of texts published by Gallimard in 1973: *L'homme du commun à l'ouvrage*.[28] The 'common man at work', as Dubuffet sees himself, is the addressee of his art theory and at the same time the authority in whose name Dubuffet carries out his attacks on hierarchically structured, elitist culture. At the same time, 'l'homme du commun' is the name for the

26 Letter to René Auberjonois (28 August 1945) in Dubuffet, *Prospectus et tous les écrits suivants*, VOL. 2, p. 240.

27 Dubuffet, *Asphyxiante Culture*, p. 26.

28 The idea of the 'homme du commun' plays a major role throughout. Dubuffet's admiration for the work of Louis-Ferdinand Céline and his use of argot bear witness to this important role, as do Dubuffet's literary experiments in phonetic transcription, which he explains as an attempt to write 'like a pig'. See Jean Dubuffet, *Lettres à J.B.: Lettres à Jacques Berne (1946–1985)* (Jacques Berne ed.) (Paris: Hermann, 1991), pp. 192, 207 (1 November 1970 and 11 May 1971), regarding the text *Une clef pour toute chose* by Gérard Singer. See also Jacques Berne (ed.), *Dubuffet* (Paris: Éditions de L'Herne, 1973), pp. 389–90. On p. 207, Dubuffet writes: 'C'est incroyable ce que c'est rare, des textes écrits comme un cochon, je veux dire vraiment tout à fait comme un cochon, c'est introuvable.'

artists he collects under the label Art Brut: mineworkers like Augustin Lesage, 'Verdingbuben' (indentured child labourers) like Adolf Wölfli, governesses like Aloïse Corbaz, winegrowers like Heinrich Anton Müller, postmen like Ferdinand Cheval, or factory workers like Josef Wittlich, who become artists either by disposition, by decision, or by the onset of a mental illness that condemns them to a life in an institution. They begin to build another, fictitious world according to their own wishes, ideas, and ideals in place of the broken world that has become uninhabitable for them. Dubuffet's high esteem for the common man is linked to an estimation of the value of creativity, which, in his view, as a capacity of the individual is necessarily directed against the normativity of culture and is available to everyone as a resource. Anyone can sing or dance; it is only culture that stifles this original creativity by enforcing certain guiding principles regarding what deserves recognition as an artistic result and what should be disregarded. Dubuffet dreams of a city in which there are no spectators but only actors, of a society in which everyone shares equally in the recognition that this utopian society bestows on the results of creative activity, without distinction.[29]

*

Born in 1901 into a family of wine merchants in Le Havre, Dubuffet attended the École des Beaux-Arts in his native town at the age of fifteen. Against his father's wishes, he enrolled at the Académie Julian in Paris in 1918 and came into contact with artists such as Suzanne Valadon, Raoul Dufy, Fernand Léger, and Max Jacob, and took part in the Sunday meetings at Daniel-Henry Kahnweiler's house. Disappointed with his artistic work, he left the Académie. In 1924 he gave up all artistic endeavours for the next eight years, worked temporarily as a technical draughtsman in Buenos Aires, and finally founded a wholesale wine business in 1930, which he leased out in 1934 in order to try his hand at being an artist one more time. When the business threatened to go bankrupt in 1937, he took over the management again before finally deciding to live as an artist in 1942. In the autumn of 1944, he had his first exhibition at René Drouin's renowned

29 Dubuffet, *Asphyxiante Culture*, p. 96.

gallery, and from then on things went from strength to strength. Supported by the influential writer, editor at the Gallimard publishing house, and publisher of the *Nouvelle Revue française*, Jean Paulhan, and with the help of his school friends Raymond Queneau and Georges Limbour, he quickly gained access to the Parisian art and intellectual milieu. It was also Jean Paulhan who accompanied Dubuffet on a trip to Switzerland in 1945, where, with the help of the painter René Auberjonois, Dubuffet became acquainted with works by Aloïse Corbaz, Adolf Wölfli, and Heinrich Anton Müller in the institutions of Lausanne and Bern. Paulhan wrote the text *Guide d'un petit voyage en Suisse au mois de juillet 1945* about this trip, in which Le Corbusier and Paul Budry also took part.[30]

From then on, Dubuffet's activities as an artist, collector, and theorist were closely intertwined. In 1948, Dubuffet founded the Compagnie de l'Art Brut, whose members included André Breton, Jean Paulhan, and Charles Ratton. Works of Art Brut were acquired at a rapid pace. As early as 1948, 102 works were shown in a room set aside specifically for this purpose at the Gallimard publishing house, and in 1949 an exhibition of over 200 works by 63 artists was shown at the Drouin Gallery. Dubuffet acquired entire bodies of work, among others with the assistance of the Geneva psychiatrist Charles Ladame. In 1951, he fell out with Paulhan and Breton and dissolved the Compagnie de l'Art Brut, which now had more than 60 members. He then shipped the collection to New York, where the painter Alfonso Ossorio took it into his care and looked after it until 1962, without making it accessible to the public. Dubuffet moved to Manhattan in 1951 and gave the lecture 'Anticultural Positions' at the Arts Club in Chicago. Marcel Duchamp, whom he had met in New York (alongside Jackson Pollock, Yves Tanguy, and Clement Greenberg), helped him write it. Greenberg published a text in which he compared Dubuffet—to his disadvantage—with Pollock,[31] but at the same time considered him to be the most interesting of the French painters and the only one during the

30 Published in *Les Cahiers de la Pléiade* 1 (April 1946), pp. 197–216.

31 Clement Greenberg, 'Review of Exhibitions of Jean Dubuffet and Jackson Pollock', *The Nation* 164(5) (1 February 1947): 137.

preceding decade to have any originality,[32] an assessment with which William S. Rubin would agree a few years later.[33]

In the same year that the Collection de l'Art Brut returned to Paris (1962), Dubuffet had a solo exhibition at the Museum of Modern Art in New York. In 1964, his *Hourloupe* paintings were presented for the first time at the Palazzo Grassi in Venice, he began his *catalogue raisonné*, the *Catalogue des travaux de Jean Dubuffet*, and took part in documenta III in Kassel—his second documenta participation after 1959, followed by a third in 1968. In 1967, Dubuffet donated a considerable number of his own works to the Musée des Arts Décoratifs in Paris after the museum had shown a large Art Brut exhibition. The collection, which was housed on the Rue de Sèvres, remained closed to the public until 1976, the year the Collection de l'Art Brut opened in Lausanne, whose first long-term director was Michel Thévoz. In addition to large public commissions (*Quatre arbres* in front of the Chase Manhattan Bank, New York, 1972, the *Jardin d'émail* in Otterlo, 1973, and the *Tour aux figures* near Paris, built in 1988 according to plans from 1967), Dubuffet realized the *Closerie Falbala* and the *Cabinet logologique* in Périgny-sur-Yerres on a site he had acquired in 1969 as three-dimensional architectural variations of his *Hourloupe* technique. A year before his death on 12 May 1985, his works were exhibited in the French pavilion at the Venice Biennale.

It is obvious that the theorist of the anti-cultural and Art Brut is an extremely successful, strategically adept participant in the culture that he is so keen to condemn and against which he polemicizes in all his texts and letters. Not only does he succeed in establishing and defending the term Art Brut as a brand by threatening legal sanctions for any use that seems illegitimate to him;[34] he also succeeds in anchoring both his collection

32 See Aruna D'Souza, 'I think your work looks a lot like Dubuffet: Dubuffet and America, 1946–1962', *Oxford Art Journal* 20(2) (1997): 61–73.

33 William S. Rubin, *Dada and Surrealist Art* (New York: Harry N. Abrams, 1969), p. 409: 'Dubuffet, in my estimation the only major painter to emerge in Europe after World War II, stood outside the main trends of French art and, for many years, was far more appreciated in America than in Europe.'

34 Letter to E. de Wilde (15 August 1965) in Dubuffet, *Prospectus et tous les écrits suivants*, VOL.4, p. 560n35. See also the letter to Eric Charpentier (21 September 1965) in Dubuffet, *Prospectus et tous les écrits suivants*, VOL. 4, p. 561.

and his own work institutionally by combining an exhibition of Art Brut works with a donation of his own works, as illustrated by the Donation Dubuffet to the Musée des Arts Décoratifs in 1967. By initially winning Breton over to the Compagnie—Breton had collected outsider art earlier than he had and had drawn his attention to the work of Pascal Maisonneuve, for example[35]—only to finally snub him by throwing him out, he copied Breton's strategy of maintaining his position as the pope of surrealism over decades, albeit one that was gradually losing its lustre. Dubuffet was no different in his dealings with Jean Paulhan, whom he first ridiculed as a grand eunuch with a pseudo-episcopalian entourage on the occasion of an exhibition of Heinrich Anton Müller's works in the rooms of the *Nouvelle Revue française*,[36] before finally falling out with him when he received the Prix Littéraire de la Ville de Paris (25 March 1951).

There are other facts that illuminate the seemingly paradoxical relationship between culture and subversion in Dubuffet's practice: in 1975, Bernard Vernier-Palliez, who had recently been appointed president of Renault, revoked a commission granted to Dubuffet by his predecessor. It was a commission to design a square on the factory premises, and work had to be stopped. Dubuffet sought legal recourse through institutions of the state, of which he claimed to know only one face, the face of the police, and sued Renault.[37]

What appears to be a contradiction, which his apologists try to explain away by stylizing Dubuffet as a double agent attempting to destabilize the 'system' from within,[38] is best understood as an example of the logic that has prevailed since the middle of the nineteenth century.

35 Letter to André Breton (28 May 1948) in Dubuffet, *Prospectus et tous les écrits suivants*, VOL. 2, p. 265.

36 Letter to André Breton (29 January 1949) in Dubuffet, *Prospectus et tous les écrits suivants*, VOL. 2, p. 284.

37 See Flora Lewis, 'An Outraged Artist Battles With Renault', *New York Times* (6 May 1977), p. 23. Dubuffet won the case in the end, but renounced the right to execute the work. See also Jean Dubuffet and Claude Simon, *Correspondance, 1970–1984* (Paris: L'Échoppe, 1994), pp. 25–29.

38 See Lucienne Peiry, *Art Brut: The Origins of Outsider Art* (New York: Rizzoli, 2006), p. 8. See also Michel Thévoz, *L'art brut* (Geneva: Skira, 1975), p. 50.

Since the middle of the nineteenth century, the transgression and contestation of the concept of art and culture has been seen as the decisive characteristic of artistic practice and the discourse that accompanies it. Subversion of culture is not antagonistic to its affirmation; rather, the phenomenon of subversion is part of the logic of the dialectics of culture in its Western manifestation. To claim that Dubuffet became entangled in contradictions, whereby his life's work—both theoretical and artistic—would have to be disavowed,[39] ignores the fact that contradiction is part of the centrifugal practice of permanent transgression that characterizes the art of modernism. It no longer unfolds solely in the interplay between academy and salon, but—as one is inclined to say: necessarily—must be directed against its own concept in the process of its differentiation and diversification. The outsider is one of those figures who paradigmatically represent the process of the dialectic of transgression.

To invoke the a-cultural and savage, the uncultivated and the uncultured as an ideal in order to be able to criticize the idea of culture, belongs to a tradition that began in the middle of the eighteenth century. Its protagonists, the most prominent of whom is Jean-Jacques Rousseau, tended to pit nature against culture, the wild against the civilized, the raw against the cooked, the authentic against the artificial.[40] What is being negotiated in this dialectic, which contrasts the loss of what has been authentic with the result of this loss, the corrupted present, is the question of whether the world we inhabit is to be understood as the best of all worlds, or whether it must be understood as the result of blind coincidence, if not the product of a flawed creative force. Dubuffet repeatedly draws parallels between the position of Art Brut and savageness and freedom as synonyms of the state of nature.[41] This is the state of an original perfection that encompasses not only nature, but also man as a natural being. It is the sin of culture to have

---

39 See Antonia Dapena-Tretter, 'Jean Dubuffet & Art Brut: The Creation of an Avant-Garde Identity', *Platform* 11 (Autumn 2017): 12–33.

40 See Jean-Jacques Rousseau, *Abhandlung von dem Ursprung der Ungleichheit unter den Menschen* (Ursula Goldmann ed.) (Weimar: Böhlaus Nachfolger, 2000 [1765]), p. 21. Claude Lévi-Strauss also operates with these opposites in *Le cru et le cuit* (Mythologiques, VOL. 1) (Paris: Plon, 1964).

41 For example, Dubuffet, *Asphyxiante Culture*, p. 92.

alienated man from this state of nature, and it is the sin of culture-creating man to have acquired this culture as second nature instead of the first and true one. The fight against culture serves to regain the original perfection of the world and thus also to regain man's position in this well-ordered world.

In Dubuffet's thinking, the figure who represents this position of reconciliation after restoring the established orderliness of the world and finding a home in this world (and therefore not in society) is the outsider. In many cases, this outsider is the mentally ill, the *aliéné*, but Dubuffet insists that there is as little an art of the mentally ill as there is an art of the dyspeptic.[42] Mental illness facilitates alienation, no more and no less. What he thus rejects is the idea that mental illness has a reasonable place in the medical system, and at the same time he rejects the differentiation between somatic and mental illness. It is logical that, in rejecting the concept of mental illness, he also rejects the concept of *art psychopathologique*,[43] which opens up the possibility of placing himself outside the tradition of doctors such as Hans Prinzhorn and Walter Morgenthaler or artists such as Max Ernst or André Breton. Prinzhorn and Morgenthaler attempted to counter society's ignorance of the creations of artists interned as mentally ill with an appreciation that did not shy away from comparisons with Grünewald, and artists like Ernst and Breton saw in the artworks of the internees formulations and procedures that could serve as models for their own practice.

The new and unknown that Dubuffet finds in ideal form in the works of the mentally ill replaces for him what the works of non-European artists had been for the protagonists of cubism or German expressionism: works that were formally unusual and were therefore (mis)understood as innovative; something alien was misinterpreted as expressions of a wild, noble

42 Jean Dubuffet, 'L'art brut préféré aux arts culturels' in *Prospectus et tous les écrits suivants*, VOL. 1, p. 202.

43 The term *art psychopathologique* was coined in 1950 on the occasion of the *Exposition internationale d'Art psychopathologique* at the Clinique Ste Anne. See Robert Volmat, *L'art psychopathologique* (Paris: Presses Universitaires de France, 1956). Dubuffet had loaned 18 drawings, but distanced himself from Volmat's objectives. See also Dubuffet, *Prospectus et tous les écrits suivants*, VOL. 2, pp. 512–13.

humanity free of the burden of civilization. What distinguishes Dubuffet's outsider is that he is to be found in the middle of Europe and not on the islands of the Pacific or in the heart of Africa. He lives invisibly in the midst of the culture that overlooks and ignores him, in a state of social non-being, as a part without a share.[44] Although he lives in a state of social exclusion and disadvantage, of internment and suffering, construing him as reconciled to the world allows for the assumption that it is culture that has alienated man from his originally harmonious position in the world, that it therefore requires an inversion of this alienation, an alienation from the world or a second-order alienation, so that it may evoke a state that at least reminds us of one that was lost. The mentally ill person as the ideal figure of the outsider stands outside the struggles of culture and anti-culture; he is the a-cultural, the third instance, that cannot be grasped by any dialectic, the nothing that exists within the invisible and works within this invisible.

In many passages in his texts, however, Dubuffet attempts to make it clear that the figure of the *aliéné*, the *homme du commun*, or the art of Art Brut are to be understood merely as ideal poles or regulative ideas,[45] whose heuristic value is nevertheless not diminished by the fact that what they denote cannot be found in pure form. Even if they are only understood as projections back into a state of nature that never existed, as a backdrop or point of contrast they make it possible to give contour and sharpness to the critique of culture. Dubuffet thus concedes that the poles he needs in order to be able to criticize culture are in relation to one another, and that these relations can be of a different kind. Their intensity results from the degree of reciprocal influence and interpenetration. They are not juxtaposed as stable positions outside time, but influence each other mutually and thus have changing semantics. To speak of a *maieutic of nothingness* and to restrict this in the same breath in the sense that one can only speak of a 'so-called' nothingness is not merely a consequence of perspectivism. Rather, this so-called nothingness is also the result of its transformation

44 Jacques Rancière, *Der Hass der Demokratie* (Berlin: Matthes & Seitz, 2011), pp. 44ff.

45 Dubuffet, *Bâtons rompus*, no. 99. Dubuffet, *Wider eine vergiftende Kultur*, pp. 91–92.

in the course of historical development. For what appears to be nothing was only declared as such in the course of cultural evolution. It was either made invisible by being declared nature or it was—as cultural production—made invisible by being reduced to a nullity, to nothingness, to worthless junk. What appears as nothingness is the sediment of the cultural, covered by layers of time, sunk to a fathomless bottom; wrecked pieces of the cultural that have become unrecognizable, translated back into the natural or consigned to heedlessness as garbage.

The *aliéné* now succeeds where the cultivated artist must fail: he is able to construct a world from these ruinous remnants which, as a non-intentional counter-world to that of culture, preserves the memory of the lost state of nature. While the cultivated artist denies the contingency of his historical as well as his artistic and cognitive position due to his mistaken belief that there is a consistency and logical coherence to his thinking and an inner continuity in the course of historical evolution, the *aliéné* fully surrenders to this contingency. Since, on the one hand, the state of nature can only be imagined as a corrupted residue of culture that has become worthless and, on the other hand, culture has no normative function, all original creation, which could actually be a mimetic re-creation of the world in its authentic form, is impossible. The fragmented ideal world, undetectable under the rubble and remnants of culture, can no longer be reconstructed, and what incentive for its mimetic repetition should a world be that is to be rejected in its entirety as the production of suffocating culture?[46] Neither a creation based on the ancients, as demanded by classicist aesthetics,[47] nor a creation that attempts to recreate nature's well-orderedness by imitating it is possible. Only a creation that attempts to create a different world from the existing remains is possible. This technique of *bricolage*, which Lévi-Strauss associates with Art Brut,[48] replaces both the

46 On the topos of the state of nature and its functionalization in Rousseau's critique of culture, see Iring Fetscher, *Rousseaus politische Philosophie* (Frankfurt am Main: Suhrkamp, 1988 [1960]), pp. 20–48.

47 Johann Joachim Winckelmann, *Gedanken über die Nachahmung der griechischen Werke in der Malerey und Bildhauerkunst*, 2nd EDN (Dresden and Leipzig: Walther, 1756), p. 16 and *passim*.

48 Claude Lévi-Strauss, *La pensée sauvage* (Paris: Plon, 1962), p. 26: 'Comme le

technique of *imitatio* and that of *inventio* from the classical concept of creation, which was associated with the figure of the *alter deus*.[49] God is now opposed by a figure of lesser dignity, the *demiurge*, whom Christianity falsely identified with the biblical Creator God.[50] However, he is not a creator, but a craftsman,[51] and he is, if not the evil god of Marcion, at least a figure of subordinate dignity and low ability who stands between the evil and the alien god.[52]

The artist of Art Brut as the *homme du commun* has more in common with the demiurge, the engineer and technician, the tinkerer and hobbyist than with the god-like genius artist of the Renaissance and Classicism. He is driven by the desire to build a new world out of the remnants of a world poisoned by culture that corresponds to his dreams, no matter how clumsily it is assembled, screwed together at an angle, and nailed together crookedly.

*

---

bricolage sur le plan technique, la réflexion mythique peut atteindre, sur le plan intellectuel, des résultats brillants et imprévus. Réciproquement, on a souvent noté le caractère mythopoétique du bricolage: que ce soit sur le plan de l'art, dit "brut" ou "naïf"; dans l'architecture fantastique de la villa du facteur Cheval, dans celles des décors de Georges Méliès.'

49 See Julius Caesar Scaliger, *Poetices libri septem* (Lyon: Antonium Vincentium, 1561), critical edition by August Buck (Stuttgart: Friedrich Frommann, 1964), 1.2, p. 3A. See also Thomas Leinkauf, 'Der Begriff des Schönen im 15. und 16. Jahrhundert' in Heinrich F. Plett (ed.), *Renaissance-Poetik / Renaissance Poetics* (Berlin and New York: De Gruyter, 1994), pp. 53–74; here, p. 72. See Ernst Kris and Otto Kurz, *Die Legende vom Künstler* (Frankfurt am Main: Suhrkamp, 1980 [1934]), pp. 64ff.

50 See Hans Blumenberg, 'Nachahmung der Natur—Zur Vorgeschichte der Idee des schöpferischen Menschen' (1957) in *Wirklichkeiten, in denen wir leben* (Stuttgart: Reclam, 1981), pp. 55–103; here, pp. 68–69.

51 Kurt Rudolph, *Die Gnosis: Wesen und Geschichte einer spätantiken Religion* (Göttingen: Vandenhoeck & Ruprecht, 1994), p. 70.

52 See Adolf von Harnack, *Marcion: Das Evangelium vom fremden Gott* (Leipzig: J. C. Hinrichs, 1924), pp. 89, 169. See also E. M. Cioran, 'Der böse Demiurg' (1969) in *Die verfehlte Schöpfung* (Frankfurt am Main: Suhrkamp, 1979), pp. 7–20; here, p. 12. See also Gerhard May, *Creatio ex Nihilo: The Doctrine of 'Creation out of Nothing' in Early Christian Thought* (A. S. Worrall trans.) (London and New York: Bloomsbury, 2004 [1978]), pp. 53–61.

Dubuffet removes the Art Brut artist and *aliéné* from the grasp of medical systematics and places him in a landscape of the a-cultural, where he is both the most ordinary and the most unusual, the Everyman and at the same time the only and radically Me-Man. This solitary figure, who is like everyone else, who is more craftsman than genius, and yet at the same time the inventor of an unknown third way beyond *imitatio* and *inventio*, shares some characteristics with the figure of the *idiota* of Nicholas of Cusa (1401–1464). In his *Idiota* dialogues of 1450, the figure of the layman (*idiota*) confronts the figure of the scholar and philosopher and engages in a conversation that forces the scribe to admit that his book and school knowledge is inferior to the intuitive knowledge of the spoon carver. For it is as such that the layman appears in the dialogue *Idiota de mente*:

> The layman took a spoon and said: 'The spoon has no archetype other than the idea created by our mind. For even if a sculptor or a painter takes the prototypes of the things he endeavours to recreate, I do not do so, for I create spoons and bowls and pots out of wood and clay. I am not imitating the shape of any natural object. Such forms of spoons, bowls, and pots can only be created by human art. Therefore, my art consists more in creation than in the imitation of creaturely forms, and in this it is more similar to infinite art'.[53]

The art of the spoon carver differs from the art of painters and sculptors in that it does not imitate cultural models. At the same time, his work is not an imitation of nature, as his creations owe themselves solely to his creative power, to the idea created or arising exclusively in his mind. The fact that they exist can be derived neither from a Platonic archetype nor from a model found in nature; they are neither re-creations in their essence nor re-creations in their appearance. His works cannot be derived or foreseen in any respect; they enter the realm of the existing only through the creative process, the carver's creative activity. This is more of a creation (*magis perfectoria*) than an imitation, and in this it is superior to the art of

53 Nikolaus von Kues, *Idiota de mente / Der Laie über den Geist* (Renate Steiger ed.) (*Schriften des Nikolaus von Kues in deutscher Übersetzung*, Heft 21; lateinisch-deutsche Parallelausgabe) (Hamburg: Meiner, 1995), nos 61–63, pp. 14–15.

painters and sculptors. For his method of creating is most similar to 'infinite art'. According to the spoon carver, this infinite art derives from absolute eternity:

> It is therefore only absolute eternity that is infinity itself, which is without origin. Therefore, everything finite is produced by the infinite origin. [ . . . ] Every finite art therefore originates from the infinite art. And so infinite art will necessarily be the archetype of all art, the origin, centre, goal, unit of measurement, measure, truth, accuracy, and perfection.[54]

All archetypes and models, whether ideas or formations of nature, are finite because they are forms; all art that is dedicated to imitating them is a finite art that derives from the finite and is therefore of a lower rank. Only the art of the spoon carver is derived from the infinite and is therefore of incomparably higher dignity. But 'the infinite no mind can reach. Therefore [it] becomes inexpressible, ungraspable, if one uses names attached to the movement of the mind. [ . . . ] So there is only one ineffable word, which is the exact name of all things'.[55] The ineffable word is, of course, the name of God, and it was the prerogative of God to endow man with a spirit so that he possesses the art of creating himself in equal measure: 'Therefore, everything that is contained in absolute art in full truth is contained in our spirit as the true image. Therefore, the spirit is created by the art of creation, as if art wanted to create itself'.[56] In contrast to the art of mimesis or imitation (imitating nature or the ancients), the art of the spoon carver is not to be understood as the skill of simply producing forms. Rather, it is the true imitation and realization of the creative power of God himself.[57]

---

54 Nikolaus von Kues, *Der Laie über den Geist*, pp. 14–15.

55 Nikolaus von Kues, *Der Laie über den Geist*, p. 21.

56 Nikolaus von Kues, *Der Laie über den Geist*, p. 113.

57 Gerhard Krieger, 'Conceptus Absolutus: Zu einer Parallele zwischen Wilhelm von Ockham, Johannes Buridan und Nicolaus Cusanus' in João Maria André, Gerhard Krieger and Harald Schwaetzer (eds), *Intellektus und Imaginatio: Aspekte geistiger und sinnlicher Erkenntnis bei Nicolaus Cusanus* (Amsterdam: Grüner, 2006), p. 15.

This is not the only aspect that connects the *idiota* of Nicholas of Cusa with Dubuffet's *aliéné* and *homme du commun*: the power of the Creator manifests itself in its purity in his creations. What all three have in common is that all scholarly knowledge is alien to them. So says the *idiota*: 'I don't know the scriptures'.[58] And in the *Dialogue on Wisdom*, he confidently opposes the arrogant speaker, who asks in amazement why he thinks he is wise: 'This is perhaps the difference between you and me: you think you are knowledgeable when you are not; therefore you are arrogant. But I recognize that I am an ignorant man; therefore I am more humble. In this I am much more instructed'.[59] He contrasts the 'wisdom out in the streets' with the book knowledge that the speaker places so much emphasis on: 'That is what I said: that you are led and deceived by an authority. Someone has written this word and you believe him. But I say to you: wisdom calls out in the streets, and it is her call that she herself dwells in the highest heights'.[60] It is of great significance that Nicholas of Cusa's *idiota* asserts that wisdom in its 'natural purity' is not to be found in books, but that wise men arrived at their wisdom by ingesting 'natural food'.[61] Here we find a topos that, by means of the metaphor of natural food, contrasts the natural and uncultivated with the unnatural, deformed by bookish wisdom, and that is reflected in Dubuffet's preference for the raw and uncooked.[62]

---

58 Nikolaus von Kues, *Der Laie über den Geist*, p. 117.

59 Nikolaus von Kues, *Der Laie über den Geist*, pp. 6–7.

60 The passage is derived from Proverbs 1:20: 'Wisdom cries aloud in the streets and makes her voice heard in the squares. She cries out in the loudest tumult, at the entrance of the gates, she speaks her words in the city.' See Nikolaus von Kues, *Der Laie über den Geist*, p. 82.

61 Nikolaus von Kues, *Der Laie über den Geist*, p. 82.

62 See Jean Dubuffet, 'Anmerkungen für die Schöngeister' in *Malerei in der Falle*, Schriften Band I (Andreas Franzke ed., Elke Kronjäger trans.) (Bern and Berlin: Gachnang und Springer, 1991), p. 53.

CHAPTER ONE

# The Rejection of the World

## The History of the Word *Idiot*

The *idiota* of Nicholas of Cusa is of course not identical with the idiot of the present. Rather, the German translation of the *Idiota* dialogues equates him with the layman, who has a history that is different from that of the idiot but runs parallel to it. The layman, whose Greek origin identifies him as 'belonging to the people',[1] figures in the eleventh and twelfth centuries as a counter-figure to the priest.[2] He was not ordained, was not allowed to administer the sacraments, and was not allowed to preach. In the High Middle Ages, other aspects were added: he is the uneducated, the unlearned, the one who does not know how to read and write, and is equated with the *illiterate*. In a dictionary from 1561, *Die Teütsch Spraach* by J. Maaler, there is a definition that makes layman and idiot synonymous: 'Ley who is not ordained. Laicus. Ley A person who has no intellect, a simple, simple-minded and ignorant person. Idiota'.[3] Both *idiota* and *laicus* are ultimately also equated in Johannes Rasch's *New Calendar* from 1590, whereby Rasch explicitly opposes a derogatory meaning: 'das ich die wörtlein idiot, vnglert, lay, gmain mann, pöfel vnd dergleichen, aus oder zu verachtung schreibe, sundern das man diejenigen, die nicht studiret, anderst nit nennen kann, wie die gelerten wissen'.[4] The intention to deny the legitimacy of the laity's

1 On this and in the following, Wilhelm Braun, 'Stichwort "Laie"' in Elisabeth Charlotte Welskopf (ed.), *Das Fortleben altgriechischer sozialer Typenbegriffe in der deutschen Sprache*, VOL. 5 (Berlin and New York: De Gruyter, 1981), pp. 235–61.

2 So also in Thomas of Celano, *Vita prima S. Francisci Assisiensis*, ed. a patribus Collegii S. Bonaventurae, Analecta Franciscana, X (Quaracchi, 1926). See Herbert Grundmann, *Religiöse Bewegungen im Mittelalter* (Darmstadt: Georg Olms, 1977 [1935]), p. 165.

3 Braun, 'Stichwort "Laie"', p. 242.

4 Johannes Rasch, *Neu Kalendar* (Rorschach am Bodensee: Leonhart Straub, 1590), Q2b: 'That I do not write the words idiot, uneducated, layman, common man, populace, and similar, not out of condescension, but for the reason that we have no other words

criticism of the official church in many cases leads to describing them as stupid, thus equating the *laicus* and the *idiota* with the heretic.[5]

The layman and the *idiota* thus enjoy an existence that links them with the common man and with the uneducated before the meaning of *idiota* shifts to the pejorative, a shift that the term 'layman' has not undergone. At the same time, however, the *idiota* has had its own career since the seventh century. In Beda Venerabilis (672/673–735), he is the uneducated or,[6] as in Beda's commentaries on the Proverbs of Solomon and his homilies, the simple-minded man who finds God's favour.[7] But in a ninth-century source, Ermoldus Nigellus' poem in praise of Louis the Pious, the author defends the cult of relics with the words: 'Quis nam idiota ferat demens, non corpora patrum / Sanctorum merito rure colenda fore', 'What foolish idiot can say that the bodies / of holy fathers are not worthy to be venerated in the countryside.'[8] In parallel to the character trait of simplicity, foolishness as dementia, as an absence of spirit, as stupidity, now becomes

---

for them, as the scholars know.' Hans Schulz, *Deutsches Wörterbuch* (Strasbourg: Institut für Deutsche Sprache, 1901), p. 281. See also Marie Simon, 'Stichwort "Idiot"' in Welskopf (ed.), *Fortleben altgriechischer sozialer Typenbegriffe*, VOL. 5, p. 292.

5 See Grundmann, *Religiöse Bewegungen im Mittelalter*, pp. 30, 495.

6 Bede the Venerable, *In Evangelium S. Lucae, in Venerabilis Bedae Anglosaxonis Presbyteri Opera Omnia*, J.-P. Migne (series ed.), Patrologiae Latina, VOL. 92 (Paris: J.-P. Migne, 1862), col. 501C.

7 Beda Venerabilis, *Liber primus homiliarum genuinarum*, HOM. 9, *In die festo Innocentium*, In *Opera Bedae Venerabilis presbyteri, Anglosaxonis: viri in divinis atque humanis literis exercitatissimi: omnia in octo tomos distincta, prout statim post praefationem suo elencho enumerantur: additum rerum et verborum indice copiosissimo* (Basel: per Ioannem Hervagium, 1563), col. 912: 'qui vero infra, simplices vel Idiotas, fidei tamen non fictae constantia fortes aeque denuntiant'. See also Bonizo Sutrensis, *Liber ad amicum sive de persecutione ecclesiae*, Patrologiae Latina, VOL. 150 (Paris: J.-P. Migne, 1854), col. 818.

8 Ermoldus Nigellus, *Carmen elegiacum de rebus gestis Ludovici Pii, ab anno 781 usque ad annum 826*, Patrologiae Latina, VOL. 105 (Paris: J.-P. Migne, 1851), col. 633A; German translation in Ermoldus Nigellus, *Lobgedicht auf Kaiser Ludwig, und Elegien an König Pippin* (Theodor Gottfried Martin Pfund trans.), Georg Heinrich Pertz, Jacob Grimm, Karl Lachmann, Leopold Ranke and Karl Ritter (eds), *Die Geschichtschreiber der deutschen Vorzeit in deutscher Bearbeitung*, VOL. 3 (Berlin: Wilhelm Besser, 1856), p. 90.

evident. An anonymous author distinguishes between the fool and the simple-minded in a biography of Norbert of Xanten, who behaved like a *fatuus*, a fool, among the uneducated, the *idiotae*,[9] while an eleventh-century priest, Gualterus Tarvanensis, used *insipiens* (ignorant), *stultus* (stupid, foolish), and *idiota* synonymously.[10] Finally, in his work *Opus synonymorum* from 1220, Joannes de Garlandia considers all the different forms of folly and idiocy to be synonymous: 'Est fatuus, stolidus, erroneus, insipiensque, / Inscius, et brutus, simplex, idiotaque, stultus / Indoctus, simul insipidus conjungitur illis, / Inconsultus, et eligius cui verba negantur', 'He is foolish, stupid, errant, unwise, / ignorant and brutish, simple, idiot, stupid / Uneducated, at the same time insipid is joined to them, / Unconsulted, and to whom more words are denied'.[11]

In the Cluniac and Cistercian monasteries, the uneducated, those unable to read and write, were used as cheap labour and for menial tasks such as simple sacristan services.[12] As men who had joined the monastery at a mature age, the *conversi*, *illiterati* or *idiotae* were regarded as monks of a lower rank who could not be called upon for missionary work and were deliberately barred from any 'spiritual education' in order to keep them in their subordinate position.[13]

9 *Vita S. Norberti auctore canonico Praemonstratensi coaevo*, Patrologiae Latina, VOL. 170 (Paris: J.-P. Migne, 1854), col. 1259A.

10 Gualterus Tarvanensis, *Vita Caroli Boni, comitis Flandriae*, Patrologiae Latina, VOL. 166 (Paris: J.-P. Migne, 1854), col. 942C.

11 Joannes de Garlandia, *Opus synonymorum*, Patrologiae Latina, VOL. 150 (Paris: J.-P. Migne, 1854), cols 1589C–D.

12 Eberhard Hoffmann, *Das Konverseninstitut des Cisterzienserordens in seinem Ursprung und seiner Organisation* (Freiburg: Universitäts-Buchhandlung Otto Gschwend, 1905), p. 13.

13 Karl Schreiner, 'Zisterziensisches Mönchtum und soziale Umwelt: Wirtschaftlicher und sozialer Strukturwandel in hoch- und spätmittelalterlichen Zisterzienserkonventen' in Kaspar Elm (ed.), *Die Zisterzienser: Ordensleben zwischen Ideal und Wirklichkeit*, Ergänzungsband (Cologne: Rheinland-Verlag, 1982), p. 123. Note 100 cites the view that even the admission of the uneducated man, the *rusticus idiota*, into the monastic community was seen as a threat to *discretio*, the differentiation of class. See Brian Stock, *The Implications of Literacy: Written Language and Models of Interpretation in the Eleventh and Twelfth Centuries* (Princeton, NJ: Princeton University Press, 1983), pp. 28ff. Hildegard von Bingen's criticism of the dissolution of class boundaries in the

The topos of simplicity, which combines the *idiota* with deep piety and religious fidelity, has its origins in the Acts of the Apostles. Until the twelfth century, the apostles were commonly referred to as 'homines idiotae et sine litteris'.[14] Other adjectives such as *indoctus* are added to distinguish them from the sophists, and the doubling of *idiotae* and *sine litteris* serves to emphasize the simple and unpretentious nature of the apostles, who defend the truth of the gospel against the chatter of the world.[15] At the same time, the term is used to characterize people without knowledge of Latin. But it changes in the course of an ever more finely developed awareness of rhetorical possibilities, until even authors writing in Latin, regardless of their command of Latin, call themselves *idiotae*. They incorporate the figure of ignorance into their writings in order, for example, to differentiate between knowledge of God and secular knowledge (*litteratus seculi*), which is ignorance with regard to knowledge of God (*Idiota Dei*).[16] And finally, the word even lent itself to becoming the laudatory epithet of a fourteenth-century author, Raimundus Jordanus, whose text *Idiota sapientissimus de statu et conditione religiorum* from 1381 was often published together with works by Bernard of Clairvaux and St Augustine from the sixteenth century onwards.[17]

The association of the *idiota* with the quality of simplicity lived on into the sixteenth century. The poet Benedetto Varchi (1502–65) describes the father of Florentine historiography and inventor of the legend that

monastery has become well known; see Lothar Hardick, 'Franziskus, die Wende der mittelalterlichen Frömmigkeit', *Wissenschaft und Weisheit* 13(3) (1950): 129–41; here, p. 130.

14 For this and the following, see Johannes Schneider, 'Das Wort *idiota* im mittelalterlichen Latein' in Welskopf (ed.), *Fortleben altgriechischer sozialer Typenbegriffe*, VOL. 4, pp. 132–57.

15 While Bernard of Clairvaux certainly opposed the sophistry and small-mindedness of the scholastics, his praise of simplicity was intended more as a warning against people's curiosity about topics beyond what was permitted. On the role of the *idiota* among the Cistercians, see also John Saward, *Perfect Fools* (New York: Oxford University Press, 1980), pp. 65–68.

16 Schneider, 'Das Wort *idiota*', p. 138.

17 See Cédric Giraud, 'La réception des *Meditationes sive orationes* d'Anselme de Cantorbéry à l'âge de l'imprimé', *Revue de l'histoire des religions* 230(4) (2013): 75–102.

Charlemagne rebuilt Florence, Giovanni Villani (1280–1348), as a 'uomo assai semplice e idiota, ma fedelissimo però e diligentissimo scrittore', 'a very simple and uneducated man, but a very faithful and diligent writer'.[18]

*Idiota* thus has a history that is constructed around the semantic core of simplicity. Surrounding this core, illiteracy and a lack of command over the language of the educated, belonging to the lower social classes, and a rejection of theological sophistry complete the picture. The transitions to folly and foolishness, stupidity and dullness are fluid, as the *idiota* can be a *fatuus*, a person considered stupid, or a person who only behaves like a *fatuus*. The legal literature of the Middle Ages makes it clear that whether a person is in fact an idiot or only pretends to be one makes no difference.[19] No medical vocabulary or diagnostic tool was as yet available to distinguish the asocial from the mentally handicapped, which is why the language of the law treats both equally.

## Revaluation of Values

When the *idiota* enters the stage in the Acts of the Apostles, a story of inversion begins. The most important protagonist of this drama of inversion is the former persecutor of Christians, Saul, who transforms into Paul. In Acts 4:13, as already mentioned, the disciples of Jesus are described as unlearned and uneducated simple people, *sine litteris et idiotae*.[20] But it is less the *idiota* than the synonymous *stultus*, the fool, that is the decisive figure for Paul's strategy of the revaluation of values: 'Nos stulti propter Christum, vos autem prudentes in Christo: nos infirmi, vos autem fortes:

---

18 Quoted from Thomas Maissen, *Von der Legende zum Modell: Das Interesse für die französische Vergangenheit während der italienischen Renaissance* (Basel: Helbing und Lichtenhahn, 1994), p. 92.

19 See Irina Metzler, 'Intellectual disability in the European Middle Ages' in Michael Rembis, Catherine J. Kudlick and Kim E. Nielsen (eds), *The Oxford Handbook of Disability History* (Oxford: Oxford University Press, 2018), pp. 55–70; here, p. 66. See also Irina Metzler, *Fools and Idiots? Intellectual Disability in the Middle Ages* (Manchester: Manchester University Press, 2016).

20 Acts 4:13: 'Videntes autem Petri constantiam, et Joannis, comperto quod homines essent sine litteris, et idiotæ admirabantur', 'then they saw the boldness of Peter and John and realized that they were unlearned and simple people; they were amazed'.

vos nobiles, nos autem ignobiles', 'We are fools for Christ's sake, but you are wise men in Christ. We are weak, you are strong; you are respected, we are despised' (1 Cor 4:10).[21] And in 1 Cor 1:19–29, it says:

> Scriptum est enim: Perdam sapientiam sapientium, et prudentiam prudentium reprobabo. Ubi sapiens? ubi scriba? ubi conquisitor hujus sæculi? Nonne stultam fecit Deus sapientiam hujus mundi? Nam quia in Dei sapientia non cognovit mundus per sapientiam Deum: placuit Deo per stultitiam prædicationis salvos facere credentes. Quoniam et Judæi signa petunt, et Græci sapientiam quærunt: Nos autem prædicamus Christum crucifixum: Judæis quidem scandalum, gentibus autem stultitiam, Ipsis autem vocatis Judæis, atque Græcis Christum Dei virtutem, et Dei sapientiam: Quia quod stultum est Dei, sapientius est hominibus: et quod infirmum est Dei, fortius est hominibus. [ . . . ] Videte enim vocationem vestram fratres, quia non multi sapientes secundum carnem, non multi potentes, non multi nobiles: Sed quæ stulta sunt mundi elegit Deus, ut confundat sapientes: et infirma mundi elegit Deus, ut confundat fortia: Et ignobilia mundi, et contemptibilia elegit Deus, et ea, quæ non sunt, ut ea quæ sunt destrueret: Ut non glorietur omnis caro in conspectu ejus.

> For it is written, I will destroy the wisdom of the wise, And will bring to nothing the understanding of the prudent. Where is the wise? where is the scribe? where is the disputer of this world? hath not God made foolish the wisdom of this world? For after that in the wisdom of God the world by wisdom knew not God, it pleased God by the foolishness of preaching to save them that believe. For the Jews require a sign, and the Greeks seek after wisdom: but we preach Christ crucified, unto the Jews a stumblingblock, and unto the Greeks foolishness; but unto them which are called, both Jews and Greeks, Christ the power of God, and the wisdom of God. Because the foolishness of God is wiser than

21 See also the reference to 1 Corinthians 4:10 by John Chrysostom in the second homily on the incomprehensibility of God, in Philipp Mayer (ed.), *Des Johannes Chrysostomos ausgewählte Homilien* (Nuremberg: Stein, 1830), p. 190.

> men; and the weakness of God is stronger than men. [ . . . ] For ye see your calling, brethren, how that not many wise men after the flesh, not many mighty, not many noble, are called: but God hath chosen the foolish things of the world to confound the wise; and God hath chosen the weak things of the world to confound the things which are mighty; and base things of the world, and things which are despised, hath God chosen, yea, and things which are not, to bring to nought things that are: that no flesh should glory in his presence. (KJV)

In the second letter he challenges the Corinthians accordingly: 'Utinam sustineretis modicum quid insipientiæ meæ, sed et supportate me', 'May you endure a little foolishness from me! Yes, bear with me!' And he continues: 'Nam etsi imperitus sermone, sed non scientia, in omnibus autem manifestati sumus vobis', 'For though I am inexperienced in speech, yet not in knowledge, but in everything we have become manifest to you'.

Paul stands before the Christian community in Corinth, torn apart by religious struggles, as a representative of the true faith:

> Puto enim quod Deus nos Apostolos novissimos ostendit, tamquam morti destinatos: quia spectaculum facti sumus mundo, et Angelis, et hominibus. Nos stulti propter Christum, vos autem prudentes in Christo: nos infirmi, vos autem fortes: vos nobiles, nos autem ignobiles. Usque in hanc horam et esurimus, et sitimus, et nudi sumus, et colaphis cædimur, et instabiles sumus, Et laboramus operantes manibus nostris: maledicimur, et benedicimus: persecutionem patimur, et sustinemus: Blasphemamur, et obsecramus: tamquam purgamenta hujus mundi facti sumus, omnium peripsema usque adhuc.

> For it seems to me that God has put us apostles on display at the end of the procession, like those condemned to die in the arena. We have been made a spectacle to the whole universe, to angels as well as to human beings. We are fools for Christ, but you are so wise in Christ! We are weak, but you are strong! You are honored, we are dishonored! To this very hour we go hungry and thirsty,

> we are in rags, we are brutally treated, we are homeless. We work hard with our own hands. When we are cursed, we bless; when we are persecuted, we endure it; When we are slandered, we answer kindly. We have become the scum of the earth, the garbage of the world—right up to this moment. (1 Cor 4:9–13)

The apostles are 'as those consecrated to death'; they act as if they were not acting, live as if they were not living. But therein lies the error of the world and its people, even the angels. For the spectacle offered by the apostles is that of scum and folly only with the proviso that the world does not know that redemption has already happened. The apostles' actions in this world are irrelevant, as they have been living in the state of salvation for which the Christian community in Corinth is still waiting. From the perspective of salvation, all worldly actions appear as folly, and all worldly views of salvation see only despicable weakness, scum, and excrement.

The inversion of the values of strength and power that the New Testament tells begins with the story of the helpless child in the stable and ends with the martyred and wretched Son of God on the cross. This story is reinforced by Paul. Added to this is his conversion story, which is itself an inversion story: the hunter of Jesus' disciples becomes first a blind, helpless man, but ultimately the most powerful builder of the theological foundation of Christianity. The book of Acts of the Apostles (Acts 9:1–19) reports how Saul of Tarsus, the persecutor of Christians, falls to the ground as if struck by lightning on his way to Damascus, where he wants to search the synagogues for Jesus' followers, and hears a voice: 'Saul, Saul, why are you persecuting me?' When Saul asks who is speaking, the voice replies: 'I am Jesus, whom you are persecuting'. The light that had blinded Saul before he fell to the ground has now given way to complete darkness: he is blinded and has to be taken to the city by his companions, who had heard the sound but seen no one. There he stays for three days without being able to eat or drink. He is finally healed through the mercy of a disciple named Ananias, whom God commands to seek out the notorious persecutor of Christians and lay hands on him. Then 'it fell from his eyes like scales, and he received his sight; and he arose and was baptized' (Acts 9:18).

The apostle does not recognize the truth because he has painstakingly studied the Scriptures and their interpretations in order to gain knowledge about which view of the world and its Creator would be the right one. His theological knowledge does not bring him to the truth, and it is doubtful that his old faith was anything more than an opportune excuse to indulge his passion as a hunter of Christians. The new truth does not come to him by way of study, but strikes him like a bolt of lightning and forces him to convert through the sheer force of its manifestation. The conversion experience empties all his previous knowledge of its content and makes him receptive to a new knowledge for which nothing has prepared him. Realization occurs instantaneously and out of nowhere as the devaluation of all values or as their complete reversal.[22]

## The Abolition of Time

Before Nicholas of Cusa makes the *idiota* the heroic representative of a higher knowledge that is far superior to scriptural knowledge, it is Saint Francis of Assisi who associates ignorance with apostolic fidelity and thus with the true following of Christ. This not-knowing is not the erudite not-knowing of Nicholas of Cusa, who declared the cognition of the unknowability of God to be the highest form of knowledge by speculating on scale and number and the comparability of proportions and ratios[23] (tellingly, the inspiration for this thought comes to him as a sudden night-time experience on the crossing from Constantinople to Italy).[24] Instead, Saint

22 The *idiota*, which in the case of the apostles has a positive connotation, also appears in the Corinthian letters in a negative sense, however, when it refers to the ignorant who do not understand the teaching and praise of God. 1 Corinthians 14:16: 'Ceterum si benedixeris spiritu: qui supplet locum idiotæ, quomodo dicet, Amen, super tuam benedictionem? quoniam quid dicas, nescit.', 'Otherwise, if you praise with the Spirit, how can he who takes the place of an ignorant man say Amen to your praise? He does not know what you are saying.' As already indicated, this ambivalence will continue to characterize the *idiota* in the following centuries.

23 See Ulrich Offermann, *Christus—Wahrheit des Denkens: Eine Untersuchung zur Schrift 'De docta ignorantia' des Nikolaus von Kues*, Beiträge zur Geschichte und Theologie des Mittelalters, VOL. 33 (Münster: Aschendorff, 1991), pp. 63–64.

24 See Johann Uebinger, 'Der Begriff *docta ignorantia* in seiner geschichtlichen Entwicklung', *Archiv für Geschichte der Philosophie* 7(1) (1895): 10.

Francis' not-knowing is the renunciation of knowledge and comes exclusively from the ecstatic immersion in the suffering of Christ, whom the believer emulates.[25]

Born Giovanni di Pietro di Bernardone in Assisi in 1181 or early 1182, Francis, the son of a wealthy cloth merchant, receives a school education befitting his background and learns to read, write, and do arithmetic.[26] He also studies French courtly poetry, which awakens in him the desire to lead the life of a knight. Driven by this desire, he wants to take part in the war against the Hohenstaufen dynasty in Apulia, but on the way there he is overtaken by a vision of God asking him to abandon the worldly life of a knight and turn to spiritual service instead. The resulting process of renunciation and repentance spans a long period of time as a painful transformation of the wealthy young man into an eccentric who is said to have lived with beggars on a pilgrimage to Rome. After a dream in which God asks him to 'rebuild his house', he begins to renovate churches and chapels in the surrounding area, misunderstanding the vision as a literal mission. He takes money and goods from his parents' trade for this purpose, which leads to conflict with his father. As all attempts to persuade him to lead a 'bourgeois' life are to no avail, he has to defend himself in a trial brought against him by his father, with the bishop as judge. It is this scene that marks his final conversion: he renounces his father, strips off his clothes, and rejects his inheritance. From now on, he wants to follow the naked Crucified One as a naked man.[27]

Saint Francis uses the designation *idiota* for his companions and for himself and uses it in parallel with the distinction between clergy and laity.[28] Thus, he writes in the *Testament*: 'Officium dicebamus clerici secundum alios clericos, laici dicebant: Pater noster; et satis libenter manebamus in

---

25 Thus, hagiographic literature celebrates him as a perfect *idiota*. See Joseph Lortz, *Der unvergleichliche Heilige*, p. 82.

26 For a biography and bibliography on St Francis, visit istcap.org.

27 See Bonaventura, *Stimulus divini amoris* (Brixen, 1599), p. 20. See also Kurt Ruh, 'Zur Grundlegung einer Geschichte der franziskanischen Mystik' in *Kleine Schriften*, VOL. 2 (Berlin and New York: De Gruyter, 1984), pp. 118–44; here, p. 121.

28 See Francis of Assisi, 'Epistola toti Ordini missa' (1223), §39, in *Sämtliche Schriften: Lateinisch/Deutsch* (Dieter Berg ed.) (Stuttgart: Reclam, 2014), p. 160.

ecclesiis. Et eramus Idiotae et subditi omnibus', 'We prayed the officium like other clerics, the laity said the Lord's Prayer; and we loved to linger in the churches. And we were uneducated and subservient to all'.[29] Saint Francis and his companions are also referred to as *simplex et idiota* in the later biographies, the *Legend of the Three Companions* and the *Vita secunda* by Thomas of Celano.[30]

By suffering the sufferings of the Lord, Saint Francis tries to become like him. In the text of True Joy,[31] he describes his wanderings on a winter night in search of shelter, which he is refused after knocking on the door

29 Francis of Assisi, *Sämtliche Schriften*, p. 349.

30 Thomas of Celano, *Vita Secunda S. Francisci Assisiensis* in *Legendae S. Francisci Assisiensis saeculis XIII et XIV conscriptae ad codicum fidem recensitae a patribus collegii, Analecta Franciscana* 10 (Quaracchi: Typographia Collegii S. Bonaventurae, 1927), pp. 127–268, here p. 145. *Die Dreigefährtenlegende des heiligen Franziskus: Die Brüder Leo, Rufin und Angelus erzählen vom Anfang seines Ordens* (Engelbert Grau and Sophronius Clasen eds) (Werl [Westfalen]: Dietrich-Coelde-Verlag, 1972), 7.21. See also Ruh, 'Zur Grundlegung', p. 130. Thomas of Celano entitled a chapter in the *Vita secunda* 'De sancta simplicitate'. In the *Legenda Perusina*, edited by Marino Bigaroni, '*Compilatio Assisiensis' dagli scritti di fr. Leone e compagni su S. Francesco d'Assisi dal Ms. 1046 di Perugia*, 2nd EDN (S. Maria degli Angeli: Porziuncola, 1992), pp. 56–58, Francis reports that God himself had asked him to live as a new fool in the world: 'Et dixit Dominus michi, quod volebat, quod ego essem unus novellus pazzus in mundo'. See also Achim Wesjohann, 'Individualitätsbewußtsein in frühen franziskanischen Quellen? Eine Suche nach Indizien' in Gert Melville and Markus Schürer (eds), *Das Eigene und das Ganze: Zum Individuellen im mittelalterlichen Religiosentum* (Münster: LIT Verlag, 2002), pp. 225–67; here, p. 243. The *Legenda Perusina*, however, uses the word *pazzus*, which can also mean madness. See also the descriptions and self-descriptions of Aegidius, one of Francis's companions, in Friedrich Pösl, *Leben und goldene Sprüche des seligen Aegidius von Assisi, Laienbruders und dritten Jüngers des hl. Franciscus: Nach den Bollandisten bearbeitet von Friedrich Pösl* (Passau: Ambrosi, 1847), pp. 7–8, 50. On the significance of *simplicitas*, see Achim Wesjohann, 'Simplicitas als franziskanisches Ideal und der Prozeß der Institutionalisierung des Minoritenordens' in Gert Melville and Jörg Oberste (eds), *Die Bettelorden im Aufbau: Beiträge zu Institutionalisierungsprozessen im mittelalterlichen Religiosentum* (Münster: LIT Verlag, 1999), pp. 107–68; esp. pp. 160–61, where Aegidius asks Minister General Bonaventure whether an uneducated person (*idiota*) can love God as much as a learned person (*literatus*).

31 Thomas of Celano, *Vita Secunda*, pp. 198ff. See also the embellished version of the same narrative in *I fioretti*, CHAP. 8, edited by Luigi Luzzatti (Milan: Istituto Editoriale Italiano, 1917), p. 48.

of a monastery with the words: 'Vade; tu es unum simplex et idiota', 'Go away! You are a simpleton and an uneducated man'. As a homeless man, covered with dirt, bleeding from his wounds, and half-frozen, Saint Francis lives through the suffering of the defenceless child of God, whose parents were denied shelter on the night of his birth. And it is not without significance that he, the *idiota*, is chased away not from the door of just any house, but from the gate of a monastery.

Among other things, Saint Francis justifies his renunciation of knowledge by referring to 2 Cor 3:6, where Paul writes: 'The letter kills, but the spirit gives life'. And he criticizes the believers in the Word with an argument also used by Nicholas of Cusa's *idiota*, namely the assertion that they care only about acquiring knowledge in order to 'be considered wiser among others and to acquire great riches'.[32] Saint Francis is concerned with the rejection of every form of worldly good, be it prestige, fame, or wealth. It was especially his insistence on complete poverty, which he saw as a commandment of apostolic succession, that brought him into conflict with the Curia, which initially still saw him as a renewer of the Church. A poor monk appeared to Pope Innocent III in a dream, holding up the facade of the Lateran Cathedral with his right arm and shoulder, which had fallen into ruin. The pope reads the Lateran Cathedral as a symbol of the Holy Church, and the monk as the Poverello, to whom he grants permission to live in communal poverty with his confreres and to do penance as an itinerant preacher, integrating him and his order into the organizational structure of the Church through the commandment of tonsure and the obligation of absolute obedience. However, it was during Saint Francis' lifetime that the ideal of poverty came under pressure due to the rapid growth of the order. To accommodate the Franciscans, Pope Innocent IV developed the legal construction that the Church was the owner of all the Franciscans' property, and that they could therefore comply with the ideal of poverty, as they merely made use of goods without owning them. However, this led to the de facto secularization of the order and a competitive relationship with the parish clergy. After any discussion of the question of Christ's refusal of property had been suppressed under sustained

32 Francis of Assisi, *Sämtliche Schriften*, p. 185.

pressure by Pope Nicholas III in the bull *Exiit qui seminat* of 1279, Pope John XXII reversed the argument in 1323 and declared in the bull *Cum inter nonnullos* that the view that Christ and the apostles had lived without any possessions was heretical. This put an end—albeit temporarily—to the poverty controversy.

The fact that the *Parousia*, the second coming of Christ, had failed to occur had already posed a problem for Paul, whose Damascus experience set the pattern for many other incidents of conversion. But this problem was seriously exacerbated more than a thousand years later in the conflict between Saint Francis and the Roman Church. Whether Paul understands the time after Christ's death and resurrection as an interim period between redemption and the Second Coming, or whether he denies it any relevance, since it is only the redemption through Christ's birth and resurrection that counts, and all time is thus abolished and passes directly into God's eternal reign, is a controversial question.[33] If time has been fulfilled with the birth of Christ, as Paul writes in his letter to the Galatians (Gal 4:4), then all time after that is without meaning. Redemption has already taken place, people are already living in a state of grace (see Col 2:12–13), and all worldly activity is an activity in the mode of as if:[34] to act as if one were not acting; to live as though one were not alive. Since the state of grace has been reached and redemption has been accomplished, worldly life is deprived of all meaning, and what masquerades as worldly wisdom is foolishness in view of the fact that time has been fulfilled.

However, the fact that historical time has not come to an end through eschatological rupture poses the question as to how the position of the Church in the world can be justified in an intermediate age which sits

---

33 The former position is represented by Hans-Alwin Wilcke, *Das Problem eines messianischen Zwischenreichs bei Paulus* (Zurich and Stuttgart: Zwingli, 1967), pp. 99ff. The opposite position can be found in Rudolf Bultmann, *Geschichte und Eschatologie* (Tübingen: Mohr [Paul Siebeck], 1964), pp. 44ff. See Giorgio Agamben, *Die Zeit, die bleibt* (Frankfurt am Main: Suhrkamp, 2006 [2000]), pp. 83ff.

34 See Christian Strecker, *Die liminale Theologie des Paulus: Zugänge zur paulinischen Theologie aus kulturanthropologischer Perspektive* (Göttingen: Vandenhoeck & Ruprecht, 1999), pp. 230ff. See Erich Gräßer, *Das Problem der Parusieverzögerung in den synoptischen Evangelien und in der Apostelgeschichte* (Berlin and New York: De Gruyter, 1977).

between the resurrection of the Son of God and the Last Judgement. The Church responds to the non-occurrence of Christ's return with the secularization of the expectation of salvation; as long as justice has not yet been pronounced on the Last Day, it is the Church whose congregational jurisdiction is to be seen as the 'highest anticipation of future judgement'.[35] It acts as the keeper of the treasure of salvation and grace and ensures that the fulfilment of the promise is not suspended, but merely delayed.

The difficulty initially lies in organizing the Church; instead of the equality of all believers before the Last Judgement, a structure of institutionally authorized and systematically organized religious knowledge is established in the dispute over the correct interpretation of the fact that God does not return. The name of this structure is theology. It excludes opposition or heterodoxy as heresy from the realm of legitimate convictions. And it had become necessary when Christianity 'wanted to make itself possible in a world that it actually denies'.[36] To establish an institution in a world that does not want to end, for the purpose of preserving the faith in promised salvation until it becomes reality, requires having to deal with the challenge of exercising power. In the name of salvation, suspended for the time being and indefinitely, those whose whole mind strives to exchange this rejected world for a better one must be convinced that this world can serve as a temporary home despite its depravity. The Catholic Church has found itself in this dilemma since the middle of the fourth century, after Constantine's gradual conversion to Christianity, which was followed by his successors' resolute protection of the new religion until it was elevated to the status of state religion in 380 CE. In this moment, both spiritual and secular power converged in one institution; a power that the Church by no means hesitated to exercise, as demonstrated by the rapid onset of discriminatory measures against pagan elites and sanctuaries.[37]

35 Tertullian, *Apologeticum*, cited in Franciscus Oehler (ed.), *Septimi Florentis Tertulliani* (Halle: Halae Saxonibus, 1849), p. 200. See Hans Blumenberg, 'Säkularisierung: Verweltlichung durch Eschatologie statt Verweltlichung der Eschatologie' in *Die Legitimität der Neuzeit*, pp. 46–62.

36 See Franz Overbeck, *Über die Christlichkeit unserer heutigen Theologie: Streit- und Friedensschrift* (Leipzig: E. W. Fritzsch, 1873), p. 10.

37 See Johannes Hahn (ed.), *Spätantiker Staat und religiöser Konflikt*, Millennium-Studien, VOL. 34 (Berlin and New York: De Gruyter, 2011). See also Wolfgang Speyer,

The Franciscans were also faced with the task of having to adapt to the world, as they were successful in it precisely because they rejected it. The order grew rapidly, and it is significant that from 1224, partly due to his worsening eyesight and declining health, Francis withdrew from the business of regulating religious life and devoted himself to meditation and prayer in the solitude of Monte La Verna. Finally, the advocates of a strict ideal of poverty also capitulated to the demands brought about by the expansion of the order; they submitted to the growing pressure of the Church or split off (Fraticelli). Ugolino dei Conti di Segni, later Pope Gregory IX, took over as protector of the order in 1220 and prepared the integration of the mendicant crder into the Church's power structure.

Saint Francis does not reject the Church; he is subject to it, just as he is subject to everyone. The conflict, which ultimately ends to his disadvantage and to the detriment of the Fraticelli, revolves around the question of the legitimacy of property and the exercise of power. What Saint Francis insists on is the legitimacy of his refusal to exercise the right to property. But what Francis may have had in mind—subordination to the Church as an institution in the world and at the same time fidelity to the ideal of *imitatio* and *conformitas Christi*—cannot be realized; there is no third party to the 'vita perfecta et apostolica'[38] on the one hand and the institutionalization of this teaching in the form of an organization on the other. Because it is this organization which has to represent the semantics of the world's unworthiness in this world, and has to reconcile the dubiousness of this world's existence with its own continued existence.

However, Saint Francis does not reject earthly life and the world either. On the contrary, he celebrates life as the alphabet in which divine love is expressed. The fact that he takes off his clothes in the marketplace of Assisi is not a renunciation of the world because it is not worth living in it, or because the shorter the life, the quicker salvation can be won. Instead, it means the rejection of the paternal heritage and all markers of a certain social status; it also means the return to a state of nature before this world

---

*Büchervernichtung und Zensur des Geistes bei Heiden, Juden und Christen* (Stuttgart: Hiersemann, 1981), pp. 120–66.

38 Herbert Grundmann, *Studien zu Joachim von Floris* (Wiesbaden: Springer, 1927), p. 187.

has been socially codified. It is a second-order naturalness, that of the naked Christ as a symbol of the extreme humiliation of the Son of God, the complete revaluation of all social values and hierarchies. The affirmation of this second-order naturalness goes hand in hand with the affirmation of first-order naturalness, the animal and plant world, to which he dedicates the *Canticle of the Sun*. In the affirmation of this perfection, which is the affirmation of the God-ordained perfection of the material, visible, and natural world, the criticism of the social form of the Church is included. The affirmation of the natural is synonymous with the criticism of the social as an aberration.

At the same time, the rejection of the right to property is the rejection of the right to exercise power. John XXII refuses the Franciscan ideal of poverty, since, from the Church's perspective, a right to use things without owning them does not exist. To be allowed to use things presupposes the legal right to use them, especially when it comes to things that are consumed through use, such as food. Having a right means having power over the object that one has the right to use. Therefore, on the one hand, there is a close connection between the subjective right as law (*ius*) and the power (*potestas*) that one exercises over the object of this right, and, on the other, the possession (*proprietas*) and the de facto power (*dominium*) that one has over an object, regardless of whether this power is legitimized by the *ius* or not. In the late Middle Ages, these terms were used by different parties in different ways depending on their intentions.[39] For example, there are serious differences in the use of the term *ius*, which is understood on the one hand as a law to be obeyed and on the other as a right to which one is entitled.[40] Ockham adds a further layer to the common distinction between *ius naturale* and *ius positivum*, namely that between the *ius fori*, the law of man, and the *ius poli*, the heavenly law.[41]

39 See Brian Tierney, *The Idea of Natural Rights* (Grand Rapids, MI: Eerdmans, 2001), pp. 104–70.

40 See Marsilius of Padua, *Defensor pacis* (Hanover: Hahnsche Buchhandlung, 1932 [1324]), 2.12 and 2.13; William of Ockham, *Opus nonaginta dierum* (1332–34) in H. S. Offler (ed.), *Opera politica*, VOLS 1–2 (Manchester: Manchester University Press, 1940–63).

41 For a further differentiation of *ius naturale* in Ockham, see Arthur Stephen McGrade, *The Political Thought of William of Ockham: Personal and Institutional*

Ockham equates natural law, which is understood as the law that gives legitimacy to the positive law created by human legislation, with *ius poli*, the heavenly law. His argument against John XXII is that by *ius utendi*, the right to the use of an object when necessity dictates or permits it, he could only have meant a positive right; consequently, natural law must remain unaffected by it and, if John XXII insisted that the Franciscans had to exercise a right and thus exercise power, this was merely a human right that could be overridden by the *ius poli* or *ius naturale*, which lay outside human power and disposition. He insists that 'fratres minores, in rebus quibus utuntur, non habeant aliquod ius positivum, habent tamen aliquod ius in eis, scilicet ius naturale', 'the fratres minores, [ . . . ] regarding the things they use, do not [have] a positive right, but they do have a right, namely a natural one'.[42] Consequently, there is a right to use without the obligation to own the object used; the natural or heavenly right gives the individual the right to renounce the provisions of earthly law and to position himself outside the right defined by this law without simultaneously falling victim to social death.

The question of whether property can be just goes to the heart of any discussion about the legitimacy of positive law, or the question of whether law can be just is decided by this question. Mirabeau would sum this up as follows:

> En un mot, le partage des biens est la première loi de la societé, & le tronc, pour ainsi dire, de toutes les autres lois: qu'on ne m'oppose pas l'example des Sauvages qui vivent en commun de chasse & de la pêche.
>
> In a word, the division of property is the first law of society, and, as it were, the root of all other laws; do not contradict me here with the example of the savages who live in common by hunting and fishing.[43]

---

*Principles*, Cambridge Studies in Medieval Life and Thought, 3rd SER., VOL. 7 (Cambridge: Cambridge University Press, 1974), pp. 173–76.

42 Ockham, *Opus nonaginta dierum*, p. 561.

43 Victor de Riquetti, marquis de Mirabeau, *L'ami des hommes, ou Traité de la population*, VOL. 1 (Avignon, 1758 [1756]), p. 3. Translated by LE.

Further, Locke writes that without property there is no injustice.[44] Saint Francis' rejection of the right to property can be derived from the nagging doubt as to whether this right might have its origin in injustice. The question that needs to be clarified is its genesis: Was Adam the owner of the entire earth? And was the person who, after the expulsion of Adam from paradise, took possession of a piece of land or an object for the first time a thief who robbed the community of what had belonged to everyone?[45] Did the origin of property lie in the usurpation of a power that violated the rights of the community? The theories that attempt to clarify the paradox of the first property resort to different models of how the injustice associated with a pre-legal application of a right can be explained, and thus the usurpation of power could be framed as in accordance with the law.[46] The model that proves to be the least problematic is that in a state of natural abundance, property does not represent a restriction of the rights of a third party, since the latter will be able to find what is their own elsewhere; there is, so to speak, enough for everyone. The fact that the claiming of a property right means the exclusion of someone else from ownership of the same thing is then a negligible trifle. In contrast, Rufinus (*c.*1192), probably born in Assisi, educated in Bologna, and later Archbishop of Sorrento, assumes that the first acquisition of property was in fact injustice, which was subsequently transformed into law through human legislation.[47] Other writers, however, understand the sin that came into the world through Adam as the moment through which inequality entered the world. Property is thus understood either as a corrective to this

44 John Locke, *An Essay concerning Human Understanding* (Philadelphia, 1854 [1690]), BOOK 1, p. 370. On the question of the abuse of property, see Daniel Loick, *Der Missbrauch des Eigentums* (Berlin: August, 2016). See Niklas Luhmann, 'Am Anfang war kein Unrecht' in *Gesellschaftsstruktur und Semantik*, VOL. 3 (Frankfurt am Main: Suhrkamp, 1993), pp. 11–64; here, pp. 36–37.

45 See Robert Filmer, *Patriarcha and Other Political Works* (Peter Laslett ed.) (Oxford: Basil Blackwell, 1949), p. 273.

46 See Luhmann, 'Am Anfang war kein Unrecht', pp. 11–64.

47 Heinrich Singer, *Die Summa Decretorum des Magister Rufinus* (Paderborn: F. Schöningh, 1902), p. 4. See Rudolf Weigand, 'Die Rechtslehre der Scholastik bei den Dekretisten und Dekretalisten' in Rudolf Weigand (ed.), *Ius canonicum*, VOL. 16 (Pamplona: Ediciones Universidad de Navarra, 1976), pp. 61–90; here, p. 63.

inequality or as a punishment for Adam's original sin.[48] It is part of the logic of the problem that the element of work comes into play at this point: not only does the first human couple have to atone for the sin of having violated God's commandment in paradise through the sweat of their brow and in pain, work also serves as an argument in the context of the discussion about property in order to justify it as legitimate: anyone who works continues God's work of creation and acquires a right, for example, to control the land that he or she cultivates.[49] At the same time, work links property to the individual physical possibilities of the person in question, whereby they are entitled to what they can cultivate with their hands. The category of labour thus limits the scope of the possible acquisition of property. Only money, with the help of which labour and land can be purchased, and which can be used for its own multiplication, decouples property from labour and adds to the natural inequality of human beings a second and more serious facet: social inequality, the cruelest form of which is serfdom and slavery. For this reason, Thomas Aquinas warns against money as the root of all sin: not only does money harbour the danger of becoming independent as an end instead of serving as a means; its danger also lies in the fact that it can be used to acquire further goods, powers, and rights, thereby enabling people to acquire more than they can manage on the one hand, or use and utilize on the other.[50] According to Thomas Aquinas, property that was acquired by force and goes beyond what is useful is robbery.[51]

The question of whether property can be legitimate is thus linked to the question of which right—the *ius positivum* or *ius fori* or the *ius naturale* or *ius poli*—can be regarded as a legitimate right. Together with the question of the legitimate exercise of power, it converges in the problem of the time that remains. Is the time that has begun, and seems to last, an interim period or is it already the time of grace?

---

48 Tierney, *The Idea of Natural Rights*, p. 141.

49 Tierney, *The Idea of Natural Rights*, p. 143.

50 Thomas Aquinas, *Summa theologica*, 1.2.84. See Anthony Parel, 'Aquinas' Theory of Property' in Anthony Parel and Thomas Flanagan (eds), *Theories of Property from Aristotle to the Present* (Ontario: Wilfred Laurier University Press, 1979), pp. 89–114.

51 Thomas Aquinas, *Summa theologica*, 2.66.2 ad 3.

Saint Francis tries to solve this problem by attempting, as the *alter Christus*, to annul time by transcending the power of the first Christ. He is first described as the *alter Christus*—the second Christ—in the circular letter of Elias of Cortona, which he wrote shortly after Saint Francis' death.[52] This topos is used again in the early fourteenth-century collections of legends, the *Fioretti* and the *Actus Beati Francisci et Sociorum Eius*,[53] written between 1327 and 1340. It can be assumed with some reason that it was not only his exegetes who understood Saint Francis to be not only equal to the Son of God but superior to him.[54] What definitely goes beyond *conformitas* and *compassio*, while initially allowing us to construe likeness to Christ, are the stigmata that Saint Francis received on Monte La Verna two years before his death. They play a decisive role when Elias of Cortona undertakes to link Francis with Moses, John the Baptist, and Christ through a multitude of cross-references, so that the saint is able to take on several functions: he functions as a mediator of the Old Covenant, as a prophet who points to the coming Christ, and as the one to whom reference was made, as a mediator of the New Covenant between man and God. By fulfilling time anew as the new Christ, Francis not only declares all historical time that has passed since Christ, but also Christ's abolition of time, irrelevant. It is this double abolition of time that, after establishing equality of essence in a first step, elevates him above Christ in a second step and thus

52 Johannes Schlageter, 'Rundbrief des Bruders Elias zum Tod des St. Franziskus' in Dieter Berg, Leonhard Lehmann and Johannes-Baptist Freyer (eds), *Franziskus-Quellen: Die Schriften des heiligen Franziskus, Lebensbeschreibungen, Chroniken und Zeugnisse über ihn und seinen Orden* (Kevelaer: Butzon & Bercker, 2009), pp. 180–86. For a biography of Elias of Cortona, see Heinrich Rybka, *Elias von Cortona* (Leipzig: Naumann, 1874). For an assessment of the role of Elias of Cortona in the formation of legends, see Vincent Isenberg, *Die Stigmatisierung des Franziskus von Assisi* (Bochum: Ruhr-Universität Bochum, 2019).

53 See Achim Wesjohann, *Mendikantische Gründungserzählungen im 13. und 14. Jahrhundert* (Berlin: LIT, 2012), p. 120. See also Paul Sabatier (ed.), *Actus Beati Francisci et Sociorum Eius* (Paris: Librairie Fischbacher, 1902). On the various legends and their periodization, see also Sophronius Clasen, *Legenda antiqua S. Francisci* (Leiden: E. J. Brill, 1967).

54 In this sense, Helmut Feld, *Franziskus von Assisi, der Zweite Christus* (Mainz: Philipp von Zabern, 1991). See also Feld, *Franziskus von Assisi* (Munich: C. H. Beck, 2013 [2001]).

removes him from the jurisdiction of the Church. No attempt by the Church to defend the arrangement with the world by pointing to the delay of the event of salvation can stand if historical time collapses under the pressure of an eschatological rupture, which no longer correlates with the return of the Son of God, but with the appearance of the Poverello. The basis of his defence of the ideal of poverty and his rejection of wealth, money, and power is the assertion that, with him as the second Christ, time has come to an end for the second time and has been fulfilled. This is also why the Church's justification—that it must continue to fill, until the Second Coming, the role that the judge will finally assume on the Day of Judgement—is no longer valid. Saint Francis is therefore not calling for a return to the *perfectio apostolica*; it is not about the restoration of an ideal original state, but about the fact that from now on there is no more time. Since there is no more time and therefore no more in-between time, all forms of worldly possessions and the exercise of power lack any justification. With his ideal of poverty, Saint Francis is not advocating a backward-looking utopia. Rather, he is calling for the establishment of a different world under the sign of suspended, abolished time.

## CHAPTER TWO

# Fools

### *The Ship of Fools* by Sebastian Brant

With the *idiota* of Nicholas of Cusa, the idiot has one last brilliant appearance in the wake of the apostles and of Saint Paul and Saint Francis, before being relegated to the margins for a few centuries. From that moment, the main roles in the game between society and its outsiders will be played by the fool and the jester, two figures who have little in common with the *idiota*, who, as a knowing ignoramus, masters the art of creation out of nothing.

The *Ship of Fools* by Sebastian Brant (1457–1521), first published in Basel in 1494, makes no mention of the *idiota* in its Latin version of 1497. Brant's work, which is inspired by Latin satirical poetry such as that of Juvenal, has replaced the *idiota* with the Fool, who populates the entire earth and rules it with his fool's clapper. Like a mental epidemic, foolishness disrupts the social order. Arrogance, stupidity, pride and greed, lust, selfishness, and arrogance dominate people and drive them towards their end, where nothing but eternal torment awaits them in hell. Full of references and quotations from the Old and New Testaments, from classical literature such as Ovid's *Metamorphoses* or Virgil's *Georgics*, and full of allusions to heroines and heroes who are failures and tragic victims of their own or others' wickedness from pagan and biblical stories, the poem proves to be an erudite polemic against the rampant corruption and stultification of its time. Wherever Brant looks, people cheat and lie to each other, give in to drunkenness, torment their children, and betray their duties. They have no table manners and follow only their basest instincts, cannot keep their mouths shut in church and never miss an opportunity for quick sex, whereby a large portion of the blame naturally falls on the unchaste women who tempt the defenceless men with their charms.

On the doomed ship of fools that has set sail for an unknown destination with great certainty (satire 108), people, especially those probably best described as 'common people', crowd around and indulge in their folly. It is noticeable that only in a few instances are the princes and the higher clergy brought into play, as if they were exempt from the madness of folly. Brant does not see folly at work everywhere, but only among the common people. Brant mentions the princes in the satire 'On the Decline of Faith', but immediately asks for leniency after having made them responsible for the decline of the Holy Roman Empire of the German Nation. For him, the clearest sign of decay is the fact that the Turks have conquered the Christian possessions in Asia Minor and are now ready to occupy Italy and from there to advance into the European heartland. Brant vehemently campaigns for the princes and estates to stand behind Maximilian I (1459–1519, elected king in 1486, emperor from 1508) and jointly defend themselves against the Islamic enemy. Brant does not, it seems, want to put the fool's cap on any king or emperor, abbot, bishop, or pope; it is exclusively the lower classes who shake the fabric of society with their foolishness. This distinguishes his dance of folly from the dances of death to which he refers (satire 85), in which representatives of all classes and social strata are led out of life by merciless death without distinction. In the *danses macabres* all social inequalities are levelled before the great equalizer and all worldly honour melts away. It is, however, the craftsmen and peasants, the lowly clerics and monks, the beggars, quacks, and merchants, who have to board the ship of fools and whose licentious behaviour, short-sightedness, and greed make a mockery of any notion of honour and morality. Brant does not forget the pagans and heretics, especially the Hussites, whom he lumps together with prostitutes, panderers, suicides, and doubters in one paragraph; they are not even worthy of the attempt to be converted by law and commandment. The world ruled by foolishness is the world of the lower classes, the uneducated and illiterate, who lack the insight that they must bow to the authority of secular and ecclesiastical masters in order for the *ordo* to be re-established. In many instances, Brant's poem follows the topos of the decay of customs and the glorification of the past, which can even be found in Greek and Roman literature combined with the idea of a golden age.[1] The idea of the golden age is in Brant's poem (satire 83, 'On Contempt of Poverty') linked to the idea of shared property ('da hat niemand geachtet Geld oder etwas besessen allein', 'no one held money in esteem, and no one owned anything just for himself') and, related to this, general peace, which comes to an end as soon as an individual works a piece of land and thus claims it for himself.

It also seems that the following eulogy to the virtuous acceptance of poverty should be endorsed by the poor themselves. Brant offers them the good advice that they can still go begging, even if it is seen as bad: 'A poor man has *this* freedom / That he can still go begging / Even though people look at him badly; / And even if they give him nothing at all, / His goods remain as light as before' (emphasis in original). For the poor, the freedom from the burden of worldly goods that comes with poverty should be worth living in social ostracism. Brant merely warns the rich that they should be free of the guilt of the extortionate or unjust acquisition of property. In this way, the poor can console themselves for their misery with the fact that their existence is pleasing to God, whereas the rich should be able to continue to enjoy their prosperity as long as they are aware of the futility of everything worldly and take precautions for their salvation.

Whereas Nicholas of Cusa and the authors who wrote the legends of the Poverello placed the intuitively gained knowledge of the *simplex* and *illiteratus* above the acquired knowledge of the book scholar, Sebastian Brant takes the exact opposite position when he writes about the 'Bagpiper of Nickelshausen' (satire 11, 'Contempt of Holy Scripture'): 'Now one has so much of Scripture / Of the Old and the New Covenant, / one doesn't need any further testimony / nor music and preaching / from the bagpiper of Nickelshausen'. He is referring here to the preacher Hans Böhm,[2] a shep-

1 See Margarethe Billerbeck, 'Stoizismus in der römischen Epik neronischer und flavischer Zeit' in Hildegard Temporini and Wolfgang Haase (eds), *Aufstieg und Niedergang der römischen Welt*, VOL. 2 (Berlin and New York: De Gruyter, 1986), pp. 3116–51; here, pp. 3126ff. See also Reinhart Koselleck and Paul Widmer (eds), *Niedergang: Studien zu einem geschichtlichen Thema* (Stuttgart: Klett-Cotta, 1980); Reinhart Koselleck, 'Fortschritt und Niedergang: Nachtrag zur Geschichte zweier Begriffe' in *Begriffsgeschichten* (Frankfurt am Main: Suhrkamp, 2006), pp. 159–82.

2 August Schäffler, 'Böhm, Hans' in *Allgemeine Deutsche Biographie*, VOL. 3 (Leipzig: Duncker & Humblot, 1876), pp. 62–64.

herd who was probably born around 1458 in a place called Helmstadt in Lower Franconia, perhaps as a descendant of immigrant Bohemians. The orphan had to work as a shepherd boy, apparently learned neither to read nor write and was unable to pray the Lord's Prayer, as was revealed in the interrogation following his arrest. In the spring of 1476, after Our Lady appeared to him, Böhm began preaching in Niklashausen, a village in the Tauber Valley, which was already a place of modest pilgrimage, and attracted a large number of believers within a very short time. The preacher not only demanded signs of atonement, such as the burning of jewellery and fine cloth, but also called for an end to the oppression of the lower classes and peasants by the nobility and the high clergy. The Prince-Bishop of Würzburg had him arrested as early as 13 July 1476. The large crowd that came to see the 'holy youth' the following day and marched to the Würzburg fortress was put to flight by a cannonade from the fortress ramparts. Mounted soldiers caused a bloodbath among those fleeing. When the authorities came to realize that Hans Böhm had, without knowing it, placed himself in the tradition of the respected Franciscan preacher Johannes Capistranus, it became necessary to accuse the obviously harmless and naive young man of heretical views and get him out of the way as quickly as possible. On 19 July, he was burned at the stake along with two other defendants.

Since the Prince-Bishop of Würzburg had tried to erase the memory of the piper of Niklashausen by having the Church of St Mary destroyed in order to disperse the continuing pilgrimage,[3] it was from the nineteenth century onwards that legends arose. These narratives made him the propagandist of a socialist revolution and of the Peasants' War that broke out shortly after his death.[4] This myth-making continued into the 1970s, when Rainer Werner Fassbinder made his agitprop film *Niklashauser Fart*, his first television production, which can be considered Fassbinder's first thesis

---

3 The humanist Johannes Trithemius, bishop of Sponheim and later abbot of the Schottenkloster in Würzburg, wrote a report on Hans Böhm in 1514, inspired by Sebastian Brant's *Ship of Fools*. See Richard Wunderli, *Peasant Fires: The Drummer of Niklashausen* (Bloomington, IN: Indiana University Press, 1992), pp. 67ff.

4 For example, Herman Haupt, *Die religiösen Sekten in Franken vor der Reformation* (Würzburg: A. Stuber's Buch- und Kunsthandlung, 1882), pp. 57ff.

film, a genre mix with static shots, long dialogues about the necessity of revolution, and a five-minute smashing performance by Amon Düül II.[5]

Hans Böhm, the uneducated fool, is attacked by Brant not so much for the content of his sermon, but because he seems to believe that something should be added to the Old and New Testament and thus to the corpus of church tradition, the basis of the claim to catholicity. Since the emergence of new religious orders in the mid-twelfth century, such as the Waldensians and Humiliati, the fact that lay people dared to preach had provoked resistance from the clergy and exposed the itinerant preachers to accusation of heresy, which they often paid for with their lives.[6] The Waldensians demanded that not only clergymen appointed by the Pope, but any lay person, even women (!), be allowed to preach and not require ordination. After they had been banned from preaching under Pope Alexander III in 1179, Innocent III allowed the Humiliati to preach morally, but they were still barred from preaching dogmatically.[7] A direct attack on the church's *ordo* concept consisted in the view that a layperson was also allowed to administer sacraments as long as he led a flawless life. The Waldensians even went so far as to deny 'immoral' clergy the *meritum* by virtue of which priests and laity alone were entitled to administer sacraments and preach the word of God. Such a conviction undermined the Church's exclusive claim to exercise the officium.

It is significant in this context that the Humiliati and Waldensians began to produce vernacular translations of the Bible in order to proselytize in the cities. Here, too, they met with determined resistance from the Church, which had the translations confiscated and burned wherever possible. After 1242, the Dominicans were forbidden to translate sermons or other writings from Latin into the respective vernacular languages. It comes as no surprise that the associations of devout women that emerged alongside the mendicant-order movement, called Beguines in the Netherlands and German-speaking countries and Papelards in France,

5 See Michael Töteberg (ed.), *Rainer Werner Fassbinder*, VOL. 2 (Reinbek: Rowohlt, 2002).

6 See Grundmann, *Religiöse Bewegungen im Mittelalter*, pp. 70ff.

7 Grundmann, *Religiöse Bewegungen im Mittelalter*, pp. 78ff.

also faced accusations of heresy, as they preached as laywomen and based their faith not on knowledge of the Scriptures but on visions and mystical experiences.[8] Here, too, the problem of voluntary poverty played a role in the conflict with the clergy, earning the Beguines accusations of hypocrisy and sometimes harsh criticism.[9] The fact that the beguines described their ecstatic experiences with words that, in the secular sphere, refer to erotic encounters or even sexual union must have seemed particularly questionable to the representatives of the Church. For example, Mechthild of Magdeburg writes, among other things, that she stands naked before the heavenly bridegroom, lets herself be 'rubbed' by him, and both are completely 'love-sick' from lip-kissing.[10] Significantly, Mechthild of Magdeburg introduces her work, which is regarded as the first great creation of religious German prose literature, by stating that she is a very 'simple little girl' (Latin: *puella simplicissima*).[11] Sebastian Brant's criticism of the piper of Niklashausen stands in the tradition of ecclesiastical condemnation of the presumption of the laity to have direct access to knowledge of God and to be able to dispense with the mediating role of the clergy. This claim goes hand in hand with a turn to the vernacular and the renunciation of book knowledge. Book knowledge is countered by an intuitive or existential knowledge that is fed by the *cognitio Dei experimentalis*, the bodily experience of encountering, if not, as in the case of many Beguines, uniting with God. However, what applies to the piper—the combination of illiteracy, mystical vision, simple social background, and social criticism—does not in most cases apply to the Beguines. The beguinages were not refuges for

---

8 Grundmann, *Religiöse Bewegungen im Mittelalter*, pp. 319ff. Kurt Ruh, 'Beginenmystik: Hadewjich, Mechthild von Magdeburg, Margarete Porete' in *Kleine Schriften*, VOL. 2, pp. 237–49.

9 For example, see Erhard Lommatzsch, *Gautier de Coincy als Satiriker* (Halle: Niemeyer, 1913), pp. 26–31.

10 P. Gall Morel (ed.), *Offenbarungen der Schwester Mechthild von Magdeburg oder Das fliessende Licht der Gottheit* (Darmstadt: Wissenschaftliche Buchgesellschaft, 1980). See Peter Dinzelbacher, *Deutsche und niederländische Mystik des Mittelalters* (Berlin and Boston: De Gruyter, 2012), pp. 99ff.

11 Balázs J. Nemes and Elke Senne (eds), *Mechthild von Magdeburg, Lux Divinitatis: Das liecht der gotheit. Der lateinisch-frühneuhochdeutsche Überlieferungszweig des 'Fließenden Lichts der Gottheit'* (Berlin and Boston: De Gruyter, 2019), pp. 20–21.

destitute women facing social challenges; their inhabitants were mostly from the nobility or urban patriciate,[12] who had decided to 'leave the world', as Saint Francis describes his conversion in the *Testament* after his encounter with the lepers.[13]

With his criticism of the piper of Niklashausen, whom he declares to be a fool, Sebastian Brant rejects as negative what had distinguished the *idiota* in the tradition from Francis to, with a different theoretical interest, Nicholas of Cusa, and had made him appear equal, if not superior, to the book scholar, as it had allowed one to place him close to the apostles and thus the followers of Christ: simplicity of mind, humility, renunciation of the world, trust in the goodness of God and in the efficacy of a law that was superior to the merely human. The Fool in Sebastian Brant is therefore not the successor of the *idiota*, but a distortion. Whereas it was the *idiota* who accused the spiritual institutions of being too worldly and demanded that they renounce the world, it is now a representative of the spiritual and secular authorities who outlines the area of validity of both the secular and the spiritual. At the same time he banishes the layman from this area and criticizes him for being too worldly, for devoting himself to the mundane business of acquiring property and amusements, which, at the same time, is declared to be his only legitimate field of action. And while it was the *idiota* who set his *simplicitas* against the loquaciousness of school wisdom and insisted on the value of his intuitively acquired knowledge, it is now the humanistically educated poet who assigns the loud-mouthed, drum-beating, pipe-blowing village idiot, preaching on an inverted barrel, his designated place in the order of things and hierarchies and forbids him to interfere in matters of which he knows nothing.

The *ordo* that Sebastian Brant defends encompasses not only the order of social hierarchies, but also the order of knowledge. In satire 34 ('Fool Today as Yesterday') and 66 ('Wanting to Explore All Lands'), he denounces a curiosity that turns to the physical world as its legitimate object of interest without seeking support from theological justifications. Brant argues that no acquisition of knowledge about the external world is of value if it does

12 Grundmann, *Religiöse Bewegungen im Mittelalter*, p. 188.

13 Francis of Assisi, *Sämtliche Schriften*, p. 97.

not also serve self-knowledge. This self-knowledge is to be equated with the recognition of the relativity and necessary incompleteness of possible knowledge (hence the accusations against Dikaiarchos, a Greek geographer and philosopher and student of Aristotle, that he had measured the Alps but not the depth of the hole in which he was condemned to sit, or the ironic remark about the conversion of units of measurement producing little knowledge) and with the recognition of one's own finiteness: 'What need dwells with a man / That he seeks greater things than he is? / He does not know what good will come to him, / When he experiences such high things / And does not know the time of his death, / Which runs away like a shadow' (satire 66). To want to find out something about the world that goes beyond the limits of where religion places man with regard to God and his creation is presumption and hubris. If God is to be thought of as the totality of all that is both possible and real, it is not given to man to attain comprehensive knowledge of the totality of this reality. Otherwise, he would go beyond the likeness of God to an equality in essence with his Creator. At the same time, the world does not represent divine perfection, since the attribute of perfection belongs to him alone, the Creator God. This is why it is a futile effort, if not heretical insubordination to the authority and greatness of God, to concern oneself with the measurement and exploration of the finite and necessarily imperfect.[14]

> On the one hand, the maximum version of the concept of the perfection of the Creator and the world requires us to say that nothing more perfect *could* have been made; on the other hand, the maximum version of the concept of divine power requires us to say that no real work of this Creator ever realizes the maximum of what he could have achieved in terms of greatness and perfection. There is no way out of this dilemma.[15]

---

14 See Hans Blumenberg, 'Der Prozess der theoretischen Neugierde' in *Die Legitimität der Neuzeit*, pp. 263–530. Bernhard von Clairvaux had identified curiosity as a source of pride and old and new guilt. See Gerhard Winkler (ed.), *Bernhard von Clairvaux: Sämtliche Werke lateinisch / deutsch*, VOL. 2 (Innsbruck: Tyrolia, 1992), pp. 39–40.

15 Blumenberg, 'Nachahmung der Natur', p. 87.

Brant decides to solve this dilemma by calling for a renunciation of curiosity. Man must be modest, since his curiosity is an insult to God's omnipotence and the inexhaustibility of his potential to have created this world in one way or another, or, in his boundless freedom, not to have created it at all.[16] However, Brant concedes the possibility that the exploration of distant parts of the world is justifiable if this is conducive to self-knowledge: to travel in order to increase one's wisdom, one must 'overlook', that is, forgive, the fact that not all senses are directed towards God (satire 66).

In *De testimonio animae*, Tertullian (*c.*160–220 CE) had warned against the curiosity with which Christian theologians searched pagan texts for arguments to substantiate Christian truth. Instead, he asked that the simple and unrefined soul be honoured, which he invokes below:

> Sed non eam te advoco, quae scholis formata, bybliothecis exercitata, academiis et porticibus Atticis pasta sapientiam ructas. Te simplicem et rudem et impolitam et idioticam compello qualem te habent qui te solam habent, illam ipsam de compito, de trivio, de textrino totam. Imperitia tua mihi opus est, quoniam aliquantulae peritiae tuae nemo credit. Ea expostulo quae tecum homini infers, quae ex temetipsa aut ex quocumque auctore tuo sentire didicisti.

> But it is not you I call upon, who are educated in schools, versed in libraries, fed intellectually in the academies and Attic halls, who belch forth wisdom from yourself. I address you, who are simple and unrefined, uneducated and ignorant, as with people who have you alone and nothing else, the soul, just as it comes from the alley, from the street corner, from the workshop. It is your lack of experience that I need, because no one believes that you have even a little experience. I want to ask you what you

16 Hans Blumenberg, 'Der Cusaner: Die Welt als Selbstbeschränkung Gottes' in *Die Legitimität der Neuzeit*, p. 604n78: 'The will to create and the plan of creation are as such contingent: God could not have created and he could have created something else. But his actions cannot be measured against these statements of possibility, because "possibility" also springs from divine determination.'

> bring with you into the human being, how you have learned to feel from yourself or through your creator, whoever he may be.'[17]

Just as the wisdom of Nicholas of Cusa's *idiota* can be found on the streets, Tertullian finds it among craftsmen, in the alleys, and in workshops. By invoking an inherent need for knowledge in ordinary people, he follows on from the Aristotelian tradition to which Thomas Aquinas adhered. From the first sentence of Aristotle's *Metaphysics*, which has been effective for centuries—'All men by nature desire to know'[18]—Thomas Aquinas had drawn the conclusion that, since the desire for knowledge is a natural characteristic of man, it is also good: 'Omnis ergo scientia speculativa bona est et honorabilis'.[19]

The extent to which perfect knowledge would be possible without the only perfect thing—namely, God—becoming unknowable presents a dilemma that had corroded the systemic position occupied by the question of the legitimacy of curiosity. In Brant, this position is restructured by abolishing the duality between *idiota* and *doctus* and dissolved in favour of *auctoritas*. Knowledge is legitimate only if it occurs within the framework of what is permitted by the Church. It may be true that it is given to man to want to know, but judgement about permissible curiosity is made depending on the right measure and the appropriateness of the object of curiosity in view of the infinity and omnipotence of God, which transcends all measure and of which only the Church is entitled to have knowledge. The *idiota*, who from Tertullian to Saint Francis was recognized as having a special capacity for knowledge, is relegated to the darkness of ignorance, from which Sebastian Brant evokes his distorted image and afterimage, the fool, in order to use this defamation to ridicule the unregulated and undisciplined, which escapes ecclesiastical sanction.

---

17 E. F. Leopold (ed.), *Septimi Florentis Tertulliani*, VOL. 1 (Leipzig: Tauchnitz, 1839), p. 179; translation by Heinrich Kellner at tertullian.org.

18 Aristotle, *Metaphysik: Schriften zur ersten Philosophie* (Franz F. Schwarz trans. and ed.) (Stuttgart: Reclam, 1970), p. 17.

19 Thomas Aquinas, *Divi Thomae Aquinatis Doctoris Angelici Commentaria in tres libros Aristotelis De anima* (Rome: Apud haeredem Hieronymi Scoti, 1570), LECTIO PRIMA, p. 1.

The *Ship of Fools* is not in the tradition of Shrovetide,[20] against which Brant rails in no uncertain terms (satire 110b), and it is not a poem of a 'topsy-turvy world' that shows what the merely conventional world looks like behind its facade. In Brant's poetry, no hollow order is unmasked, but in the name of order rebelliousness, intoxication, and even if only temporary, the suspension of social protocol and excess are denounced as immoral and reprehensible. The world may be in a phase of perversion, but it is not in a state of inversion. The poem is about a restoration of order, in which the mob, which insists on its right to reshape this order according to its will, must be put back in its place. The *Ship of Fools* is a deeply restorative, conservative poem.

Brant uses a powerful symbol of a perverse world in the chapter on the downtrodden fool (satire 78). The woodcut opening the chapter shows a man in a cowl and wearing a jester's cap, slumping to the right with his hand raised defensively, being attacked by a donkey, the attribute of the jester. The donkey has reared up on its hind legs and appears to be pushing the man to the ground with its front legs. The following text makes it clear that the donkey stands for all the folly that holds man down—quarrelsomeness, melancholy and dejection, lack of understanding and irascibility—and the author, as he reports, hides in a bush in the vain hope, as the woodcut shows, that the donkey will overlook him and spare him. Man is the victim of his own faults and weaknesses as well as of his lack of insight into his own condition, which he could very well change. The motif of a donkey riding a man, or a man carrying a donkey, seems to have been widespread in folk art throughout Europe from the fifteenth century onwards. It came to prominence at the end of the eighteenth century: in *Capricho* No. 42 by Francisco de Goya (1746–1828), which is part of a six-part series of depictions of donkeys within the cycle *Los Caprichos* (1799), two men are seen bending under the weight of donkeys sitting on their backs. As the commentaries suggest, the donkeys refer to the nobility and

---

20 See Dietz-Rüdiger Moser, *Fastnacht—Fasching—Karneval: Das Fest der 'verkehrten Welt'* (Graz: Edition Kaleidoskop, 1986). See also the entry 'Fastnacht / Karneval' in Christoph Auffarth, Jutta Bernard and Hubert Mohr (eds), *Metzler Lexikon Religion*, VOL. 1 (Stuttgart and Weimar: J. B. Metzler, 2005), pp. 356ff.

clergy, who are holding down the lower classes. 'It is precisely the poor people and useful classes of society who carry the donkeys on their backs, that is, they alone bear the entire weight of the tax burden'.[21] However, Goya's etching does not allow for a clear distinction between perpetrator and victim: the man and the animal in the rear plane of the picture seem to form one body, and the head of the man at the back paradoxically overlaps that of the man at the front, above whom the donkey seems to hover, rather than to rest on him, despite his bent posture. This aporetically constructed formation of power relations, which can also be found in other *Caprichos* by Goya (for example in No. 33, with the comparable fusion of the limbs of the violent quack and his victim), ascribes as much responsibility for his situation to the victim as to the perpetrator, but does so from a different perspective and in a different historical situation: Brant uses the metaphor of the donkey to assign responsibility, if not guilt, to the victim for his humiliation. Nothing and no one prevents him from freeing himself on the narrow path of virtue and obedience except his own lack of insight into his state of subjugation to divine right.[22] In contrast, Goya constructs the victim's shared responsibility from the perspective of a resignation resulting from doubt about the possibility of enlightenment. The folly in the *Caprichos* is not a world out of joint that needs a restorative correction to heal, but a society in which man does not dare to take the decisive step into a future in which he gets rid of that which oppresses him. What he lacks is not insight into the rightfulness of the established order, but the insight that he lacks nothing to free himself from his self-inflicted immaturity except the will to establish his own rights.[23]

---

21 Quoted from Werner Busch, 'Goya und die Tradition des "capriccio"' in Max Imdahl (ed.), *Wie eindeutig ist ein Kunstwerk?* (Cologne: DuMont, 1986), pp. 41–73; here, p. 69.

22 See Sebastian Brant, *Das Narrenschiff*, SATIRE 47, 'Vom Weg der Seligkeit'.

23 The motif of the donkey bearers is taken up again in the video work *Inverso Mundus* (2015) by the artist collective AES+F, in which a young couple carry two donkeys through a digitally smooth backdrop to the Toccata from Jacques Kauffmann's *Suite Gothique*. The scene is at the end of a long tableau vivant that plays out on up to seven screens, in which young people with model appeal indulge in slow movements in a twisted hedonism, older people 'fight' with the young in slow-motion battles and both

## *Praise of Folly* by Erasmus of Rotterdam

Only a few years after the publication of *The Ship of Fools*, in 1509, the humanist and theologian Erasmus of Rotterdam (1466–1536) wrote his *Praise of Folly*, dedicated to the English scholar Thomas More. It is said that the text was conceived during a spell of boredom on the journey from Italy to England, and as an imagined conversation with his distant friend to pass the time—a chat about folly.[24] First published in Paris in 1511, later in Strasbourg, and translated into German in 1534, this text is one of the bestsellers of modern European literature.

Comparing the two texts has its challenges—one written in stanzas, the other in free prose; one dominated by the voice of an authorial speaker, the other rendered in the tone of ironic inauthenticity; one imbued with the gravity of a task and a reproach, which the other dispenses with through laughter. The ironic refraction and double-coding of the text through the introduction of the figure of Folly as the speaker of a speech that applies to herself allows Erasmus the freedom of inauthenticity; he can have *Stultitia utter* all the impertinences, caustic observations, relentless denunciations, and vehement accusations with which he laments the folly of the world, without restricting his own freedom through pre-emptive self-censorship. This did not save the text from the Index, but the Index itself proved to be nothing more than temporary folly.

The word 'idiota' appears three times in Erasmus' text: when he mentions Pythagoras' esteem for the 'simple citizens' instead of the scholars and great men of the realm ('Rūrsum inter hominēs, idiōtās multīs partibus antepōnit doctīs ac magnīs'), when he makes fun of the grammarians, who know how to make an impression on the 'stupid mothers and simple-minded fathers' through an appearance of importance ('ut stultīs māterculīs et idiōtīs patribus'), and finally, in connection with the 'foolishness of the cross', when he mentions the 'dull-witted and sluggish apostles' ('Neque aliā ratiō-ne mederı voluit quam per stultitiam crucis, per apostolōs idiōtās

---

sexes roll around each other in a continuous hallucinatory fumble without ever coming close to each other.

24 Erasmus of Rotterdam, *Lob der Torheit* (Heinrich Hersch trans.) (Hamburg: Nikol, 2019).

ac pinguēs: quibus sēdulō stultitiam praecipit'),[25] which Christ thought he had to use alongside the cross for the work of redeeming humanity, while at the same time anxiously ensuring that they never relied on their 'own wisdom' but depended entirely on him.

The meaning of the term 'idiota', therefore, has no sharp contours. It ranges from simple in the positive apostolic sense to stupid and uneducated to dull-witted and daft. The *idiota* thus no longer has an insightful or functionally relevant position in the debate, which revolves around the value of knowledge and faith, curiosity and modesty, as well as the moral constitution of society, which Erasmus takes apart with zeal and irony. In contrast to Brant's text, folly has now spread to all social classes, and Erasmus subjects the kings, popes, and princes, whom Brant had spared, to unforgiving, biting mockery. After first sketching an image of the good ruler,[26] he contrasts this ideal with the reality of the selfish, uneducated, passion-driven libertine and narcissist, who is concerned with nothing less than the fate of his subjects. He is followed by a whole procession of sycophants, the 'most obsequious, contemptible, repugnant and depraved',[27] who ensnare the prince with every kind of flattery as long as he allows them to enrich themselves and lead a life of opulence. This is followed by criticism of the papacy and the clergy, who, stupid and oblivious to their task, imitate the life of princes, amass wealth, indulge in gluttony, start wars, and sin against Christ. The 'godless popes',[28] through their heartless reign, mercilessly shed the blood of thousands of innocent people; they consider poverty to be 'vulgar', compassion soft, the cross, symbol of their faith, tasteless.[29] Although Christ was without possessions and the apostles left everything behind to follow him (Luke 18:28), the representatives of the apostolic see enjoy their estates and abundant sources of income such as customs duties and the sale of indulgences. Tirelessly amassing money,

25 See Desiderius Erasmus, *Encomium moriae; sive, Declamatio in laudem stultitiae* (Tilburg: Tilburg University Press, 2019), pp. 38, 58, 96.

26 Erasmus, *Lob der Torheit*, pp. 105–06.

27 Erasmus, *Lob der Torheit*, p. 108.

28 Erasmus, *Lob der Torheit*, p. 114.

29 Erasmus, *Lob der Torheit*, pp. 113–14.

they delegate the task of pastoral care to the lower ecclesiastical ranks, who, as guardians of their sheep, know nothing better than to shear their fleeces.[30]

It goes without saying that the grammarians, rhetors and philosophers, and other 'scholarly riffraffs'[31] are spared as little as the learned theologians with their sophistry.[32] However, Erasmus attacks the pious, the religious, and the monks with the same sharp pen.[33] What they present to their fellow human beings as simplicity and innocence of spirit is to him 'ignorance, rudeness, and impudence', and he is outraged by the 'brazen, impertinent mien' with which they beg for bread and harass all 'taverns, carts, and barges'. He also accuses those who reject property of hypocrisy, because they are not interested in being like Christ, but in being unlike one another.[34] It is only towards the end of her eulogy that Folly treats the zealous practitioners of apostolic simplicity with a little less malice when she says: '[T]hey care nothing for the body, they spurn and flee money as if it were garbage; if they are forced to occupy themselves with earthly things, they do so only sullenly and reluctantly; they have as if they had nothing, and they possess as if they had nothing'.[35] Erasmus thus distinguishes between the performance of the pious, who out of vanity and arrogance pretend to be exemplary to their fellow believers, and true followers of Christ, for whose characterization he chooses the words with which Paul had described life under the eschatological proviso, the life of the 'As-If'.

Nevertheless, Erasmus has little respect for the Christian religion because, he says, 'it has a certain kinship with folly and has no relation at all to wisdom'.[36] In the passage already mentioned,[37] where he speaks of the 'foolishness of the cross', he accuses Christ and God the Father alike of

30 Erasmus, *Lob der Torheit*, p. 117.

31 Erasmus, *Lob der Torheit*, p. 129.

32 Erasmus, *Lob der Torheit*, p. 120.

33 Erasmus, *Lob der Torheit*, pp. 96–97.

34 Erasmus, *Lob der Torheit*, p. 97.

35 Erasmus, *Lob der Torheit*, p. 138.

36 Erasmus, *Lob der Torheit*, p. 135.

37 Erasmus, *Lob der Torheit*, p. 133.

having intended to keep the apostles and the first human couple in spiritual dependence and to deny them the possibility of knowledge by denouncing knowledge as 'poison for beatitude' and, as he writes with regard to Paul, as 'a seed of pride and corruption'. After a lengthy discussion on the correct understanding of the sacraments, he comes to the conclusion that the pious, who reject the body, and the non-pious disagree on every point and accuse each other of frenzy, but that it is to the pious that the word frenzy applies more properly. With reference to Plato (*Phaedrus* 245b, where Plato distinguishes the delusion of love from the frenzy caused by the Muses), Erasmus compares the lover who 'is beside himself' with the believer seized by religious rapture. But Erasmus is not concerned with the theological justifications of the true faith or the condemnations of the false faith, but, after proving his biblical solidity and his knowledge of the ancient authors, compares the exalted believer with the madman. He contrasts both with Wisdom, which remains strangely pale throughout the text. It may seem obvious that Folly does not have much to say about her, but there is a passage in which she, like the donkey in Aesop's fable, dons the 'lion's skin of scholarship'[38] and takes the reader on a whirlwind tour through the history of the mind-body problem since Plato in order to prove that the bliss of Christians is only a kind of frenzy and folly. Erasmus' appeal to examine the 'thing itself' is an expression of trust in the ability of the human mind to subject its objects of knowledge—whether creations of the mind or objects of nature—to critical scrutiny in order to gain knowledge about the world that is intersubjectively valid. It is possible for humans to gain knowledge as an 'adaequatio intellectus et rei'.[39] It is

38 Erasmus, *Lob der Torheit*, p. 136.

39 See Martin Heidegger, *Platons Lehre von der Wahrheit* in *Wegmarken* (Frankfurt am Main: Vittorio Klostermann, 1978 [1967]), p. 216: 'Truth has for the occidental for a long time meant the correspondence of the thinking conception with the thing; it has been the basis of thought: *adaequatio intellectus et rei*.' See also Martin Heidegger, *Sein und Zeit* (Frankfurt am Main: Vittorio Klostermann, 1977), GA 2, pp. 285ff., 297. On the change in his conception of truth away from the principle of correspondence towards the rhetoric of unconcealment, see Martin Heidegger, *Vom Wesen der Wahrheit* (Frankfurt am Main: Vittorio Klostermann, 1988), GA 34, pp. 8–20; see also Martin Heidegger, 'Vom Ursprung des Kunstwerks' (1935/36) in *Holzwege*, GA 5 (Frankfurt am Main: Vittorio Klostermann, 1977), pp. 1–77; here, pp. 44ff.

therefore not surprising that, at the end of the discussion of the frenzy of the faithful, a section is devoted to the description of the mentally ill in a state of manic exaltation: 'They speak incoherently and not at all like human beings, for they utter only senseless sounds, and their facial expressions change every moment. Sometimes they are happy, sometimes depressed, sometimes crying, sometimes laughing, sometimes sighing; in short, they are really beside themselves'.[40]

Like Brant, Erasmus also links human curiosity and the human will to knowledge with the fact that humanity is no longer living in the Golden Age. All the 'learned stuff' was unnecessary and alien to the 'simple generation of the Golden Age' ('simplex illa aurei saeculi gens'),[41] and their religious timidity prevented people from gaining experience about the size and movement of the stars, for example, as they considered it a sin to exceed the limits prescribed for them. It was only through the invention of the *arts* (*artes*) that the things that made people's lives a constant torment came into the world. The arts can be understood as compensatory media for the loss of natural security and innocence that accompanied the end of the Golden Age. Knowledge as a substitute for lost happiness results from the loss of pristine, happy simplicity and the loss of nature as a teacher. By denouncing the sciences and arts as compensatory forms for the loss of nature, whose 'creations [ . . . ] are in every respect more excellent [than] those of made-up art',[42] Folly draws on the topos of the state of nature, from which man has sinned by distancing himself through culture. If Folly invokes the vice of folly as a virtue that makes life possible for man, who is alienated from the state of nature, it simultaneously invokes Wisdom and

40 On the symptoms described by Erasmus, see Dietrich von Engelhardt, 'Der Kranke und seine Krankheit in der Literatur' in Heinrich Schipperges, Wilhelm Doerr and Hans Schaefer (eds), *Der Mensch in seiner Eigenwelt: Anthropologische Grundfragen einer theoretischen Pathologie* (Heidelberg: Springer, 1991), pp. 29–51; here, p. 49.

41 Erasmus, *Lob der Torheit*, p. 48; *Encomium moriae*, p. 36. This topos is repeated in Rousseau, for whom the *artes inutiles* and the *sciences frivoles* are signs of decay and decline. See Fetscher, *Rousseaus politische Philosophie*, p. 56. In the same sense, see also Chateaubriand, *Essai sur les révolutions* (Paris: Ladvocat, 1826), p. 294–95: 'When the Swiss were still upright, they knew nothing of literature and art. But when they began to lose their morality, Haller, Tissot, Gessner and Lavater appeared.'

42 Erasmus, *Lob der Torheit*, p. 50.

knowledge as the torments under which man has been groaning ever since, forced to submit to the law, which as his own is able to save him in his homelessness. Wisdom is folly from the perspective of the fool who does not want to admit to himself that the happiness he associates with the idea of the natural state in paradise cannot be regained. The man of whom Folly speaks is the man who derives his actions neither from Christ's commandment nor from the commandments of nature, but who, irrevocably cast out of the safety of a prehistoric bliss, has had to place himself at the centre of his own world. The rift between truth and madness, reason and folly no longer runs between two forms of behaviour and understanding of the world, one of which is to be found on the side of God-ordained and natural well-orderedness and the other on the side of human blindness and hubris begotten by sin. Rather, the rift runs through man himself. Instead of folly, which is always only a distorted reflection of an imagined or dreamed ideality, madness emerges at the end. It pulls man into a vortex that no longer resembles the overwhelming vision of God and the exalted union with the Son of Man or is set in motion by the gravitation of vice, laziness, and baseness as the 'natural' characteristics of man, but by the inner, autonomous dynamics of a 'world-eccentric' existence.[43] The frenzy, the madness, the foolishness are no longer moral states of aberration with regard to the perfection of the world desired by God, which man defiles through his sinful behaviour, or caused by his shamefully inadequate nature as a rejected, flawed being, but, as a disease, madness is one possibility of being human. This possibility of failing as a human being and sinking into spiritual disintegration and illness no longer retains any of the magic of Platonic enthusiasm,[44] which Marsilio Ficino had tried to revive as *furor poeticus* a few years before Brant and Erasmus at the end of

---

43 Max Scheler, *Die Stellung des Menschen im Kosmos* (Munich: Nymphenburger Verlagshandlung, 1947), p. 82.

44 Plato, *Ion* (Friedrich Daniel Ernst Schleiermacher trans.) (Berlin: Akademie Verlag, 1984), 534a: 'For a poet is a light being, and winged and holy, and is not able to write poetry until he has become enthusiastic and unconscious and reason no longer dwells in him. For as long as he still holds on to this possession, every man is incapable of writing poetry or speaking oracles' (Translated by LE).

the fifteenth century.[45] The human being that Erasmus conceives of is the human being who creates his own nature. This creation of a self corresponds to the creation of a science of man, in which madness is diagnosed as a disease. It is still influenced by the ancient doctrine of the humours and is far from establishing itself as an independent discipline. However, at the beginning of the sixteenth century, in the discourse on idiocy, folly, and wisdom, the raving maniac, the madman, the mentally ill person emerges as a figure with his own profile as the result of a progressive diremption. In this hour of the birth of the mentally ill person, it is already foreseeable that this will also lay the seed for a moral approach to his illness, which will determine the treatment of madness for a long time to come.

### Opicinus de Canistris and Hugo van der Goes

Just how closely the madman, who together with the fool took the place of the *idiota*, was interwoven with the moral concepts of sin and transgression, repentance and punishment, as well as the themes, ideas, and neuroses, the idiosyncrasies and mannerisms of his time, is shown by the fates of a cleric in Avignon and a painter in what is now Belgium, who were separated from each other by just over a hundred years. The first, Opicinus de Canistris (1296–1353), served as a priest at the court of Pope John XXII in Avignon, the other, Hugo van der Goes (1435/40–1482), was a successful painter in Ghent. Opicinus was born in Lomello near Pavia, trained as a priest in Genoa, and was ordained in Parma in 1320. His writings include a critique of Marsilius of Padua and Louis the Bavarian, from whose troops Opicinus fled to Valenza in 1329 after they had conquered Pavia. From there, Opicinus went to Avignon, where he found employment as a scribe at the papal court. In his autobiography, which has been preserved in two manuscripts, he describes how he was struck down by an illness on 31 March 1334, as a result of which he lost his speech and his memory. His right hand is paralysed and will never regain its full strength, even in the years that follow, during which he slowly recovers. Opicinus experiences

45 Marsilio Ficino, *Opera Omnia* (Lyon: Antonium Vincentium, 1557), pp. 116ff. On *furor poeticus* in general, see Christoph J. Steppich, *Numine afflatur*: *Die Inspiration des Dichters in der Renaissance* (Wiesbaden: Harrassowitz, 2002), pp. 146ff.

his illness as a punishment for his sins and views his protracted convalescence as the recovery of his powers of faith, which, he is convinced, are ultimately even stronger than before the illness. Alongside his autobiographical writings, he produces large-format drawings with complex depictions in which planetary orbits overlap with cosmological bodies, and figures blend into maps. The rediscovery of the two manuscripts kept in the Vatican, one published by Richard Salomon, the other by Muriel Laharie and Guy Roux,[46] led to a controversy as to whether Opicinus had suffered a stroke or a severe schizophrenic episode. This has consequences for the extent to which one perceives his style and content as remaining in the realm of the conventions of his time or as showing traits of deviance and mental illness.

The fact that it is not possible to distinguish whether his anthropomorphizing depictions of celestial bodies and seashores, planetary orbits and continents are to be understood as religiously grounded or hallucinatory-pathological, based on contemporary, conventional knowledge, which he modifies, or on delusions,[47] sheds light on Erasmus' thesis that religious frenzy cannot be distinguished from mental illness. In addition, if one wants to decide on Opicinus' mental state, there is the historical, mental, and cultural distance that separates the contemporary viewer from him and prevents direct access to the enigmatic pictorial inventions of the sick cleric. His statements leave no doubt that Opicinus was ill and experienced himself as ill, but today's nosological classifications do not do justice to the understanding of illness and health at the time.

---

46 Richard G. Salomon, *Opicinus de Canistris: Weltbild und Bekenntnisse eines Avignonesischen Klerikers des 14. Jahrhunderts* (London: Warburg Institute, 1936), 2 VOLS.; REPR. Lichtenstein: Kraus Reprint, 1969. Guy Roux and Muriel Laharie, *Art et Folie au Moyen Âge: Aventures et Énigmes d'Opicinus de Canistris* (*1296–1351?*) (Paris: Le Léopard d'Or, 1997).

47 On the debate, see Serena Masolini, 'Crossing Lines between the Mediterranean, the *Ecclesia Specularis*, and the Self: Notes on a Recent Book on Opicino de Canistris' in *Mediterranea: International Journal for the Transfer of Knowledge* 4 (2019): 255–66. See also Karl Whittington, *Body-Worlds: Opicinus de Canistris and the Medieval Cartographic Imagination* (Turnhout: Pontifical Institute of Mediaeval Studies, Department of Publications, 2014). Sylvain Piron, *Dialectique du monstre: Enquête sur Opicino de Canistris* (Brussels: Zones sensibles, 2015).

Hugo van der Goes also suffers an episode of illness, which he describes as punishment for sins committed. The artist, who was listed as a freeman of the Ghent Painters' Guild in 1467, entered a monastery of the Windesheim Congregation at the Rood Klooster near Brussels as a *conversus* ten or eleven years later. Due to his fame as a painter, who was even visited by the future Emperor Maximilian I, he enjoyed a special position in the monastery, which caused envy and resentment among the monks. On his way back from a trip to Cologne in 1482, he was overcome by 'a strange illness in which he fantasized, constantly saying that he was damned and condemned to eternal damnation. Whereby he also wanted to harm himself physically and fatally if he were not violently stopped from this attempt by bystanders'.[48] Just as David cheered up the melancholic Saul by playing the harp, the abbot tries to heal the sick man, who sees himself as a prodigal son, through music. But van der Goes never recovers; he dies in 1482, probably without having produced a single painting any more. The chronicler Ofhuys sees the painter's illness as a punishment for the arrogance and pride he had developed due to his success and mentions that after his return, the *conversus* humbly ate his meals with the other lay brothers and not, as before, with the monks in the refectory. Whether van der Goes' illness was actually caused by the fact that he could no longer bear the tension between worldly fame and the monastic-ascetic ideal and collapsed under its weight can only be speculated.[49] The Windesheim Congregation, which he had joined, was under the considerable influence of its most famous member, Thomas à Kempis, whose *Imitation of Christ* was, second only to the Bible, one of the most widely read and most popular books printed in Europe.[50] In it one finds all the warnings against worldly pleasures and exaggerated curiosity that are now quite familiar to us. If the monastery chronicler's report is correct, van der Goes' illness and the content of his delusions reflect what the monastic community in

48 This is the report of the chronicler Gaspar Ofhuys quoted in Jochen Sander, *Hugo van der Goes: Stilentwicklung und Chronologie* (Mainz: von Zabern, 1992), p. 17.

49 Margot Wittkower and Rudolf Wittkower, *Künstler: Außenseiter der Gesellschaft* (Stuttgart: Klett-Cotta, 1989 [1963]), p. 129.

50 Johann Michael Sailer (ed.), *Das Buch von der Nachfolgung Christi* (Sulzbach: Seidel, 1845).

which he lived burdened him with as guilt. There is nothing original or interesting about the content of his delusions; rather, they are directly dependent on semantics that had determined his life and that of his fellow monks even before his collapse. The madness does not catapult him out into a space of the asocial, but rather sucks him into the centre of his social world, in which he is now torn apart as its prisoner by its contradictory forces. But at the same time, caution is required, both as concerns the self-testimonies of Opicinus and the documents of Brother Ofhuys: both have only a limited number of hermeneutic tools at their disposal with the help of which they can categorize what has just tried to elude categorization and seems to have slipped away. Their efforts to understand themselves or the other person take place within a narrowly defined terrain. Even the sick person hallucinates only what he already knows something about, and his counterpart will be able to record only what corresponds to his previous understanding of the meaning of madness. The absolutely alien, if it is possible at all, escapes one's own grasp as well as that of the other. It either sinks into silence or into insignificance. In either case, since there are no words for the absolutely alien, it eludes transmission and disappears into the nothingness of the never-happened. To 'turn to the thing itself', as Erasmus demands in a good Husserlian way,[51] is then a decision the appropriateness of which becomes contingent, since what 'the thing' is remains questionable. Viewed from the inside, where delusional content is perceived as truth, and from the outside, in which case it is perceived as madness, the truth of each delusional experience is *the thing itself.* What it was that caused the cheerful pre-Enlightenment philosopher from Rotterdam to believe that his mind could cleanly separate the jumble of belief, madness and delusion, hallucination and delirium from the core of reality that must be hidden within it remains a mystery.

For the core of reality is madness, or rather madness reveals the interior of the social semantics that produce its forms of expression.

51 Edmund Husserl, 'Philosophie als strenge Wissenschaft' (1911) in *Vorträge und Aufsätze*, Husserliana, VOL. 25 (Dordrecht: Kluwer Academic Publishers, 1987), p. 21.

CHAPTER THREE

# Jurodivyj

On 28 November 1931, the Paris-based Russian intellectual Boris Zajcev (1881–1972) published a text entitled *Istorija russkoj duši* (History of the Russian Soul) in the Parisian newspaper *Vozroždenie*. In this review of the book *Svjatye drevnej Rusi* (The Saints of Ancient Rus) by Georgij Fedotov, he says,

> The assumption of an ugly, disfigured countenance, a humility that consists in provoking aversion [ . . . ] one must admit that our 'Dostoyevskyism', which is rooted in some morbid traits of the soul, is an unpleasant affair. [ . . . ] The image of the saint as a humiliated and almost persecuted, half-naked and hungry being was somehow particularly close to Rus. Only Byzantium knew holy jurodivye—this is almost completely alien to the West (but again: Francis of Assisi!).[1]

The Poverello from Assisi, who had shed his clothes in the marketplace of his home town to follow the naked Christ, is associated by Zajcev with the figure of the jurodivyj, the figure of the Russian ascetic, beggar, troublemaker, madman, and fool, whose many scandalous characteristics include his nakedness. Naked or only scantily clad, the jurodivyj wanders through the cities, unwashed and unkempt, with long hair and heavy chains or weights forged onto his body. According to Zajcev, he is the product of an 'unpleasant Dostoyevskyism', a predilection for the grotesque and the abject, the repulsive and the revolting, rooted in pathological traits of the Russian soul.

---

1 Quoted in Christian Münch, *In Christo närrisches Russland: Zur Deutung und Bedeutung des jurodstvo im kulturellen und sozialen Kontext des Zarenreiches* (Göttingen: Vandenhoeck & Ruprecht, 2017), p. 293. In addition to this account, in the following I rely primarily on Sergey A. Ivanov, *Holy Fools in Byzantium and Beyond* (Oxford: Oxford University Press, 2006); Priscilla Hunt and Svitlana Kobets (eds), *Holy Foolishness in Russia: New Perspectives* (New York. Slavica Publishers, 2011); Cezary Wodziński, *Saint Idiot* (Paris: Difference, 2012).

In his review, Zajcev intervenes in a debate that in nineteenth-century Russia had ennobled the holy fool as the epitome of the Russian soul, after he had been, for centuries since the beginning of the Eastern Roman Empire, subjected to an eventful history of admiration and veneration on the one hand and hatred, contempt, and persecution on the other. The jurodivyj is an idiot, an ascetic, a prophet, a provocateur, and a lover. He dares to put a stop to bloodthirsty tsars and to slap bishops for their hypocrisy, he defecates in public, visits brothels, he riots in church and throws stones at passers-by, he dances with prostitutes by day and prays and atones by night, he wears women's clothes and sleeps with the dogs on the dung heap like Job. He allows himself to be tormented and abused, insulted, beaten, and spat upon and puts all his ambition into being the lowest of the low, the most despicable of sinners and the scum of the earth.

When Zajcev formulated his aversion to the 'unpleasant Dostoyevskyism', Russian nationalism seized upon the figure of the jurodivyj. The figure of the ascetic had already played an important role in the debate between the 'Slavophiles' and the 'Westerners' after 1812. The debate was intensified by the publication of Petr Čaadev's 'First Philosophical Letter' in the journal *Teleskop* in 1836. In this text, Čaadev criticized Russia as a nation that had contributed nothing to the progress of the human spirit and was hopelessly inferior to the West as a historical entity,[2] an assessment against which the Slavophiles, led by the historical philosopher and lay theologian Aleksey S. Chomjakov (1804–1860), argued, drawing on the jurodivyj.[3] Now the courage of the jurodivyj was one of the characteristics of the Russian national character, which opposes the cruelty of the tsars. His spiritual simplicity and material poverty stand in contrast to the 'erudition and sophistication' of the West, which led to luxury and depravity. The unity of the Russian church and the unity of faith and life in Christian Orthodox Russia are contrasted with the fragmentation of life in post-Enlightenment Europe and stylized as the expression of a higher truth that manifests itself

---

2 Münch, *In Christo*, p. 263n453.

3 On Chomjakov, see Jennifer Wasmuth, 'Östliche Orthodoxien: Die Verbreitung des 'Sobornost'-Konzepts in den östlichen Kirchen' in *Europäische Geschichte Online* (EGO) (16 April 2012).

in the Russian national soul. Chomjakov, who published only in German and French, summarizes the contrast between Russia and the West with the words: 'Ce que la sagesse de l'Occident ignorait, l'ignorance de l'Orient le lui enseigne', 'What the wisdom of the West has not recognized, the folly [*jurodstvo*] of the East teaches it'.[4]

The jurodivyj belongs in the tradition of the early Christian figure of the salos, which was particularly widespread in Syria and Egypt. The salos—the madman, the possessed—appears in the context of koinobitic and anachoretic monasticism, whose protagonists practise a life in a monastic community (*koinobitism*) or as hermits and ascetics separated from the community (*anachoretes*).

However, the first figure of salos is not a man, but a woman. As early as the fourth century, there are reports of an unnamed person, who later comes to be called Isidora. She lives in a convent in the Thebais in Upper Egypt and is mistreated, ridiculed, and harassed by the other nuns because of her simple-mindedness. Without ever speaking a word, she performs menial tasks in the convent kitchen, washes and cleans, and eats leftover food. In a vision, the hermit Piteroum, who lives nearby, is told to go to the monastery as he will find a woman there who leads a life more pleasing to God than his own and whom he will recognize by a crown. The person who is finally presented to him is Isidora, her head wrapped in dirty rags, and when Piteroum prostrates himself before her, this not only provokes the astonishment and horror of the assembled nuns, but also the objection of the simple-minded woman, who refuses to be worshipped by the saint. When her resistance is of no avail, she leaves the convent unnoticed and disappears without a trace. Neither the rest of her life nor the time and place of her death are known.[5]

In the centuries that followed, two men in particular shaped the type of salos as a parallel figure to the Western *idiota*: Symeon of Emesa (sixth century), whose life is recorded in the *Vita Symeonis Sali* by Leontius of

4 A. S. Komjakov (Chomjakov), *L'église latine et le Protestantisme au point de vue de l'Église d'Orient* (Lausanne and Vevey: B. Benda, 1872), p. 111.

5 W. K. Lowther Clarke, *The Lausiac History of Palladius* (New York: Macmillan, 1918), CHAP. 34, pp. 118ff. See Ivanov, *Holy Fools*, pp. 51ff.

Neapolis (Cyprus, mid-seventh century),[6] and Andrew of Constantinople (tenth century), about whom Nikephoros reports in a biography based on the Vita of Symeon and which probably integrates earlier texts in the form of a compilation.[7]

Symeon travels with his elderly mother to Jerusalem, where they both take part in the celebrations of the Raising of the Cross. There, Symeon meets a young man, John, who also comes from present-day Syria and is accompanied by his father and his young wife, whom he had married only a year earlier. After visiting the holy places, the two families decide to travel back together, and their journey takes them to Jericho, where they marvel at the numerous monasteries built on the banks of the Jordan. The young men ask each other in amazement who might live in those buildings. They assume it must be the angels of God. The moment of conversion follows: undecided as to whether they should continue on the path of life or the path of death, on which they see their parents and the young woman advancing, they throw the dice. It turns out in Symeon's favour: he looks towards the Jordan, towards the monasteries, towards life, and 'overjoyed, they embrace and kiss each other and forget about the path of death, all their possessions, their wealth and their parents'.[8] The two friends leave their families and initially spend a week in a monastery dedicated to Saint Gerasimos, where they are encouraged by Abbot Nikon in their decision to lead the life of ascetics. They are drawn to the desert, where they will spend the next thirty years together under great hardship. However, Symeon later undergoes a second conversion: he doubts that life in the solitude of the desert will bring him any further spiritual merit,[9] as the scriptures say that it is more important to seek the salvation of one's neighbour than

6 Leontius of Neapolis, 'Vita S. Symeonis Sali confessoris' in *Hesychii Hierosolymitani presbyteri, Olympiodori Alexandrini, Leontii Neapoleos in Cypro episcopi, opera omnia*, Patrologia Graeca, VOL. 93 (Paris: J.-P. Migne, 1865), cols. 1669ff.

7 See Lennart Rydén, *The Life of St Andrew the Fool*, pp. 27–28. See Jan Hofstra, *Leontius von Neapolis und Symeon der Heilige Narr* (Drachten: Karmel, 2008). See Münch, *In Christo*, pp. 70ff. See Derek Krueger, *Symeon the Holy Fool: Leontius's Life and the Late Antique City* (Berkeley: University of California Press, 1996).

8 Leontius of Neapolis, 'Vita S. Symeonis Sali confessoris', cols. 1675A–1676C.

9 Leontius of Neapolis, 'Vita S. Symeonis Sali confessoris', cols. 1703A–1704A.

one's own (1 Cor 10:24). John fears that the devil has given rise to these doubts and reminds him of the promise they had made to each other: never to leave each other. He begs him to continue serving God with him in the silence of the desert, but Symeon confirms his decision: to go into the world in Christ's name in order to expose it to ridicule.[10] He asks his friend to 'consider him dead',[11] which is why it makes no difference whether he stays with him or not, whereupon John gives up his resistance. He accompanies his friend part of the way but, in tears, turns back after repeated requests.

Symeon, eager to visit the holy places once again, goes to Jerusalem, from where he sets off for Emesa, today's Homs, three days later. The chronicle of Leontius tells of his spectacular entry into Emesa: outside the city gates, Symeon finds the carcass of a dog on a dung heap. He ties one end of the rope holding his robe together around one of the dead animal's legs and, dragging the dead dog behind him, he enters the city. As soon as he enters, he is mocked as mad and beaten by children whose school he passes.[12] This is followed by a series of provocations and scandalous acts: Symeon disrupts the service, throws nuts at worshippers, extinguishes candles, storms the place of the lectern and overturns the merchants' tables as he flees from the angry citizens, who offer their wares in front of the church and almost beat him to death.[13]

The account of Leontius is full of stories in which the saint appears to behave like a fool: he gives away a merchant's goods instead of selling them,[14] he undresses in front of a woman who accuses him of attempting to rape her, whereupon he in turn receives a beating. He empties himself in public without shame, and instead of going to the men's bath, he goes to the women's bath when he is asked by his only confidant in the city, a deacon named John, to purify himself.[15] When his companion John, who

10 Leontius of Neapolis, 'Vita S. Symeonis Sali confessoris', cols. 1703A–1704B.

11 Leontius of Neapolis, 'Vita S. Symeonis Sali confessoris', cols. 1703A–1704D.

12 Leontius of Neapolis, 'Vita S. Symeonis Sali confessoris', cols. 1707A–1708D.

13 Leontius of Neapolis, 'Vita S. Symeonis Sali confessoris', cols. 1709A–1710A.

14 Leontius of Neapolis, 'Vita S. Symeonis Sali confessoris', cols. 1709A–1710B.

15 Leontius of Neapolis, 'Vita S. Symeonis Sali confessoris', cols. 1712C–1714C.

had stayed behind in the desert, sends two monks to have him give them spiritual advice, he insults them, calls both John and the two brothers idiots and scalds their lips with hot wine in order to force them to keep quiet.[16] When a man who lives near Emesa wants to convince himself that the salos is only faking his foolishness, he goes into town and meets Symeon in the company of two prostitutes. Convinced that Symeon is fornicating with the two women, he tells himself that the saint is possessed by Satan. Then Symeon approaches him, hits him, drops his clothes, dances in front of him and says: 'Come and play, there is no deceit here'. To prevent the man from telling anyone else that he has been able to read his thoughts, Symeon seals his lips.[17] Leontius admits that his words are not enough to describe all the follies that Symeon commits: sometimes he limps, sometimes he dances, sometimes he trips up passers-by, and sometimes he slides around on his backside. At the new moon, he rolls on the ground, utters unintelligible sounds, and behaves as if he is possessed by demons.[18] But Leontius also never tires of repeating that Symeon is only playing at being a fool, and he reports numerous miracles in which the saint converts Jews or enables prostitutes to lead an honourable life, saves the deacon from being unjustly hanged, or forces a man never to beat his slaves again. Acts that seem completely mysterious are given meaning after the fact: he whips columns that remain upright when an earthquake shakes the city, he kisses children's eyes and forbids their teachers to chastize them because they have a long way to go. As it turns out, that way is to lead to death by plague.[19] When Symeon has performed a healing or worked a miracle, he withdraws as quickly as possible in order to conceal his authorship. His holiness remains hidden in the light of day, and only in the darkness of night, in prayer and in conversation with the deacon John, does he reveal himself. His unrecognisability and concealment continue beyond his death: when he feels his end approaching, he hides under a bundle of brushwood in his shelter. After two days, his absence is noticed; those who find him

16 Leontius of Neapolis, 'Vita S. Symeonis Sali confessoris', cols. 1719B–1722B.

17 Leontius of Neapolis, 'Vita S. Symeonis Sali confessoris', cols. 1725B–1728A.

18 Leontius of Neapolis, 'Vita S. Symeonis Sali confessoris', cols. 1726B–1726C.

19 Leontius of Neapolis, 'Vita S. Symeonis Sali confessoris', cols. 1715D–1718B.

want to bury him, without prayers and without having washed the body, in a cemetery intended for strangers. However, a glassblower, whom Symeon has converted to Christianity, hears heavenly choirs singing as the men carry the body past. He hurries after them and buries Symeon with his own hands. Later, he tells the town about the angels' singing. The deacon John also hears about this, but when he goes to exhume the body in order to bury it in accordance with the customs of the time, he finds the grave empty. It is at this moment that the inhabitants of Emesa realize that Symeon was not a fool, but that in their blindness they had misjudged his true nature.[20]

In his biography of Symeon, Leontius uses sources such as the *Historia Lausiaca* by Palladius, in which the story of Saint Isidora, discussed earlier, is told, the *Pratum Spirituale* by John Moschus, and the *Historia Philothea* by Theodoret of Cyrrhus.[21] In addition, in the introduction to his text he refers to the now familiar passages in Paul's letters to the Corinthians and also has Symeon himself—in the dialogue with John, whom he leaves behind in the desert—refer to Paul. However, the theme of inversion, which Paul presents and which is played out by Saint Francis, Sebastian Brant, and Erasmus, is given a new meaning in the biography of Symeon. The motif of inversion continues to resonate: people come to realize the folly of their actions as soon as they realize that the person they thought was an idiot and a fool has the wisdom of the one blessed by God. The same motif resonates in the idea that the salos reflects the madness of worldly activity back into the world in a kind of distorted mimesis. That the truth shows itself more clearly as soon as the foolish world becomes aware of its folly, recognizing itself in the distorting—and precisely therein truthful reproduction of its true nature by the figure of the idiot, is a logic based on the assumption that human beings are too foolish to recognize that the world has already been saved. To have abandoned the

20 Leontius of Neapolis, 'Vita S. Symeonis Sali confessoris', cols. 1743C–1746B.

21 Hofstra, *Leontius*, pp. 246ff. The *Pratum spirituale* by Johannes Moschus (c. 540/550, Damascus–620, Rome) is in Patrologia Graeca, VOL. 87, PART 3, cols 2951–3116. The *Historia philothea* by Theodoret of Cyrrhus (393, Antioch–*c.*460, Cyrrhus) is in Pierre Canivet and Alice Leroy-Molinghen, *Histoire des moines de Syrie* (*Philothea* I–XIII = *Sources chrétiennes* 234) (Paris, 1977).

state of redemption after the redemptive act of Christ is the folly of man; to remember the error of man and to demand the correction of this error is the task of the fool. In anticipation that the fact of salvation will be confirmed, all life is shaped as a life in the mode of As-If. The believers live as if they were not living, and they describe themselves as the scum they are not. It is this logic of the inversion of truth and folly that Chomjakov invoked in 1872.

The actions of the salos, unlike those of Saint Francis and the fools of the Catholic Middle Ages, are certainly rooted in this logic of inversion, and this logic undoubtedly comes into play at the moment of Symeon's death, when the residents of Emesa realize the truth about the saint. However, the interplay between negation and affirmation, between contrastive doubling and duplication of doubling, is more complicated across long stretches of the saint's life than could be captured by the concept of inversion. Not only does the salos reflect as foolish that which understands itself as reason, but he also praises as wise that which the world rejects as foolishness. The folly of the salos does not offer a vision of the world as it could be should those who are blinded abandon their misguided ways and their misdeeds; it does not offer a way out through a cathartic dialectic that sketches a conception of the world along the fault line between reason and madness.

For the salos plays; his idiocy is the staging of an insanity that can multiply in an endless game of negation of negation. The idiot can be the idiot who mimes the wise man, who plays an idiot, but is actually an idiot who mimes the idiot imitating a wise man. The miming, the play, which Paul describes as a characteristic of the arch-imitator, Satan, contradicts in itself every concept of holiness; miming the idiot is itself a reprehensible act. When the *idiota* Saint Francis confronts the representatives of the Church with his *simplicitas* as a virtue, he does so in a gesture of perfect sincerity, which is guaranteed by his simplicity: he cannot do otherwise. But the salos can always do otherwise. And so he closes off the possibility of meaning by withdrawing his actions from the world's grasp in a conundrum of ambiguities. The non-sense of the world is total.

This non-sense leaves no room for reconciliation, as it could manifest itself in the dialectic of reason and insanity, inversion and reconstitution. For in contrast to Paul's conversion, in the course of which one kind of knowledge is replaced by another, and a new subject is constituted in the moment of the 'self-emptying' of the subject as it existed before, the 'self-emptying' of the salos, for which there is the concept of *kenosis* in Eastern Church religiosity,[22] is a complete form of self-abandonment. It is no longer followed by a reconstitution that revises the erasure of the self. Paul had written in his letter to the Philippians (Phil 2:7–8): '[Christ] renounced himself, taking the form of a servant, being made in the likeness of men, and being found in appearance as a man; he humbled himself and became obedient to the point of death, death on a cross'. The salos practises *kenosis* as a complete *imitatio Christi* insofar as he extinguishes the last indications that his actions could be in accordance with God. Not only does he deny his holiness; rather, he divests himself of his humanity. He transforms himself into a nonhuman.[23]

It is logical and at the same time in contradiction to the *imitatio* topos that the salos hardly speaks. It follows from his transformation into a non-human that he neither preaches nor teaches. He does not establish a dogma, he does not found a religious order and has no confreres (only the deacon John as a confidant). He mostly babbles, and at best he utters short sentences. His *kenosis* is evident in the fact that he does not correct the image the world has of him, but hides his holiness. He conceals what he does in the mysteriousness of his seemingly absurd and laughable actions, instead of opening up the meaning of his actions to people's understanding through a teaching. There is no doctrine to proclaim, and there is no need for institutions to preserve it through the ages, since time has long since been fulfilled and the time that remains is meaningless, empty time.

22 See Georgi Fedotov, *The Russian Religious Mind*, VOL. 1 (Cambridge, MA: Harvard University Press, 1966 [1946]), p. 128–29.

23 Renate Lachmann, 'Der Narr in Christo und seine Verstellungspraxis' in Peter von Moos (ed.), *Unverwechselbarkeit: Persönliche Identität und Identifikation in der vormodernen Gesellschaft* (Cologne: Vandenhoeck & Ruprecht, 2004), p. 405.

His being dead to the world reflects the unworthiness and depravity of the world, which is not worthy of salvation. The fact that the salos saves the prostitutes, slaves, and pagans, forcing the miserly and violent to repent, is not an attempt to change the world for the better, but the practice of love in defiance of the depravity of the world. However, this practice of charity also has its antithesis: when the salos delivers to death the children who will die of the plague with the sign of his kiss instead of saving them, this gesture of a sexually charged and questionable tenderness reveals a mercilessness that corresponds to the depravity of the world.[24] The concern that Symeon expresses when he forbids the teachers to chastize the children he has marked with the kiss is an expression of the paradoxical love that is paired with this implacability. His kiss is not only a kiss of death, like the kiss of Judas, it is also a reversal of the act of marking the saved, of whom we are told in Ezekiel 9:4. During the destruction of Jerusalem, only those righteous who have the Greek τ sign marked on their foreheads are to be saved from God's wrath. Saint Francis used to sign his letters and texts with this sign, and he painted it on the wall in a niche in the chapel of Fonte Colombo. It can also be found at the bottom of a letter to Brother Leo, in which he tries to encourage him and free him from his doubts. Just as the τ sign as an abbreviation of the cross stands for salvation, which will triumph over the misery of the world, the kiss of Symeon stands for death, to which the world is consecrated.

How far Franciscan folly is from the folly of the salos is also shown by the varying meaning of nakedness. The nakedness of Saint Francis is *conformitas Christi*, following the naked and crucified Christ and recalling the original sinlessness of the world. For it was only after the Fall that Adam and Eve realized that they were naked. Recognition of nakedness and guilt are as interlinked as nakedness and innocence. It is only in the socially constructed world, alienated from its purpose, that nakedness becomes sin. In taking off his clothes, Saint Francis reminds us of the possibility of being human in a state of grace. In doing so, he gets rid of the signs of social identification and at the same time rejects his natural descent, his own sonship. By becoming naked, he becomes both visible and non-identifiable; his return to the 'state of nature' is both a rejection of the naturalness

24 Krueger, *Symeon the Holy Fool*, p. 46.

of his origin and a dedication of his physicality to God. Nudity thus takes on an important role in the interplay between society and the outsider, who becomes both indistinguishable and visible or recognizable. As a naked person, he becomes human, thus erasing the difference from those from whom he previously distinguished himself as a social being.

In the context of Orthodox religiosity, there is also the idea that the ascetic's nakedness testifies to his angelic innocence and that, as a naked man, he is clothed in the white robes of incorruptible life.[25] In contrast, however, Symeon's nakedness denotes the repulsive and abject nature of human existence. His nakedness is not a *memoria* of paradisiacal innocence, but a sign of depravity, the repugnance of which is heightened by the fact that Symeon allegedly indulges in sexual debauchery or dances in public. The emaciated body, tortured by hunger and thirst, cold or heat, rolling in the dirt or twitching ecstatically, gives no cause for hope or consolation. To show it is to expose it as abject. His nakedness is not an Adamite nakedness, and all the less so because in late antiquity and in early Christian society, those who tore off their clothes and showed their bare bodies were considered to be possessed by demons or by the devil. The saint who mimes the sinner in order to humiliate himself before the world adds to the shame of his nakedness the stigma that it is not the holy nakedness of Christ that he is reminding the audience of in his drama, but the obscene nakedness of the possessed. Naked, the ascetic takes up a wrestling match with the demons.[26] The body he shows is a corpse.

The conflict between God the Creator, the flawed Demiurge, and God the Redeemer determines the absoluteness with which the salos rejects the world. The world as it is, is not worth saving; the world that was worth saving has long since been saved through the incarnation of God in Christ. With him, the God of love takes up his reign and replaces the Old Testament God of law. Christ rejects the law-abiding Pharisees and scribes because they did not follow the law according to the spirit, but only according to the letter (Matthew 5:20; Mark 12:38). Paul will proclaim the end of the age of the law and the beginning of the age of love: 'So then love is the fulfilment of the law' (Romans 13:10). 'For Christ is the end of the law'

25 Münch, *In Christo*, p. 205.

26 Lachmann, 'Der Narr', p. 397.

(Romans 10:4; see also Romans 6:15). Finally, Marcion (*c*.85–*c*.160) rejects all of God's creation as well as the God of the Old Testament. He accepts only the God of love, the foreign God who calls man from the 'dreadful homeland', the world, into the 'blessed foreign land'; he transfers him from the state of the law into the state of love, in which the foreign God undoes the deed of the 'known God'.[27] The salos, dead to the world, knows no eschatological reservations. Everything happens under the sign that redemption is done and the continued existence of the world has become meaningless, a scandal to God the Redeemer. Only the practice of love can counter this scandal.

Unlike the word 'idiota', which first acquired its pejorative meaning in its migration from Greek into Latin and via Middle Latin into the Western European vernaculars, the word 'salos' began its career with precisely this meaning as a negative term for the possessed and the insane.[28] The etymology is unclear: the word possibly comes from the Syriac 'sakla' or 'sela', which means 'to repel, disgust'.[29] Other derivations refer to σάλος (swaying, dizziness, restlessness) and σαλεύω (to be restless or upset, to shake or agitate).[30] Before it appears in a religious context where it denotes the holy fool, it stands for a person who is either mentally confused or extraordinarily stupid.[31] In any case, the history of the word is exactly the opposite of the case with *idiota* in the West.

---

27 Harnack, *Marcion*, pp. 2–3.

28 The word *idiota* appears in some hagiographic texts of the Eastern Church written in Greek (Lachmann, 'Der Narr', p. 384). However, it does not appear in Leontius's text.

29 Lachmann, 'Der Narr', p. 384.

30 Claudia Ludwig, *Sonderformen byzantinischer Hagiographie und ihr literarisches Vorbild: Untersuchungen zu den Viten des Äsop, des Philaretos, des Symeon Salos und des Andreas Salos* (Berliner Byzantinistische Studien 3) (Frankfurt am Main: Peter Lang, 1997), p. 291.

31 Ivanov, *Holy Fools*, pp. 32–33; Metzler, *Fools and Idiots?*, pp. 36–37. Metzler writes on p. 57 that *salos* is often used synonymously with *moros*, which in Galen's *De locis affectis* (192 CE) stands in the same series as terms such as *morosis*, *mania*, *lethargos*, *phrenetis*, *paraphrosyne*, *apoche* and *melancholia*, which are scarcely differentiated from one another. In the Septuagint, on the other hand, *epileptos* stands for the insane (Ivanov, *Holy Fools*, p. 14), and the inhabitants of Constantinople regard Andrew as an epileptic (Wodziński, *Saint Idiot*, p. 126). The terms vary and therefore cannot be taken as clinically valid diagnostic terms.

Six saloi are venerated as saints in the Eastern Church, as well as other saints who bear the characteristics of the salos.[32] However, the tradition of the Byzantine salos died out in the tenth century. The Council in Trullo of 692 (actually the Quinisext Council, held in a domed hall, troulos, of the palace of Constantinople) had declared the salos to be possessed.[33] It proves extremely difficult to unravel the game of the mad ascetic who pretends to be a saint, and the sage, who mimes a madman who could be a sage, etc. The council proclaims that those who behave like madmen should be punished and treated in the same way as those who are actually mad. After his holiness has been called into question, the salos is disqualified as a possessed person and handed over to exorcism.[34] Another factor contributing to the extinction of the salos tradition is the Arab conquest of Syria, Palestine, and Egypt. The 'real' martyrs in the conquered territories, who paid with their lives for following Christ, made the veneration of ascetics and fools in Christ 'superfluous'.[35] After the conquest of Constantinople, Russian foolishness in Christ, *jurodstvo*, finally took over the legacy of the saloi, 'which had been made possible by contact with Byzantine ascetic models and the reading of the *Vitae* translated into Old Church Slavonic'.[36]

The Old Russian word *jurodivyj* also migrated from the profane realm into the religious sphere with its originally negative meaning. Its root is considered to be *urod*, which means deformed. In the end, the jurodivyj comes to denote a weak-minded person, a madman, or one who is possessed.[37] Another derivation is from an Old Slavic word (*uródъ* / ǫródъ), which combines the privative prefix *ǫ* with the word *rod* and denotes someone who lives without a home (*rod*), does not belong to any group,

32 Wodziński, *Saint Idiot*, pp. 355–56.

33 Hans-Georg Beck, *Das byzantinische Jahrtausend* (Munich: C. H. Beck, 1994), p. 285.

34 'Those who now pretend to be possessed and by bad behaviour flaunt the condition of those [possessed] in a feigned manner, it seemed right to punish in any case and to subject them to hard exercises and sufferings of the kind to which the truly possessed are rightly subjected for redemption from demonic possession.' Quoted in Münch, *In Christo*, p. 68.

35 Ivanov, *Holy Fools*, pp. 130–31.

36 Lachmann, 'Der Narr', p. 381.

37 Lachmann, 'Der Narr', p. 384.

and has no offspring.[38] The pejorative meaning originally attached to the word and used in Slavic until the fifteenth century receives a melioration in religious literature only when it is used in the semantic field previously occupied by 'salos'. The deformed, homeless, and possessed idiot becomes the fool of God.

The characteristics of the salos can be found in the jurodivyj: he roams the city naked or scantily clothed, he is usually completely alone, behaves like a madman during the day and hides his holiness from the public. He sleeps on dung heaps and drinks sewage or water from puddles, his body is covered in faeces and dirt. He is beaten and abused, ridiculed and tortured. He is silent or slurs his words or speaks in incoherent sentences. According to legend, Nicholas of Trani (1075, Steiri, Boeotia–1094, Trani, Apulia) is said to have spoken only and incessantly the words *Kyrie eleison*. The glossolalia of the jurodivyj makes him appear to be an imbecile or a prophet speaking in riddles. His foreignness, which even appears in the biography of Andrew Salos,[39] is often due to the forgetting of or actual ignorance about his origins and becomes an essential part of the legend. For example, Prokop of Ustjug (d. 1303) is reported to have come from 'German soil' and converted from the impure faith of his homeland to the true faith of the East. A similar story is told about Isidore of Rostov (d. 1474), who is said to have come from Brandenburg. Through his foreignness, which connects the jurodivyj with the strannik, the pilgrim, he proves to be eternally unhoused on earth. Barely able to speak or delirious in foreign tongues, of unknown origin and strange and bizarre in his behaviour, he is despised as a barbarian.[40]

Until the nineteenth century there was a variety of jurodivye, including a small number of women.[41] The only canonized female saint is Ksenia of Petersburg (1719/1730–1803), who also represents one of the rare cases of

38 Münch, *In Christo*, pp. 33–34.

39 Andreas was Scythian; see Münch, *In Christo*, pp. 73–74.

40 Wodziński, *Saint Idiot*, p. 226.

41 See the list in Münch, *In Christo*, pp. 459ff. Elena Jurodiva, about whom the Dutchman Isaac Massa wrote a report in 1610, became known but was not canonized. Münch, *In Christo*, pp. 126ff.

transvestism: after the death of her husband, an officer, she initially retired to a convent before returning to St Petersburg. In public, she could be seen only in her deceased husband's military uniform and could be addressed only by his name.[42] The story of Griša von Kočetovka (1851–1906), who can only be found in women's clothing—adorned with children's toys, intended to emphasize his childlike innocence—represents a reverse case. Unlike Ksenia, however, he does not reject his sexual identity, but chooses a homosexual orientation: he remains a man and becomes the bridegroom of Christ, whom he wants to marry.[43]

Unlike the salos, the jurodivyj interferes in public affairs. The best-known reports are based on the legend that a man named Nicola rebelled against Ivan the Terrible (1530–1584, tsar from 1547) when he had the city of Pskov sacked and hundreds of people killed in 1570. A German adventurer named Heinrich Staden, who took part in Ivan's campaign, tells of a rich peasant named Mikula who confronted the tsar. In response to the peasant's words, 'Enough! Turn back!', the tsar stops the destruction of the city. The legend continues to develop through various stages and in various reports by English and German travellers, in which Mikula becomes Nicola, the chance encounter between the bloodthirsty tsar and the rich peasant turns into a kind of pilgrimage by the ruler to the holy fool, who, instead of blessing him, hurls insults at him, calling him a bloodsucker from the window of his house. The final version is found in the report of the English traveller Giles Fletcher, who, sixteen years after the siege of Pskov, adds the episode that Nicola offered the tyrant a piece of raw meat. Ivan refuses the gift on the grounds that it is forbidden to eat meat during Lent, whereupon Nicola, using the diminutive form of Ivan, Ivaška, mockingly asks the tsar why 'is it a sin to eat the flesh of an animal during Lent, and not a sin to destroy as many people as he has already done?'[44] On the

42 Natalia Diefenbach, *Die Vita der hl. Xenia von St. Petersburg* (*Journal für Religionskultur* 223) (Frankfurt am Main: Goethe-Universität, 2016). Sergei Shtyrkov, 'The Unmerry Widow: The Blessed Kseniia of Petersburg in Hagiography and Hymnography' in Hunt and Kobets (eds), *Holy Foolishness in Russia*, pp. 281–304. Ivanov, *Holy Fools*, pp. 350–51.

43 Münch, *In Christo*, pp. 211ff.

44 Münch, *In Christo*, p. 112; there also in detail on the various versions of the legends.

one hand, the episode portrays Ivan as a man-eater; on the other, it portrays Nicola, who is nicknamed Symeon in folklore and called Nicola Salos, as a saint who, on account of his holiness, is exempt from following religious rules. Symeon also eats raw meat during Lent.[45] The legend thus places Nicola close to the Byzantine ascetic. Like the latter, he is indifferent to all the temptations and enticements of the world and thus exempt from the social and religious norms to which even the tsar must adhere. The seemingly blasphemous act demonstrates the *apatheia* of the jurodivyj and the holiness that overrides all normative criteria. At the same time, it reveals the hypocritical nature of the tyrant, who slaughters thousands of people without pity, and yet wants to present himself as committed to the letter of the law. Just as the tsar's hypocrisy is an inversion of true piety, the apparent blasphemy is the inversion of actual blasphemy. The inversion of the hierarchical relationships between the secular and religious spheres, modelled on the Diogenes-Alexander legend, follows this logic: it is not the tsar but the saint (who has mutated from a rich peasant to a salos) who has the greater and true power and authority.

The model developed in the legends of Nicola Salos is also followed by other stories in which encounters between jurodivye and representatives of secular power are subsequently reported. For example, Ioann Vlasatyj of Rostov (d. 1572), into whose biography the story of Arsenij of Novgorod (d. 1570) was woven,[46] or Vasilij Blažennyj (Basil the Blessed of Moscow, d. 1557) fearlessly confront the tsar, prevent atrocities, or ostentatiously challenge the power of the ruler.[47] Their position remains ambivalent; on the one hand they oppose tsarist injustice, on the other hand they socialize—in their own idiosyncratic way—at court.[48] However, it is indisputable

See also Ivanov, *Holy Fools*, pp. 291ff.

45 Leontius of Neapolis, 'Vita S. Symeonis Sali confessoris', cols. 1729A–1730A.

46 Ivanov, *Holy Fools*, p. 278, assumes that Ioann of Moscow and Ioann of Rostov are identical.

47 See Ivanov, *Holy Fools*, pp. 300–1, 320. Basil is feared by Ivan because of his ability to read his thoughts. Arsenii or Ioan Vlasatyi and Basil are all three equally praised for having prevented the bloody conquest of Novgorod.

48 Wodziński, *Saint Idiot*, pp. 266ff. See also Dmitrij S. Lichacev and Aleksandr M. Pancenko, *Die Lachwelt des alten Russland* (Munich: Fink, 1991), p. 170.

that towards the end of the sixteenth century, under Ivan the Terrible and his son and successor, Fyodor I (1557–1598, tsar from 1584), the jurodivyj enjoyed a prestige that had not been granted him before and would not be granted again afterwards. Under Fyodor, who described himself as a fool but was in fact intellectually disabled, the veneration of the jurodivyj reached an unprecedented level. Ioann of Rostov and Basil the Blessed are given state funerals; both burials in the Cathedral of the Protection and Intercession of the Virgin on the Moat in Moscow (better known as St Basil's Cathedral) are accompanied by miracles and healings, storms and catastrophes. Ivan the Terrible is said to have carried Basil's coffin himself, and after Basil's reburial in 1588 in the cathedral associated with his name, signs and miraculous healings continue to occur.

Even before the sixteenth century, while the game between society and outsider in the case of the jurodivyj was characterized by the multiplication of inversions and reversals between play and existence, truth and simulation, Ivan the Terrible and Fyodor I added new facets to this puzzle.

Ivan the Terrible wrote two letters to monks under the pseudonym 'Parfeni, the Jurodivyj',[49] in which he resorts to the topoi of self-incrimination: 'Who can I, a stinking dog, teach anything? [ . . . ] I, who live in drunkenness and fornication, wantonness, filth and murder, to whom can I, a rotten and defiled destroyer of souls, be a teacher?'[50] What looks like an exaggerated version of the stereotypical formula of one's own unworthiness turns out to be part of a complex play, in which Ivan denies his superiority by ostentatiously humiliating himself and identifying with the jurodivyj. Just as Nicola Salos's apparent blasphemy allows him to place himself above the tsar, so the tsar's disguise as a jurodivyj allows him to co-opt the latter as a pawn in his intrigues and to usurp the values associated with him. Not only does he commit blasphemy against the ascetic's sanctity, he also reveals himself to be its master by committing blasphemy. On the one hand, he violates the concept of holiness insofar as he imitates the simulation game of the jurodivyj without being legitimized to do so; he plays holiness without holiness. On the other hand, however, by imitating holiness without holiness,

49 Wodziński, *Saint Idiot*, p. 263.

50 Quoted in Ivanov, *Holy Fools*, p. 286.

he lays claim to the superiority of the secular sphere he governs in comparison to the religious sphere. By robbing the sphere of the sacred of its sanctity without any irony and tainting it with his mimicry, he proves himself to be its master. Similarly with Fyodor I: Ivan's son, who is indeed an imbecile, dons the mask of the good-natured fool.[51] Foolishness as a voluntarily donned disguise conceals spiritual disability, simplicity embraced as a gift of grace covers up creaturely stupidity. But nothing impairs the strength and power of the ascetic ideal more permanently than the respect paid to it by a talentless, mentally disabled tsar who is not master of his senses and his actions. When the jurodivyj achieved his highest recognition in the political life of the tsarist empire, his descent began.

As the decisions of the Council in Trullo show, the figure of the salos has always been viewed with suspicion, as there is uncertainty as to how to deal with the multiplying inversion of the reversal and inversion of worldly folly and the uncertainty as to whether this folly is actual foolishness or actual play. His repulsive appearance justifies the veneration of the salos, just as it justifies his social ostracism. Insofar as his strangeness can be regarded as proof of his holiness, it justifies the ascetic's veneration; but insofar as his behaviour can be regarded as an arbitrary disregard for the social order, as a scandal, it provides the reason for its exclusion and negative sanctioning. For the social order, like the holiness of the salos, is also an expression of God's will; nonconformity and asocial behaviour are then signs of blasphemous disregard for the God-ordained and God-compliant constitution of society.

Something similar happens to the figure of the jurodivyj. Time and again, clerical resolutions place him in the vicinity of pseudo-prophets and those possessed by demons who are to be driven out of their homes. Ivan the Terrible, who himself imitated the jurodivyj in order to profit from his aura of sacredness and at the same time damage it, complained in 1551 about false prophets who ran around naked and barefoot, with long flowing hair, shaking and howling. At the so-called Synod of a Hundred Chapters of the same year, there was a demand for measures against false preachers wandering around alone, monks who had left their

51 See Ivanov, *Holy Fools*, pp. 303–4.

monasteries and entertained pernicious customs, which were described as Hellenistic heritage and superstition. These included certain games, the singing of diabolical songs, dancing and drinking, and all kinds of buffoonery.[52] The measures were never implemented, but were incorporated into various decrees in the following decades, which forbade the jurodivyj from attending church services and were generally directed against the jurodstvo, whose protagonists were described as work-shy, lice-ridden, and quarrelsome troublemakers whose 'disgusting yapping' disturbed the faithful.[53] The Code of Tsar Aleksei Mikhailovich of 1649 can ultimately be seen as a turning point in the relationship with the jurodivyj, in which not only the concept of superstition introduced during the Hundred Chapter Synod is firmly established, but also the accusation of blasphemy is made against the jurodivyj for the first time, for which the code orders burning at the stake as punishment, a form of execution that had been 'imported' from Europe. Finally, the Great Moscow Council of 1666/67 condemns jurodstvo as hypocrisy, which for the next 250 years relegates it to the recesses of a church-run society and state, at best tolerated in popular piety. The defining criterion for the distinction between the 'venerable fathers' and the contemporary jurodivyj is that the latter acted out of a thirst for recognition and glory:

> There are some hypocrites and seducers who live in the middle of towns and villages, in the habitus of anachoretes or inclusives, with long hair and wearing a monk's habit. Others are forged in iron chains. They also walk naked and barefoot through towns and villages in the world out of a desire for recognition, so that they may receive fame from the people and be revered as saints, and in this way, they seduce the simple and ignorant. But we command that you henceforth give no more credence to such, for it is evident that they do not do this in God and not in truth, and certainly not with a sound mind.[54]

52 E. Duchesne (ed. and trans.), *Le Stoglav, ou les cent chapitres* (Paris: É. Champion, 1920), CHAP. 92, pp. 242ff.

53 Münch, *In Christo*, p. 135.

54 See Gabriele Scheidegger, *Endzeit: Russland am Ende des 17. Jahrhunderts* (Bern: Peter Lang, 1999), quoted in Münch, *In Christo*, pp. 136ff.

The condemnation of the jurodivyj is linked to the reform efforts of Patriarch Nikon (1605–1681), which led to the schism of the Russian Orthodox Church in 1652 and the secession of the Old Believers, the Raskolniki.[55] Nikon attempted to reform and correct the rites and textbooks of the church and to enable uniform practice with the non-Russian Orthodox churches, as errors had crept into the scriptures and rites over time through the copying of Byzantine sources. These reform efforts met with resistance from representatives of the clergy, who, after the fall of Constantinople (1453) and the Council of Ferrara-Florence (1431–1445), at which attempts to unite the Eastern and Western Churches had failed, saw themselves as the keepers of the only orthodox faith and declared Moscow the third Rome.[56]

Nikon was deposed at the Great Council of Moscow in 1666/67, not least because of his thirst for power and the intransigence with which he defended the view that spiritual power was superior to secular power. However, his defeat was of no use to his enemies. His opponent, the protopope Avvakum (1621/22–1682), dies at the stake in exile in Siberia,[57] after which secular power triumphs in the conflict between the two competing religious camps. The final point was the dissolution of the patriarchate in 1721, which Peter the Great (1672–1725), Tsar from 1682 to 1721 and Russian emperor from 1721 to 1725, replaced with the Holy Governing Synod, which consisted of clerics and laymen appointed by the tsar and was suspended only in 1918.[58]

In this conflict between secular and spiritual authority, between Old Believers and reformers, between a burgeoning Russian nationalism and

55 Raskol initially meant only those who rebelled against the church authorities and was then transferred to the so-called Old Believers, becoming synonymous with the schism that split the Russian Orthodox Church from 1666. See Georg B. Michels, *At War with the Church: Religious Dissent in Seventeenth-Century Russia* (Stanford, CA: Stanford University Press, 1999), pp. 106ff.

56 Renate Lachmann in Lichacev and Pancenko, *Lachwelt*, p. *vii*.

57 See Pierre Pascal, *Avvakum et les débuts du raskol* (Paris and The Hague: Mouton, 1969 [1938]).

58 James Cracraft, *The Church Reform of Peter the Great* (London: Macmillan, 1971), pp. 70–71, 112ff.

European Enlightenment absolutism, the jurodivyj figures either as a religious figure of identification for the Raskolniki or as a symbol of a backward-looking, medieval piety that needs to be overcome, and also takes on the traits of political troublemaker and potential insurgent. Instrumentalized by Avvakum and his fellow believers in the conflict with the reform-minded authorities, the jurodivyj now actually becomes the religious, social, and political outsider, a role whose performance had been his task for centuries. For the first time, jurodivye were executed, partly because they questioned the authority of the ruler. In 1672, the year of Peter the Great's birth, Afanasij of Nizhnij Novgorod was publicly burned to death in Moscow for calling the monarch, Aleksei Mikhailovich (1629–1676), a heretic, an apostate, and a persecutor of the faithful.

The jurodivyj no longer occupied an ambivalent position in the game between apostolic radicalism and heretical deviation or between orthodoxy and its institutional deformation, but now fulfilled a symbolic function in the conflict between state and individual, absolutist claims to omnipotence and the subjective claim to deviance. Here, the rationalist-economic criterion of indolence and asociality begins to play just as important a role as the religious and political argument. It is flanked and supported, in a way typical of modern times, by the emerging medical science, which provides the criterion of mental illness as justification for the ostracism of the jurodivyj in the social and religious sphere.[59]

The fact that Ksenia of St Petersburg was canonized by the Russian Orthodox Church in 1988 proves that the fate of the jurodivyj was not yet sealed. She represents the model of the jurodstvo which, reduced to faithfulness and asceticism, can be combined with ideas of a piety that is in the service of Russian nationalism, not much different from 1931, when Boris Zajcev refers to the use of the jurodivyj by the Slavophiles. It is not the idiot-performer, beaten half to death because of his repulsive nudity and obscene behaviour, who is elevated to the status of a saint by the Orthodox Church, now close to the post-Soviet regime. Rather, it is the personification of a seemingly specifically Russian piety, which is suitable for defining a national character by distinguishing it from Western forms of piety. The

59 Ivanov, *Holy Fools*, pp. 345ff.

dual function of the outsider on whom both affirmative and critical-subversive aspirations and tendencies can be projected is evident here as well as in the texts written during the Soviet era that refer to the jurodivyj.[60] It is also obvious in the actions of the Collective Actions Group, the Blue Noses Group, and Moscow actionism in post-Soviet Russia.[61] Oleg Kulik's actions, with which the artist became known in the 1990s, derive their specific content from the significance of the dog in the Cynic tradition,[62] which is echoed in the jurodivyj's closeness to dogs as ostracized animals—he sleeps with them to find warmth in the cold of the winter night, but even they abandon him.[63] Naked like the jurodivyj and on all fours, barking and biting, sometimes led on a leash by a fellow artist, Kulik (b. 1961, Kiev) quickly caused a sensation in the art world.[64] He certainly knows how to push the buttons of scandal and provocation, and he allows the Western art scene in particular to flatter him as the lapdog of their art carnival to satisfy their own lust for show and sensationalism. And yet, the fusion of the lunatic and the animal retains its unwieldiness against the backdrop of the *kenosis* of the jurodivyj. Kulik 'empties' himself of his humanity and becomes the animal with which Symeon associates himself when he enters Emesa to begin his martyrdom among humans. The chain functions both as an attribute of the biting dog and as a hallmark of the saint, and the howling, yowling, and mooing of Kulik in some of his performances finds its parallel in the jurodivyj's renunciation of human language. Aleksandr Brener's (b. 1957, Alma Ata) act, in which he challenges Boris Yeltsin to a boxing match to protest against the war in Chechnya

---

60 See Marco Sabbatini, 'The Pathos of Holy Foolishness in the Leningrad Underground' in Hunt and Kobets (eds), *Holy Foolishness in Russia*, pp. 337–52.

61 Natalia Ottovordemgentschenfelde, *Jurodstvo: Eine Studie zur Phänomenologie und Typologie des Narren in Christo; Jurodivyj in der postmodernen russischen Kunst: Venedikt Erofeev 'Die Reise nach Petuški', Aktionismus Aleksandr Breners und Oleg Kuliks* (Frankfurt am Main: Peter Lang, 2004).

62 See in particular Krueger, *Symeon the Holy Fool*, pp. 90–107.

63 See the reports on Andrew of Constantinople and Prokopij of Ustjug in Lichacev and Pancenko, *Lachwelt*, p. 142.

64 On Kulik, see Gesine Drews-Sylla, *Moskauer Aktionismus* (Munich: Fink, 2011), pp. 167–244.

(*Boxing Champion*, 1995), is understood as a reference to the resistance that Nicola Salos puts up to the tsar.

Kulik and Brener are among the best-known representatives of post-Soviet Russian art, which resorted to the means of fictitious idiocy in order to counter the emerging authoritarian and corrupt state apparatus ruled by oligarchs. Less well-known collectives such as ETI ('Expropriation of the Territory of Art'), which spelled the word 'dick' with their bodies on Red Square in front of Lenin's mausoleum in 1991 and whose members risked prison for it,[65] caused a sensation with their carnivalesque interventions. In order to protect them from being convicted of disturbing public order, Grigory Gusarov, the co-organizer of the action performance, draws connections to Russia's centuries-old culture of laughter and tries to soften the taboo-breaking that is supposedly a characteristic of Russian folk culture.[66]

The artist Leonid Nikolaev also slips into the disguise of the idiot, putting a blue bucket on his head as part of the *Lenya Ebnutyi—Our President*! action and running atop a car belonging to the FSB secret service in the middle of Moscow's embankment. By calling himself *Ebnutyi* (the fucked-up one), he follows the pattern of self-humiliation and masking as an idiot.[67] Vojna (War), the collective of which Nikolaev is a member, also follows the tradition of provocation and obscene intervention, and attempts to set itself apart from the predecessors of Moscow actionism by claiming that its members want only to make politics instead of political art. Vojna operated on the fringes of the art field, for whose representatives, such as Kulik and Anatoly Osmolovsky, they had nothing but contempt. They finally propelled themselves into illegality by setting fire to a prisoner transport vehicle.[68]

Kulik, however, supports Vojna after a sex performance in Moscow's Timiryazev State Biological Museum in 2008. During that event, members

65 Matthias Meindl, *Reiner Aktivismus? Politisierung von Literatur und Kunst im postsowjetischen Russland* (Cologne and Weimar: Böhlau, 2018), p. 12.

66 Meindl, *Reiner Aktivismus?*, p. 45.

67 Meindl, *Reiner Aktivismus?*, p. 151.

68 Meindl, *Reiner Aktivismus?*, p. 44.

of the group had indulged in sexual intercourse among showcases and display boards, while comrades-in-arms displayed posters with the slogan 'Make sex to support the little bear', which pointed towards Medvedev. In his defence of Vojna, Kulik references the tradition of the jurodivyj to explain why the police did not arrest the provocateurs.

The police and prosecutors exercise less restraint four years later, when they arrest the three members of Pussy Riot, Maria Alyokhina (b. 1988, Moscow), Yekaterina Samutsevich (b. 1982, Moscow), and Nadezhda Andreyevna Tolokonnikova (b. 1989, Norilsk), who perform a punk prayer against the alliance between the Orthodox Church and the Putin government with two female colleagues in Moscow's Cathedral of Christ the Saviour. Samutsevich and Tolokonnikova had also been members of Vojna. The three women were sentenced to two years in prison for hooliganism.[69] Samutsevich was released on appeal in October 2012, while Alyokhina and Tolokonnikova were released under an amnesty in December 2013. However, if Putin had hoped that this was the end of the matter, he was mistaken: in 2014 Pussy Riot protested in Sochi against the conditions in Russian prison camps and the repression of dissidents, and in 2020 they incurred the wrath of the state when they tried to shoot a video about police violence in St Petersburg, in which extras were to mime police officers in action. As if reality wanted to overtake the video's message, a real police unit marched into the film studio and put an end to the shoot.[70]

Tolokonnikova herself gives evidence in the courtroom on 7 August 2012 that the musicians saw themselves as jugglers, jesters, and jurodivye. In her plea one day later, she claims the seriousness of the jurodstvo for their performances and actions.[71] In a turn against the Orthodox Church

---

69 See Sandra Frimmel, *Kunsturteile: Gerichtsprozesse gegen Kunst, Künstler und Kuratoren in Russland nach der Perestroika* (Cologne, Weimar and Vienna: Böhlau, 2015), pp. 276ff.

70 'Nadeschda Tolokonnikowa: Pussy Riot bei Videodreh durch russische Polizei gestoppt', *Die Zeit* (10 February 2020). An overview of actions until 2025 is provided on Pussy Riot's website (pussyriot.love/actions).

71 Münch, *In Christo*, pp. 19–20, note 15. See Svitlana Kobets, 'From the Tabennisi Nunnery to Pussy Riot: Female Holy Fools in Byzantium and Russia', *Canadian Slavonic Papers* 60(1–2) (2018): 87–107. Kerith M. Woodyard, 'Pussy Riot and the Holy Foolishness of Punk', *Rock Music Studies* 1(3) (2014): 268–86.

and the government supported by it, she references the same figure, which is also claimed by the institution against which the agitation is directed. The jurodivyj as a saintly outsider functions as the ancestor both of an anti-Western, religiously based nationalism and of an anti-authoritarian art activism that is directed against this nationalism and its accompanying phenomena: homophobia, xenophobia, and misogyny. The prerequisite for the jurodivyj's dual function as a surface on which to project both opposing intentions is his character as a multiply coded figure of both extreme obedience and fearless transgression, of unreserved *conformitas* and unconditional non-conformity. Conservative forces that systematically persecute women artists use the jurodivyj as a figure to identify with in order to profile themselves as threatened by forces against which resistance is merely self-defence. For activists critical of the system, on the other hand, the jurodivyj serves as a figure in order to criticize the current political constellation by reproducing the mythical-historical confrontation between the saints and the power of the state.

Contrary to Tolokonnikova's reference to the jester, however, this game of inversions is not one that could be equated with the game that the jester or the juggler plays with society. For the jester is characterized by a kind of osmotic sensitivity towards the multitude of fine subtleties of meaning in the social sphere to which he reacts parodistically or ironically, mimicking or counteracting them, which he reflects or acts against, whose offerings he takes up or which he undermines. The fact that Gusarov believes he can mitigate the potential of the affront to Lenin, the saint revered by the state, through his reference to Russia's culture of laughter indicates that the intermittent, temporary manifestation of the carnivalesque does not have the subversive power that is often attributed to it but, on the contrary, has an affirmative effect. The freedom of laughter is always a temporally limited freedom.[72] Just as the carnival does not last forever, but rather

72 Mikhail M. Bakhtin, to whom the concept of Russian laughter culture goes back, admits this himself. See Michail M. Bachtin, *Literatur und Karneval: Zur Romantheorie und Lachkultur* (Frankfurt am Main: Fischer Taschenbuch Verlag, 1990), pp. 33, 38. See Wolf Iro, *Tertium non datur: Ideologie und Soziologie in Isaak Babels Konarmija* (Frankfurt am Main: Peter Lang, 2001), p. 12: '(Carnival) as a conscious deviation from the socially instituted norms represents the temporary suspension of everything systemic tolerated by the system, an alternative way of life for a limited period of time.'

represents the exception as a contrast to normality, the actions of the juggler and jester are also temporally and functionally limited. Like the monkey at the signal of his tamer, the court jester jumps at the command of his master. His function is completely dependent on the wishes and desires of his owner, and the juggler performs his tricks as long as it pleases the spectators, on whose goodwill his existence depends.

The carnival functions as an outlet, and for this reason it stabilizes the system.[73] 'The carnivalesque counterculture is [ . . . ] instrumentalized, even co-opted [ . . . ].'[74] Its social function is evident, its dialectical entanglement with society and its neuroses, its entire pathogenic metabolism of self-consumption and self-constitution is obvious. That the fool is sacred is the wishful thinking of society, which holds him up as its counter-image. By establishing him as a contrasting figure, it produces the appearance of a possible different world. If society, to which the jester supposedly holds up a mirror, were not the colossus ploughing through time, whose gravitational forces nothing can resist, there would be no jester. He pushes hard on the social gears that produce and nourish him. The little laughter that he evokes, the reprieve that he makes possible, the dream of disinhibition, the illusion of liberation allows the participants in society to see themselves as free in the face of the alternative that the fool seems to provide and to which the citizen temporarily associates himself.

Nevertheless, the fool allows one to think and even live in a different social state for a certain period of time. Although this state has only the character of a simple negative mirror-image, it opens up a gap through which to look at the utopia that the Christian logic of inversion was about. In its ecstatic distortion and intoxication, the carnival offers no solution; it is revolution on trial, unserious-evil and parodistic, but at least it keeps alive the memory that social realities could also be different.

Furthermore, in the religious context and in contrast to the above, the juggler has a specific connotation that is difficult to reconcile with the

73 The disciplining and regulating function of carnival was already known in the sixteenth century. See Karl Friedrich Flögel, *Geschichte des Grotesk-Komischen* (Leipzig: Werl, 1862), pp. 203–4.

74 Iro, *Tertium non datur*, p. 15.

image of the buffoon as the producer of a deeper insight disguised in merriment, which fools are supposedly able to convey, and of which Tolokonnikova may well have been aware during her plea in court. For when Bernard of Clairvaux, like Saint Francis later, describes himself as an *ioculator* (juggler),[75] this is to be understood as an act of extreme self-abasement, as jugglers and jesters, like dancers and musicians, were at the very bottom of the social hierarchy of most medieval societies as representatives of a sinful trade. The jester or juggler metaphor does not refer to the jester's function of holding up a truth to society in the distorted mirror of his funny grimaces, but to the intention of humiliating himself as the lowest among the lowest: 'Humiliatio est via ad humilitatem', 'humiliation is the path to humility'.[76] In addition, the jurodstvo knows neither irony nor pause. In its pure form, the jurodivyj is neither capable of irony nor of temporarily refraining from his actions. The spectacle of idiocy by day has the same unconditionality as prayer by night; the idiot-mimicry is of the same actuality as the dialogue with God, the multiply coded actions follow only one goal: to convey a single and cruel truth, that the world deserves only to end and that life is worth living only as if one were already dead. There is no trace of cheerful or even redeeming laughter. The jurodivyj is as deadly serious as Nadezhda Andreyevna Tolokonnikova.

---

75 See Saward, *Perfect Fools*, p. 60. See Wesjohann, 'Simplicitas', p. 142, note 225, where he refers to the tradition of the juggler metaphor among Cistercians and Franciscans.

76 Bernard of Clairvaux, quoted in Saward, *Perfect Fools*, p. 60.

CHAPTER FOUR

# On Some of Andrei Tarkovsky's Films

The 'First Philosophical Letter' by Petr Chaadaev, mentioned earlier, and a reply by Aleksandr Pushkin dated 19 October 1836, which was never sent to the author, also play a role in the film *Mirror* (1975) by Andrei Tarkovsky (1932–86). Halfway through the film, an unknown woman asks Ignat, the son of the invisible hero of the story, to read from Pushkin's text a passage underlined in red:

> There is no doubt that the schism separated us from Europe and that we did not take part in any great event that moved it; but we had our own task. It was Russia, with its enormous size, that absorbed the Mongol conquests. The Tartars, with us at their backs, did not dare to cross the western borders. They returned to their deserts and Christian civilization was saved. For this reason, we had to lead an existence that was actually Christian and made us strangers to the Christian world.[1]

Pushkin thus contradicts Chaadaev and claims an important role for Russia in relation to Europe, whose Christian civilization it had saved from destruction through its enormous sacrifice in pushing back pagan conquerors. It is quite obvious that Tarkovsky applies this argument to the historical moment in which he is living and sees Russia as a preserver and

---

1 Translated by LE. Quoted in Christian Zehnder, 'Erneuertes Gestern? Zum Verhältnis von Selbstopferung und Rückkehr bei Andrej Tarkovskij' in Norbert P. Franz, *Tarkovskij Klassiker: Beiträge zum Ersten Internationalen Tarkovskij-Symposium an der Universität Potsdam*, VOL. 2 (Potsdam: Universitätsverlag Potsdam, 2016), pp. 409–31; here, p. 415: 'Il n'y a pas de doute que le schisme nous a séparé du reste de l'Europe et que nous n'avons pas participé à aucun des grands évènements qui l'ont remuée; mais nous avons eu notre mission à nous. C'est la Russie, c'est son immense étendue qui a absorbé la conquête mongole. Les Tartares n'ont pas osé franchir nos frontières occidentales et nous laisser à dos. Ils se sont retirés vers leurs déserts, et la civilisation chrétienne a été sauvée. Pour cette fin, nous avons dû avoir une existence tout à fait à part, qui en nous laissant chrétiens, nous laissait cependant tout à fait étrangers au monde chrétien.'

protector of Europe, as demonstrated by the enormous sacrifices made by the Russian civilian population and the soldiers of the Red Army in the fight against Hitler. As is clear from many of Tarkovsky's own testimonies, he repeatedly contrasts 'the West' with 'the East', whose higher degree of spirituality he contrasts with the materialism and egocentricity of the West. Thus, he writes in *Sculpting in Time*:

> The East has always been closer to the eternal truth than the West [ . . . ]. Just compare Western and Eastern music. The West screams: Here—that's me! Look at me! Listen to how I know how to suffer and love! How unhappy and happy I may be! Me! Me!!! Me!!! The East, on the other hand, does not say a single word about itself! It loses itself completely in God, in nature, in time, and it finds itself in all of this. It is able to discover everything in itself.[2]

The discourse on spirituality is therefore, if not nationalistic, at least a discourse on the supposedly specific qualities of two 'cultures'. The willingness to make sacrifices or to offer oneself as a sacrifice is evidence of the respective degree of spirituality.[3]

The victim is indeed at the centre of numerous films by Tarkovsky. Even the child hero in *Ivan's Childhood* from 1962 is prepared to risk his life to fight the Nazis after escaping from an extermination camp. And he does indeed end up sacrificing his life: when the Red Army conquers Berlin, his portrait is found in files with pictures of prisoners of war executed by the Gestapo.

Four years later, the actor Kolya Burlyaev, who had played Ivan, played the impostor but ultimately successful bell caster Boriska in Tarkovsky's 1966 epic *Andrei Rublev*. The film is about the Russian icon painter Andrei Rublev (c. 1360–1430), whose *Trinity* (Tretyakov Gallery, Moscow) is one of the most famous works of Russian painting. The film is divided into eight chapters, preceded and followed by a prologue and an epilogue, and deals with the painter's doubts and his struggle to explore the scope of

2 Andrej Tarkovskij, *Die versiegelte Zeit* (Leipzig and Weimar: Gustav Kiepenheuer, 1989), p. 245.

3 Tarkovskij, *Die versiegelte Zeit*, pp. 246ff.

religious art in the face of violence, poverty, and injustice, which are sometimes depicted in stark images.

Boriska, whose father had never told him the secret of the correct metal mixture for casting bells, claims to the soldiers who come to his plague-ravaged village in search of his father that he knows the recipe. The soldiers take him with them and he is commissioned to cast the bell for the cathedral. It is clear that the boy is risking his life while he examines the clay with the expression of an expert and commands his assistants as if he possesses knowledge that he completely lacks. When the clapper finally sets the bell vibrating and sends its sound across the plain, Boriska collapses. The last scene shows Rublev and Boriska sitting on the plain next to a pole, the boy in the arms of the older man, an image very reminiscent of the Pietà, in which the boy assumes the position of the dead Christ. At the same time, however, he has heroically conquered his fear and has successfully become the creator of a work, even though neither the knowledge of the ancients, of tradition, nor nature as master came to his aid. As *idiota*, he risked his life for a work, the creation of which was solely dependent on his intuition. Inspired by the boy's achievement, Rublev decides to take up icon painting again, which he had decided to give up after the gruesome events of the conquest of the city of Vladimir that he had witnessed.

An idiot, Durochka, played by Tarkovsky's wife at the time, Irma Raush (who also played the mother in *Ivan's Childhood*), has accompanied Rublev ever since she witnessed how, instead of painting, he merely hurls and smears paint at the wall of Vladimir Cathedral—an iconoclastic act that terrifies the idiot. Wordlessly, she follows what is happening around her with wide eyes. Her 'animal nature' is emphasized in the scene when the Tatars throw pieces of meat to the starving crowd as if they were a pack of hungry dogs; Durochka follows the Tatar leader, who wants to make her his wife, and rides off with him, to Rublev's horror. This farewell is also the rejection of the painter-monk's radical spiritualization and self-torture, which, until Rublev is saved by Boriska's willingness to make sacrifices, leads to the suffering of numerous people in his surroundings. Thus, it is Rublev's refusal to execute the frescoes in Vladimir that causes his painter's assistants and stonemasons to leave the building site, whereupon they are blinded by the Grand Duke's henchmen. He himself becomes a murderer when, in order to save Durochka, he kills a Tatar who is about to rape her.

Mention must be made of another victim figure, the juggler, who entertains his 'proletarian' audience with crude jokes in the first scene after the prologue, whereupon he is arrested and taken away by soldiers, but reappears at the end of the film and falsely accuses Rublev of having betrayed him. What looks like an Entwicklungsroman, a novel charting the development of the protagonist, is, to a greater extent, a narrative that closes in on itself in the form of an unwinding spiral, whose protagonists would remain trapped in a cycle of sin and atonement if Boriska did not take it upon himself to dispel this state of condemnation through his sacrifice and open up the possibility of liberation.

In *Nostalghia* (1983), Tarkovsky's first film shot in Western exile, in Tuscany and Rome, the mathematician Domenico, who is considered mad, and the Russian writer Andrei Gorchakov, who suffers from homesickness, each have—or want to make—a sacrifice. Domenico lives alone in a rundown house in which he had locked up his family for seven years to wait for the end of the world before the police cleared the house and took his wife and children away. Domenico believes it is his task to save the world by performing a great deed, but one that is very easy to accomplish: Gorchakov must carry a candle through the drained pool of the sulphur baths at Bagno Vignoni. After Gorchakov has initially ignored the wish and returned to Rome, he learns that Domenico is also in Rome. Upon enquiring through an interpreter whether Gorchakov has complied with his wish and learning that he hasn't, the writer returns to Bagno Vignoni. The scenes of him trying to carry the burning candle through the pool are complemented by the scenes of Domenico's self-immolation. Standing on top of the equestrian statue of Marcus Aurelius in the Capitoline Square, Domenico gives a speech, at the end of which he douses himself with petrol and bursts into flames. At the same time, Gorchakov succeeds in a third and final attempt to place the burning candle on the edge of the pool, whereupon he dies. In his speech, Domenico demands that the so-called healthy should eat, drink, and sleep with him and his peers, the so-called sick, in order to be united as a society. In the style of modern cultural criticism lamenting the general decline of society,[4] he calls for a return to the point at which humanity had turned in the wrong direction, and laments the state of the world, in which a madman must tell the sane that they should be ashamed of themselves. Domenico calls for an inversion of the situation: it should snow in August (an allusion to the snow miracle that led to the founding of Santa Maria Maggiore in Rome in the fifth century),[5] and the sun should shine at night. The difference between the agitated Domenico and the picturesque but passive 'lunatics' scattered on the steps should undoubtedly be understood as a difference between the inspired seer of God and the merely mentally ill. Like Domenico, who introduces his speech by saying that he is not a 'whole person' because his mind cannot be where his body is, Gorchakov is also divided in two: his body is in Italy, while his spirit is with his family in Russia. This self-alienation ultimately leads to his death, a wordless sacrificial death that contrasts with Domenico's voluble suicide. While the latter is staged as a public beacon of protest, Gorchakov's sacrifice goes unnoticed and takes place in the solitude of the night.

Finally, the concept of sacrifice gives Tarkovsky's last film its title: *The Sacrifice* (1986). The opening shots show the former actor Alexander planting a dead tree on the seashore with his young son, the 'little boy', who is mute due to a throat operation, and monologuing about the meaning of everyday rituals. As it turns out, it is Alexander's birthday, and the postman Otto brings him a letter addressed to 'Myshkin' from the 'Idiotists', an allusion to Alexander's former profession as an actor, in which he played the character of Prince Myshkin from Dostoyevsky's novel. After returning to the house and before dinner is served, a television broadcast announces a (probably nuclear) catastrophe, the exact nature of which remains unclear. Deeply shaken, Alexander, who in the previous monologue had expressed

---

4 See Koselleck and Widmer, *Niedergang*, pp. 214ff.

5 See Hanns Hubach, *Matthias Grünewald: Der Aschaffenburger Maria-Schnee-Altar: Geschichte—Rekonstruktion—Ikonographie* (Mainz: Gesellschaft für Mittelrheinische Kirchengeschichte, 1996), pp. 131–98. An English version of the speech can be found at shihlun.tumblr.com/post/65503144065/domenicos-speech-in-andrei-tarkovskys-nostalghia.

his weariness at the fact that he is all words but never acts, swears to sacrifice everything he holds dear to God:

> I am giving you everything I have. I'm leaving my family, whom I love. I'm destroying my home and I'm giving up little boy. I will become mute. I will never speak to anyone again, I will renounce, renounce everything that binds me to life, if only you will make everything as it was before, as it was this morning, as it was yesterday. And that you take this deadly, agonizing and deep terror away from me. Yes, everything! Lord, help me. I will do everything I have promised you.[6]

Like Rublev, Alexander commits himself to silence and to leaving his possessions and all those he loves. In order to save the world, Otto suggests that he spend a night with the maid Maria. The paradox that the one who wants to save the world is now in need of saving himself contains the element of a circularity that is at odds with itself: it also appears to determine the subsequent events, in that Alexander wakes up the morning after the night with Maria and everything actually seems to be exactly the same as the day before.[7] It is as if the television news reports had only been a bad dream or as if the rescue had already happened. And yet, although the night of love with Maria seems to have resulted in the *apokatastasis*, the restoration of the pre-apocalyptic state, and the sacrifice that Alexander felt obliged to make has therefore lost its justification, he sets fire to his house. The senseless sacrifice, with which he destroys what he loves and the meaning of which remains closed to those for whom he makes the sacrifice, nevertheless results in the 'little boy' reacquiring the ability to speak.

---

6 Quoted from Andrej Tarkovskij, *Opfer* (with images by Sven Nykvist) (Munich: Schirmer/Mosel, 1987), p. 110.

7 Alexander remembers his vow when he wakes up in his room after his night of love with Maria and bumps his foot against a table leg, one of the few scenes in Tarkovsky's work that shows a trace of humour and which Slavoj Žižek understands as a reference to the main character of *The Idiot* from Dostoevsky's novel of the same name, which he in turn places in the specifically Russian tradition of the jurodivyj. Slavoj Žižek, 'The Thing from Inner Space' in *Angelaki* 4(3) (1999): 221–31; here, p. 229.

The stalker in Tarkovsky's 1979 film of the same name is also associated with the idiot Myshkin and other characters such as Dostoyevsky's ridiculous man from his 1877 short story 'The Dream of a Ridiculous Man'. In addition, the similarity with the jurodivyj is also pointed out.[8] *Stalker* tells the story of a scout who brings people into the 'Zone'. In the 1972 novel *Piknik na obochine* (Roadside Picnic) by the brothers Arkady and Boris Strugatsky, the Zone is an area in North America that is closed to the public for unclear reasons and from which the stalker smuggles out objects to sell. The centre of the Zone is the Golden Sphere, which the main protagonists try to find because it is capable of fulfilling wishes.

There are crucial places where Tarkovsky changes the script, in preparing which the authors of the novel were involved. He replaces the Golden Sphere with the Room, and the stalker is not a fence who sells items stolen from the Zone but a kind of scout who leads visitors into the mysterious grounds. And, in a departure from the original, Tarkovsky reduces the travelling group to the stalker, a writer, and a scientist, whom he is supposed to help enter the Zone. As it turns out, the writer is a cynic and egotist who hopes to gain inspiration from visiting the Room, and the scientist wants to blow up the Room with a bomb that he carries in his rucksack, since the numinous and the sacred are contrary to scientific rationality and the Room invites all grand inquisitors and dictators to ask for their lust for power to be fulfilled. The figure of the stalker is ambivalent: many of his statements turn out to be incorrect. For example, he claims that one cannot simply walk through the Zone, as this would be far too dangerous, and that one has to use a certain technique to determine the path: he throws ribbons wrapped around a nut in a certain direction and demands that the two men do not deviate from the path he has marked out. However, it turns out that there are no consequences if they do so, and that they can even, contrary to the stalker's assertion, return to a certain place by the same route, as the scientist does in search of the rucksack he has forgotten. In the original, the reason given for throwing the

8 Cornelia Martyn, 'Die "Russische Idee" oder die Kunst als Manifestation der Gottesebenbildlichkeit in Andrej Tarkovskijs Film *Stalker*' in Franz, *Tarkovskij Klassiker*, pp. 215–36; here, p. 231. Dietrich Sagert, 'Tarkowskijs Gottesnarren' in *forum* 259 (September 2006).

screw nut was 'magnetic concentrations' that had to be avoided, whereas in the film Tarkovsky dispenses with any explanation. The fact that the stalker nevertheless insists on the necessity of his technique exposes him to the suspicion that he only intends to intimidate or impress his customers with the seriousness of his throwing actions. The drawing of matches to decide who has to go first into the 'meat grinder', a tunnel, also proves to be nonsensical, as the stalker holds out two matches of the same length to the writer, insisting afterwards that the drawing meant nothing, as the Zone itself had already decided who had to go first. At the same time, the film draws a parallel between the stalker and the unrecognized Christ when, before the group enters the 'meat grinder', it has the stalker recite the Gospel text (Luke 24:13–35) of the disciples' encounter with the resurrected Christ at Emmaus after a female voice has spoken a passage from the Apocalypse (Revelation 6:13–17); or when the writer makes fun of the stalker by putting on a crown of thorns and paraphrasing the mockery of Christ by the torturers.

When he finally arrives at the Room, the writer refuses to go in, as he has now come to the conclusion that it is not conscious wishes that are fulfilled there, but only the most secret ones. The stalker finally steals the bomb from the scientist. He begs the two travel companions not to destroy what he considers to be his dignity, his happiness, and his freedom:

> Everything that is mine, you see, is here. The ZONE. My happiness, my freedom, my dignity, everything is here. I bring those here as I am myself. The destroyed, the tortured. Here, here they have hope. And I, when they come, you see, I can help them. Nobody can help them, but I, a louse, a disgusting louse, I can. Me, I could cry with happiness because I can help them. That's all, that's all I want. I really don't want anything else.[9]

At the end of the film, after the three men have returned from the Zone without having entered the Room, the stalker carries his daughter, who is unable to walk, home. His wife puts him to bed and tries to comfort him in his despair about the men's disbelief. The girl, referred to as 'monkey',

9 Quoted from Norbert P. Franz, *Stalker: Protokoll des Films in der Original- und der deutschen Synchronfassung* (Potsdam: Universitätsverlag Potsdam, 2009), p. 99.

apparently owes her disability to her proximity to the Zone; at the same time, she has telekinetic abilities and is able to move glasses on the table. In the stalker's wife's epilogue, the stalker is described as obsessive, a condemned man, and an eternal prisoner, but the wife also emphasizes that she does not regret her sometimes painful life with him, as it constantly reminds her of the need for hope.

*Stalker* is a cinematic discourse on the question of the existence of God and the function of hope. For the scientist, hope is a palliative; for the stalker, a reason for living; for the writer, a psychological function, after success and recognition have only driven him deeper into his cynicism. What the Room ultimately is or could have been remains as unclear as the role of the stalker between scout and moron. The imperative of disinterestedness does not allow him to enter the Room himself; the writer is paralysed by his fear of his most secret desires, the scientist by a sudden apathy after the stalker's intervention, which prevents him from setting his work of destruction in motion. The cinematic discourse thus leaves the question of the character of the Room and that of the stalker unanswered. If, as Cornelia Martyn suggests, various filmic constellations (for example, the men lying on the floor) refer to icon paintings depicting the Transfiguration of Christ,[10] the question arises as to the logic of such a constellation, in which there are disciples but no Christ. Martyn also refers to the proximity of the scene in front of the Room to Andrei Rublev's *Trinity*. As the three men gaze into the Room, which they dare not enter, it begins to rain down on them; the rain, as a symbolic connection between the heavenly and the earthly, sets in just when the men succumb to their doubts and dare not go any further. Similarly, in the final image, the table over which the girl moves the glasses thanks to her telekinetic power can be seen as analogous to the table around which the three angels are grouped in Rublev's painting, at which they sit and where the drinking cup is located. Just as a dog joins Gorchakov in *Nostalghia*, a dog joins the stalker—a reference to the role of the dog in the Cynic tradition.

*Stalker* gains its power by not answering the questions about what the protagonists in the film might be looking for, just as it keeps the purpose

---

10 Martyn, 'Die "Russische Idee"', pp. 223ff.

of the Room in suspension; not to mention the question of whether the Room is to be understood as a metaphor for God. The miraculous (the telekinetic abilities of the 'monkey') mixes with the banality and the harshness of the daily life of the stalker and his wife, who—and this is perhaps the only unambiguous element in the film—is in love with him in a way that she herself can hardly comprehend. If religiously charged iconographic markers such as the Trinity or Transfiguration are used to suggest a religious reading by means of a sacralization of the profane, they are simultaneously invalidated, as they are always incomplete, inconsistent, or flawed in one respect or another.

The ambivalence with which *Stalker* deals with its subject reflects the Janus-facedness that has already been noted several times and which characterizes the figure of the jurodivyj. Like the jurodivyj, the stalker is a reprobate, a 'disgusting louse', and yet he has the capacity for cognisance of the numinous. His fervour is the fervour of the idiot, who, although his pretension to knowledge of the Zone proves to be theatrical nonsense, unswervingly clings to the proclaimed correctness of this knowledge, a knowledge of praxis.

CHAPTER FIVE

# The Idiot in the Asylum

Erasmus of Rotterdam's statement that the Christian religion 'has a certain kinship with folly and no relation at all to wisdom'[1] refers to a process of complication that is only partly correctly named 'secularization': the natural sciences are increasingly becoming instruments of world knowledge, and the church's authority is beginning to wane in the face of their results. The fact that religious furore can hardly be distinguished from the furore of lunacy brings faith and its forms of expression closer to delusion. The laicization of society means that the possibility of integrating mystical content and its modes of experience into the structure of socially accepted schemata without friction disappears.[2] For centuries to come, medicine, which from then on claimed to be responsible for the health of the mind and soul as the science of man, would attempt to develop a nomenclature in which the idiot would find his place alongside the imbecile and the madman (and their numerous relatives).

At the same time, however, the appearance of linearity associated with history is deceptive.[3] The impression that the nosological and etiological instruments were continuously sharpened from the beginning of the modern era or the French classical period (from the middle of the sixteenth century to the end of the eighteenth century)[4] is complicated, if not refuted, by the finding that the European Middle Ages knew many ways of reacting to madness, insanity, or idiocy; many more ways than, in retrospect, the narrative of the progressive liberation of the human race from the darkness of the Middle Ages is prepared to admit.

---

1 Erasmus, *Lob der Torheit*, p. 135.

2 Michel Foucault, *Psychologie und Geisteskrankheit* (Frankfurt am Main: Suhrkamp, 1968 [1954]), p. 124.

3 Michel Foucault, *Wahnsinn und Gesellschaft* (Frankfurt am Main: Suhrkamp, 1973 [1961]).

4 Ulrich Johannes Schneider, 'Foucault und die Aufklärung' in *Das Achtzehnte Jahrhundert* 23(1) (1999): 13–25.

The spectrum of ways of dealing with the insane ranged from strict segregation in leprosy houses and other architectural structures from times of epidemics[5] to almost complete ignorance of the difference between illness-related functional failure and other forms of asociality and dysfunctionality, to the more recent use of institutions of internment and asylums, in which the mentally ill are locked up, segregated from other sick and asocial people, criminals, and crooks.

In medieval society, the mentally disturbed or disabled outsiders were the object of social care and medical attention as well as victims of exorcism and procedures of exclusion. They were either disregarded or healed, cared for or chased away; they were subjected to the torment of exorcism, or locked away and forgotten in their misery. Their fate depended on their gender, origin, class position, and wealth, and on the benevolence of their family, their integration into the rural community or urban environment, and ultimately on the extent to which society's actions towards them were determined by views on and attitudes towards curability and thus perfectibility.[6] With the beginning of the modern era, however, categories of work and economics began to play a role. The asocials, among whom the insane are counted, serve as cheap labour until it becomes clear that this subsidized human resource is beginning to harm the competitive economy outside the asylum. What remains is the institution of internment. From the eighteenth century onwards, its existence was justified by ideas of moral recovery, welfare, and philanthropy.

The appearance of the madman in Erasmus' *Praise of Folly* marks the beginning of the career that the mentally ill will take from here on in within the European system of medical and human sciences, moral philosophy, and theology. In this web of intersections, the idiot can only be dimly perceived, and his image is increasingly overlaid by other images. While the texts of the Middle Ages spoke not only of *stultus*, *idiota*, and

5 Sebastian Brant mentions the 'Dummenloch' in Basel, which had served as accommodation for people with smallpox before the lunatics and beggars were housed there.

6 See Dirk Matejovski, *Das Motiv des Wahnsinns in der mittelalterlichen Dichtung* (Frankfurt am Main: Suhrkamp, 1996), p. 273.

*fatuus*, but also of *furor* and *insanus*,[7] it is the agitated, almost uncontrollable madman, driven by myriad fears and hallucinations and an inner restlessness, who gradually and over the course of a lengthy process steadily comes to the fore. His contours remained vague for a long time until, at the beginning of the eighteenth century and then increasingly a hundred years later, specialist medical texts attempted to redefine the complex of madness, idiocy, dementia, insanity, manic insanity, among others. They set in motion a process of clarification and differentiation that replaced outdated diagnoses and etiologies with new ones, developed new descriptive parameters and clinical definitions, and subjected the game between the outsider and society to new rules. In this game, the madman and society are in a mimetic relationship with one another. The madman, the maniac, the mentally ill each reflects the fears, phobias, and neuroses of society itself. And his form changes like the content of his madness, depending on which society locks him away in the madhouse.

In English literature from 1700 onwards, the figure of the idiot or *natural fool* is known. He cannot be legally prosecuted, and his condition persists from birth without any hope of recovery.[8] Similarly, in Diderot and d'Alembert's *Encyclopaedia* of 1754, the idiot is characterized as having an almost complete lack of mental faculties and intellect by nature. His weakness of mind is innate and cannot be remedied, whereas the imbecile has merely lost his powers of reason. In the short section that the *Encyclopaedia* devotes to the idiot, Diderot and d'Alembert then make the well-known derivation from the Greek, which identifies the idiot with the private man, but they add a remarkable facet: 'C'est-à-dire, celui que nous appellerions aujourd'hui un *sage*', 'This means: He is what we would now call a *sage*.'[9]

---

7 Leontius of Neapolis, 'Vita S. Symeonis Sali confessoris', cols. 1739 and *passim*.

8 Parnel Wickham, 'Conceptions of Idiocy in Colonial Massachusetts' in *Journal of Social History* 35(4) (Summer 2002): 935–54; here, p. 940. Matejovski, *Das Motiv des Wahnsinns*, p. 65.

9 Translated by LE. *Encyclopédie, ou dictionnaire raisonné des sciences, des arts et des métiers*, VOL. 8 (Neufchâtel: Société typographique de Neuchâtel, 1765), pp. 497ff. Emphasis in the original.

Zedler's *Universal Lexicon* (1731–1754) understands the idiot differently: here he is described as clumsy and untalented, illiterate but admissible as a witness in court cases, 'a simple-minded and clumsy fellow who has learned nothing'. Zedler otherwise uses a variety of expressions and terms to describe mental deviations: crazy, insane, *mente captus*, frenzied, irrational, nonsensical, senseless, mad, furioso, debilitas, imbecillitas, a weak mind, devoid of the power to reason, idiots.[10]

In the German-speaking world before 1801, the term 'Idiotismus', which is derived from 'Idioten', refers to linguistic and dialectal peculiarities and only developed into a term denoting mental abnormality or weakness in the following decades under French influence.[11] Far from achieving any terminological clarity, both in France and in Germany, authors competed with each other in discovering and establishing ever newer categories and sub-categories, and in the course of an even finer adjustment of observational instruments, unfortunately also at the expense of sound scientific knowledge, limited phenomena were inflated to clinical categories of significance. One example is the finding of amaurotic-paralytic forms of idiocy, which Karl Scheffer, a doctor working in Budapest, believed he could easily link to the 'Jewish race' after a preliminary mapping of the

---

10 See Johannes Gstach, *Kretinismus und Blödsinn: Zur fachlich-wissenschaftlichen Entdeckung und Konstruktion von Phänomenen der geistig-mentalen Auffälligkeit zwischen 1780 und 1900 und deren Bedeutung für Fragen der Erziehung und Behandlung* (Bad Heilbrunn: Julius Klinkhardt, 2015), pp. 84ff.

11 Gstach, *Kretinismus*, p. 161. The designation of a dictionary for special dialectal or sociolectal expressions as an *Idiotikon* is still common today. The best known is certainly the *Schweizerisches Idiotikon*. See https://www.idiotikon.ch/ (last accessed 13 March 2021). When Marx and Engels write of the 'idiocy of rural life' (Karl Marx and Friedrich Engels, 'Manifest der Kommunistischen Partei' in *Werke*, VOL. 4 (Berlin: Dietz, 1959), pp. 459–93; here, p. 466), this refers to the parcelled-out way of life and economy of the peasants and is subsequently falsely equated with idiocy right up to Adorno; *Minima Moralia* (Frankfurt am Main: Suhrkamp, 1989 [1951]), p. 25. See Eric Hobsbawm's introduction to *The Communist Manifesto* (Hamburg and Berlin: Verso, 1999), p. 18: 'Marx undoubtedly shared the contempt and ignorance of the rural milieu that was widespread among city dwellers at the time. However, the phrase does not refer to "stupidity", but to the "narrow horizons" or "isolation from the many-sided society" in which people lived in the countryside'. Marx otherwise used the I-word in the pejorative sense that was already common in his day; see Marie Simon, 'Stichwort "Idiot"', p. 294–95.

various manifestations of mental impairment.[12] The fact that this state of affairs was judged critically by contemporaries themselves is evidenced by statements such as that of the physician Friedrich Nasse (1778–1851). He had worked primarily in Bonn and wrote in the first issue of the *Zeitschrift für psychische Aerzte* (1818): 'Whoever now speaks to us of madness, of insanity, of mental illness, we must first of all ask him what he understands by these terms'.[13]

In France, Philippe Pinel attempted in 1801 to distinguish the idiot—characterized by 'nullité de caractère', among other things—from the debile and the cretin.[14] Nevertheless, in 1838 Jean-Étienne Esquirol still complained that there was a great deal of confusion regarding the precise meaning of the word:

> Sauvages, Sagar, Vogel ont appelé l'idiotie amentia, imbecillitas ingenii, fatuitas, Linné la nomme morosis; Cullen et Fodéré démence innée; Dufour et Pinel en ont fait un genre de folie qu'ils désignent sous le nom d'idiotisme.
>
> Sauvages, Sagar, and Vogel have called idiocy *amentia, imbecillitas ingenii, fatuitas*; Linné calls it *morosis*; Cullen and Fodéré *démence*

12 Karl Schaffer, 'Beiträge zur Nosographie und Histopathologie der amaurotisch-paralytischen Idiotieformen' in *Archiv für Psychiatrie* 42 (1906): 127–60. On the efforts of brain-anatomical and pathological literature from the mid-nineteenth century, see Erwin H. Ackerknecht, *Kurze Geschichte der Psychiatrie* (Stuttgart: Enke, 1967), p. 74, who writes of 'mostly unsuccessful efforts', which were 'mostly insignificant or even worthless'. Similarly, Robert Castel, *Die psychiatrische Ordnung: Das goldene Zeitalter des Irrenwesens* (Frankfurt am Main: Suhrkamp, 1979 [1976]), p. 129: 'Fantastic and often contradictory statistics, underestimation of nevertheless recognized facts, such as those of inheritance, obscure casuistry of the relationships between different types of causes (predominant, secondary, directly effective, indirectly effective, etc.)—all this is considered conclusive. By hook or by crook, the medical school of error wants to assert Falret's dictum: "One thing is certain: madness is far more often caused by moral causes than by physical ones"'.

13 Friedrich Nasse, 'Ueber die Benennung und vorläufige Eintheilung des psychischen Krankseyns' in *Zeitschrift für psychische Aerzte* (Leipzig, 1818), p. 17.

14 Philippe Pinel, *Traité médico-philosophique sur l'aliénation mentale* (Paris: Brosson, 1809 [1801]), pp. 139, 181ff.

> *innée*; Dufour and Pinel made it a subcategory of madness with the name of *idiotism*.[15]

Like d'Alembert, he understands idiocy as a condition and not as a disease and thus declares it to be incorrigible. While he concedes that the forms of idiocy are innumerable,[16] he also attempts to distinguish between imbeciles and idiots and, following Pinel, the cretins, whom he describes as 'idiots or imbeciles who live in the ravines of the mountains'.[17] In a discussion of Esquirol's report on inmates of the asylum in Charenton,[18] published in the *Annales d'hygiène publique et de médecine légale*, reference is made to the cretins in the Pyrenees and the Alps, whose illness is subsequently referred to as 'endemic idiocy'.[19] Imbecility and insanity are seen as diseases of civilization and as phenomena of moral degeneration, whereas idiocy is understood as an incurable condition given to the individual by nature and as the absence of all mental faculties.[20]

In the German version of Esquirol's work from 1838, *Imbecilité* is translated as *Blödsinn*. Blödsinn is now used as a generic term for idiocy and so-called adult stupidity. At the same time, in the German translation of Marc's *De la folie, considérée dans ses rapports avec les questions médico-judiciaires* (1844), *démence* is used synonymously with *insania* and is now supposed to encompass idiocy, stupidity, and confusion.[21] In 1838, Busch and Gräfe used idiocy as a generic term for insanity and distinguished four degrees of insanity—in the first, insanity is accompanied by paroxysms

15 Jean Étienne Esquirol, *Des maladies mentales*, VOL. 2 (Brussels: Maloine, 1838), p. 76. Similarly, W. C. Ellis, *Traité de l'aliénation mentale, ou de la nature, des causes, des symptômes et du traitement de la folie* (Paris: Rouvier, 1840), pp. 198ff.

16 Esquirol, *Des maladies mentales*, p. 103.

17 Esquirol, *Des maladies mentales*, p. 110.

18 Jean Étienne Esquirol, *Rapport statistique sur la maison royale de Charenton pendant les années 1826, 1827 et 1828* (Paris, 1829), pp. 101–51.

19 F. Heyer, *Beiträge zur Lösung der Idiotenfrage* (Berlin: August Hirschwald, 1861), cited in Gstach, *Kretinismus*, pp. 157–58.

20 John Forbes and John Conolly (eds), *The British and Foreign Medical Review*, VOL. 1 (London, 1836), p. 276. Ackerknecht, *Kurze Geschichte der Psychiatrie*, p. 44.

21 Charles Chrétien Henry Marc, *Die Geisteskrankheiten in Beziehung zur Rechtspflege*, Karl Wilhelm Ideler trans. (Berlin: Voß, 1844), p. 311.

of passion, in the second by a lack of judgement, in the third by gradual degeneration, and in the fourth by a state of complete apathy—the first two of which are to be regarded as transitional states from madness and folly to insanity.[22]

Although a student of Esquirol, Édouard Séguin, the founder of integrative education in France, puts aside the static concept of idiocy as a 'condition', instead placing the idiot at the end of a developmental continuum, from which he or she can be brought up to a certain point by the caring attention of the doctor or teacher. His work *Traitement moral, hygiène et éducation des idiots*,[23] published in 1846, draws on the experiences that his other teacher, Jean Itard, had with Victor of Aveyron, a 'wild child' whom Itard had managed to teach simple tasks and rudimentary writing skills.[24] Itard's two texts from 1801 and 1807 on Victor contain the central parameters for describing the extreme poles of savagery and civilization: on the one hand, the savage, who owes nothing of what he does and can do to human education, but everything to nature;[25] on the other hand, the civilized, whose civilization consists precisely in being able to imitate with the greatest possible precision what the human environment represents. Itard also points out that the process to which he subjects Victor is partly aimed at awakening new needs in him that the boy would not even feel in his natural state. In other words, the aim is first to turn him into the deficient being that needs culture and institutions in order to remedy his weakness, which results from his rudimentary endowment with instincts.[26]

22 Busch, Gräfe et al. (eds), *Encyclopädisches Wörterbuch der medicinischen Wissenschaften*, VOL. 17 (Berlin: Veit et Comp., 1838), pp. 635ff., 642–43.

23 Édouard Séguin, *Die Idiotie und ihre Behandlung nach physiologischer Methode* (S. Krenberger trans.) (Vienna: Graeser, 1912).

24 See Lucien Malson, *Wolf Children and the Problem of Human Nature: With the Complete Text of The Wild Boy of Aveyron by Jean-Marc-Gaspard Itard* (New York: Monthly Review Press, 1972). François Truffaut's 1970 film *L'Enfant sauvage* refers to Itard's report. Four years later, Werner Herzog released *The Enigma of Kaspar Hauser*. The difference between the two films lies in the fact that Truffaut's discourse is about the relationship between nature and civilization, while Herzog's is about the relationship between society and the individual.

25 Malson, *Wolf Children*, p. 91.

26 See Arnold Gehlen, *Der Mensch: Seine Natur und seine Stellung in der Welt* (Frankfurt am Main: Klostermann, 2016 [1940]), pp. 30, 37.

Like Séguin, Itard also takes the position that the state of the disabled person or the 'wolf child' arrested in his natural state can be changed. However, Séguin's position in particular remains contradictory: on the one hand, he concedes developmental opportunities to the idiot and thus becomes one of the pioneers of integrative education, whose influence continues to have an impact well into the twentieth century; on the other hand, however, he uses the criterion of development to draw a distinction between mental illness as a process and idiocy as stasis. The idiot becomes the object of pedagogical attention as a child persisting in lifelong infancy, who cannot be educated, but whose well-being must be ensured. This goal is achieved above all by the child's unconditional obedience, which is already practised in educational institutions such as the Retreat, an asylum founded near York in 1796.[27] There and subsequently even under Pinel, however, the concern is primarily for the insane, whose illness is regarded as a self-inflicted perversion whose cure or correction requires above all the strengthening of willpower. Although the idiot is not regarded as a pervert who is himself to blame for his aberration, Séguin applies the model of moral cure to the idiot as well, thus subjecting him to the same protocol as the madman, albeit with the proviso of care and caution normally reserved for the child.[28] Finally, in 1891, Paul Sollier combines the concept of moral education with the concept of degeneracy.[29] He emphasizes the concept of moral insanity,[30] again taking up the well-known distinction between idiots and imbeciles:

> The idiot can always show a certain good-naturedness, the imbecile is egotistical, often malicious, even towards those who mean well by him. With the idiot you achieve more through gentleness, with the imbecile more through fear. The former is timid, the latter presumptuous; the former industrious, the latter a stubborn

27 See Thomas Hoffmann, *Wille und Entwicklung* (Wiesbaden: Springer, 2013), p. 144.

28 Séguin, *Die Idiotie*, pp. 70–71, 168ff.

29 J. Bogousslavsky and O. Walusinski, 'Marcel Proust and Paul Sollier: The Involuntary Memory Connection' in *Schweizer Archiv für Neurologie und Psychiatrie* 160(4) (2009): 130–36.

30 Paul Sollier, *Psychologie de l'idiot et de l'imbécile* (Paris: Germer Baillière et Cie, 1891), p. 114. Hoffmann, *Wille und Entwicklung*, p. 162, speaks of 'moral imbecility'.

> sluggard; the former good-natured, the latter malicious. The judgement of the one is weak, the judgement of the other is wrong; the will of the one is weak, the will of the other is unstable.[31]

However, Sollier goes one step further than his predecessors by making a further distinction between idiots and imbeciles, which will become important later: 'The idiots are extra-social, the imbeciles are anti-social'.[32]

Its aim is to discipline the anti-social, the imbecile, and other dangerous creatures: it goes without saying that they 'as harmful and dangerous creatures must be rendered benign'. From the middle of the nineteenth century, this discourse of morality increasingly shaped the discourse on the idiot. Formulations such as that of the 'moral nullity' of the cretin[33] support the concept of a 'moral idiocy'.[34] At the same time, the question arises as to whether idiocy is hereditary, and it is largely answered in the affirmative. In this context, Esquirol's concept of idiocy, which is based on a largely unchangeable condition and excludes both development and cure (but nevertheless calls for care), is revised by the proponents of the idea of *moral idiocy*, analogous to *moral insanity*, who assume a gradual and slow degeneration caused by 'demoralizing influences' or 'moral degeneration'.[35] The concept of *moral insanity* was developed almost simultaneously with Esquirol and prior to Sollier by James Cowles Prichard in England in his book *A Treatise on Insanity and Other Disorders Affecting the Mind*, published in 1835, and in 1856 the psychiatrist James George Davey published an article, 'On Moral Idiocy'.[36] Krafft-Ebing finally brings imbecility and weakness of character together. 'Moral idiocy' is a trait of the 'inferiorly

---

31 Sollier, *Psychologie*, p. 220.

32 Sollier, *Psychologie*, p. 74.

33 Julius Clarus, review of Guillaume Ferrus, *Mémoire sur le goître et le crétinisme* (Paris: J.-B. Baillière, 1851), in *Schmidt's Jahrbücher der in- und ausländischen gesammten Medizin*, VOL. 69 (Leipzig, 1851), pp. 274–76; here, p. 275.

34 Gstach, *Kretinismus*, p. 168.

35 Heinrich Deinhardt and Jan Daniel Georgens, *Die Heilpädagogik mit besonderer Berücksichtigung der Idiotie und der Idiotenanstalten*, VOL. 1 (Leipzig: Fleischer, 1861), p. 355 et al.

36 James George Davey, 'On Moral Idiocy' in *Association Medical Journal* (September 1856), pp. 783–86.

organized', whose other mental powers are hardly affected by his complete lack of empathy or, as Krafft-Ebing writes, 'altruism'.[37] Whereas in 1838 Busch and Gräfe were still pleading for delicacy in dealing with idiots,[38] now, since his imbecility is a moral defect, he is threatened with being sent to a workhouse, a penitentiary, or a lunatic asylum.

These theories of 'moral idiocy' became popular from the middle of the nineteenth century. They were linked to attempts to base character traits and mental deficits on anatomical features, in particular of the skull. The attempts at physiognomics by the Swiss priest Johann Caspar Lavater, which were published in four volumes between 1775 and 1778, were used for this purpose. They were systematized by the German anatomist Franz Joseph Gall, who worked in Austria and France, and after 1805 were presented as a science under the name of *phrenology*, which was used not only in asylums but also in the colonies in the service of the colonial rulers' racist eagerness to measure and categorize.[39] This was followed by a character study that correlated psychological traits, intelligence, and emotional abilities with certain skull shapes, culminating in Cesare Lombroso's *L'uomo delinquente* (1876) shortly before the end of the nineteenth century. Lombroso had formulated a related approach earlier in *Genio e follia* (1864), in this case with regard to the dark side of genius, which is often accompanied by madness and other psychological and character defects.[40]

It is this synthesis of anatomical research with heredity and degeneration theory and the view of a moral deficit on the part of the sick person

---

37 Heinrich Krafft-Ebing, *Lehrbuch der Psychiatrie auf klinischer Grundlage* (Stuttgart: Ferdinand Enke, 1890), pp. 714ff.

38 Busch and Gräfe, *Encyclopädisches*, p. 647. A prominent representative of the 'moral treatment' of the mentally ill in France was François Leuret (1797–1851). See Ackerknecht, *Kurze Geschichte der Psychiatrie*, p. 50.

39 James Poskett, *Materials of the Mind: Phrenology, Race, and the Global History of Science, 1815–1920* (Chicago, IL: University of Chicago Press, 2019).

40 Lombroso's predecessors are the French psychiatrists Félix Voisin. *Des causes morales et physiques des maladies mentales et de quelques autres affections nerveuses, telles que l'hystérie, la nymphomanie et le satyriasis* (Paris: J.-B. Baillière, 1826); Moreau de Tours (*La psychologie morbide dans ses rapports avec la philosophie de l'histoire, ou De l'influence des névropathies sur le dynamisme intellectuel* (Paris: Victor Masson, 1859).

that leads to illness—as outlined by Sollier—being seen at the end of the nineteenth century primarily in terms of the disruption of social order. To eliminate this disorder, not only pedagogical or medical, but increasingly also carceral measures were to be used. For Kraepelin, the concept of illness is primarily a concept of value.[41] Illness as an irritation of the interaction of social forces is anti-social, the sick person represents a non-value, and treatment and disciplining therefore falls not only within the remit of healing and care, but also within the remit of the police authorities. Kraepelin devotes an entire chapter to 'enemies of society' under the generic term of psychopathic personalities. He writes: 'The nature of degeneracy makes it seem self-evident that its carriers complicate and endanger the coexistence of people in the most diverse directions'.[42] In his view, it is not so much socialization as predisposition that causes people to slide into a life of crime. In particular, he views the unwillingness of society's enemies to integrate themselves into work processes as problematic. Even if he disagrees with Lombroso on individual points, he considers his thesis of the 'born criminal' to be proven and correct, which is why educational attempts are at best useful for children, but otherwise penal institutions or the detention centres of asylums are the last destination of the born criminal, who should be prevented from passing on his anti-social dispositions by severing the spermatic cord.[43] It is not long before these corrective-discipline-oriented recommendations are translated into preventive recommendations. In 1920, the lawyer Karl Binding and the psychiatrist Alfred Hoche wrote the book *Die Freigabe der Vernichtung lebensunwerten Lebens* (Allowing the Destruction of Life Unworthy of Living), in which they advocated the killing of the mentally disabled and idiots as 'mentally dead'.[44] Their arguments were based primarily on economic considerations.

---

41 Hoffmann, *Wille und Entwicklung*, p. 187.

42 Emil Kraepelin, *Psychiatrie: Ein Lehrbuch für Studierende und Ärzte*, VOL. 4 (Leipzig: Johann Ambrosius Barth, 1915), p. 2076.

43 Kraepelin, *Psychiatrie*, pp. 2082, 2101, 2106, 2110.

44 Karl Binding and Alfred Hoche, *Die Freigabe der Vernichtung lebensunwerten Lebens* (Leipzig: Felix Meiner, 1920), p. 49.

It is not a long way from here to the 'euthanasia' measures of the Nazis and the mass extermination of the mentally disabled.[45]

The journey of the idiot from his blurred position as a Janus-faced outsider on the fringes of the social sphere into the darkness of the asylum follows a winding path. It seems to be synonymous with his elimination from the realm of the social and his segregation into the black heart of nature. And yet it ends in the centre of society insofar as his journey shows what modification society, which expels the idiot from itself, makes to itself. It changes from a hierarchically stratified to a functionally diversified society that begins to organize itself around the central categories of productive forces and relations of production, categories that gain contour in the formation of what will be called capitalism. The fact that the idiot mutates from his position between fool and wise man, between dork and saint, into the dull nullity that should be eliminated for economic reasons, shows how whether or not someone is allowed to survive is decided by means of calculations in which expenditure is set off against profit.[46]

This process of totalizing the economic goes hand in hand with the totalization of morality. For the medium of morality, there can be no area that is beyond its reach.[47] While cost-benefit calculations override every moral obstacle that could protect those who are weak, sick, and debilitated from the machinery of capitalism, the moral framework that denounces anyone who cannot meet the demands of usefulness as unworthy of living continues to prevail. While these two totalities—that of the economy and

45 Hans-Walter Schmuhl, *Rassenhygiene, Nationalsozialismus, Euthanasie: Von der Verhütung zur Vernichtung 'lebensunwerten' Lebens, 1890–1945* (Göttingen: Vandenhoeck & Ruprecht, 1987).

46 Bénédict Augustin Morel also makes an economic argument when he complains: 'The idiots, imbeciles, cretins and epileptics, in other words: masses of socially worthless people stream back into the asylums, where they settle and take the place of the truly insane'. The 'truly insane' have a completely different social value from the social nullities of idiots and cretins. Quoted in Castel, *Die psychiatrische Ordnung*, p. 288.

47 Niklas Luhmann, *Die Moral der Gesellschaft* (Frankfurt am Main: Suhrkamp, 2008), p. 336: morality is a 'mode of communication that circulates throughout society. It cannot be differentiated as a subsystem, cannot be concentrated in a specific functional system in such a way that moral communication can only take place in this system and nowhere else'.

that of morality—are established in their only seemingly paradoxical complementarity, a process of internal social erosion is taking place. At its centre we find the phenomenon of alienation. The concept of alienation as a philosophically and economically charged instrument of criticism of the effects of capitalism on society, of functional diversification, and the consequences of emerging class antagonisms attempts to understand this society as a lost unity.[48] Alienation can be understood as a category which, focusing on disintegration, aims at integration. At the same time, the concept of *aliénation* is to split off from this unity what cannot be integrated or what is not worth integrating. Just as in the economic sphere the reality of alienation becomes the precondition of capitalist economic activity, the demand for the unity of society in the psychiatric and moral sphere is enforced by means of the concept of *aliénation*. While society exposes itself internally to the risk of ever-increasing tension up to the point of collapse, it works on the production of a coherence that tolerates nothing contradictory to it—merely something that resembles a piece of deadwood or a total nullity, the idiots in the dark. Functional diversification and alienation in the economic sphere produce the ideologeme of a totality whose actors are the social engineers in sanatoriums and psychiatric chairs.[49] This totality, even if it is the purest ideology, produces social reality by concealing disintegration within society and at the same time bringing about the almost complete elimination of a conceivable third that lies outside the horizon of the social.

In the seemingly aimless game of concepts, distinctions, categorizations, rubrics, and quibbles of medical science, which gained in relevance

48 See Karl Marx, 'Ökonomisch-philosophische Manuskripte' (1844) in *Marx-Engels-Werke*, VOL. 40 (Berlin: Karl Dietz, 2012), pp. 515, 517.

49 Foucault, *Wahnsinn und Gesellschaft*, p. 388, writes of the connection between alienation as a concept of economic analysis and *aliénation* as a psychological concept, and claims that madness has become the paradoxical condition of the continued existence of the bourgeois order. However, the aim here is to show relations, not causalities, which either smack of pathos or of a telos that is ultimately only fantasized. On the relationship between thinking oriented towards functional equivalences and thinking oriented towards causalities, see Niklas Luhmann, 'Funktion und Kausalität' in *Soziologische Aufklärung I* (Opladen: Westdeutscher Verlag, 1991 [1970]), pp. 9–30; here, in particular, pp. 25–26.

throughout the nineteenth century, the idiot is distinguished from the imbecile, who now assumes the role of the anti-social, while the idiot sinks into silence as the 'spiritually dead'. What had been particular to the *idiota* as a master of organizing the conceivable possible—his insistence on a position beyond socially practised knowledge, on the value of intuition, the value of thinking for oneself, the privilege of unmediated or non-socially mediated knowledge—is taken away from him and erased. In his place, the imbecile appears as the socially categorizable anti-social under the sign of morality, shaped by utilitarian thinking, which identifies the pathological enemy of society with the recalcitrant. The idiot, on the other hand, disintegrates into a leftover, into nothingness that can and must be cleared away.

To keep in check the imbecile who in his inferiority, ruthlessness, and selfishness is worse than any other human being, is the task of the doctor who begins to occupy a supra-juridical position. It is up to him to determine the diagnosis and the cure, and thus at the same time to pass judgement and impose punishment. He is educator and guardian, judge and enforcer; he establishes the laws whose implementation he supervises and whose observance he sentences the idiots, imbeciles, lunatics, and madmen to.[50] Thus ends the asylum of the idiot in the mechanics of a delirious medicine. His separation from society as a half-human, whether mentally crippled or physically deformed, ends with the intrusion of the moral into the sphere of medical diagnostics. The stasis in which Esquirol has imprisoned the idiot is countered by a dynamic model of degeneration,[51] mixed with social Darwinism and anti-Semitism. Now the doctor, as the guardian of social values, assumes the right to judge inferiority or superiority, and subjects the idiot to a judgement that hits him, like it does his fellow sufferers, guiltless and guilty, with destructive force. While psychiatry expels the idiot from the social sphere into the underworld of a black, mute, and

50 See Emil Renaudin in *Annales médico-psychologiques* 6 (1845), p. 240, where he writes that the effective management of asylums by doctors is a question of 'unity of power'.

51 At the same time, there are also approaches that assume that idiocy can be cured, such as that of the director of the deaf-and-dumb institution in Berlin, C. W. Saegert, *Ueber die Heilung des Blödsinns auf intellectuellem Wege* (Berlin: Self-published, 1846).

featureless nature, it draws him back into the realm of its own social technology as the thing to be eliminated. Thus, it claims a validity far beyond the boundaries of its discipline. By totalizing itself with the help of morality, it totalizes morality, from whose grasp and from whose verdict no defect and no biological disposition is safe. It develops into the instrument of a politics of erasure. It gives the decision-making power to doctors and judges, politicians and bureaucrats to pronounce guilt and consign to destruction that which has no guilt at all.

Sollier's internal distinction between the idiot and the imbecile would be of little interest if it were merely part of the seemingly endless and pointless sequence of classifications and the slow process of inventing categories and concepts that are only relevant (if at all) in the discourse of specialization; yet it is significant because it suggests the figure of the idiot as 'extra-social' and thus the possibility of positioning him outside society, a possibility that Foucault and Dubuffet will make use of later.

Sollier's interest lies in the imbecilic, the anti-social. He moves and is active, he acts and agitates, he disturbs and subverts, cannot be located, eludes capture; a fugitive, he is lazy, indolent, and deviously renitent, good for nothing. In this construction of the born anti-social, Sollier, as a representative of the bourgeoisie of the late nineteenth century, creates the 'proletarian monster'[52] or the proletarian who endangers the ruling class as a monster. It is this aspect that actually distinguishes Sollier's reflections from the bulk of other contemporary theories.

In Foucault's statements, the distinction made by Sollier reappears when he writes (here the idiot is identical with the 'person afflicted by *aliénation*'):[53]

---

52 Wolfgang Jantzen, 'Die Entwicklung des Begriffs Imbezillität als Beispiel des gesellschaftlichen Umgangs mit Minderheiten: Ein Beitrag zur Ideengeschichte von Psychiatrie und Behindertenpädagogik', lecture delivered at the Arbeitstagung der Dozenten für Sonderpädagogik in deutschsprachigen Ländern, Essen, October 1980.

53 There is a reference to Sollier in Foucault's papers, but it is not illuminating in our context (http://eman-archives.org/Foucault-fiches/items/show/5947). Dubuffet's strategic avoidance of naming influences and references is notorious, and a lack of references therefore does not mean very much.

> The madman is not completely alien to the world of reason: he represents much more the perverted reason that is constantly thrown off course with every intellectual movement. In him the dangerous alternation of reason and unreason takes place incessantly, while *aliénation* rather denotes the moment of rupture. The person afflicted by *aliénation* is completely on the side of nonsense, the madman in the reversal of sense.[54]

Of course, it would be pointless to question Foucault's distinctions between dementia, imbecility, idiocy, melancholy, and hypochondria[55] for their consistency or correspondence with certain categories of nineteenth-century medical literature. What is relevant here, however, is the idea that there is a realm of complete estrangement in which this 'person afflicted with *aliénation*' is located, which does not appear to be identical with the madman, but can rather be identified with the idiot.

As part of his cultural critique, Dubuffet develops the ideal pole of an absolute a-sociality. It is from this icy region of complete social and cultural remoteness that the forces of the subversions that 'break the hourglass' originate. It should have become clear by now how much this thinking owes to eschatological discourse, whose protagonists do not hope for an improvement of worldly conditions, but for their complete elimination. Nevertheless, Dubuffet's thinking is not a secularized eschatology 'as a translation of theological content into its secular self-alienation, but [ . . . ] a reshuffling of positions that have become vacant'.[56] The hope for a transcendent force that would give worldly and human industriousness in its aimlessness a vanishing point by determining its end has become empty. The vacant place in the system of transcendence is occupied by the socially and culturally non-existent, the a-social, the social nullity.

When Dubuffet takes up Sollier's category of the a-social, he ascribes to him, the idiot, the active role of the one who breaks the hourglass. In a way, he affirms Sollier's identification of the imbecile with the proletarian;

54 Foucault, *Wahnsinn und Gesellschaft*, pp. 403–4.

55 Foucault, *Wahnsinn und Gesellschaft*, pp. 198–99.

56 Blumenberg, *Die Legitimität der Neuzeit*, p. 75.

but the proletarian, according to Dubuffet, only wanted the revolution, and the revolution was only the reconstruction, in inverted form, of what it had tried to destroy. The revolution of the proletarian has failed; it has disappointed the hopes that it seemed to justify. This is why the dialectic of the revolution itself must be suspended. In the *homme du commun*, the figure of the 'extra-social' lives on in Dubuffet's thinking as a vague figure of a radicalism that is located in a social nowhere. This *homme du commun*, removed from the dialectic of class antagonisms, no longer aims for revolution but practises subversion. Passive and silent, invisible outside the realm of the social, unmoving, in Dubuffet's thinking the idiot returns from the black hole at the heart of nature and from the darkness to which psychiatry had banished him.

CHAPTER SIX

# The Redeemer

Nietzsche uses the term idiot in its common pejorative meaning to attack his opponents. In *The Antichrist*, for example, he uses the verbal cudgel of the I-word to defame Kant.[1] And 'idiot' stands alongside 'woman and masses' as a synonym for enormous stupidity.[2] In this respect, its use by Nietzsche is therefore no different from its use in the medical literature of his time, which has found its way into everyday language since the middle of the nineteenth century. The idiot is a weak, morally and physically degenerate prat, a jerk, a moron.

At the same time, however, in *The Antichrist* Nietzsche uses the figure of the idiot to denounce Jesus as a product of 'degeneracy'. This is in opposition to the heroicization of Jesus as conceived by the French historian of religion Ernest Renan in his book *Vie de Jésus* (1863), which was heavily criticized by Nietzsche. Thus, Nietzsche writes:[3]

> To make a hero out of Jesus! —And what a misunderstanding of the word 'genius'! Our whole concept, our cultural concept of 'spirit' has no meaning at all in the world in which Jesus lives. Speaking with the rigour of a physiologist, a completely different word would be more appropriate here: the word idiot.

Nietzsche associates it with a 'pathological irritability of the sense of touch', a 'childishness that has, as it were, receded into the spiritual', and

1 Friedrich Nietzsche, *Der Antichrist* in *Kritische Studienausgabe*, 2nd EDN (KSA) (Giorgio Colli and Mazzino Montinari eds) (Berlin: De Gruyter, 1988), VOL. 6, p. 177: 'What destroys faster than working, thinking, feeling without inner necessity, without a deeply personal choice, without desire? than the automaton of "duty"? It is virtually the recipe for décadence, even for idiocy [ . . . ] Kant became an idiot.' For further use, see David Marc Hoffmann, 'Idiot' in Henning Ottmann (ed.), *Nietzsche Handbuch* (Stuttgart: Metzler, 2011).

2 Nietzsche, *Der Antichrist*, §53, p. 235.

3 Nietzsche, *Der Antichrist*, §29, p. 200.

'delayed and undeveloped puberty in the organism as a consequence of *degeneration*'.[4]

By trying to delineate the image of Jesus in starker terms, Nietzsche draws the idiot into a complex argument which is subject to constant change as the text progresses.

Initially, Nietzsche's *Antichrist*, which he completed in September 1888 and which was intended as part of the 'Revaluation of All Values',[5] was aimed at condemning Christianity. The accusations are well known: the devaluation of life in this world as a sham, the revaluation of the sham hereafter as the real world, revaluation of weakness as virtue, cult of compassion, justification of a culture and politics of the underprivileged, the weak and the muckrakers, justification of a politics of resentment. Nietzsche poses the following questions and answers at the beginning of the text:

> What is good? —Everything that increases the feeling of power, the will to power, the power itself in people.
> What is bad? —Everything that comes from weakness.
> What is happiness? —The feeling that power is growing, that resistance is being overcome.
> Not contentment, but more power; not peace at all, but war; not virtue, but efficiency (virtue in the Renaissance style, *virtù*, virtue without morals).
> Let the weak and misfits perish: the first sentence of our love of humanity. And they should also be helped.
> What is more harmful than any vice? —The compassion with all the wicked and weak—Christianity . . .[6]

Nothing stands in greater contrast to Nietzsche's philosophy of an unreserved affirmation of this world, of life, and of a morality beyond good and evil than Christianity with its moralistic suspicion of all strength as violence and all inequality as injustice. This Christianity, which, according

4 Nietzsche, *Der Antichrist*, §29, p. 200; §31, p. 202; §32, p. 203.

5 Friedrich Nietzsche, letter to Paul Deussen, 26 November 1888.

6 Nietzsche, *Der Antichrist*, §2, p. 170.

to Nietzsche, no decent person could profess,[7] is to be put on trial. This process cannot exclude the founding figure of Jesus, but the further the text advances, the more clearly Nietzsche distinguishes the founder of the religion from the religion itself and the institutions that refer to him. He is convinced that, on the one hand, the herald of the Good News was opposed to the 'Jewish church' and, on the other, that the founding of the 'Christian church' represents a perversion of the actual content of the Gospel.[8]

The idiot Christ, initially a figure of degeneration, seems to be one of those misfits whom Nietzsche wishes to be helped to perish. But the more the figure of Jesus himself comes to the fore and is outlined against the backdrop of both the Jewish and the Christian church, the picture changes. Jesus becomes the betrayed one, whose revolt against the Pharisees and Philistines is as pointless as his death on the cross. This death is considered pointless because Jesus cannot prevent the doctrine of an institution, the church, from being built on his gospel.

He further adds: 'This "joyous messenger" died as he lived, as he taught—not to "redeem people", but to show them how to live'.[9] A little earlier in the text, Nietzsche describes how one should live if one wants to live according to the gospel:

> In the whole psychology of the 'Gospel' the concept of guilt and punishment is missing; likewise, the concept of reward. 'Sin', any distance between God and man is abolished, —that is precisely the 'good news'. Beatitude is not promised, it is not dependent upon conditions: it is the only reality—the rest is a sign to speak of it [ . . . ] The life of the Saviour was nothing other than this practice, —his death was also nothing different . . .[10]

---

7 Nietzsche, *Der Antichrist*, §50, p. 229: 'If there is still no lack of those today who do not know how indecent it is to be a "believer"'.

8 Nietzsche, *Der Antichrist*, §36, p. 208: 'That humanity is on its knees before the antithesis of what was the origin, the meaning, the right of the Gospel, that in the term "church" it has canonized precisely that which the "glad messenger" felt to be beneath him, behind him—one searches in vain for a greater form of world-historical irony.'

9 Nietzsche, *Der Antichrist*, §35, p. 207.

10 Nietzsche, *Der Antichrist*, §33, p. 205.

The life and death of Jesus constitute the practice of saying yes to life as a life of bliss. We no longer have to hope and wait for this: it has come to pass. The death of Jesus is not a promise that man looks forward to being fulfilled in the future, but part of a practice of redeemed existence as the impossibility of denial:

> Denial is precisely that which is quite impossible for him. Similarly, there is no dialectic, there is no idea that a belief, a 'truth' could be proven by reasons ('his *proofs* are inner "lights", inner feelings of pleasure and self-affirmations, nothing but "*proofs of power*"').[11]

Thus, within a few passages, the weak, degenerate idiot Jesus becomes the conqueror of the negation of life, whose proofs are 'proofs of power' beyond all dialectics.[12]

Nietzsche repeatedly emphasizes the meaning of Jesus' 'practice',[13] and accentuates it in such a way that it can only be understood as directed against doctrine, the formation of a system, and the formation of the church. This practice is a practice of love and a practice of non-distinction: 'That he makes no distinction between strangers and natives, between Jews and non-Jews [ . . . ]; that he is not angry with anyone, does not disdain anyone. That he neither allows himself to be seen in courts of law nor to be called upon ("not to swear")'.[14] And: 'Do not resist, do not be angry, do not blame . . . But also, do not resist evil, —love it . . .'[15]

Nietzsche conceives of Paul as a contrasting figure to the idiot Christ, 'the genius in hatred, in the vision of hatred, in the relentless logic of hatred. [ . . . ] His need was power; with Paul, the priest once again wanted power—he could only use concepts, doctrines, symbols with which to tyrannize the masses and form armies'.[16] And: 'Paul was not at all an idiot'.[17]

---

11 Nietzsche, *Der Antichrist*, §32, p. 204.

12 See in particular Heinrich Detering, *Der Antichrist und der Gekreuzigte: Friedrich Nietzsches letzte Texte* (Göttingen: Wallstein, 2010).

13 Nietzsche, *Der Antichrist*, §§ 33, 35, 38, 39, 42.

14 Nietzsche, *Der Antichrist*, §33, p. 204.

15 Nietzsche, *Der Antichrist*, §35, p. 208.

16 Nietzsche, *Der Antichrist*, §42, p. 215–16.

As a 'dysangelist',[18] the theorist Paul, who 'nails the Saviour to the cross', perverts the gospel, which preaches the practice of love,[19] into its opposite, into a system of hatred. It is he, according to Nietzsche, who has 'taken the centre of gravity from life'.[20] While Jesus may be the *decadent* one who, in his idiocy, still believes in the persuasive power of his practice while already dying on the cross, Paul is the nihilist who does not even need life, but only the death of Christ for his ideology,[21] and constructs his doctrine of the negation of life on this basis. Nietzsche's contempt and rejection are directed at the theological system based on this negation, at the institution that passes it on, the church, and at its founder and herald, Paul.

Besides the negation of life, which deprives life of all meaning, it is the category of pity against which Nietzsche's anger is directed. The pathos of pity, as an ideology for the lowly, for those who have come up short, establishes a politics of resentment. By envying and denying those with ambition their right to privileges, the lowly make everything low and pull everything that aims for the higher down to themselves. Christianity as a 'collective movement of all kinds of elements of rejection and apostasy [ . . . ] as an aggregate formation of forms of decadence that crowd together and seek each other'[22] is the ideology of vengefulness that seeks to destroy everything grand, and the ideology of the sick who begrudge the strong their health. Nietzsche's tirades against Christianity, in which religious criticism is mixed with institutional criticism, culminate in the

> most terrible of all accusations [ . . . ]; [the] parasitism as the only practice of the church; with its paleness, its ideals of 'Holiness', it drinks up all blood, all love, all hope for life; the hereafter as the

17 Nietzsche, *Nachgelassene Fragmente 1887–1889*, p. 237.

18 Nietzsche, *Der Antichrist*, §42, p. 216.

19 On Jesus as a lover, see Friedrich Nietzsche, *Jenseits von Gut und Böse* in *Kritische Studienausgabe*, 2nd EDN (KSA) (Giorgio Colli and Mazzino Montinari eds) (Berlin: De Gruyter, 1988), VOL. 5, §269, p. 225: '[A]nd who finally, having become aware of human love, had to invent a God who is entirely love, entirely able to love, —who has mercy on human love, because it is so poor, so ignorant!'

20 Nietzsche, *Der Antichrist*, §43, p. 217.

21 Nietzsche, *Der Antichrist*, §42, p. 216.

22 Nietzsche, *Der Antichrist*, §51, p. 231.

> will to negate all reality; the cross as a sign of the most hideous conspiracy that has ever existed—against health, beauty, wellbeing, bravery, spirit, goodness of the soul, against life itself.

What follows from this is the need to 'revalue all values!'[23]

The rhetorical effort with which Nietzsche condemns Christian churches and their ideologies, however, masks the nuances in his assessment of the figure of Jesus himself. Of course, his condescension also applies to the 'epilepsoid' character,[24] the unmanly weakling, the unheroic idiot. However, the positioning of this loner against both the Jewish and the Christian church, which perverts his gospel, contains an esteem of Jesus as a positive typological prefiguration, as an instance of reference and orientation for Nietzsche, who on the one hand suffers from his loneliness and on the other stylizes this loneliness into the heroism of distance, the outlines of which become increasingly clear over the course of the last two years before the onset of mental illness. He writes in a prophetic tone, evoking an imagined future community:

> Only we, we free spirits, have the prerequisite for understanding something that nineteen centuries have misunderstood—that righteousness that has become instinct and passion, which declares war on this "sacred lie" more than any other lie . . . One was unspeakably distant from one's loving and cautious neutrality, from that discipline of the spirit with which alone the guessing of such strange, such tender things is made possible: one wanted at all times, with an impudent selfishness, only one's advantage in it, one has built up the church from the opposition to the Gospel . . .[25]

---

23 Nietzsche, *Der Antichrist*, §62, p. 253.

24 See Nietzsche, *Nachgelassene Fragmente 1887–1889*, p. 237, FRAG. 14[38]: 'Type Jesus. Jesus is the antithesis of a genius: he is an idiot. [ . . . ] The fact that the real male instincts—not only the sexual ones, but also those of struggle, pride, heroism—never awoke in him, that he remained retarded and childlike at the age of puberty: that belongs to the type of certain epileptoid neuroses.' Nietzsche also counts St Francis among these characters: 'The kindred natures: Francis of Assisi (neurotic, epileptic, visionary, like Jesus)'; Nietzsche, *Nachgelassene Fragmente 1887–1889*, p. 160, FRAG. 11[365].

25 Nietzsche, *Der Antichrist*, §36, p. 208.

Nietzsche constructs a typological parallelization of Christ and himself, the representative of the 'liberated spirits', the 'Hyperboreans', who find life and happiness beyond the north, the ice and death in an 'experience of seven solitudes'. 'This book belongs to the very few', and perhaps, Nietzsche speculates, his listeners and readers have not even been born yet; because: 'Only the day after tomorrow belongs to me. Some are born posthumously'.[26] This pathos of loneliness, of the outsider, of the untimely, and of the prophet, which is portrayed in the figure of Zarathustra, who descends from his 'azure solitude' to the people,[27] pervades Nietzsche's late writings. When he writes in *Ecce Homo* that he always understood philosophy as a practice of solitude, 'in ice and high mountains', where the 'solitude is immense', 'six thousand feet beyond man and time',[28] this is an expression of his opposition to and distance from the contemporary world. At the same time, Jesus as an idiot embodies a simultaneously repulsive and fascinating mixture of frailty and sublimity. Even those who understand Nietzsche's last letters as testimonies of spiritual collapse cannot avoid taking into account the orientation towards the figure of the crucified, which is already manifested with sufficient clarity in the choice of the title *Ecce Homo*. The idiot Jesus as victim of the prophet of hatred, Paul, serves Nietzsche as a prefiguration of himself in being prophetically ahead of humanity and a victim of contemporary society. The redeemer as an idiot and paradigmatic outcast, whom the crowd mocks and whose death they demand, functions as a metaphor for the necessary outsider status of the exceptional man. Nowhere is this clearer than in the double-coded reprise of the story of betrayal, when Nietzsche inserts a word from Zarathustra in the preface to *Ecce Homo* as though citing himself and at the same time as a reference to the betrayed Christ: 'only when you have all denied me will I return to you'.[29]

26 Nietzsche, *Der Antichrist*, pp. 167, 169.

27 Friedrich Nietzsche, *Ecce Homo* in *Kritische Studienausgabe*, 2nd EDN (KSA), VOL. 6, §6, p. 343.

28 Nietzsche, *Ecce Homo*, §1, p. 335.

29 Nietzsche, *Ecce Homo*, Preface, p. 261.

In *The Antichrist*, as mentioned, the idiot does not function as an independent figure, but rather as an amplifier in relation to Jesus. He is of merely indirect interest, as he can serve to further enhance Nietzsche's self-fashioning as a distant loner by way of typological recourse to Jesus. Nietzsche proceeds in a similar way with another figure, a dark and exotic one, that accompanies him in his later notes alongside the idiot and which he subjects to the same process of inversion as Jesus: the Chandala.

In the *Manusmriti*, an Indian codex of laws from the period between 200 BCE and 200 CE, the term *chandala* refers to casteless people at the lowest end of the social order, who owe their existence to the union of a female Brahmin, a member of the highest caste, with a male Sudra, a member of the lowest caste, and to whom the *Manusmriti* permits all forms of violence and degradation.[30] Nietzsche drew his knowledge of these legal texts from a more than dubious source, a translation by the French anti-Semite Louis Jacolliot from 1876, who put forward the adventurous thesis that the 'Semitic races' were descendants of Chandalas who had escaped from India.[31]

In numerous instances, Nietzsche denounces Christian morality as chandala morality or describes Christianity as a chandala religion, as the religion of the poor and disenfranchized. His invectives against Christianity are combined with his criticism of socialism, whose representatives he defames as riff-raff and as chandala apostles.[32] But there is also a remarkable nuance here; in a sudden departure from his glorification of the Laws of Manu as formulations of an ideology of harshness beyond all arbitrariness,[33] in the spring of 1888 he subjects the text, which he now calls a 'holy lie',[34] to criticism as an attempt by the Brahman caste to cement its social power.

30 See *The Laws of Manu* (Max Müller ed., G. Bühler trans.), The Sacred Books of the East, VOL. 25 (Oxford: Oxford University Press, 1886), p. 404 and *passim*.

31 See Andreas Urs Sommer, 'Ex oriente lux? Zur vermeintlichen "Ostorientierung" in Nietzsches *Antichrist*' in *Nietzsche-Studien* 28 (1999): 194–214. See also Jörg Salaquarda, 'Dionysos gegen den Gekreuzigten' in Jörg Salaquarda (ed.), *Nietzsche* (Darmstadt: Wissenschaftliche Buchgesellschaft, 1996 [1980]), p. 313n2.

32 Nietzsche, *Der Antichrist*, §57, p. 244.

33 Nietzsche, *Der Antichrist*, §57, p. 243.

34 Nietzsche, *Nachgelassene Fragmente 1887*–1889, p. 439.

Now the chandala, who had hitherto joined the resentful 'socialist rabble', stands as a positive contrasting figure to the Brahmanical 'hatchery for theologians' and 'school of stultification': '[It] must be the chandalas who had intelligence and even the interesting in their favour. They were the only ones who had access to the true source of knowledge, empiricism.'[35] And at the beginning of *The Antichrist* he writes:

> Let us not underestimate this: we ourselves, we free spirits, are already a 'revaluation of all values', a bodily declaration of war and victory against all old concepts of 'true' and 'untrue'. The most valuable insights are found at the latest; but the most valuable insights are the methods. All methods, all the prerequisites of our present scientificity, have for thousands of years been held in the deepest contempt; on account of them one was excluded from intercourse with 'honourable' people—one was regarded as an 'enemy of God', as a denier of truth, as an 'obsessive'. As a scientific character you were chandala . . . We had the whole pathos of humanity against us.[36]

After subjecting the chandala to his fury as a representative of the weak and lowly and condemning him for daring to claim equality of rights, Nietzsche now revises his assessment. The chandala is transformed into an empiricist who turns against the sacred lie of the Brahmanic religion and for this reason is subjected to contempt and violence by the priestly caste. Empiricism as a method functions as a means of reason to reveal the hypocrisy of religion. This inversion of the image of the chandala corresponds with a fragment from the spring of 1888:

> The chandala of former times is on top: ahead of the blasphemers, the immoralists, the permissive of every kind, the artists, the Jews, the minstrels—basically all disreputable classes of people—[ . . . ] we immoralists are the strongest power today: other great powers need us . . . we construct the world in our own image.[37]

35 Nietzsche, *Nachgelassene Fragmente 1887*–1889, p. 386.

36 Nietzsche, *Der Antichrist*, §13, p. 179.

37 Nietzsche, *Nachgelassene Fragmente 1887*–1889, p. 438.

In the course of the revaluation of values resulting from the criticism of the institution of the church and of Christianity as an ideology, the chandala, the outsider, with whom the immoralist Nietzsche identifies, has grown into the strongest force. The time of the few, which is mentioned at the beginning of *The Antichrist*, will be the time of the chandalas, and like Jesus they have grown from despised muckrakers and sycophants, enviers and degenerates to that class of people for whom Nietzsche reserves the highest honour: 'free spirits' who have already achieved the 'revaluation of all values'. For nineteen centuries the free spirits were the dregs and scum of the world, but now, with the beginning of the great revaluation, they are 'on top'—together with other 'disreputable' people, the possessed, gamblers, and immoralists.

The overlapping strategies of revaluation are intertwined: Nietzsche's revaluation moves from considering the idiot Jesus as a weak degenerate to holding him up as a representative of a force that affirms existence. Further, initially associated with the socialist rabble, the chandala, like Jesus with regard to the institution of the church, turns into a hero of resistance against the mendacious and stultifying theology of Brahmanism. In this revaluation, which happens to both figures in the course of the text, they are simultaneously revalued as representatives of the great revaluation of values, which itself, however, exhibits characteristics of the inversion for which the preacher of hatred, Paul the non-idiot, stands, the 'genius of chandala-hate made flesh'.[38] Just as Paul claims that he and his co-religionists are the scum of the world, Nietzsche declares that he and the free spirits, among whom he counts the chandalas and Jesus, have been counted among the scum, and just as Paul sees the time of revaluation as having come after the resurrection of the Son of God, Nietzsche sees it as having come after the death of God. The poles of re-evaluation have the same names, the mechanisms of re-evaluation follow the same logic, even the evaluation of love as superior to the law or overriding the law connects the two.

But the re-evaluation is now directed against the representative of the first inversion, who had used the same procedures, the same names, and

38 Nietzsche, *Der Antichrist*, §58, p. 246.

the same logic as Nietzsche himself. The metaphors stand parallel to one another, the poles of recognized and rejected values, the respectable masses and the despised individual, the wise man considered stupid and the fool considered wise, the apparent truths and the real truths, the time scheme of oppression and contempt followed by triumph and victory—the matrix remains intact, while the semantics swap places. The names remain stable—Jesus, chandala, idiot—but the index jumps from negative to positive and vice versa.

Whether this inversion of the inversion is to be understood as a 'dialectical suspension'[39] or rather as an undialectical contestation is worth discussing. The answer to the question depends on the relevance one wants to assign to Nietzsche's programme of the revaluation of values. The figure of speech of the 'Umwertung', revaluation, is one of a revolution in which the antithesis appears as a reversal of the thesis. The semantic difference between thesis and antithesis is due to the different 'points in time'[40] at which Nietzsche and Paul find themselves: the historical distance and the fact that, just as Paul refers to Judaism, Nietzsche refers to Paul, but also to the history that has taken its course since Paul. The set of referents is different, and the form of the reference changes through the context of relations into which Nietzsche can and must place his inversion in order to give it weight. For this reason, to call Nietzsche's attempts at a revaluation of values a dialectical abolition of Pauline thought is as misleading as the attempt to speak of an 'identification' of Nietzsche with Jesus.[41] Nietzsche with a crown of thorns in the year 2002 is as simplistic and repulsively ideological as his equation with the chandala a hundred years earlier.[42]

---

39 Salaquarda, 'Dionysos gegen den Gekreuzigten', p. 300.

40 Hans Blumenberg, 'Ernst Cassirers gedenkend' (1974) in *Wirklichkeiten, in denen wir leben*, pp. 163–72; here, p. 171.

41 See Detering, *Der Antichrist*, pp. 111, 202n26. See also Andreas Urs Sommer, *Kommentar zu Nietzsches Der Antichrist, Ecce Homo, Dionysos-Dithyramben, Nietzsche contra Wagner* (Berlin and Boston: De Gruyter, 2013), p. 380.

42 Eugen Biser, *Nietzsche: Zerstörer oder Erneuerer des Christentums?* (Darmstadt: Wissenschaftliche Buchgesellschaft, 2002). Arthur Moeller van den Bruck, 'Tschandala-Nietzsche' in *Die moderne Literatur* (Berlin and Leipzig: Schuster & Loeffler, 1902), pp. 13–52.

The figure of the idiot, as introduced by Nietzsche, is, as mentioned at the beginning, influenced by the medical literature of his time. It is documented that his library contained a copy of a book by a little-known colleague of Paul Sollier, Charles Féré, who worked at the Bicêtre Hospital.[43] The work, published in Paris in 1888, is entitled *Dégénérescence et criminalité*, and its author refers to the well-known theories of Lombroso and the anatomical observations of German and Austrian doctors on the skulls of criminals to support his thesis of a 'folie morale'.[44] And it is quite plausible that this book influenced Nietzsche's physiological theses on 'degenerescence'.

The question of Nietzsche's reception of another book received more attention than Nietzsche's reading of Féré's work. We are talking about Fyodor Dostoyevsky's *The Idiot*. The novel, written between 1867 and 1868 in Geneva and Milan, was published serially in the journal *Russkii Vestnik* from January 1868 to February 1869. The story of Count Myshkin, who returns to St Petersburg after a stay in a Swiss sanatorium where he was treated for epilepsy and becomes embroiled in the intrigues and tragedies of a society that is losing its inner cohesion before he is once again overcome by derangement, quickly received an intensive international reception, which continues to this day and is reflected in numerous theatre and film adaptations.[45]

---

43 Paolo Stellino, *Nietzsche and Dostoevsky* (Bern: Peter Lang, 2015), p. 111.

44 Féré mentions Benedikt, Schwekendiek and Flesch. Féré, *Dégénérescence*, p. 71ff.

45 Harald Bluhm, 'Dostojewski- und Tolstoi-Rezeption auf dem "semantischen Sonderweg": Kultur und Zivilisation in deutschen Rezeptionsmustern Anfang des 20. Jahrhunderts' in *Politische Vierteljahresschrift* 40(2) (1999): 305–27. Horst-Jürgen Gerigk, *Dostojewskij, der "vertrackte Russe": Die Geschichte seiner Wirkung im deutschen Sprachraum vom Fin de siècle bis heute* (Tübingen: Attempto, 2000). In 2021, a production of *The Idiot* took place at the Thalia Theater in Hamburg, directed by Johan Simons. And of course, on 11 November 2021, on the 200th anniversary of the author's birth, *Der Spiegel* ran the headline 'Was für ein Idiot!'. *The Idiot* also inspired the unsuccessful cinema adaptation *L'Amour braque* by Andrzej Żuławski in 1985 (*Love and Violence*). The far-reaching reception of Dostoevsky's *Idiot* is also shown by the revisiting of Ippolit's question as to whether it was true that Myshkin believed that it was beauty that would save the world in Nick Cave's 'Nature Boy' on *Abattoir Blues / The Lyre of Orpheus* (2004). 'Beautiful World' on the same album is both a hymn to genius outsiders and to the concept of inspiration: 'Send that stuff on down to me!' In

While it remains unclear whether Nietzsche had read *The Idiot*,[46] the strong impression the author made on him is clear. On 23 February 1887, he reported from Nice to Franz Overbeck that he had discovered a work by Dostoyevsky, whose name was previously unknown to him, but which he would soon describe as one of the 'most beautiful strokes of luck in my life'.[47] The book is entitled *L'Esprit souterrain*. Published by Plon in 1886, *L'Esprit souterrain* is the more than idiosyncratic combination of two texts by the Russian writer translated into French, namely the 1847 story entitled 'The Landlady' and *Notes from Underground*, published in 1864.[48] Nietzsche reads this and other books by Dostoyevsky only in French translation, as indicated in a postcard to Heinrich Köselitz dated 27 March 1887.[49]

Nietzsche frequently refers to Dostoyevsky in the following years. In a posthumous fragment from the spring of 1888 with the heading 'Jesus:Dostoyevsky' Nietzsche repeats his criticism of Renan and writes:

> I know of only one psychologist who has lived in the world where Christianity is possible, where a Christ can arise at any moment. That is Dostoyevsky. He intuited Christ: [ . . . ] But can one make a mistake worse than turning Christ, who was an idiot, into a genius?[50]

In the light of his doctrine of decadence, Christ appears as *décadent* and Dostoyevsky as his ideal chronicler. Nietzsche describes the world of the Gospels as

> a world like something out of a Russian novel, in which society's effluvia, nervous disorders, and 'childish' idiocy seem to have a

---

1997, Cave wrote 'Idiot Prayer', the prayer of a man about to be interned. In 2020, he released a livestreamed solo concert of the same title.

46 Sommer, *Kommentar*, p. 10.

47 Friedrich Nietzsche, *Götzen-Dämmerung* in *Kritische Studienausgabe*, 2nd EDN (KSA) (Giorgio Colli and Mazzino Montinari eds) (Munich: Deutscher Taschenbuch Verlag, 1988), VOL. 6, §45, p. 147.

48 Stellino, *Nietzsche and Dostoevsky*, p. 25.

49 Nietzsche Source—Digitale Kritische Gesamtausgabe Werke und Briefe (eKGWB), BVN-1887, 822.

50 Nietzsche, *Nachgelassene Fragmente 1887*–1889, p. 409.

> rendezvous. [ . . . ] One would have to regret that a Dostoyevsky did not live in the vicinity of this most interesting *décadent* [Christ], I mean someone who knew how to feel the gripping charm of such a mixture of the sublime, the sick, and the childish.[51]

While there is thus no question that Nietzsche was inspired by Dostoyevsky, it remains questionable whether the figure of the idiot Myshkin is responsible for the fact that Nietzsche's image of Jesus changes in the course of writing *The Antichrist*. As there is no evidence that he read the novel, it is more plausible to understand the inversion of the figure of Jesus, flanked by the outsider figures of chandala and the idiot, as the result of a logic that configures the relationship between outsider and society, and not only in Nietzsche. Nietzsche seeks and finds prefigurations of his loneliness and his position of revolt, and his 'honesty'[52] forces him to admit that he does not occupy the position of power in his time, but that of powerlessness, social weakness, and irrelevance. Whoever owns the day after tomorrow is today a chandala, he is scum, an idiot, an outsider, and a victim like the man who is crucified by a church that invokes his teachings. Just as Nietzsche uses Jesus as an image of himself—even the phrase about being born posthumously can be understood as a non-religious adaptation of the idea of resurrection—he strips him of the religious connotations and allows him to appear anew as a practitioner of love who affirms the here and now. He shares the qualities that characterize Jesus and the idiot, who serves to give the sublimely ill Redeemer a profile: remoteness from the world, alienation from society and culture, incomprehension of any form of dialectics, rejection of scriptural knowledge, and possession of an insight that unfolds its persuasive power as an 'inner light':

51 Nietzsche, *Der Antichrist*, §31, p. 202. See also Nietzsche, *Nachgelassene Fragmente 1887–1889*, p. 267, where he declares the 'anemic saint of Nazareth' to be a member of a 'species' 'such as Dostoiewsky knows, —touching, depraved and twisted freaks with idiocy and rapture, with love . . .'

52 See Friedrich Nietzsche, *Also sprach Zarathustra* in *Kritische Studienausgabe*, 2nd EDN (KSA) (Giorgio Colli and Mazzino Montinari eds) (Munich: Deutscher Taschenbuch Verlag, 1988), VOL. 4, p. 312: 'Where my honesty ends, I am blind and also want to be blind. But where I want to know, I also want to be honest, namely hard, strict, narrow, cruel, implacable.' See also Nietzsche, *Der Antichrist*, §32, p. 204.

> Culture is not even known to him by hearsay, he has no need to fight against it—he does not deny it . . . The same applies to the state, to the whole bourgeois order and society, to work, to war—he has never had any reason to deny 'the world', he has never suspected the ecclesiastical concept of 'the world' . . . Denial is precisely what is quite impossible for him.[53]

It is this distance of the idiot, alienated from reasoning and argumentation, from the dialectic of social reason, his uninvolved astonishment and ability to remain untouched, watching social processes in amazement and without the possibility of understanding, that Jesus shares with him. This results in both of them being strangers to the law, in the face of which the only alternative is love.

At this point, we should once again remember Marcion, the heretic and compiler of an early biblical canon, who contrasts the evil God of the law with the strange God of love. It is the God of love who enables man to forgive the God of creation, the flawed demiurge, for the failure of his creation. At the same time, the grace that God bestows on man is that of undeserved love and the grace of redemption, the enjoyment of which is not made possible by good deeds or by abiding by the law. When Nietzsche writes that every relationship of distance between God and man has been abolished, he means to say that the categories of guilt and sin have been overcome. Man already lives in the time of grace. Man is already redeemed by the undeserved love of God, which cannot be earned, and by the death of the Son of God, whose practice of death is identical with his practice of life. Any need for dialectics and mediation has become superfluous.

Of course, Nietzsche is not a proponent of a philosophy of love. However, the argumentative figure of love contains a moment of abrogation that has already been encountered elsewhere: the moment of the abrogation of time. Marcion declares the debate about the necessity and timing of the redemption of the world to be superfluous, since the world has already been redeemed: with the God of the New Testament, the law has not been fulfilled, as Paul believes, but has been suspended and replaced by the love

53 Nietzsche, *Der Antichrist*, §32, p. 204.

of the foreign God. In a similar way, Nietzsche erases time in his conception of the Redeemer: redemption has already happened, all mediation has imploded, all dialectics have ceased, all processes have come to a standstill. The church as an institution is a betrayal of the fact that redemption has already taken place. The abolition of time as a consequence of the practice of love is the way out of the false dialectic of repetitive inversions. Through the implosion of all mediation, law and knowledge evaporate. World knowledge becomes worthless.

Nietzsche signs the letter to Overbeck, in which he reports on his discovery of Dostoyevsky, 'Faithfully your old friend N, homo illiteratus'.

CHAPTER SEVEN

# The Idiot Revolting

While Nietzsche sinks into the dark depths of his illness and his sister works on the great forgery of his philosophy, the Nietzsche cult establishes itself within a very short period of time. It takes hold of artists in particular—writers and musicians as well as visual artists—in France and Germany. From 1900 onwards, Nietzsche became a fashionable phenomenon or, as Gottfried Benn wrote, 'the greatest phenomenon of charisma in the history of ideas'.[1] The wave of enthusiasm is so strong that it provokes countercurrents within a very short time. As early as 1893, the philosopher Ludwig Stein turned against the Nietzsche cult, followed by Ferdinand Tönnies, who even devoted an entire book to the subject in 1897, entitled *Der Nietzsche-Kultus*.[2] As W. Paulsen writes, the reception of *Zarathustra* in particular took place in the form of an 'osmosis',[3] gradually encompassing other areas and currents, including non-artistic ones, 'from theology to free thought, from capitalism to socialism, from conservatism to Bolshevism, from internationalism to nationalism, from atheism to anthroposophy, [which] are made lively with streams from Nietzsche and witty with quotations from him.'[4] In 1905, four young artists in Dresden were inspired by a Nietzsche quote when they were looking for a name for the artists' group they intended to found.[5] They called the group Die Brücke,

1 Quoted from Andreas Urs Sommer, *Nietzsche und die Folgen* (Stuttgart: Metzler, 2017), p. 94.

2 Sommer, *Nietzsche und die Folgen*, p. 115.

3 Quoted from Silvio Vietta and Hans-Georg Kemper, *Expressionismus* (Munich: Fink, 1983), p. 135.

4 Thus the theologian and cultural philosopher Ernst Troeltsch in 1922, quoted from Sommer, *Nietzsche und die Folgen*, p. 95.

5 Nietzsche, *Also sprach Zarathustra*, §4, pp. 16–17: 'What is great about man is that he is a bridge and not an end: what can be loved about man is that he is a transition and a demise I love those who do not know how to live, except as those who perish, for they are those who pass over.'

and their manifesto brims over with the Nietzschean creative spirit: 'Anyone who can truly express what urged him to create belongs among us'.[6] It is no different with the almanac of Der Blaue Reiter, which was published in 1912. Here, too, there is talk of the inner necessity with which the soul urges expression, and all questions of form are pushed aside with the remark that inner necessity alone lends a given work of art the decisive quality of authenticity. Accordingly, and in a way that was groundbreaking for its time, its own works and those of colleagues were reproduced alongside examples of folk glass painting, African masks, Japanese paintings, and children's drawings in order to substantiate the claim that the question of style was secondary to the question of the urgency of unrestricted expression. 'Inner necessity' as the decisive buzzword owes its legitimacy to Nietzsche's creative heroism[7] and the imperative force of inspiration he reclaimed: 'One hears, one does not seek; one takes, one does not ask who gives; like a flash of lightning, a thought lights up, with necessity, in form without hesitation'.[8]

The attribution of authenticity to the creations of children and to works of non-European art is the result of a misunderstanding. What does not correspond to one's own convention appears as unencumbered by conformist compulsion, whereas it is merely subject to an unknown drive. It is as far removed from subjective immediacy and expressive truthfulness as the academic school exercises that Kandinsky and his comrades-in-arms are revolting against. The child or the sculptors from Cameroon, New Caledonia, Mexico, or the North American West Coast owe their reputation for following solely their subjective and expressive will to a logic of projection that appropriates the foreign and the alien. As the work's inherent nature and otherness remain inaccessible, the European artists

---

6 Quoted from Magdalena M. Moeller (ed.), *40 Jahre Brücke-Museum Berlin: Dokumente der Künstlergruppe Brücke* (Munich: Hirmer, 2007), p. 40.

7 Nietzsche, *Nachgelassene Fragmente 1887*–1889, p. 247: 'This style has this in common with the great passion, that it disdains to please; that it forgets to persuade; that it commands; that it wills . . . To become master of the chaos that one is; to force one's chaos to become form; necessity in form: to become logical, simply unambiguous, mathematics; to become law—that is the great ambition here.'

8 Nietzsche, *Ecce Homo*, p. 339.

charge it with their own content, making it available to their own theoretical and artistic intentions. Carried by the spirit of Nietzschean 'Artistenmetaphysik' (*artist's metaphysics*—the pretence that artists have privileged access to higher knowledge), the merely foreign is misunderstood as the authentic, which supposedly represents the creative impulse in an uncorrupted form.

## The Art of Forgetting

The turn against the academic requires the need to unlearn. Where authenticity is not achieved because of a lack of immediacy—unfortunately, one does have a choice—one looks for the roots of the creative under the academic rubble that has piled up over the centuries and which one is now beginning to clear away. The idea that it is easier to work where there is less to unlearn can already be found in Joshua Reynolds (1723–92). In his third academy speech of 14 December 1770, he writes:

> And, indeed, I cannot but suppose that the ancients saw an easier task before them than the moderns. They had probably little or nothing to unlearn, as their manners were nearly approaching to this desirable simplicity; whereas the modern artist, before he can see the truth of things, is obliged to remove a veil, with which the fashion of the times has thought proper to cover her.[9]

The praise of *simplicitas* that Reynolds intones here can often be found in the *Discourses on Art*, and he defends himself against possible attacks from academic colleagues by pointing out that he prefers genius in less respected colleagues to the tastelessness of the more highly rated ones. To him, Gainsborough is the protagonist of praiseworthy simplicity, and he compares him to 'those men who, [ . . . ] without knowing the right expressions, succeed in conveying the lively and strong impression of an energetic mind'.[10] Imitation of the ancients is recommended precisely because they, the ancients, had worked closer to the 'origins', which is why following

9 Joshua Reynolds, *Discourses on Art* (Edward Gilpin Johnson ed.) (Chicago: A. C. McClurg, 1891), p. 130.

10 Reynolds, *Discourses on Art*, pp. 412, 426.

them meant having to remove fewer of the veils and layers that various epochs had spread over them.

That the paradigm of the primordial, which has been replaced in the course of civilization and, where it still persists, is corrupted and weakened, motivates the exoticism and primitivism of European artists, is as well known as the fact that this search for the original takes place in the context of colonialism and imperialism. The phantasm of the 'natural state' led artists such as Gauguin, Nolde, and Pechstein to search for the forgotten source of human expressiveness in the South Seas, while Picasso and Braque found the decisive inspiration for the formal innovations of cubism in the collections of the Trocadéro. German expressionism also greatly draws inspiration from non-European arts. The supposedly 'primitive', which the expressionists, under the influence of Nietzsche, equated with untamed real life, also drew their attention to the 'indigenous' in their own culture. The recourse to the woodcut, which is considered typically German, stands for this, as does the interest in Bavarian votive images. Enthusiasm for nature, painting outdoors, and nudity as a way of life and as a pictorial motif are evidence of anti-cultural turns towards the natural. Paul Klee wrote the summa of the doctrine of necessary unlearning in 1912:

> There are still primordial beginnings of art, the kind you tend to find in ethnographic collections or at home in your children's room. Don't laugh, reader. Children can do it too, and there is wisdom in the fact that they can do it too! The more helpless they are, the more instructive examples they offer us, and we must also protect them from corruption at an early age. Parallel phenomena are the work of the mentally ill, so neither childish behaviour nor madness is a dirty word here that could be used to describe what is meant. All this is to be taken seriously, more seriously than all the art galleries when it comes to reform today. If, as I believe, all of yesterday's tradition is really petering out, [ . . . ] then a great moment has come and I welcome those who are working on the coming reformation.[11]

---

11 Paul Klee, diary entry from 1912, later edited. Quoted from Manfred Clemenz, *Der Mythos Paul Klee* (Cologne, Weimar and Vienna: Böhlau, 2016), p. 70.

Klee names the three practices from which the art of forgetting could be learned: the practice of the 'primitive', the 'mentally ill', and the child. Their respective discovery took place in phases, but culminated in the first decade of the twentieth century in the great wave of anti-cultural revolt decisively initiated by Nietzsche. Traces of this exercise in the art of forgetting can still be found in Willi Baumeister's reflections in *The Unknown in Art*, when he writes: 'The original artist abandons the known and the skilful. He pushes forward to point zero. This is where his state of enthusiasm begins. Original production is not based on comparable skill; in this sense, the original artist in the state of enthusiasm has no skill'.[12]

The revaluation of non-European art and the art of children took place under the flag of Rousseau and his critique of civilization, preceded by phases of curiosity and the 'discoveries' of the art of China and Japan, for example. These 'discoveries' are, as already mentioned, linked to imperialist-colonialist conquests, in the context of which, on the one hand, European thinking of superiority develops and consolidates, and, on the other hand, this thinking begins to question itself, as it becomes aware of its own relativity in a world it wants to conquer. Yet for all its efforts, thinking that is fascinated by its Other remains a dialectical form of thinking. It remains true to itself by separating itself from itself, and it unfolds its full assimilative and repressive power by distancing itself from itself and thereby seeming to be able to integrate what is foreign to it. Some misunderstand the tropical as the originally paradisiacal;[13] others are

12 Willi Baumeister, *Das Unbekannte in der Kunst* (Stuttgart: Curt E. Schwab, 1947), p. 155.

13 Hence Nolde's and Gauguin's horror at the real conditions in the places of longing, whose criticism of the colonial power was resolute, but also motivated by the fact that the colonial masters had spoiled their dream of paradise. See Nana Badenberg, 'Südsee-Insulaner als Kunsttrophäen: Mai 1914: Nolde in Neuguinea, Pechstein in Palau' in Alexander Honold and Klaus R. Scherpe (eds), *Mit Deutschland um die Welt: Eine Kulturgeschichte des Fremden in der Kolonialzeit* (Stuttgart: Metzler, 2004), pp. 438–48. See also Emil Nolde, *Mein Leben* (Cologne: DuMont, 1996 [1976]), pp. 260–90, where he reports on his experiences in New Guinea. Pechstein, in turn, stylized himself in his memoirs as a genuine 'savage' who had shed the ill-fitting garb of civilization without difficulty. Interestingly, Pechstein borrows such a passage from Osborn's 1922 monograph (Max Osborn, *Max Pechstein* [Berlin: Propyläen, 1922], p. 120) to describe

concerned only with the decontextualized formal, whose qualities provide them with inspiration for their own work and whose meaning they do not care about. This conflict between art and context continues into today's discussions about the extent to which the separation between art and artefact, art gallery and ethnographic museum, can be justified. The futility of the discourse, which has developed very little since then, is expressed in the conflict surrounding the exhibition *Primitivism in 20th Century Art*, which can still be considered paradigmatic today. While the curator William S. Rubin believes in a mental affinity between modern and tribal art,[14] his opponent, Thomas McEvilley, accuses him of decontextualization with the accusation that there is no blood left on the fetishes—a remarkable hallucination about non-Western realities in which the blood apparently always flows in streams.[15] Despite the fact that debates about decolonization have become widespread and the lines of argument have diversified, it has not yet been decided whether the visions of a global culture, which would find an appropriate home in a 'Museum Global',[16] are more than new versions of the universal museums supported by Western zeal for collecting and integration. What if the idea of the universality of values is itself only a particularity of the West? What if the label of modernity, which the West is increasingly willing to attach to non-Western art practices with a sincere desire for integration or with a patronizing gesture, is merely the revenant of the colonialist-imperialist paradigm of civilization? With the help of this paradigm, in all its modifications, not only Europe but every colonialist high culture from Japan to Russia subjected the colonized peoples to its violence.

---

himself. See Bernhard Fulda and Aya Soika, *Max Pechstein: The Rise and Fall of Expressionism* (Berlin and Boston: De Gruyter, 2012), p. 150. In general, his notes on his stay in Palau are characterized by blatant distortions of the actual circumstances, of which he was well aware.

14 William S. Rubin, '*Primitivism*' *in 20th Century Art: Affinity of the Tribal and the Modern* (New York: Museum of Modern Art, 1984), VOL. 1, pp. 24, 73 and *passim*.

15 See the exchange of letters between Rubin and McEvilley in *Artforum* (New York), November 1984 and May 1985.

16 See Kathrin Beßen, Susanne Gaensheimer, Doris Krystof et al. (eds), *museum global: Mikrogeschichten einer ex-zentrischen Moderne* (Cologne: Wienand, 2018).

## Illness as a Motive and Projective Stimulus[17]

The discovery of the art of the mentally ill is a different matter. It takes place parallel to the medical discourse on the idiot, the lunatic, and the imbecile, but these two strands only occasionally intersect. Initially, the mentally ill, the melancholic, the stupid, and the insane were merely the subject of artistic interest as pictorial motifs in the works of Hogarth, Goya, and Géricault, right into expressionism. William Hogarth (1697–1764), in *A Rake's Progress*, a series of eight paintings (Sir John Soane's Museum, London), which gained great popularity as engravings published in 1735, is in the tradition of the moral condemnation of mental illness as a consequence of a dissolute lifestyle and lack of discipline. Tom Rakewell ends up in Bethlem Hospital, surrounded by masturbating lunatics who think they are kings, religious maniacs, lovesick people, among whom is a mad scientist working in vain to solve the longitude problem. The figure of the madman who is absorbed in contemplating his own wall scribblings appears here, although not for the first time.[18] Such graffiti can also be found in Wilhelm von Kaulbach's (1805–74) engraving *Das Narrenhaus* from 1835. On the wall next to the warden smoking his pipe are depictions that are probably to be understood as drawings by the inmates. In the style of children's drawings, they depict an aspect of everyday life in the madhouse that the engraving itself does not show: the beating of an inmate in the asylum, who stretches his arms upwards in horror and is abused by the warden—a reproduction of the fat, grumpy warden standing in front of the wall, with the whip hanging out of his pocket. Kaulbach seems to have calculated the image of the house of fools as a cleverly staged shock to further his career.[19] Allegedly based on the memory of a visit to an asylum in Düsseldorf, the composition claims an authenticity that it contradicts stylistically as a

17 See Werner Janzarik, 'Der bildnerische Ausdruck seelischen Krankseins als projektiver Stimulus' in Hans Gercke and Inge Jarchov (eds), *Die Prinzhornsammlung* (Königstein/Taunus: Athenäum, 1980), pp. 5–9; here, p. 5.

18 See Bernard Lens II and John Sturt, illustration to Jonathan Swift, *A Tale of a Tub* (1710) in John M. MacGregor, *The Discovery of the Art of the Insane* (Princeton, NJ: Princeton University Press, 1989), p. 17.

19 Werner Busch, *Die notwendige Arabeske: Wirklichkeitsaneignung und Stilisierung in der Kunst des 19. Jahrhunderts* (Berlin: Mann, 1985), p. 133ff.

composite of various pictorial quotations. It aims to arouse feelings of voyeuristic horror, which contemporary art theory associates with the category of the sublime. The same applies to Goya's depictions of madhouses, *Corral de locos* (*Yard with Lunatics*, 1794) and *Casa de locos* (*Madhouse*, between 1812 and 1819). Goya says of the scene from 1794, at the centre of which two wrestling madmen are being beaten by a guard, that he based it on scenes he had witnessed at the asylum in Zaragoza.[20] Both paintings are relatively small; *Yard with Lunatics* is painted on tinplate, a medium that painters reserved for cabinet pieces, as it allowed them to demonstrate their mastery of the brush. In fact, *Yard with Lunatics* was intended for the art market and was not a commissioned work, and Goya was keen to sell the work as quickly as possible to cover the costs of treating his own illness.[21] The claim to authenticity and the simultaneous calculation of success in the emerging art market, which was still predominantly aristocratic in Goya's case and already bourgeois in Kaulbach's, reveals the strategic calculation to which the autonomous artist had to submit. The evocation of 'mixed feelings',[22] as illustrated by Lucretius in the shipwreck with spectators made famous by Hans Blumenberg,[23] is brought about by the depiction of an object that arouses disgust, the titillation of which the art critic can appreciate from a safe distance. The attraction lies in the representation

20 Peter K. Klein, 'Insanity and the Sublime: Aesthetics and Theories of Mental Illness in Goya's *Yard with Lunatics* and Related Works' in *Journal of the Warburg and Courtauld Institutes* 61 (1998): 198–252; here, pp. 200–1.

21 Klein, 'Insanity and the Sublime', p. 222.

22 Bernard Le Bovier de Fontenelle, 'Réflexions sur la poétique' in *Œuvres complètes*, 8 VOLS (Paris, 1790), VOL. 3, pp. 139–40: 'On pleure les malheurs d'un héros à qui l'on s'est affectionné, et dans le même moment l'on s'en console, parce qu'on sait que c'est une fiction; et c'est justement de ce mélange de sentiments que se compose une douleur agréable, et les larmes qui font plaisir', 'One weeps at the misfortune of a hero who is close to one's heart, and at the same time one feels consolation, knowing that it is only a fiction; and it is precisely this mixture of feelings that produces a pleasant pain, and the tears that bring pleasure' (translation by LE.) See Mendelssohn's discussion of the 'mixed sensations': 'Rhapsodie, oder die Zusätze zu den Briefen über die Empfindungen' in Moses Mendelssohn, *Ästhetische Schriften* (Anne Pollok ed.) (Hamburg: Meiner, 2006), pp. 142–87; here, p. 148.

23 Titus Lucretius Carus, *De rerum natura* (Herman Diels ed.) (Berlin: Weidmannsche Buchhandlung, 1923), BOOK 2, p. 57.

of a frightening or repulsive situation, the character of which becomes all the clearer as the viewer can be touched, frightened, or otherwise moved from a distance. The painting, in Goya's case the cabinet piece, intended for intimate contemplation by connoisseurs, acts as a trigger for emotions that can be enjoyed as mediated.

The portraits of the sick made by Théodore Géricault (1791–1824) in the early 1820s, possibly commissioned by the psychiatrist Étienne-Jean Georget, a pupil of Esquirol, take on a different function. Esquirol had already commissioned works from the engraver Ambroise Tardieu in order to create a 'catalogue' of physiognomic states in various mental illnesses. Géricault's five surviving paintings probably stand in the context of similar attempts by Georget to illustrate and diagnose certain illnesses on the basis of physiognomic features.[24] Whether the five paintings that are lost to us depicted, or could have depicted, the states of the people portrayed after successful therapy remains a matter of speculation.[25]

Already in the tradition of dark Romanticism, Eugène Delacroix (1798–1863) painted the imprisoned Tasso in the dungeon in 1839. The poet, who believed himself to be exposed to intrigues at the court of the Duke of Ferrara, was accused of illegitimate affairs and appeared to be prone to violence. He was imprisoned in 1579 as a 'raving lunatic' in the Arcispedale Sant'Anna, from where, after the ban on writing letters was lifted, he eagerly corresponded with colleagues and wrote numerous texts until the Duke of Mantua freed him in 1586.[26]

The difference between Géricault's portraits and Delacroix's work is obvious: Delacroix does not produce a painting that the person who commissioned the paintings could use as a diagnostic tool (or as an aid to

---

24 Margaret Miller, 'Géricault's Paintings of the Insane' in *Journal of the Warburg and Courtauld Institutes* 4 (1941–42): 151–63. The five paintings are now in the Louvre, Paris; the Museum of Fine Arts, Springfield, Massachusetts; the Musée des Beaux-Arts, Lyon; the Museum of Fine Arts, Ghent; and the Oskar Reinhart Collection, Winterthur.

25 See Albert Boime, 'Portraying Monomaniacs to Service the Alienist's Monomania: Géricault and Georget' in *Oxford Art Journal* 14(1) (1991): 79–91. See C. Clément, *Géricault* (Paris: J. Claye, 1879), p. 317.

26 See Margret Stuffmann et al. (eds), *Eugène Delacroix: Spiegelungen: Tasso im Irrenhaus* (Munich: Hirmer, 2008).

further his career). Tasso is primarily seen as the poet who is also mentally ill, and he is interned as being mentally ill because as a poet he is a nuisance to society. In Delacroix's portrait of Tasso, the artist becomes the victim of society, which sanctions and disciplines him as he transgresses not only norms but also the boundaries of normality in his creative power. The reception of the *enthousiasmós* motif, which has defined the image of the artist since Plato and Neo-Platonism, leads to the licensing of transgression of norms and the re-evaluation of the phenomenon of mental abnormality in Romanticism. Under the influence of the cult of genius, which originates in the time of Romanticism, it becomes not only an occasional consequence of outstanding talent, but also a proof of this talent.

However, the depiction of the poet as a madman and the madman as a victim of society is already reduced in the Tasso painting of 1839 in Winterthur compared to the painting of the same motif and the accompanying drawing (private collections) from around 15 years earlier. In the painting from 1824, Tasso sits in the traditional melancholy posture in courtly dress in the right foreground, mocked by other inmates or guards (in the background, a man beats another man), but the poet, who is deep in thought, seems not to notice their presence. While this composition takes up the scheme of the Man of Sorrows, the Christ mocked by his tormentors, a further element reinforces the religious component in the drawing from 1823: here, the events take place under the sign of the cross, a cropped crucifix in the background of the picture. The scene is enriched by the depiction of a young man drawing on the floor and a woman looking through the barred window, possibly Tasso's mistress, Eleonore, the sister of the Duke of Ferrara, who is said to have approached the poet in an ambiguous manner, resulting in his incarceration in the asylum. In the double allusion to Christ through the depiction of the crucifix and through the paraphrase of Christian iconography, the pose of Tasso as the Man of Sorrows, the artist's role as an outsider and exemplary sufferer is reinforced; it is made accessible and legible to Delacroix's contemporaries and emotionally charged through recourse to a traditional visual vocabulary and an iconographic inventory.

The strands that Romanticism had started to draw out and that Nietzsche had loosely linked for the first time in *The Antichrist* were finally connected in expressionist literature and visual art: those of the madman and the idiot, the outsider and Christ as an exemplary sufferer. The 'Ecce homo pathos' of expressionist literature combines the rhetorical phrase 'behold the man' with the establishment of the madman, the insane, and the pervert as the victim and counter-figure of a pathogenic social normality as criticism of the Wilhelmine, imperialist authoritarian state.[27]

> Beggars, the poor, the destitute, the sub-proletariat and proletariat of the city, but also the sick, the dying, the ostracized, idiots, outsiders of all kinds are encountered in expressionist poems, sometimes religiously heightened in the vision of a new brotherhood encompassing all people, a 'new Sermon on the Mount', according to Paul Zech.[28]

The church, which conforms to the monarchy, is denied its claim to represent the heritage of the Redeemer. Like the scourged Christ and the mocked, imprisoned, and tortured lunatic, the bruised and battered man becomes the epitome of the revolt against the steel-and-capital machine of the state on the eve of the First World War, a bloodbath in the muddy trenches that proved to be the realization of Ludwig Meidner's (1884–1966) apocalyptic visions, which, in retrospect, look like realistic predictions and not like hellish scenarios of a soul tormented by fear. Against the backdrop of the war and its atrocities, the perversions of the lust murderers and sexual deviants who appear in the arts from 1910 onwards are anticipatory manifestations of individual madness as the reflection of the madness that, a little later, begins to take shape and become reality in society as a whole.[29]

27 Thomas Anz, *Literatur des Expressionismus* (Stuttgart and Weimar: Metzler, 2010), p. 166.

28 Silvio Vietta, *Die literarische Moderne: Eine problemgeschichtliche Darstellung der deutschsprachigen Literatur von Hölderlin bis Thomas Bernhard* (Stuttgart: Metzler, 1992), p. 302.

29 Leo Putz, *Ein Mord*, Folge IV, 1918–21, charcoal, Siegfried Unterberger Collection; Otto Dix, *Lustmörder*, 1920, etching on laid paper, private collection; Heinrich Maria Davringhausen, *Der Träumer II*, 1919, oil on canvas, Hessisches Landesmuseum Darmstadt; Heinrich Maria Davringhausen, *Der Lustmörder*, 1917, oil on canvas,

'As a sick person, he [the madman] is the product and manifestation of a sick society. The grimace of madness, distorted into the inhuman, becomes an expression of suffering from an environment that is contrary to humanity'.[30]

However, it is not the idiot but the madman to whom expressive literature and art are primarily dedicated, and there are reasons for this, which will be discussed under the heading of the 'schizophrenic sense of the world'. Certainly, the large blue eyes of *Dreamer II* by Heinrich Maria Davringhausen (1894–1970) look at the viewer with the strangeness of a person who has become incomprehensible to the world and to himself in his idiotic self-isolation, but it is the ecstatically contorted and extreme figures of Egon Schiele that lend a fitting expression to the feeling of the times.[31] The link made by Nietzsche between the idiot and Jesus is shifted to a blending of Jesus and the insane, thus eliminating the question of decadence, which is dealt with in psychiatric literature (Kraepelin) but relegated to the background by the artists. What concept of decadence or decency should still make sense at a time when the representatives of a perverted morality present themselves as 'pillars of society'?[32]

Arguments are pointless in protesting against a rotten society; the only thing that helps is the scream made iconic by Edvard Munch's pictorial invention:[33]

---

Pinakothek der Moderne, Munich. George Grosz, *Lustmord in der Ackerstraße*, folio 40 of the series *Ecce Homo*, 1916, printed 1922–23, Museum of Modern Art, New York.

30 Anz, *Literatur des Expressionismus*, p. 85.

31 Egon Schiele (1890–1918) created a large number of self-portraits between 1910 and 1918, the year of his death, in which the theatrical postures and gestures are not without reason read as paraphrases of Christ. See *Self-Portrait* (1911), Metropolitan Museum, New York.

32 George Grosz, *Stützen der Gesellschaft*, 1926, oil on canvas, Neue Nationalgalerie, Berlin.

33 There are four painted versions of Edvard Munch's (1863–1944) *The Scream* (1893, 1895 [2], 1910), three versions of a lithograph and a pen-and-ink drawing. See J. Gill Holland (ed. and trans.), *Edvard Munch: We Are Flames Which Pour Out of the Earth: The Private Journals of Edvard Munch* (Madison: University of Wisconsin Press, 2005), pp. 64–65. See Sue Prideaux, *Edvard Munch: Behind the Scream* (New Haven and London: Yale University Press, 2005), p. 166ff. Werner Timm, *Edvard Munch: Graphik* (Berlin: Henschelverlag, 1974), pp. 70–71.

> What is to be done? Only one thing! We can only scream—scream with all the strength of our poor, stifled human voice, scream that we drown out the horrible noise of what is happening, cry out that we may be heard by men, by God.[34]

In the hammering of parataxis, in the nominal style and in the renunciation of adverbs and adjectives, the writers think they have found the stylistic equivalent to their most urgent concern, the realization of a new human being and the breakthrough to a new era, the realization of the utopia, a new age, a 'humanity for the future'.[35]

Nietzsche also became a point of orientation for the expressionists because his descent into madness, combined with the pathos of his loneliness,[36] contrasted him with the hated bourgeoisie. Wieland Herzfelde's famous *The Ethics of the Mentally Ill*, which appeared in *Die Aktion* in 1914, stylizes Nietzsche alongside Hölderlin as the 'emotionally, ethically' enraptured. The entire text testifies to an effort to invert bourgeois values, to relabel the lunatic as the truly free man, whereas the citizen is trapped in a dungeon of convention and logic. Mental illness becomes a 'cosmic delusion', for which Herzfelde uses the metaphor of the mountaintop, 'which pierces our grey dome of the sky'.[37] The anti-citizen Nietzsche, to whom Munch, revered by the expressionists as a father figure, dedicated a posthumous portrait in 1906,[38] becomes, like the madman, the guarantor

34 Margarete Susman, 'Expressionism' (1918) in *Die Masken: Blätter des Düsseldorfer Schauspielhauses* 14 (1918/19): 93–96. Quoted from Thomas Anz and Michael Stark (eds), *Expressionismus: Manifeste und Dokumente zur deutschen Literatur 1910–1920* (Stuttgart: Metzler, 1982), p. 574.

35 Kurt Pinthus, *Menschheitsdämmerung: Symphonie jüngster Dichtung* (Berlin: Rowohlt, 1919), p. *xvi*.

36 See Friedrich Nietzsche, 'Der Freigeist' (1884) in *Nachgelassene Fragmente 1884–1885, Kritische Studienausgabe*, 2nd EDN (KSA) (Giorgio Colli and Mazzino Montinari eds) (Munich: Deutscher Taschenbuch Verlag, 1988), VOL. 11, p. 329.

37 Quoted from Anz and Stark, *Expressionismus*, pp. 183–86; here, p. 186.

38 There are two versions, one in the Thielska Galleriet, Stockholm, and one in the Munch Museum, Oslo. Here, too, it is Nietzsche's loneliness that plays a central role in Munch's choice of how to depict the philosopher. Thus, the passage from *Zarathustra*, 'Light am I, oh, that I were night! But this is my loneliness, that I am girded with light', is one of Munch's reference points. See Detlef Brennecke, *Die Nietzsche-Bildnisse Edvard Munchs* (Berlin: Spitz, 2000), p. 65.

of the possibility of an expression that does not allow itself to be restricted by any conventions:

> It is precisely one of the strengths of expressionism that its works aim to be the direct expression of emotional depths, that they remain free of visible mental preparation and reworking, that technical skill is never an end in itself, but always only an indispensable means of enhancing the emotional expression as much as possible and making it vivid.[39]

Yet for all their longing for originality and proximity to nature, for all their evocation of the suffering of alienation, urban loneliness, and melancholy, the expressionists did not succeed in bringing the dialectic between society and social criticism to a standstill. In the contrasting figures of the lonely drunkard, the hollow-eyed prostitute, the delirious madman or in the images of loving couples in the high reeds, the naked bathers and the landscape enchanted by its own soul forces, the deformation of the social lives on as a repetition of the divisiveness taken to an extreme. Or it is invoked as surmountable through its counter-image—in the vision of healing and a harmony between nature and the individual, community, and humanity. Insofar as expressionist art, whether literature, painting, or film, justifies itself as criticism and a vision of utopia, it remains mimetically attached to the existing, in the most banal form: as an opaque reflection of itself. But this is precisely what allows it to be normalized in turn and to be integrated into the social dynamic. In this dynamic, the madman, by means of a distorted rationality, assumes the function of reminding reason of its task: the creation of a humane world. For all its criticism of the social, expressionism believes in society's capacity for improvement, whose aberrations merely need to be corrected. The human being shown in the figure of Christ in the pictorial tradition of *Ecce Homo*,[40] presented to the

---

39 Ernst Jolowicz, 'Expressionismus und Psychiatrie' in *Das Kunstblatt* 4 (1920), pp. 273–76, quoted from Anz and Stark, *Expressionismus*, p. 192.

40 One exception is the series of prints titled *Ecce Homo* by George Grosz, created from 1915 onwards but not published by Malik until 1922/23, which depicts his disgust at social conditions in a reversal of the *O Mensch* pathos. See Carl Einstein, 'George Grosz' in *Bebuquin und die Dilettanten des Wunders* (Leipzig and Weimar: Reclam,

plebs seething with rage and demanding his death, functions as a memento of an original, naked, God-given humanity. Man's divinity is revealed in this nakedness.

It is this dialectical intertwining of expressionist cultural criticism with Wilhelminian society that attracts the scorn and derision of the Dadaists from 1916 onwards. Carl Einstein (1885–1940) took up arms against the exoticism of the expressionists ('Palauized plaster nude') and accused its representatives of having degenerated into a 'Palau academy of antiquated expressionism'.[41]

In a similar vein, Richard Huelsenbeck (1892–1974) argued that the expressionists had 'united under the pretext of inwardness [ . . . ] to form a generation that is already eagerly awaiting its literary and art-historical appreciation and is calling for a recognition as honourable citizens'.[42] In contrast to expressionism, which in Germany had merely become an 'idyll and the expectation of a good pension',[43] Dada was not an art movement, but merely used art to express its time—nothing more:

> Dada wants nothing. [ . . . ] Dada exposes itself to the danger of its own death. Dada places itself in things. [ . . . ] For the first time, Dadaism no longer confronts life aesthetically by shredding all the buzzwords of ethics, culture, and inwardness [ . . . ] into their constituent parts.

---

1989), p. 215: 'The painter of the now no longer places Christ in vainly powerful opposition to the rabble, but rather the suffering poor.'

41 Carl Einstein, 'Rudolf Schlichter' (1920) in Einstein, *Bebuquin und die Dilettanten des Wunders*, pp. 175, 178. See also Uwe Fleckner, *Carl Einstein und sein Jahrhundert* (Berlin: De Gruyter, 2006), p. 200: 'Exoticism intoxicated the Saxon primitives due to a lack of visual imagination.' Carl Einstein published issues 3 to 6 of the satirical magazine *Der blutige Ernst* with John Höxter and George Grosz and tried to make contact with Tristan Tzara. See letters dated 16 December 1919, 3 January 1920 and 30 July 1924 in Klaus H. Kiefer and Liliane Meffre (eds), *Carl Einstein, Briefwechsel 1904–1940* (Berlin: Metzler, 2020), pp. 106, 121, 373.

42 Quoted from Richard Huelsenbeck, 'Was wollte der Expressionismus?' in Richard Huelsenbeck (ed.), *Dada Almanach* (Berlin: Erich Reiss, 1920), p. 37.

43 Huelsenbeck, 'Was wollte der Expressionismus?', p. 38.

In the production of paradoxes and absurdities, the dialectic of world improvement that keeps the corrupted artistic enterprise running is to be brought to implosion: 'To be against this manifesto is to be Dadaist'. It is about a practice that can also be an aesthetic practice (but one can also just happen to be a businessman),[44] but ultimately a practice of any kind should be parallel to life, or rather life itself: 'Freedom: *Dada*, *Dada*, *Dada*, howling of the cramped colours, intertwining of the opposites and all contradictions, the grotesques and the inconsistencies: *Life*'.[45]

In the middle of the war, at the Cabaret Voltaire in Zurich, Dada begins its activities in February 1916. Huelsenbeck lists the programme items in the *Almanac*: 'Musique bruitiste, poème simultané, musique et danse nègre, dessins enfants, sculptures nègres'. This is followed by poems in te reo Māori ('Toto Vaca')[46] and sound poems as well as so-called Negro songs, which Tristan Tzara claims to have found and translated.[47] By means of an extensive Nietzsche quotation from *Beyond Good and Evil*, Huelsenbeck invokes the figure of God's buffoon, which is later followed by references to Pantagruel and St Francis: 'that's how he lies, that's how he hunts, that's how he cycles—half Pantagruel, half Francis, and laughs and laughs and laughs!'[48]

Not only does the Dadaist adapt the persona of the fool of God, he also follows the politics of non-distinction that Nietzsche ascribed to his Christ figure and that St Francis had claimed for himself when he wrote that he and his followers were uneducated and equally subject to all. It

---

44 Huelsenbeck, 'Was wollte der Expressionismus?', pp. 40–41.

45 Tristan Tzara, 'Manifeste Dada 1918' in Karl Riha (ed.), *Dada Zürich: Texte, Manifeste, Dokumente* (Stuttgart: Reclam, 2015 [1992]), p. 46. Emphasis in the original (in bold).

46 Tristan Tzara, 'Toto-Vaca' in Huelsenbeck (ed.), *Dada Almanach*, pp. 51–52. Tristan Tzara takes the poem from a volume by Karl Bücher, *Arbeit und Rhythmus* (Leipzig and Berlin: Teubner, 1909). See Christian Kaufmann, 'Dada liest ethnologische Quellen: Vom Wissen um fremde Kunstwelten zum poetischen Verstehen' in Ralf Burmeister, Michaela Oberhofer and Esther Tisa Francini (eds), *dada Afrika* (Zurich: Scheidegger & Spiess, 2016), pp. 96–103.

47 Tristan Tzara, 'Negerlieder' in Huelsenbeck (ed.), *Dada Almanach*, pp. 141–42.

48 Huelsenbeck, 'Was wollte der Expressionismus?', p. 40.

matters, however, whether one at all ascribes the strategy of non-distinction to Christ in order to be able to distil the practice of all-encompassing love from it, or, secondly, proclaims all-encompassing submission to everything in order to emphasize one's own *simplicitas*, or, thirdly, adopts a position of acceptance of everything, including the contradictory, in order to work towards the implosion of society and its values. But all three strategies lead to the attempt to be able to think of something other than what exists and what could be its dialectical opposite. What connects the idiot Christ with St Francis, the Dada idiot, and the jurodivyj is that they are lost to the world—they want to overcome its laws and declare them null and void or see themselves as having escaped them. As Daimonides explains,[49] after proclaiming his 'world-désinteressement', 'the Dadaist has finished with this life and this world. He has accorded to fifty percent. He walks through this world as a *distinguished foreigner*, on his head the camelhair sports cap, in his hand binoculars and his PHANTASTIC PRAYERBOOK'.[50] The strategy of non-distinction and indifference finds its justification in the conviction, derived from Nietzsche's perspectivism, of the arbitrariness and fictitiousness of all efforts to gain knowledge:

> He [the Dadaist] knows very well how to appreciate the intellectual advantages of all coherent systematics in a joking way, but he knows and experiences intimately their merely working-hypothetical fictitiousness, so to speak. [That is why it is the] analytical function of Dadaism, to radically clean up the basic ideas of a world that have long since solidified into a horrifyingly delusional system, to reduce them to zero [ . . . ] to let it flow into that *mare tenebrarum* of incalculable senselessness, which can only be depicted in vivid metaphorical terms through the most abstruse absurdities and ultimate insanity.[51]

---

49 His real name was Karl Gustav Heinrich Döhmann (1892–1982), who also used the name Edgar Firn. See https://dada.lib.uiowa.edu/edgar-firn. See also George Grosz, *Ein kleines Ja und ein großes Nein* (Hamburg: Rowohlt, 1955), p. 133.

50 Von Daimonides, 'Zur Theorie des Dadaismus' in Huelsenbeck (ed.), *Dada Almanach*, pp. 60, 61; emphasis in original.

51 Daimonides, 'Zur Theorie des Dadaismus', pp. 57, 59.

The fact that the 'relative result' of all philosophical efforts to gain knowledge is no more 'essential' than the 'choice between cake and cherries after dinner' justifies the rejection of any form of knowledge:

> When I scream ideal, ideal, ideal
> Knowledge, knowledge, knowledge,
> Boom-boom, boom-boom, boom-boom
> I have pretty much enumerated progress, the law, morality, and all the other nice things that various very intelligent people have discussed in thick books, to finally explain that despite everything, everyone has danced to their own personal boomboom.[52]

It is revealing that, in contrast to the expressionists, alongside the figure of the schizophrenic, madman, and lunatic, the Dadaists once again made the figure of the idiot the subject of their art. Richard Huelsenbeck dedicated a poem to him in 1916, which tells the story of his murder in seven quatrains.[53] Irritated by his surroundings and provoked by a priest, the idiot, the 'excrement of the races', is caught by henchmen and beaten to death after rioting in the church. From the very beginning, Huelsenbeck gives him the attributes of the animal: his 'gills are lowered', his surroundings tease him like a bull, he has monkey arms. The corpse, at which the children throw stones, is surrounded by hummingbirds, dung beetles make themselves at home in it, and in the end excrement returns to excrement: 'A servant shits on it'. Besides the sphere of waste and the physical, the psyche plays a comparatively minor role: the idiot stares 'stupidly at immense masses of worlds', he roars with laughter and yet is gnawed by melancholy and 'the deepest grief'. Huelsenbeck paints a portrait of the idiot as an animalistic, infantile victim of a brutalized society. Even in death, he is the lowest of the low, on whom—himself social excrement—the servant relieves himself.

Dada Zurich differs from Dada Berlin and Dada Paris, Dada Cologne and Dada Hanover. In Berlin, its provocative machinery began to make noise in the midst of the November riots and, unlike Dada Zurich, the

---

52 Tristan Tzara, 'Manifest Dada 1918' in Huelsenbeck (ed.), *Dada Almanach*, p. 124.

53 Richard Huelsenbeck, *Der Idiot* (1916), repr. in Riha, *Dada Zürich*, pp. 74–75.

participants pursued clear political goals aimed at a radical reorganization of society.[54] Huelsenbeck occupied (until the 1950s) the position of the Dada pope, dogmatically judgemental and, if necessary, exerting the power to excommunicate. This position was soon to be occupied by Breton among the surrealists. He lashed out against former companions and 'heretics' with vicious vanity and irreconcilable harshness. In the *Dada Almanach* of 1920, his malice targeted, among others, the former Uber-Dada Johannes Baader, to whom he wrote a premature and poisonous obituary under the pseudonym Hans Baumann. Baader (1875–1955) was a trained architect and probably came into contact with Raoul Hausmann around 1905 or 1906.[55] From 1918, as Franz Jung writes, Hausmann used him as a 'dummy' for his own purposes.[56]

Baader's fame is based on two spectacular actions: the interruption of court preacher Ernst Dryander's sermon in Berlin Cathedral in November 1918 and the disruption of the meeting of the Weimar National Assembly in November 1919. Hausmann reports that, as soon as Dryander had begun his sermon, Baader interjected with a loud exclamation: 'I ask you, what is Jesus Christ to you? He doesn't matter to you'.[57] Baader was arrested after a general commotion and charged with blasphemy (albeit without conviction). By disrupting the founding assembly of the Weimar Republic

---

54 See Hans Richter, *Dada: Kunst und Anti-Kunst* (Cologne: DuMont, 1964), p. 105ff.

55 On Baader, see Adrian Sudhalter, *Johannes Baader and the Demise of Wilhelmine Culture: Architecture, Dada and Social Critique, 1875–1920* (New York: New York University Press, 2005). See also Matthew Biro, *The Dada Cyborg: Visions of the New Human in Weimar Berlin* (Minneapolis and London: University of Minnesota Press, 2009), pp. 25ff.

56 Franz Jung, *Der Weg nach unten: Aufzeichnungen aus einer großen Zeit* (Berlin: Luchterhand, 1961), p. 112: 'Hausmann took him into his studio and modelled him into the Ober-Dada. I don't know what means and spiritual exercises Hausmann may have used. Hausmann pushed this Baader, an otherwise harmless and friendly man, somewhat imbecile and confusingly similar to the cigar dealer on the next street corner, in front of him as a dummy, as a punching ball. Baader moved and only spoke what Hausmann had drilled into him'. Hausmann confirms Jung's memories. See Karl Riha (ed.), *Johannes Baader, Oberdada: Vierzehn Briefe Christi und andere Druckschriften* (Frankfurt am Main: Peter Lang, 1988), pp. 142–43.

57 Quoted from Riha, *Johannes Baader*, p. 146.

with a speech based on the Book of Revelation and distributing a leaflet entitled *The Green Corpse*, which earned him arrest and interrogation, he became widely known as a fearless provocateur. The break with Hausmann and Huelsenbeck came after Baader disappeared with the entire set of speech manuscripts prior to a planned appearance in Prague on 1 March 1920, exposing his companions to the fury of an audience incited by effective advertising and ready to resort to violence.[58] After 1921, he made several unsuccessful attempts to revive Dada, spent his life from the mid-1920s as a journalist for the *Abendblatt* and as an auditor in Hamburg and, after the Second World War, as a commissioner for the refugee system in Landau an der Isar. He spent the last years of his life in a retirement home in Adeldorf, where he died in 1955.[59]

In his malice towards Baader, Huelsenbeck doesn't restrain himself from the pettiest bourgeois spitefulness. Uncertain about whether Baader's performances are signs of mental illness or merely performances of mental illness, he denounces him nevertheless as a 'cunning madhouse inmate' who first sat in an asylum in 1899.[60] The fact that Baader, as a revenant of the jurodivyj in the twentieth century, no longer allows the distinction to be made between being insane and the performance of being insane, makes Huelsenbeck fail by his own standards; he insists on a clear demarcation between madness and reason. If Dada is supposed to expose bourgeois obtuseness as persiflage, satire, or duplication and force it to implode, then Baader takes the spiral of reflections, duplications, and obscurations of ambiguities and misunderstandings a few turns too far for Huelsenbeck's taste. Insofar as Baader's enthronement (staged by Hausmann) as the head of Dada ironizes the bourgeois obsession with hierarchies and authorities, it also ironizes Huelsenbeck's obsession with the question of who 'invented' Dadaism, who is allowed to claim it for himself, and who should be regarded as its representative. Perhaps Huelsenbeck's play with pieces of bureaucratic vocabulary, with which he declared himself a 'privy councillor'

---

58 Richard Huelsenbeck, *En avant Dada* (Hanover: Paul Steegemann, 1921), pp. 37ff.

59 Riha, *Johannes Baader*, p. 151.

60 Baader was actually interned a total of seven times. See Sudhalter, *Johannes Baader*, p. 119.

and the *Almanach* the newsletter of the 'central office of the German Dada movement', was less Dadaist irony than one might have hoped, and was meant more seriously than one had feared.

Huelsenbeck's verdict also applies to an artist who is nevertheless, in the preface to the *Almanach*, mentioned several times as a participant in Dada actions—Kurt Schwitters: 'Dada rejects works such as the now famous "Anna Blume" by Kurt Schwitters fundamentally and energetically'.[61] It is clear from the context that Schwitters' works correspond too closely to tendencies that Huelsenbeck opposes: he wants to immunize Dada against the suspicion of craziness and sees the danger that the movement could become a victim of the very successful strategies of publicity that it had developed itself: too many people were trying to attract attention to themselves through 'stupid stammering'. Dada, however, could not become a mass-culture phenomenon: 'Dada is a matter for the initiated'. Schwitters (1887–1948), who came from Hanover, was refused an invitation to the Great International Dada Fair in 1920 by the Berlin circle.[62] Huelsenbeck, who had always described Dada as an art movement of the metropolises and the cosmopolitan dandies, considers the Hanoverian artist to be a provincial or, as he writes, 'a genius in a frock coat'.[63] Schwitters reacts angrily and describes Dada as 'marked brain softening plus hustling, one organizes the nonsense, cold with a remarkable business sense, and consciously behaves mindlessly and childish for a considerable entrance fee'.[64] The tone of the two opponents would later become calmer, and Schwitters would come to maintain friendly relations with other protagonists from the Dada milieu; nevertheless, he could not be smoothly assigned to Dada insofar as he always maintained the dual focus of his artistic work. The self-description as 'citizen and idiot', which he leaves in the guest book of the painter and art historian Käte Steinitz,[65] evidences the tension in which

61 Huelsenbeck, 'Einleitung' in *Dada Almanach*, p. 9.

62 Gerhard Schaub (ed.), *Kurt Schwitters 'Bürger und Idiot': Beiträge zu Werk und Wirkung eines Gesamtkünstlers* (Berlin: Fannei & Walz, 1993), p. 27.

63 Richard Huelsenbeck, 'DADA und Existentialismus' in Willy Verkauf (ed.), *Dada: Monographie einer Bewegung* (London: St Martin's Press, 1975), pp. 50–63; here, p. 59.

64 Schwitters, quoted from Schaub, *Kurt Schwitters*, p. 27.

he places his practice. He describes the task as follows: 'Merz's task is to balance opposites and distribute focal points'.[66] Such an intention to seek balance is of course not compatible with the polarization- and scandal-ridden politics of the Zurich and Berlin Dadaists. The fact that Schwitters wanted to emphasize his 'idiotic side'[67] with the *Ursonate* and other 'performances', which he staged repeatedly from 1921 onwards, and intended to evoke atavistic reactions in the audience beyond 'civilizational achievements',[68] nevertheless places him among his fellow artists who attempted something similar with their sound poems, in particular Raoul Hausmann, whose recitation of one of his poems inspired Schwitters to write his *Ursonate*, and Hugo Ball (1886–1927), the initiator of the Cabaret Voltaire. Dressed in a Dada costume with a 'shaman's hat' that gained iconic status, Ball recited sound poems in the style of Catholic mass chants.

It was Ball who, even though he turned away from Dadaism and towards Catholicism from 1917 onwards, found a catchy formula for what Dadaism meant: 'a fool's game out of nothing'.[69] Like Schwitters later, Ball attempted to realize with his sound poems an art form of the pre-civilizational or the beyond-civilizational, of that which is not compromised by any cultural-civilizational usefulness, an art in its purest form: in the use of the sound of the word, the pure phoneme, he believed he could penetrate the 'innermost alchemy of the word'.[70] If one cannot be an artist and believe in history at the same time,[71] the remaining options are either art as the practice of forgetting or as *creatio ex nihilo*. True art comes from nothing.

---

65 Schaub, *Kurt Schwitters*, p. 7.

66 Friedhelm Lach (ed.), *Kurt Schwitters: Das literarische Werk*, VOL. 5, *Manifeste und kritische Prosa* (Cologne: DuMont, 1981), p. 134. 'Merz' is the name Schwitters gave to his artistic practice.

67 Schaub, *Kurt Schwitters*, p. 94.

68 Thomas Grötz, 'Meine Herrschaften, Ihre eingerosteten Ohren klingen: Überlegungen zur *Ursonate* von Kurt Schwitters' in Schaub, *Kurt Schwitters*, pp. 41–51; here, p. 49.

69 Riha, *Dada Zürich*, p. 16.

70 Riha, *Dada Zürich*, p. 22.

71 Riha, *Dada Zürich*, p. 23.

## Art of the Mentally Ill

As described above, the depiction of the mentally ill preceded interest in their artistic creations since the beginning of the twentieth century.[72] In Paris, Auguste Marie, a pupil of Charcot, began to collect works by the mentally ill.[73] In 1907, Marcel Réja published *L'art chez les fous*, and from 1919, the art historian and psychiatrist Hans Prinzhorn (1886–1933), commissioned by the clinic director Karl Wilmanns, began to inventory and expand a collection of pictorial works that had been established in the Heidelberg clinic since 1909.[74]

In 1921, the Swiss psychiatrist Walter Morgenthaler (1882–1965) published his monograph on Adolf Wölfli (1864–1930), *Ein Geisteskranker als Künstler* (A Mental Patient as Artist), which attempts to approach the work of the interned composer, writer, geographer, and creator of myths iconographically and with great interest in the stylistic peculiarities of his works.[75] Rainer Maria Rilke and Lou Andreas-Salomé confessed to being touched and impressed by Wölfli's work.[76] A year later, Prinzhorn publishes his book *Bildnerei der Geisteskranken* (Artistry of the Mentally Ill), which was preceded by various articles in specialist journals. It undoubtedly represents a milestone in the examination of the art of mentally ill outsiders. The repeatedly discussed reception of his book—keyword 'Bible of the Surrealists'[77]—marks the preliminary climax in terms of linking the various

72 MacGregor, *The Discovery of the Art of the Insane*, pp. 11–160.

73 On the history of the *Musée de la folie*, see Allison Morehead, 'The Musée de la folie' in *Journal of the History of Collections* 23(1) (2011): 101–26.

74 See Gercke and Jarchov (eds), *Die Prinzhorn-Sammlung*. Laurent Busine and Inge Jàdi, *La beauté insensée* (Heidelberg: Wunderhorn, 1996). MacGregor, *The Discovery*, pp. 185ff.

75 Walter Morgenthaler, *Ein Geisteskranker als Künstler* (Bern, 1921; Berlin: Medusa, 1985).

76 Excerpts from the correspondence are printed in Elka Spoerri (ed.), *Der Engel des Herrn im Küchenschurz: Über Adolf Wölfli* (Frankfurt am Main: Fischer, 1987), pp. 67ff.

77 This repeatedly asserted function of Prinzhorn's book is based solely on remarks by Werner Spies in 'Genie und Irrsinn: Zur Ausstellung "Art Brut" in Paris', *Frankfurter Allgemeine Zeitung* (16 May 1967), p. 12, and Spies, 'Art Brut avant 1967' in *Revue de l'Art* 1–2 (1967): 123–26; here, p. 123, and has been repeated largely unquestioned ever since. See Gercke and Jarchov (eds), *Die Prinzhorn-Sammlung*, p. 63. See Thomas Röske,

strands in the perception of the insane: this is the first time that the medically oriented but anthropologically interested literature perceives the works of the mentally ill as 'art' (even if Prinzhorn prefers the term 'artistry'), and at the same time ensures that the value of these works gains acceptance in the art world. Not only does the madman now definitively become a role model for the practitioners of an art that has set itself the goal of causing a revolutionary upheaval of society; the methods of processing reality attributed to the madman are now also declared to be exemplary, as in Dalí's 'paranoiac-critical method'[78] and the automatic-writing methods of the surrealists. It is not without a cruel logic that in the totalitarian art policy of the Nazis, the madman and the 'degenerate' are of the highest argumentative significance when the self-proclaimed political and social-revolutionary potential of avant-garde art is combated in the exhibition *Degenerate Art*, which toured Germany from 1937 onwards. It is obvious that an art of unlearning is diametrically opposed to the intentions of any fascist, identitarian, or otherwise totalitarian system; where concepts such as people, nation, and culture are set to denote substances, any wilful unlearning is paradigmatically corrosive and subversive.

Prinzhorn's book from 1922 not only represents a milestone in the examination of the art of mentally ill outsiders, but also sits at a unique juncture between medicine, psychiatry, art history, and politics. The text is clearly influenced by the ideas of the expressionists, whose careers as avant-gardists, however, had long since turned in the direction of the academy and the museum. The book itself ultimately exerts influence, if at all, only on the surrealists and, partially, in the 1980s in Germany and the United States. At the same time, the collection of the works of the mentally ill takes place at a historical point that would not have been possible either earlier or after the end of the great barbarism: on the one hand, the time is now ripe for the perception and appreciation of the works of the mentally ill; on the other hand, no psychotropic drugs can as yet alleviate the

'Inspiration, unerreichtes Vorbild' in Röske (ed.), *Surrealism and Madness* (Heidelberg: Wunderhorn, 2009), pp. 9–19; here, p. 9. MacGregor, *The Discovery*, p. 281.

78 See Isabel Maurer Queipo and Nanette Rissler-Pipka (eds), *Dalís Medienspiele: Falsche Fährten und paranoische Selbstinszenierungen in den Künsten* (Bielefeld: transcript, 2007), pp. 14, 21 and *passim*.

intensity of the suffering, the feelings, anxieties, and longings of those who create the works.

Prinzhorn believes that he can identify basic principles of human creativity in the work of mentally ill artists. His interest is driven by the same fascination with the authentic, the non-cultural, as the work of the artists who, sixteen years earlier, had searched for methods of producing art that was not disfigured by any cultural influence. At the same time, however, he feels compelled to resort to art-historical comparisons in order to stress the value of the works of Franz Karl Bühler (1864–1940), for example, whose expressiveness he compares with that of Grünewald's and Dürer's paintings.[79] He concludes the section on Bühler (whom Prinzhorn calls Pohl) as follows: 'If this "Würgeengel" [Angel of the Last Judgement, Bühler's lost work, which Prinzhorn had printed as a frontispiece] could only arise from a schizophrenic sense of the world, then no cultivated person is capable of perceiving schizophrenic changes merely as degeneration due to illness'.[80] One must note the following two facts in this regard: firstly, unlike the expressionists and Dadaists, Prinzhorn does not pursue any anti-civilizational intentions. He is not interested in combating an ailing and corrupt culture with the madman as an argument and as a hero; rather, he is interested in integrating into the realm of culture what had previously suffered under its 'lame ignoramus'.[81] Secondly, he establishes a clear hierarchy within the various categories of image creators, with the schizophrenic at the top and the debile and the paralytic, the idiot and the imbecile at the bottom. The schizophrenic is capable of producing highly complex works that are equal in value to cultural creations, while the idiot

79 Hans Prinzhorn, *Bildnerei der Geisteskranken* (Heidelberg: Springer, 1922), p. 287. Other artists to whom Prinzhorn refers are Bosch, Brueghel, El Greco, Goya, Kokoschka and van Gogh, among others. See Thomas Röske, 'Außerhalb der Kontinuität historischer Prozesse: Wilhelm Fraenger und Hans Prinzhorn blicken auf Kunst von Außenseitern' in Susanne Himmelheber and Karl-Ludwig Hoffmann (eds), *Neue Kunst—lebendige Wissenschaft: Wilhelm Fraenger und sein Heidelberger Kreis 1910–1937* (Heidelberg: Kulturamt der Stadt Heidelberg, 2004), pp. 130–42. On Franz Karl Bühler see Martin Ruch, *Franz Karl Bühler* (Offenburg: Museum im Ritterhaus, 1993).

80 Prinzhorn, *Bildnerei*, p. 287.

81 Prinzhorn, *Bildnerei*, p. 357.

bluntly repeats himself or scribbles meaningless nonsense in his unsublimated productions.

Prinzhorn uses the term schizophrenia at a time when it has been established in medical discourse for just over ten years. Eugen Bleuler had replaced in publications from 1908 and 1911, with 'schizophrenia', the term 'dementia praecox', taken up by Emil Kraepelin and prefigured in Bénédict Augustin Morel's 'démence précoce'.[82] It is obviously a term that, although it does not fit seamlessly into the artistic avant-garde's self-perception, can be linked easily to central complexes that shape the self-image of the respective protagonists. The multiperspectivism borrowed from Nietzsche corresponds to a perceptual capacity accustomed to cubist and futurist fragmentation of form, to which in turn the concept of the dissociated ego fits better than the stupefied, single-minded subject; and the raging madman represents the anti-cultural passion for the forces of life to a greater extent than the dull, mute idiot. Just as hysteria corresponds to the ideal of convulsive beauty cultivated by the surrealists,[83] schizophrenia corresponds to an attention oriented in many directions simultaneously, a highly tense, oscillating sensitivity and alertness, a state of mind represented by restlessness and nervousness. Rather than anti-art, for Prinzhorn the art of the mentally ill is the art of the time. Upon drawing comparisons with works from non-European cultures, children's art, and 'primitive' productions from the early European period and the Middle Ages, it is therefore logical that he values the question of authenticity as secondary compared to the works' value as being significant and relevant for his time. He understands them as integral components in the European tradition, and his interest in a 'contribution to the psychology and psychopathology of creativity' recedes into the background in favour of a plea for the integration of the art of the mentally ill into the cultural fabric of his time. It is precisely because of this, however, that this art eludes the discourse on transhistorical and transcultural originality and becomes

82 See Eugen Bleuler, *Dementia praecox oder Gruppe der Schizophrenien* (Leipzig and Vienna: Franz Deuticke, 1911). Kraepelin, however, uses the term schizophrenia in his textbook published in 1915.

83 Ackerknecht, *Kurze Geschichte*, p. 82, states that Charcot's concept of hysteria was merely a great misunderstanding, the symptoms 'suggested' to the protagonists.

culture- and time-specific. By doing this, Prinzhorn distances them from the framework of expressionism and opens them up to be read by contemporaries for whom expressionism had already become art history.

As Prinzhorn writes in the passage on the artistic rank of Bühler's work, this work cannot be a product of degeneration, as the schizophrenic 'sense of the world' (*Weltgefühl*) is the feeling of the world of his epoch. Instead of declaring the schizophrenic outsider to be a counter-figure, he declares him to be the quintessential protagonist of contemporary culture: his work is a reflection of his times without being obscured by social considerations or ambitions. For this reason, formal principles and parallels between the art of the mentally ill and tribal or non-European art do not count for much in Prinzhorn's eyes:

> For it is superficial and wrong to construe similarity of the underlying mental states from similarity of outward appearance. The conclusion: this painter paints like that mentally ill person, therefore he is mentally ill, is by no means more proving and more intelligent than the other: Pechstein, Heckel et al. make wooden figures like Cameroon sculptors, therefore they are Cameroon sculptors. Anyone who tends to draw such simple-minded conclusions has no right to be taken seriously.[84]

Even in the case of formal homology, it is only the manner in which the respective artistic expression represents the intention of its creator that determines its semantic content. As has often been noted, this statement by Prinzhorn, who viewed the fascists positively from 1930 at the latest,[85] anticipates objections to the defamation strategies of the Nazis in the *Degenerate Art* exhibition from 1937. He clearly tries to find a justification for a cultural appreciation of art, especially that of schizophrenic authors, while at the same time placing less emphasis on the less 'successful' or less 'interesting' works. But he doesn't overlook these authors; he tries to understand them in their formal characteristics and, where possible, tries

84 Prinzhorn, *Bildnerei*, p. 346.

85 See Thomas Röske, 'Hans Prinzhorn—ein "Sinnender" in der Weimarer Republik' in Thomas Fuchs et al. (eds), *Wahn, Welt, Bild: Die Prinzhorn-Sammlung. Beiträge zur Museumsöffnung, Heidelberger Jahrbücher* 46 (2002), pp. 31–40.

to read intersubjective meaning into them, that is, to do them discursive justice.[86]

Shortly after Prinzhorn, Karl Jaspers published *Strindberg und Van Gogh*, a 'pathographic analysis'.[87] Jaspers compares the influence that the illness had on the work of both and comes to the conclusion that in Strindberg, whose unstable personality he emphasizes several times, the 'ideological substance' remained the same, the schizophrenic process 'only brought new material, but no idea'.[88] The situation is different with van Gogh, for whom Jaspers cautiously assumes that the illness, as with Hölderlin, enabled the emergence of new forces, 'forces that are themselves spiritual, neither healthy nor ill, but thrive on the soil of illness'.[89] Before drawing his conclusion, Jaspers refers to Prinzhorn's book and to cases of schizophrenic artists known to him, in particular Ernst Josephson and Charles Meryon.[90] He also mentions Odilon Redon, but assumes that his works are merely reminiscent of the creations of mentally ill authors, and that the artist was not ill. In a further attempt to relate 'schizophrenia and the culture of the time', Jaspers first points out that his contemporaries were 'enthusiastic about everything distant, foreign, unusual and primitive, about oriental art, about Negro art, about children's drawings'.[91] Precisely because 'we are loosened in the last foundations of existence', 'the time urges us to reflect on the last questions and on the most direct experiences'.[92] In 'bound times', on the other hand, people would be able to have deep and authentic experiences even without schizophrenia.[93] Schizophrenia thus stands for the immediate, the authentic, and the genuine in a time in

86 I take the term from Rainer Forst, 'Die Rechtfertigung des Fortschritts und der Fortschritt der Rechtfertigung' in Forst, *Die noumenale Republik* (Berlin: Suhrkamp, 2021), pp. 76–97; here, p. 81.

87 Karl Jaspers, *Strindberg und Van Gogh* (Berlin: Springer, 1926).

88 Jaspers, *Strindberg und Van Gogh*, p. 74.

89 Jaspers, *Strindberg und Van Gogh*, p. 146.

90 On Ernst Josephson, see Marina Schneede and Uwe M. Schneede, *Vor der Zeit: Carl Fredrik Hill und Ernst Josephson* (Berlin: Fröhlich & Kaufmann, 1984). On Charles Meryon, see R. Douglas Collins, *Charles Meryon: A Life* (London: Garton & Co., 1999).

91 Jaspers, *Strindberg und Van Gogh*, p. 149.

92 Jaspers, *Strindberg und Van Gogh*, p. 150.

93 Jaspers, *Strindberg und Van Gogh*, p. 151.

which all ties have become friable. In contrast to this immediacy, creations that are reminiscent of schizophrenia in their syntax, their content, their formal language, appear as vapid imitations: 'Do we see a dance around something that is wanted, sought, but which is only realized as screaming, as staging, as violence, as self-intoxication and self-absorption, as shallow immediacy and a stupid will to primitiveness, even as cultural hostility, and which is real and deeply visible in individual schizophrenics?'[94] Consequently, it is the experience of being unbound, of a freedom bordering on disorientation, that demands and enables the schizophrenic's boom in the cultural sphere as a placeholder for the authentic. Schizophrenia functions both as an illness that expresses the truth about the culture beyond the walls of the institution—like the latter, it is a phenomenon of the corrosion of bonds and norms—and as a counter-phenomenon to the disordered, unfounded, and disoriented nature of this culture. Without intrinsic value, neither good nor bad, the significance of the illness is measured solely by whether or not it has actually enabled something new to emerge in the work of the artists concerned.

Insofar as it has this catalytic effect in the production of the new, it has value, because this newness is at the same time profound and authentic in contrast to a time and culture that merely relies on rapid imitation and—and for Jaspers this seems to be the central flaw and problem of this art practice—becomes antagonistic to culture.

Jaspers mentions the Sonderbund exhibition of 1912, in which paintings by the expressionists were grouped around van Gogh's works in 'strange monotony', and he asks whether van Gogh was the 'only sublime and reluctant madman among so many who want to be mad'.[95] He comes to the conclusion that the disunion of the subject, who is and at the same time knows what he is, stands in contrast to the disunion of the schizophrenic, whose actual madness stands in contrast to the simulated, longed-for, imitated madness of those for whom madness becomes an existential leitmotif in their inner turmoil. The madman, disenfranchized from reason and unconscious of his madness, has the privilege of leading a life of self-conformity compared to the healthy person who suffers from his state of disunion.

94 Jaspers, *Strindberg und Van Gogh*, p. 151.

95 Jaspers, *Strindberg und Van Gogh*, p. 150.

The 1912 exhibition brought together 125 works by van Gogh, whose paintings had exerted a decisive influence on the expressionist generation since the first exhibitions in Germany (Paul Cassirer organized ten van Gogh exhibitions in Berlin between 1901 and 1914; a van Gogh exhibition organized by Ernst Arnold and Emil Richter took place in Dresden in 1906, which deeply impressed the Brücke artists).[96] Whether the fact that van Gogh is said to have suffered from a mental illness (the diagnoses vary—fact is that he became the epitome of the artist to whom the stereotype of 'madness and genius' applies in the popular imagination)[97] was significant in terms of the impact of his work is doubtful. In his 1904 monograph, Julius Meier-Graefe describes him as the 'freest, healthiest' and at the same time excessive artist:

> It was gruesome to see how he painted: an excess in which the paint splashed around like blood. He did not feel himself, was one with the element he was depicting, painted himself in the blazing clouds in which a thousand suns threaten the earth with destruction, in the trees screaming up to the sky in horror, in the terrible expanse of its plains.[98]

In any case, there is no mention of mental illness.

Although from different perspectives and with different results, Prinzhorn and Jaspers both look at a present that they both see as being characterized by a schizophrenic sense of the world. Jaspers emphasizes the cultural hostility of those whom he accuses of being epigones imitating

---

96 Walter Maria Feilchenfeldt, *Vincent van Gogh & Paul Cassirer, Berlin: The Reception of van Gogh in Germany from 1901 to 1914* (Cahier Vincent 2) (Zwolle: Waanders, 1988). See Magdalena M. Moeller, *Wege des Expressionismus* (Munich: Hirmer, 1985), pp. 13–14. See Daniela Wilmes, *Wettbewerb um die Moderne* (Berlin: De Gruyter, 2012), pp. 28ff.

97 The diagnoses range from epilepsy, schizophrenia, manic-depressive illness, Ménière's disease, digitalis intoxication, porphyria and anxiety-happiness psychosis. See W. K. Strik, 'Die psychische Erkrankung Vincent van Goghs' in *Der Nervenarzt* 68 (1997): 401–09. The stereotype of the mad genius also leads to absurd marketing gags such as cut-off ears as erasers in the museum shop of the Städel in Frankfurt at the time of the *Making van Gogh* exhibition in 2019/20.

98 Julius Meier-Graefe, *Vincent van Gogh* (Munich: Piper, 1910 [1904]), pp. 5, 32.

a genius truly creating the new, whereas Prinzhorn emphasizes the artistic and cultural value of those achievements, which he regards as equal to established works. In both arguments, it is no longer about the anti-cultural function of the madman, as in expressionism and Dadaism. Neither is it about the madman as a rebel who throws his maltreated humanity into the battle against a murderous social machine. Rather, it is about their integration into this society because they exemplify characteristic traits of their time. It is no longer their outsider status that is decisive, but their inherently paradigmatic, contemporary character. Jaspers positions van Gogh (who was regarded as truly mentally ill) against his expressionist imitators, while Prinzhorn places the brilliant Bühler-Pohl in the great line of expressive art since Grünewald. This successfully establishes the creativity of the mentally ill as valid: in Jaspers' case, it is to be regarded as positive if it succeeds in producing something new; in Prinzhorn's case, if the creations follow on from the non-classical masterpieces of art history.

The extent to which the French surrealists, who were introduced to Prinzhorn's book by Max Ernst, were also able to understand the text, remains unclear. Most of them probably only took note of the illustrations. Asserting the relevance of the collection and the book through the argument of reception is in any case a tricky strategy, as neither Breton nor Eluard, neither Aragon nor Artaud had to fall back on insights that only *Artistry of the Mentally Ill* could have conveyed to them. And the repeated comparison, made for the first time by Werner Spies, between Max Ernst's *Oedipus*, depicted on the cover of *Cahiers d'Art* in 1931, and August Natterer (1868–1933)[99] is based on a rough visual analogy, around which there are more contradictions than similarities.

*

99 Werner Spies, *Max Ernst: Collagen. Inventar und Widerspruch* (Cologne: DuMont, 1975), pp. 183–84. Natterer's (*Prinzhorn* calls him Neter) *Wunderhirte* is one of the most frequently illustrated works from the collection. See Inge Jádi and Bettina Brand-Claussen (eds), *August Natterer: Die Beweiskraft der Bilder. Leben und Werk. Deutungen* (Heidelberg: Wunderhorn, 2001), p. 143.

However, one person who was in no way impressed by Prinzhorn's collection, even though he recognized the publication's great impact among the surrealists, was Jean Dubuffet:

> I visited the Prinzhorn Collection in Heidelberg in 1948 or 1949. I was one of the first to see it after the war. They took it out of the packing cases for me. I spent three days going through it. I was disappointed. There were too few patients represented, and he didn't have many artistically important examples.[100]

With Dubuffet, however, caution is required when it comes to evaluating his assessments, as he often proceeds strategically in order to secure the fame of being a pioneer for himself and his discoveries. His mostly scathing remarks about other artists (with the exception of Paul Klee), his brutal break-ups of his relationships, his insistence on his sole authorship of Art Brut, all serve to create a singular status for himself and make comparisons impossible. Lines of tradition are denied and possible derivations are preemptively blocked off. Given that the avant-garde as a system began to lose consistency after the Second World War, Dubuffet is forced to raise the temperature of the discussion when the question of subculture or counterculture (or even the destruction of culture through permanent revolt) is posed, in pop, performance art, and music in particular, and no longer in the traditional media of painting or sculpture. The question of subversion, which is linked to the avant-garde as a system, leads Dubuffet to blatant self-contradiction and rhetorical power-mongering. To wish for the downfall of a culture in which one has achieved some prestige and fame is not a consistent position. In order to silence such questions, the volume is turned up. In 1976, Dubuffet added a new facet to culture in the form of his museum, and he obviously was never further away from destroying it than in that year. On the contrary: his entire practice of collecting, selecting, and judging the art whose creators are by definition not allowed to have any awareness of being artists robs them of any form of autonomy.[101] Dubuffet, who assigns himself a position within culture

---

100 Interview with John MacGregor in Dubuffet, *Prospectus et tous les écrits suivants*, VOL. 4, p. 46.

101 Letter to Peter Selz (30 December 1961) in Dubuffet, *Prospectus et tous les écrits*

because he is not worthy of being called an Art Brut artist ('I am not worth it'),[102] exercises sole and absolute power over who is accepted into the inner circle of Art Brut or expelled from it again, as happens to Louis Soutter and Gaston Chaissac.[103] Dubuffet's strategy of instrumentalizing the mute and alienated work of Art Brut and its creators leads to an absolute position of power on the part of its mentor, promoter, and collector, which finds a parallel only in the absolute power that nineteenth-century psychiatry intended to establish, and succeeded in exercising, over the hospitalized patient in the form of the omniscient, judging doctor, who is prosecutor and judge in one person. Since the opening of the museum in Lausanne, a flood of publications has been devoted to Art Brut; new positions have been identified and incorporated into Art Brut, such as the

---

*suivants*, VOL. 2, p. 349: 'la fonction de l'artiste exige capitalement qu'il ne se sache pas un artiste, qu'il l'oublie au moins tout à fait au moment qu'il opère, et que l'effet de l'ouvrage d'art exige pareillement que le mot d'art ne puisse être formulé, ne puisse d'aucune façon venir à l'esprit dans le moment que cet effet s'exerce'. '[ . . . ] l'art véritable ne peut être que là où son nom ne saurait être prononcé, tout le reste n'étant que grimaces ou exercices scolaires sans signification ni intérêt', 'The function of the artist requires above all that he does not see himself as an artist, that he forgets it at least at the moment when he is active; and the effect of the work of art equally requires that the word art cannot be formulated at all, cannot come to mind in any way at the moment when art exerts its effect . . . True art can only be where one does not know how to pronounce its name; all the rest is nothing but grimaces and academic exercises without meaning or interest' (translated by LE).

102 Interview with John MacGregor in Dubuffet, *Prospectus et tous les écrits suivants*, VOL. 4, p. 58.

103 On the Chaissac–Dubuffet relationship, see Christian Delacampagne, *Outsiders* (Paris: Mengès, 1989), pp. 106–19; Sarah Wilson, 'From the Asylum to the Museum: Marginal Art in Paris and New York, 1938–1968' in *Parallel Visions: Modern Artists and Outsider Art* (Los Angeles: Los Angeles County Museum of Art, 1992), pp. 120–49, here p. 132; Dominique Allan Michaud, *Gaston Chaissac: Puzzle pour un homme seul* (Paris: Gallimard, 1974), where Dubuffet's disparaging remark about Chaissac, that he had become a professional artist, is quoted (p. 62), as well as Chaissac's bitter remark that *Art Brut* had made a career, whereas he had been rejected (p. 72). Dubuffet did not comment on Louis Soutter until 1970 (Dubuffet, *Prospectus et tous les écrits suivants*, VOL. 3, pp. 301–2). He had been aware of his work since 1946 at the latest (see the Letter to René Auberjonnois [29 December 1949] in Dubuffet, *Prospectus et tous les écrits suivants*, VOL. 4, p. 129). Soutter was a school friend of Auberjonois and a second cousin of Le Corbusier.

works of the patients from the Künstlerhaus Gugging. Glossy magazines such as *Raw Vision* are constantly discovering new artists and working towards a flourishing art market whose economic potential is demonstrated at art fairs such as the Outsider Art Fair in New York. While Art Brut and the art of the mentally ill have always been merely an overlooked inner side of culture, culture now completely lacks its opposite. Not because the societies of the global North were characterized by the virtue of integration and tolerance, but because the new is the cultural fuel of the attention economy. Even more so in times of cognitive capitalism, the game between outsider and society is a fictional one. Instead of the binarity on which Dubuffet's (and other) theories of outsiderhood thrive and that enables a seemingly easily recognizable distinction, any possibility of differentiation between periphery and centre, marginality and mainstream is now lost in the field of culture, in the white noise of everyone communicating with everyone through every conceivable channel about every conceivable topic. If culture is understood as a system of observing the production and dissemination of values in the art field, then there are stars and failures, global players and poor losers, top prizes and flops, but no one who is fundamentally excluded from observation and evaluation and thus from a possible career in the cultural system. The new, which capitalist economies demand, bears the name of the outsider in the cultural field, since it is easier to package and sells better. And since he is misunderstood, he can also be a genius. Endowing him with moral dignity as a marginalized person serves to valorise him. This value, if it endures, can also be translated into economic capital. It is not surprising that this valorisation of the outsider goes hand in hand with unbroken star hype around stars and the admiration not only of the public but also of curatorial circles for great artists. These two poles are analogous to the relationship between value creation and value preservation, between the powers of constituting and the powers of the constituted, between invention and institutionalization. From these poles, democratic and capitalist societies draw their self-transformative power.

CHAPTER EIGHT

# Actionism, Fluxus, and Pop

## Performance of Regression

Dubuffet's belief that creation out of nothing has the power to unhinge culture is linked to the traditional media of painting and sculpture, even if his *Coucou Bazar* is a work that combines theatre, sculpture, music, and image.[1] His improvisations, which he performs on the piano with bandaged hands, are etudes in the art of forgetting. But what he is not aware of, or does not want to be aware of, are the attempts of an art form to take forgetting to an extreme by means of wilful regression. This art makes use of the body—the artist's body and the bodies of protagonists who have to perform or endure certain actions. Almost without warning, Vienna witnesses a group of artists briefly arrive on the scene who no longer stop at creating images, but instead work with real bodies, real blood, real pain, and real agony. The Viennese actionists Brus, Frohner, Mühl, Nitsch, Schwarzkogler, and Schilling took their inspiration from a variety of sources: 'These incunabula of new ugliness are a growth of surrealism, the Cobra Group, Dubuffet, expressionism, Art Brut, and graffiti'.[2] But they go far beyond their role models. The gloominess and, to this day, shocking ruthlessness with which the artists in the Viennese Perinetkeller destroy

---

1 *Coucou Bazar* was performed three times (1973 at the Guggenheim Museum in New York, 1974 in Paris and 1978 in Turin). While the composer İlhan Mimaroğlu created the music for the first two performances, Dubuffet performed his own compositions in Turin, which were released on the Sub Rosa label in 2014. In 1961, he published eleven pieces improvised with Asger Jorn as *musique brut*.

2 Veit Loers, 'Als die Bilder laufen lernten: Zur Ästhetik des frühen Wiener Aktionismus' in Dieter Schwarz and Veit Loers (eds), *Von der Aktionsmalerei zum Aktionismus: Wien 1960–1965* (Klagenfurt: Ritter, 1988), p. 11; emphasis in the original. Other role models were action painting à la Pollock, Yves Klein and the happenings of Allan Kaprow and Robert Rauschenberg, which were already documented at the time. See Hal Foster, 'Viennese Actionism' in Hal Foster, Rosalind Krauss et al. (eds), *Art Since 1900* (London: Thames & Hudson, 2004), p. 464.

and experiment on themselves and others, rummage through bodies and materials, mess around with liquids on orifices, work on pain and despair, have no parallel. Although the actions of the Viennese actionists are still performative and largely respect aesthetic difference (with the exception of the actions with animals), they stand out in the art history of the twentieth century as disturbing, deeply irreconcilable solitaires. They reduce life to a point where it can no longer be referred to as human, but only as the body.[3]

In their rejection of language, the Viennese actionists adopt a moment of Dadaist revolt. All that remains is the scream: 'Language has been lost. You can still find it in growling and hissing, in screaming and swallowing . . .'[4] What they also distance themselves from are the practices of conformist provocation with which Arnulf Rainer and Friedensreich Hundertwasser are successful. Insulting the public (Arnulf Rainer, 1951) is a tried and tested tool for attracting attention, right up to the subtle Handke, who was ultimately awarded the Nobel Prize. And how conventional Hundertwasser's nude performances are becomes clear when one compares them with images of the shocking early performances by Nitsch or Mühl. It is true that some of Brus' performances, such as the stroll with the face painted white (*Wiener Spaziergang*, 1965), also slip into a strangely harmless Pierrot aesthetic, which is not made any more radical by the fact that Viennese police officers, who ultimately take him to a police station to establish his identity, form the escort in the pictures. But these unsuccessful works are the exception. Much more than Rainer, who in his Messerschmidt[5] paraphrases and overpaintings ultimately only acts as a petty-bourgeois iconoclast, aware of the value of scandalization, the

3 See Otto Mühl, 'Die Materialaktion' in Loers and Schwarz (eds), *Von der Aktionsmalerei zum Aktionismus*, p. 270: 'now it is understandable that the human being is not treated as a human being in the material action, but as a body.'

4 Günter Brus, 1960, quoted from Loers and Schwarz (eds), *Von der Aktionsmalerei zum Aktionismus*, p. 12.

5 Franz Xaver Messerschmidt (1736–1783) was an Austrian sculptor, working primarily in Vienna and Bratislava, who became known for his character heads, which bordered on caricature and the grotesque, and became of interest to the literature on the psychopathology of art. See Antonia Boström, *Messerschmidt and Modernity* (Los Angeles: Getty Publications, 2012).

Viennese actionists create works of conscious regression that actually prevent themselves from being appropriated. While Mühl, under the influence of Freud's and Reich's psychoanalysis, Nitsch, influenced by Jung's theory of archetypes, and Schwarzkogler work on a possible art of healing, Brus approaches regression through pain:

> The IDIOT is surrounded by whitish MUD—A glass of lemonade is knocked over—I split my head in half with a WOODEN HACKLE—Someone pulls the cord—The arm falls out of the joint—I stab the CRIPPLE—BLOODLESS SELFMUTILATION—The tongue of the invalid sticks to the ice-cold steel [ . . . ]. The lemon-yellow idiot drives the NAIL through his kneecap.[6]

The martyred animal, the actor bound to the cross and doused in blood, the self-mutilating idiot and imbecile form a pandemonium of pain and disfigurement, of mistreatment and regression into a sphere of the inhuman, which is invoked to remind us of the restoration of the human. The highly reflective, staged regression uses the idiotic, the seemingly feeble-minded, to remind us of a lost reason, not unlike what the expressionists and Dadaists had attempted. But where the expressionists failed because of their ambition and the Dadaists because of their tendency towards clowning around, the Viennese actionists avoided the risks of affirmation associated with dialectics. The universe of pain is absolute.

As many of Nitsch's work titles suggest (*Stations of the Cross*, *Wall of the Flagellation*, *Triptych of the Blood of Christ*, *Entombment*), one of the main reference points of his art—alongside Dionysus and Orpheus torn apart by the Maenads—is Christ offering himself as a sacrifice. When Frohner, Mühl, and Nitsch performed *Blood Organ* in 1962, the symbol of the lamb, which is nailed upside down to a cross and disembowelled, played a central role. Nitsch claims the role of the vicarious sufferer for himself. In the magazine *Blutorgel* (Blood Organ) he wrote: 'In my art (a form of devotion to life), I take upon myself what appears to be a negative, perverse, and obscene pleasure in order to spare you the shame and disgrace

6 Günter Brus, text for the planned magazine *Das Fieber*, 1965, quoted from Loers and Schwarz (eds), *Von der Aktionsmalerei zum Aktionismus*, p. 342.

that would result'.[7] It is no different with Brus, whose 1970 *Ordeal* in Munich represents an extreme act of self-torture, even if the soteriological aspect is less prominent than in Nitsch's work eight years earlier. Nonetheless, the staged debility goes hand in hand with the rhetoric—expressed in the manifestos and visually present in the works—of a vicarious, redeeming, para-Christian function of the protagonists.

If Yves Klein (1928–62), to whom the Viennese actionists refer, is never far from irony and mischievous falsification, the artists from Vienna, despite Mühl's sometimes odd titles, lack any ironic distance from their own practice and any sense of play. This statement is true even though Nitsch, for example, feels committed to the idea of carnival and the tradition of 'laughter culture' as outlined by Bakhtin.[8] The *Orgien Mysterien Theater*, which Nitsch had been performing at Prinzendorf Castle since the early 1970s, is, like carnival, a temporary, ritually framed transgression or reversal of rules and hierarchies. Excess and transgression are means of abreaction;[9] however, they fulfil a stabilizing function, as the relief of urges is limited in time and as strictly formalized as the social existence against whose alienating mechanics the excess is directed.

When the Viennese actionists, together with Peter Weibel, Gerhard Rühm, and Oswald Wiener, among others, organized the Zockfest at the 'Gasthaus zum Grünen Tor' on 21 April 1967 (three years before the start of the Prinzendorf productions), the excess got out of hand: the audience threw body parts of a lamb at Nitsch; he responded by chasing the spectators and showering them with blood. The whole performance ends in a brawl, which is broken up by two hundred helmeted police officers with dogs.[10]

---

7 Quoted from Foster, 'Viennese Actionism', p. 466.

8 Hermann Nitsch, *Orgien Mysterien Theater* (Salzburg: Residenz, 1990), pp. 53–54: 'carnival represented a Dionysian escape from the ascetic confines of Christianity, pagan elements that had been suppressed came to the fore [ . . . ] the demons and pagan gods that had apparently been banished by Christianity were also brought back to mind at many carnival festivals'.

9 A recording of the *Akustisches Abreaktionsspiel* produced by WDR (Aktion 38b) from 1972 is available at https://www.youtube.com/watch?v=QxN88Z_H6JI.

10 Thomas Dreher, *Performance Art nach 1945: Aktionstheater und Intermedia* (Munich: Fink, 2001), p. 272.

Just over a year later, on 7 June 1968, the Kunst und Revolution (Art and Revolution) action struck the final chord. The action was introduced in a speech by Mühl, who insulted the memory of American senator Robert F. Kennedy, who had been killed a few days earlier: 'Another naught less'. Peter Weibel in turn denigrates the then Austrian Finance Minister Stephan Koren (1919–88), who had lost a hand in World War II:

> [W]hen one-handed people are allowed to rule with their own hands and without authority, when the crippled Koren shakes lies and promises out of his sleeve, when the crippled Koren's left hand does not know what his right hand is doing, then he has it easy, because his arm hangs loose and empty, because there is no right hand at all on the body of the crippled Koren.[11]

While Weibel is still speaking—interrupted by interjections from the audience, to which Valie Export reacts by switching the microphone and the light on and off—Brus enters the stage, urinates and defecates, vomits, and performs masturbation movements to the sound of the Austrian national anthem. Mühl begins to whip a masochist who reads pornographic texts, and Wiener explains the input-output relationship between language and thought with the help of a wireless microphone in the midst of the increasing tumult, as if he wanted to explain the dynamic that had just shaped the relationship between Weibel and the audience.

Mühl is imprisoned for four weeks, and Rühm, Weibel, Wiener, and Brus are sentenced (Brus to six months in jail) and go into exile (Brus and Wiener go to Berlin) instead of being jailed.[12]

Nitsch would later endeavour to press the anarchic nature of these actions into scripted form and drift into the theatrical, academic, and myth-laden, which earned him a professorship at the Städelschule in Frankfurt; Schwarzkogler died in 1969 from a fall from a window; Weibel, despite an incomparable career as a museum curator and director of the Zentrum für Kunst und Medien (Centre for Art and Media) in Karlsruhe, worked on self-heroicization as a great artist; Brus withdrew into the medium of drawing, Mühl slipped into the totalitarianism of his

11 Quoted from Dreher, *Performance Art nach 1945*, p. 273.

12 See Dreher, *Performance Art nach 1945*, p. 278.

psycho-commune and into paedophilia.[13] However, the repulsive and disgusting nature of their early actions permanently and thoroughly protected the art of the Viennese actionists from being too smoothly turned into something socially constructive. The seemingly senseless affront precludes not only reconciliation, but also the idea of an improvement of society. There is nothing positive that the insults and obscenities could point to as their negative. The polymorphous perverse does not have the healthy individual of ego psychology as its dialectical counterpart. It even lacks—and it is important to emphasize that this only applies to the early actions up to 1968—the negative-mimetic reference to social reality as inversion: what the Viennese actionists realize, the staged maximum regression without a goal, is a third that lacks the potential for perfection and thus cannot be integrated into society.

## Criticism and Shamanism

The social isolation as well as the art-historically erratic position of the Viennese actionists becomes all the clearer when seen against the backdrop of the international network that connected the protagonists of Fluxus and pop art at almost the same time. There are numerous overlaps and transatlantic connections, and Japanese artists also play an increasingly important role in this context.[14] At the same time, there are numerous South-South connections, as exemplified by the influence of the Brazilian artist Hélio Oiticica (1937–80) on New Zealand's Post-Object Art.[15] Transcontinental travel enabled exchange, cooperation, and communication that had not been possible to the same extent for the protagonists of *Der Blaue Reiter* and Dadaism.[16]

How different the strategies of Fluxus and pop are, and how different the ways in which the figure of the outsider is configured by the respective

13 In 1991, he was sentenced to seven years in prison for, among other things, sexual abuse and rape of minors.

14 See Luciana Galliano, *Japan Fluxus* (Lanham, MD: Lexington Books, 2019).

15 See Jim Allen, *The Skin of Years* (Auckland: Clouds & Michael Lett, 2014).

16 For a detailed history of the elusive Fluxus phenomenon, see Ken Friedman (ed.), *The Fluxus Reader* (Chichester: Academy Editions, 1998).

protagonists, can be demonstrated by examining the practices of the two central artistic personalities of the last third of the twentieth century: Joseph Beuys (1921–86) and Andy Warhol (1928–87). The two met in 1979 at the height of their fame at Hans Mayer's gallery in Düsseldorf, before Beuys had his retrospective at the Guggenheim Museum in New York. In 1980, at Beuys' suggestion, Warhol produced a poster, *Andy Warhol for the Greens.*[17] When Beuys was in New York, Heiner Bastian arranged a photo session in Warhol's Factory. The result was a series of silkscreen prints that Warhol sprinkles with diamond dust, ostensibly as a reference to Beuys' use of materials.[18] When Warhol shows the Beuys portraits in Europe, the two travel to the opening of the exhibition at the Lucio Amelio Gallery in Naples on 1 April 1980. While Beuys patronizingly describes Warhol as a naive but revolutionary artist, Warhol confides to a German magazine that he welcomes Beuys' political activities and believes he should come to the USA and become president.[19]

In view of the vast amount of literature on both artists, it is unnecessary to attempt a summary of their respective artistic practices, when the question is how they positioned themselves as outsiders towards society. What I would like to do is experiment with the thesis that Beuys' approach to the problem of the relationship to society is one of critique, while Warhol pursues a strategy of indifference, both consequently using opposing procedures that can nevertheless be interpreted as subversive, with the figure of the idiot playing a small but illuminating role. I would like to consider the thesis that Beuys conducts the business of criticism through art in a traditional way: he points out social deficits and aberrations, names undesirable developments and shortcomings, and, with the help of an extensive syncretic theoretical apparatus, develops arguments that are intended both to motivate and explain his artistic practice, both to justify and illuminate it. His belief that it is the task of art to initiate social change led him to actual political activism as a founding member of the Green Party in Germany. His famous

17 Victoria and Albert Museum, London, acc. no. E.1883-1991.

18 Victor Bockris, *The Life and Death of Andy Warhol* (New York and Toronto: Bantam, 1989), p. 325.

19 Bockris, *The Life and Death of Andy Warhol*, p. 325.

self-fashioning with hat and fishing vest, his self-aggrandizement through myths that do not stand up to verification, the authentication of his choice of artistic materials through the biographical, all of this contributes to the creation of a persona that has become a fixture in the media and in the field of art, while at the same time cultivating the myth of the outsider. As is well known, Beuys draws on various prefigured types, in particular that of the shaman, who combines the aspects of being both marginalized and possessing deeper, esoteric knowledge. It is his privilege and duty to impart his knowledge, whose origin remains hidden from the uninitiated. In many cases, the central moment of initiation for the shaman is a serious and life-threatening illness. Beuys' experience of illness in the house of the van der Grinten brothers in Kranenburg in 1957 signifies a crisis that can be understood as such a turning point and as an initiation experience.[20] Referencing the figure of the shaman, endowed with a knowledge reserved only for him, allows Beuys to double-code his own persona.[21] By referring to the shaman, he is able to contour the claim of the avant-garde artist,[22] whose

20 See Mircea Eliade, *Schamanismus und archaische Ekstasetechnik* (Frankfurt am Main: Suhrkamp, 1975 [1951]), pp. 43ff. 'As we shall see immediately, all ecstatic experiences that determine the vocation of the future shaman exhibit the traditional pattern of an initiation ceremony: suffering, death and resurrection. From this point of view, every "sick calling" fulfils the role of an initiation, for its sufferings correspond to the initiatory tortures; likewise, the psychic isolation of a "chosen sick person" forms the counterpart to the ritual isolation and loneliness of the initiation ceremonies, and the danger of death which the sick person has experienced (agony, unconsciousness) forms the analogy to the symbolic death which is represented in all initiation ceremonies' (translated by LE). Beuys is said to have known the book. See Klaus Raschzok, 'Joseph Beuys (1921–1986) und die Figur des Schamanen im künstlerischen Werk' in Haringke Fugmann (ed.), *Schamanismus als Herausforderung* (Norderstedt: Books on Demand, 2015), pp. 158–97, here p. 162.

21 'When I do something shamanic, I take the shamanic element—undoubtedly an element of the past—to make a statement about a future possibility. I turn back by breaking through to the future'. Quoted from Burkhard Reinartz, 'Joseph Beuys und die Religion: Auferstehen muss der Mensch schon selbst', *Deutschlandfunk* (25 December 2019).

22 On the concept of the avant-garde in Beuys, see Franz-Joachim Verspohl, 'Avantgarde und soziales Bewußtsein: Das Beispiel Joseph Beuys' in *Marburger Jahrbuch für Kunstwissenschaft* 22 (1989): 241–46. In 1989 Verspohl could still claim that Beuys had not accommodated the public, 'to feel confirmed in their conventional expectations

position had become questionable at the transition to postmodernism, in such a way that it can be understood transculturally and transhistorically, rooted in a sphere of timelessness—and can therefore hardly be criticized. At the same time, he blocks the esoteric content of his teaching and his art from exoteric hermeneutics. And his supposed origin in the mythical coincides with his being ahead of his time—being avant-garde.

Shaman and avant-gardist, Beuys is also 'the idiot with the felt hat' who wants to make people realize that he is just like them. He plays humorously with the public perception (the occasions on which he was denounced as a charlatan and ridiculed as a so-called 'art professor' are legion)[23] of his own branding and its most well-known element, the hat. In this way, he can portray himself as both an outsider and a common man. Very early on, Beuys uses the figure of the tormented Christ in his strategy of representing his persona as complex as it is elusive, by drawing on a multitude of references for his own art as well as for his portrayal in the media. Not only did he create a series of religious sculptures in his early years (*Pietà*, 1951; *Crucifixion*, 1962–63), but Beuys also resorted to the iconography of the *Ecce Homo* in a context seemingly far removed from the religious sphere: on 20 July 1964, he took part in the Festival of New Art in the Audimax of the Technical University of Aachen, maltreating a grand piano[24] and handling saltpetre acid, a few splashes of which damaged the

---

of art' (p. 246). The provocation, however, is precisely the convention that the audience expects to be observed.

23 In 1979, *Der Spiegel* put his likeness on the front page and asked: 'Künstler Beuys. Der größte. Weltberuhmt fur einen Scharlatan?' Beuys signed and wrapped the issue and offered it as a multiple. See Jörg Schellmann, *Joseph Beuys: The Multiples* (Munich: Schellmann, 1992), no. 321.

24 Unlike in 1963, however, he does not chop it up. At the opening of Nam June Paik's exhibition in the private villa of gallery owner Rolf Jährling, he grabbed an axe without being asked and destroyed the piano. Friedrich Achleitner and Gerhard Rühm had already destroyed a piano on 15 April 1959 on the occasion of the second literary cabaret of the Wiener Gruppe at the Porrhaus. At the Wiesbadener Tage für neue Musik in 1962, the dismantling of a grand piano over several days in the free interpretation of Philip Corner's *Piano Activities* by George Maciunas, Dick Higgins, Ben Patterson, Alison Knowles, Wolf Vostell and Emmett Williams is probably the most scandalous event. What happens to the material of the scandal over time is shown by videos of re-performances of the action in galleries or at carnival parades, where avant-garde artists

clothes of a student, who retaliated with a punch (which Beuys is said to have returned with a hook). With a bloody nose, his right arm raised declamatorily, Beuys holds a cross in his left hand towards the camera, an image that gained iconic status.[25]

Beuys' theoretical and artistic work is characterized by a number of other allusions to Christian iconography and Christian semantics.[26] These include the washing of feet and the reference to baptism in *Celtic + ~~~~* in 1971 in the air-raid shelter in Basel, which varied a previous version in Edinburgh, but also the use of the hare as a reference to incarnation, which Beuys parallels with his own penetration of the earth and his 'resurrection' and rescue after the legendary plane crash. But there is a parallel in another respect: even if the proximity to the animals in Beuys' case is motivated by his claim to being a shaman, it also points back to the proximity of the idiot to the animal. We are not talking about the idiot of the nineteenth and twentieth centuries, but about the *idiota* of the poverty dispute and the salos of early Christianity.

Beuys' famous 1974 performance *I Like America and America Likes Me* is generally regarded as the art event that illustrates his self-creation as a shaman in a particularly impressive way. Beuys, who, after arriving at New York airport, is taken by ambulance to the René Block Gallery (and back again the same way), spends four days (from 21 to 25 May) in the gallery with a coyote, separated from the audience by a mesh screen. For the duration of the performance, he engages in a silent yet highly expressive dialogue with the animal, which ignores him, fears him, provokes him, plays with him, and tires of him. In addition to Beuys and the animal, the other protagonists of the action are daily issues of the Wall Street Journal, on which 'Little John' urinates, a flashlight, a crook, felt, a triangle, and a pile of straw. Beuys interacts with the animal as guardian, shaman, and

---

or roaring hooligans destroy pianos. Even in terms of acoustic qualities, the Wiesbaden action, which Corner learned about only later, is of a higher quality. See Gunnar Schmidt, *Klavierzerstörungen in Kunst und Popkultur* (Berlin: Reimer, 2013).

25 See Andreas Beitin and Eckhart J. Gillen (eds), *Flashes of the Future* (Bonn: Bundeszentrale für politische Bildung, 2018), pp. 172–89, here p. 172.

26 See Friedhelm Mennekes, *Christus Denken / Thinking Christ* (Cologne: Katholisches Bildungswerk, 1996).

playmate. One of the reference points here is the taming of a wolf by St Francis, as recounted in the legend of the Wolf of Gubbio.[27] Another reference point is the coyote as an animal sacred to the indigenous nations of North America on the one hand, and as an animal ostracized and persecuted by the white settlers, branded as cowardly and deceitful, on the other.[28] The coyote as nomad and paradigmatic survivor, who was not harmed by the extermination policies of the whites and who survived the efforts made by the state to get rid of him,[29] urinates on an organ of American capitalism, the Wall Street Journal, and plays a game with the foreigner as a trickster and prankster.

References to Christian iconography in teaching and work, to Rudolf Steiner's syncretism, to shamanism and spirituality by Beuys himself are documented and no longer need to be explained. What he did not explicitly refer to, but which should be emphasized here, are the complex relationships with the tradition of kynism, which can initially be established purely iconographically through the figure of the dog.

## Kynism

Kynism is generally understood to be a tradition of Greek philosophy, the most important representatives of which are Antisthenes and Diogenes of Sinope.[30] Diogenes of Sinope still sits in his pithos, a large clay storage jar, in our collective memory today, and his 'Get out of the sun' in response to Alexander the Great's question as to what he wished for has become common knowledge.[31] Diogenes is said not only to have eaten his meals at the

27 I owe the tip to Wolfger Pöhlmann.

28 See Dan Flores, *Coyote America* (New York: Basic Books, 2016), pp. 81–112, 234ff. See David Levi Strauss, *Between Dog & Wolf: Essays on Art and Politics* (Brooklyn, NY: Autonomedia, 1999 [1990]).

29 Flores, *Coyote America*. There are also further details on the 'war' against the coyotes.

30 See Margarethe Billerbeck (ed.), *Die Kyniker in der modernen Forschung: Aufsätze mit Einführung und Bibliographie* (Bochumer Studien zur Philosophie 15) (Amsterdam: B. R. Grüner, 1991). Georg Luck, *Die Weisheit der Hunde: Texte der antiken Kyniker in deutscher Übersetzung mit Erläuterungen* (Stuttgart: Alfred Kröner, 1997).

31 Not to forget Wilhelm Busch's 'Yes, yes, that comes from that' as the final sentence of the wise man maltreated by the bad boys of Corinth.

market and to have defecated there, but also to have masturbated in public, as he regarded sexual urges, similar to hunger and defecation, as predetermined by nature and thus also as positively sanctioned. One of the explanations for the term *kynism* is that he was rebuked by his contemporaries, including Plato, for this scandalous behaviour with the words that he was behaving like a dog (Greek *kyon*). The occasional depiction of Diogenes standing naked in the marketplace accompanied by a dog is based on this fable; the statue of a dog is also said to have adorned his grave. He turned the negative meaning of the insult into its opposite and adopted the word to describe himself. Finally, it was established as the name of his philosophy and that of his successors, whereby the term philosophy can only be used in a limited sense because no writings are known apart from the anecdotes and statements that have come down to us.

When Emperor Julian II (331/332 CE, emperor 361–63, died 26 June 363) turned against the kynics, one of his main arguments against them was their alleged hostility to education.[32] While he reveres Diogenes, his anger is directed at his successors, who, according to Julian, were uneducated and uncultured and merely provided themselves with an excuse to lead a dissolute and immoral life.[33] In his view, they tried to attain wisdom by the 'short route', whereas a true understanding of ancient culture, which he tried to reinstate against the barbarism of the Christians he despised and fought against, required the long and arduous study of classical literature. The metaphor of the short and the long route was in Christianity (re)transformed into the metaphor of vices and virtue as the metaphor of the narrow and the broad path, albeit with recourse to the older image of Hercules at the crossroads.[34] However, initially it only describes two different ways of gaining insight and knowledge: through intuition or through study.

32 *The Works of the Emperor Julian*, VOL. 2 (Wilmer Cave Wright trans.) (London and New York: Heinemann and Macmillan, 1913), pp. 5–72.

33 An accusation that would later also be levelled against the jurodivyj, the mendicant monks and the beguines.

34 See Erwin Panofsky, *Hercules am Scheidewege* (Leipzig: Teubner, 1930), in particular the comments on *Hercules Prodicius* and the relationship of the motif to that of female poverty and the virtues, pp. 37ff.

When Nietzsche refers to 'cynicism', he is usually referring to the kynics, but he also uses it in the sense in which 'cynicism' is used today. The respective meaning is derived from the context. And just as the meanings and value attributions change throughout his work or even turn into their opposite, Nietzsche also continuously changes the semantics of cynicism and ends with a parallelization of the kynic with the buffoon and clown (Hanswurst), in whose proximity he ultimately places himself: 'I don't want to be a saint, rather still a clown . . . Perhaps I am a clown . . .'[35] He claims to have written the text in which he makes this statement,

> [W]ith a cynicism that will become world-historical: the book is called 'Ecce homo' and is an assassination without the slightest regard for the Crucified One: it ends in thunderbolts against everything that is Christian or Christian-infected, at which one loses sight and hearing. In the end, I am the first psychologist of Christianity and, as the old artilleryman that I am, I can bring forward heavy artillery of which no opponent of Christianity has even suspected the existence. The whole thing is the prelude to the revaluation of all values, the work that lies ready before me: I swear to you that in two years we shall have the whole earth in convulsions. I am fate.[36]

At the same time, the cynicism of this book is the highest he can create:

> There is no prouder or at the same time more subtle kind of books: they sometimes attain to the highest pinnacle of earthly endeavour, cynicism; to conquer them a man must have the tenderest fingers as well as the most intrepid fists. Any kind of spiritual decrepitude utterly excludes all intercourse with them—even any kind of dyspepsia: a man must have no nerves, but he must have a cheerful belly.[37]

---

35 Nietzsche, *Ecce Homo*, p. 365.

36 Friedrich Nietzsche, Letter to Georg Brandes (20 November 1888), *Nietzsche Source—Digitale Kritische Gesamtausgabe Werke und Briefe* (eKGWB), BVN-1888,1151.

37 Nietzsche, *Ecce Homo*, pp. 302–3.

Not only is the reference to the cheerful belly, which is otherwise rarely mentioned in Nietzsche, significant in connection with kynism; the recourse to kynism also reveals from where Nietzsche took the formula of the revaluation of values, which characterizes not only his attacks on Christianity but his entire philosophy: from Diogenes Laertius' account of Diogenes of Sinope.[38] Another motif, that of the 'mad man', also goes back to Diogenes of Sinope, who went to the market with a lantern in broad daylight to look for human beings.[39] In *Fröhliche Wissenschaft*, Nietzsche describes how the madman runs into the market at daylight with a lantern and shouts: 'I seek God! I seek God!' In response to the rhetorical question of where God is, he announces: 'I will tell you. We have killed him'. Finally, ridiculed by the bystanders, the madman throws the lantern on the ground so that it breaks, repeating Nietzsche's recurring motif, which he himself coined, that he had come too early and that it was 'not yet time'. On the same day, he invades various churches and proclaims God's death.[40]

Michel Foucault dealt with the kynics in his last lecture at the Collège de France[41] and drew not insignificantly on the book *Der Kynismus des Diogenes und der Begriff des Zynismus* by Heinrich Niehues-Pröbsting.[42] Without going into its significance for Nietzsche, he points to the importance of the fact that Diogenes came from a family of coin forgers (or was

38 Heinrich Niehues-Pröbsting, 'Der "kurze Weg": Nietzsches 'Cynismus' in *Archiv für Begriffsgeschichte* 24(1) (1980): 103–22; here, p. 121. Laertius, *Leben*, p. 272: 'When Xeniades asked him how he should bury him, he said: "Lying on his face". But when asked why, he said: "Because in a short time the lower will be turned upside down".'

39 Laertius, *Leben*, p. 276.

40 Friedrich Nietzsche, *Kritische Studienausgabe*, 2nd EDN (KSA) (Giorgio Colli and Mazzino Montinari eds) (Munich: Deutscher Taschenbuch Verlag, 1988), VOL. 3, pp. 480ff.

41 Michel Foucault, *Der Mut zur Wahrheit: Die Regierung des Selbst und der anderen II: Vorlesungen am Collège de France 1983/1984* (Berlin: Suhrkamp, 2010), especially from LECTURE 5, pp. 207ff.

42 Heinrich Niehues-Pröbsting, *Der Kynismus des Diogenes und der Begriff des Zynismus* (Frankfurt am Main: Suhrkamp, 2016 [1979]). See also Peter Sloterdijk, *Kritik der zynischen Vernunft*, VOL. 1 (Frankfurt am Main: Suhrkamp, 1983), in particular pp. 203–14, 294ff. Foucault's mocking comments on Sloterdijk in Foucault, *Der Mut zur Wahrheit*, p. 234.

himself once banished for counterfeiting coins), and to the connection of this motif to the commandment of the Delphic oracle: 'Mint the coin'. The aforementioned encounter between Alexander the Great and Diogenes illustrates that the relationship between coin (*nomisma*) and law (*nomos*) is not merely a phonetic proximity when it comes to revaluing values and re-stamping laws and currencies: Diogenes reverses the balance of power by commanding the emperor to get out of the sun, since, as a direct descendant of Zeus, Diogenes is a king by birth and does not need to be trained to become king. Moreover, by renouncing all merely external possessions and being his own master, he is independent of courtiers and the law, ministers, armies, and the need for wealth in order to finance his reign. Nor can he lose his kingship, because he has always had it. This is how Seneca understands him when he describes Diogenes as the man who 'stands above the man who had everything at his feet. He was far more powerful, far richer than the world ruler of the time, Alexander. After all, it was more that the latter could not accept what was given than what the former could give'.[43]

This revaluation of values, the inversion or reversal of power and powerlessness, of relationships between conventions of honour and decency, of education and ignorance, of the beautiful and the ugly, of the true and the illusory can be found in numerous anecdotes in Laertius's biography. Starting from his basic theme, the theme of truth-speaking, *parrhesia*, Foucault ascribes to the kynic the ability to derive truth directly from his own practice of life without the mediation of a doctrine. Life itself is the practice of truth (*alethurgy*).[44] The impression of impudence and impertinence, which provokes the hostility of the public, results from the unmediatedness, the urge to speak the truth without fear and to live according to this truth. Foucault repeatedly speaks of the scandal of truth: truth itself is a scandal because it makes that which is concealed public, unveils the lie, exposes the falsehood. Kynism, despite its theoretical poverty, represents the principle of philosophical heroism.[45] The kynic is a philosophical hero,

---

43 J. M. Moser (ed.), *Lucius Annaeus Seneca des Philosophen Werke*, VOL. 5: *Von den Wohltaten* (Stuttgart: Metzler, 1829), p. 847.

44 Foucault, *Der Mut zur Wahrheit*, p. 284.

an athlete who knows no fear and no barriers when it comes to speaking the truth.[46] His life takes place in public, because a life in truth, the true life, needs no concealments or cover-ups. It is a life according to what nature demands and therefore a life of sincerity. Filled with the desire to speak the truth, the kynic is both a healer and a nomad;[47] he is driven by concern for the well-being of the people, he interferes and performs a 'physical and social interventionism'.[48] He is, as Epictetus writes, the homeless wandering *kataskopos* who belongs nowhere, a kind of vanguard of humanity, an envoy of Zeus and a scout who, 'after having carefully scouted everything, [comes] back and [ . . . ] reports the truth'.[49] The knowledge of the kynic is, precisely because he is an outsider, ahead of the knowledge of the majority, and it is this 'ahead-ness' of the kynic that also gives him the task of being the *episkopos*—guardian—of humanity.[50] He speaks to the masses in public, and he speaks in a way that the people on the street understand. Peregrinus, a kynic philosopher (100–165 CE), who is said to have converted to Christianity and, after throwing himself into the fire at Olympia and burning to death in front of the public, was seen as a resurrected man after his death, preaches to the 'idiotai' in Rome and seems to have been involved in popular anti-Roman uprisings.[51]

Diogenes of Sinope, like Epictetus, is at one point a slave, and in many anecdotes, it is reported how he inverts his lawlessness into a relationship of dominance, for example towards his future master Xeniades, when he claims that the latter must obey him even though he is his slave. And: 'Menippus tells us', says Diogenes Laertius, 'in the "Sale of Diogenes", that he was asked at his sale as a prisoner what business he was in, and his

---

45 Foucault, *Der Mut zur Wahrheit*, pp. 278–79.

46 Foucault, *Der Mut zur Wahrheit*, p. 363.

47 Joseph Grabisch (ed.), *Unterredungen mit Epiktet*, BOOK 2, CHAP. 22 (Jena and Leipzig: Diederichs, 1905), pp. 101–02, where Epictetus describes the kynic as a king to whom 'the peoples entrust themselves; [ . . . ] he must go around like a doctor and feel the pulse'.

48 Foucault, *Der Mut zur Wahrheit*, pp. 362–63.

49 Grabisch (ed.), *Unterredungen*, p. 92.

50 Grabisch (ed.), *Unterredungen*, p. 94.

51 Foucault, *Der Mut zur Wahrheit*, p. 257.

answer was: "to rule over men"'.[52] This reversal, which is repeated in the fact that Diogenes, as their teacher, educates the children of Xeniades to extreme humility, not only expresses the significance of the game of inversion, but also begins a narrative of humility and humiliation, the power of which only fully unfolds in Christianity. It is understandable that Epictetus and Peregrinus are repeatedly said to be early Christians[53] and Foucault also wavers as to whether he should describe Peregrinus as a kynic who became a Christian or as a Christian who became a kynic. In religious studies, the question of the relationship between Christianity and kynism and the question of whether Jesus should be understood as a kynic is controversial.[54] In any case, Foucault believes that he can draw a connection between kynism and Christianity, but not without emphasizing the important differences that lie above all in the significance that the virtue of obedience and the idea of an afterlife play for Paul, for the early Christian ascetics and for their later successors, the Franciscans and Dominicans, the *Domini canes* (dogs of the Lord). Paul also felt committed to *parrhesia* and had to fear for his life after the disputes with the Greek Jews in Jerusalem (Acts 9:20–31). Thus, the kynic virtue of truth-telling seems to be very close to the early Christian virtue of the courage to profess faith without reservation. The topos of nakedness, which St Francis would follow in Assisi, as did Basil in Moscow, is rooted in the concept of the 'original man' who looks with boldness into the face of God.[55] However, according to Foucault, this boldness, which is expressed in the basic trust with which the believer faces his God, is in the course of history concealed by the institutionalization of obedience. It is no longer the immediate relationship between God and man, the fervour and directness of the experience of the

52 Both episodes in Laertius, *Leben*, p. 271.

53 See Koen Vanhagendoren, 'Individuelles religiöses Erleben auf dem Hintergrund stoischer Vorgaben? Aspekte von Epiktets Gottesbild' in *Hermes* 132(4) (2004): 495–510; on the state of research, pp. 497–98. See Gilbert Bagnani, 'Peregrinus Proteus and the Christians' in *Historia: Zeitschrift für Alte Geschichte* 4(1) (1955): 107–12.

54 Hans Dieter Betz, 'Jesus and the Cynics: Survey and Analysis of a Hypothesis' in *The Journal of Religion* 74(4) (October 1994): 453–75. This also contains relevant literature and a description of the respective positions up to 1994.

55 Foucault, *Der Mut zur Wahrheit*, p. 427.

divine, that is of the highest value. The institution, the Church, intervenes and insists on the indispensability of its mediating role. In the process of forming its theological philosophy, it suppresses and indeed often criminalizes the claim to a direct experience of God.

More important than the category of obedience, however, seems to be that of the afterlife: the kynic rejects conventional social life as false because it is an unfree life.[56] The Christian ascetic, on the other hand, rejects earthly life because it is irrelevant and an error with regard to eternal life in the hereafter. From the point of view of salvation, it is either an aberration, since only salvation counts, or irrelevant because salvation has already taken place. St Francis' indifference stems from this view: from the perspective of the redemption that has already taken place, life on earth is necessarily a false life, no more than a test. There is no true life in this false life, which one must both live, since to live it is God's will, and reject, since it is full of errors, pitfalls, sins, and suffering. This life is also untrue, and here the legacy of kynism mixes with that of Platonism, since truths are eternal. What passes away, passes away because it is untrue. Only the eternal can be true.

In several respects, the Christian succession to kynism thus differs clearly from the philosophical practice of Diogenes, for whom true life is made possible by the ability to know how to make the right distinctions.[57] For him, indifference (*adiophora*) towards worldly goods is equally a part of the right life as the effort to recognize good and bad, true and false. The metaphor of the dog, which distinguishes between friend and foe and, as guardian of the house, barks at the stranger, also refers to this.[58]

56 Grabisch, *Unterredungen*, p. 97.

57 Foucault, *Der Mut zur Wahrheit*, p. 318.

58 At the transition to the sixteenth century, this ability to differentiate allowed the dog to become an assistant emblem of logic, on whose behalf it pursued the problem, depicted as a hare, sometimes as *Veritas*, sometimes as *Falsitas*. See Manfred Schneider, 'Der Hund als Emblem' in Anne von der Heiden and Joseph Vogl (eds), *Politische Zoologie* (Zurich and Berlin: Diaphanes, 2007), pp. 149–76; here, pp. 155ff.

For Diogenes, life in this world certainly offers the possibility of leading a different, a true life. His asceticism does not serve to mortify and escape from the world, but rather to assert himself in it.[59]

The question of the extent to which the figure of the salos in particular can be related to the kynics, especially Diogenes of Sinope, is answered differently in literature. While Rydén considers the parallels between the two to be coincidental,[60] Krueger assumes a positive connection: 'By linking Symeon with the dog, Leontius connects Symeon with the kynic tradition, both linguistically and metaphorically. Symeon brings this tradition back to the city, where he continues to imitate Diogenes by eating lupins and raw meat and defecating in public'.[61] The undisguised nakedness and the unconcealed life in public, the permanent provocations, the disregard for the question of burial, the tendency to self-deprecation and the way of attracting humiliation—all this connects Diogenes and the kynics with a salos like Symeon of Emesa. However, the numerous differences between the two figures suggest that Leontius, the author of the *Life of Symeon*, consciously constructed his protagonist on the model of Diogenes in order to make his actions appear comprehensible against the backdrop of late antique knowledge and to give his readers the opportunity to classify them according to their existing knowledge. In particular, it is the different role played by individual nature that distinguishes the kynics from the saloi. Where Diogenes follows his nature, Symeon rejects it. He empties himself in the market not because it is right to obey nature, but because what is natural about him no longer plays a role. Where Diogenes wants to point to the possibility of a true life in this world through the scandal of truth, Symeon has already given up the world. If at all, then the kynism of the Roman Imperial period (and only from a sociological and religious-historical perspective), but not the kynism of the Hellenistic period with Diogenes as its main representative, is a phenomenon related to Christian ascetic monasticism.

---

59 Niehues-Pröbsting, *Der Kynismus*, p. 192.

60 Lennart Rydén, *Bemerkungen zum Leben des heiligen Narren Symeon von Leontios von Neapolis*, Studia Graeca Upsaliensia, VOL. 6 (Uppsala: Almqvist & Wiksell, 1970), pp. 17–18.

61 Krueger, *Symeon the Holy Fool*, p. 103.

However, according to Foucault, kynism provided late antiquity and Christian asceticism with the matrix of a fundamental ethical experience.[62] Its elements differ in relevance from each other. If one wants to emphasize the outsider status, the renunciation of social norms and life as a scandal, one will point to similarities. But if one wants to clearly draw the caesura between antiquity and Christianity, one will emphasize the importance of the inner world in contrast to the orientation towards the hereafter or point out that the ancient kynic lacks the element of conversion that characterizes the salos and the *idiotae* Paulus and St Francis equally: Paul must first shed his Saul and St Francis, with his cloak, his feudal existence in order to become the Poverello; Symeon (like the disciples) must leave his family in order to lead a life of *imitatio Christi*. Diogenes, on the other hand, is born free, and his actions are determined by nature, which transcends everything social. It is this unchanging rightness of what nature commands that makes it possible to live a life in truth (or life as truth).[63] Those who see congruence will emphasize the role played by the element of inversion: the lowest to the highest, the slave a master, the child a god, the god crucified, the elect the idiot, the powerful the weak, the first the last and the dregs of the world, and the one consecrated to death finally being the one chosen to eternal life; but those who consider differences to be more important will emphasize that Diogenes lives his life as a scandal by day and by night, whereas the salos only plays his game during the day.

To return to my initial argument: regardless of how one answers the question of the relationship of the kynics to the saloi and the Christian ascetics, the matrix that Foucault speaks of enables different entries and combinations and also temporal extensions. It is possible to place Beuys on this matrix, even if a corresponding self-characterization is missing (at least I am not aware of one).[64] It seems completely misguided, as both

62 Foucault, *Der Mut zur Wahrheit*, p. 374.

63 There is a reference to a conversion of Diogenes, who was banished from Athens for counterfeiting (Niehues-Pröbsting, *Der Kynismus*, p. 74), but this arises from a certain moralizing reading of the counterfeiting anecdote.

64 This has occasionally been attempted; see the conference 'Christoph Schlingensief und die Avantgarde', Bielefeld, 2–4 February 2017, and the lecture by Sebastian Kirsch, https://networks.h-net.org/node/79435/discussions/177072/tagb-workshop-christoph-

hagiographic and critical journalism does, to try to determine Beuys' rank on the basis of the question of whether or not he actually was a healer or a shaman, or whether or not his persona corresponded to him as a person. Where there are no simple business interests behind his glorification, an infantile zealotry prevails that bears poor witness to the criticality that otherwise artists and the producers of discourse accompanying their work claim for themselves. Likewise, the disparagement of him as a charlatan is merely a gesture of ignorance that masks hostility towards art. The reference to a figure such as the shaman, the fool, and the idiot is in itself revealing and an interpretament. Seeing Beuys against the backdrop of kynism opens up the possibility of placing him within a specifically European history of the outsider and his relationship to society and of assigning him a place there. His restlessness, his prolixity, his interventionism, with the attitude of a healer, his complacency, his delight in scandal and his ethos of turning to the common man ('I am in search of the stupidest'),[65] then give him a different kind of profile than if he were to be stylized, positively or negatively (as happens primarily in Germany, but interestingly hardly ever in the non-German scenes), as the exceptional figure who knows no comparison in history. Seeing him against this backdrop also prevents the overly easy interpretation of his work and his behaviour as foolishness. For the fool has a choice; he pursues a profession that consists in entertaining his clients, even if it is through provocation(s). The kynic, however, like the *idiota*, has no choice. He does not practice a profession, but follows a vocation or, in other words, his nature. The frequently emphasized importance

---

schlingensief-und-die-avantgarde-bielefeld . Roxana Kath, 'Das Konzept des 'einfachen Lebens' in der Antike: Ein Beispiel für die Anwendung von Textmining-Verfahren in der Geschichtswissenschaft' in *Working Papers Contested Order / eAQUA Working Papers* 1 (2010): 71–90; here, pp. 77–78. Like Betz, she refers to the significance of kynicism for Gregory of Nazianzus and establishes a link between the ancient image of the stranger, the nomad and Christ, which culminates in the figure of the Scythian sage Anacharsis, after whom the Prussian baron Johann Baptist Cloots named himself, which in turn inspired Beuys to call himself 'Joseph Anacharsis Cloots Beuys'.

65 Beuys in conversation with Horst Schwebel, in Horst Schwebel, *Glaubwürdig: Fünf Gespräche über heutige Kunst und Religion* (Munich: Kaiser, 1979), pp. 15–42. Arnold Gehlen, *Moral und Hypermoral: Eine pluralistische Ethik* (Frankfurt am Main: Klostermann, 1969), p. 14, also saw an inevitable rapprochement of its protagonists with the 'rabble' due to the 'finality of the ego emphasis' of Christianity.

of the blending of art and life and the denial of the difference between the two spheres in Social Sculpture is then parallel to Nietzsche's practice when he writes about the idiot Jesus that his entire action is a practice of non-distinction. And it is parallel to the *alethurgia* of the kynic, which measures the value of a doctrine by its non-distinction from the practice of life. Even if one finds Beuys' pathos ridiculous, with regard to the kynic, one can place his self-assurance—with which he can claim, marching towards the viewer, 'The revolution is us'[66]—in the tradition of the kynic as *kataskopos*, as scout and messenger. The avant-gardist would then not be a figure of modernity alone, but a representative of the extraordinary human being, as manifested in the figure of the shaman, but also in the form of the kynic, the philosophical hero and the idiot disregarded by society.

## Indifference and Subversion

On 1 April 1987, a memorial service in honour of Andy Warhol is held at St Patrick's Cathedral in New York, during which the art collector and Picasso biographer John Richardson gives a eulogy for the artist, who had died in February. Among other things, Richardson said,

> Andy's aloofness, the distance he had established between himself and the world, was above all a question of innocence and art. Isn't an artist obliged to keep his distance from things? In his impenetrable innocence and humility, Andy always struck me as a *yurodstvo*—one of those holy simpletons that haunt Russian literature and Slavic villages.[67]

---

66 *La rivoluzione siamo noi*, 1972, poster for the exhibition at Lucio Amelio's gallery in Naples, WVZ no. 49.

67 Quoted from Charles F. Stuckey, *Andy Warhol: Heaven and Hell Are Just One Breath Away! Late Paintings and Related Works, 1984–1986* (New York: Rizzoli, 1992), p. 140. Richardson confuses the jurodstvo with the representatives of this ascetic path of holy foolishness, the jurodivyj. See Christian Münch, 'Narrenfreiheit um Gottes Willen: Vom Freiheitsstreben der "jurodiwye" in Russland' in *Geist und Leben: Zeitschrift für christliche Spiritualität* 92(1) (2019): 45–54; here, p. 46.

With reference to the religious iconography of his late works, his Catholic origins, his charity, and the regularity of his churchgoing, Warhol was stylized as a religious artist after his death.[68] Of course, the question of whether this stylization by Richardson and in later biographies is correct or not is not of interest here; what is of interest is the connection between this characterization as jurodivyj, on the one hand, and one specific feature of Warhol's statements and his artistic practice, on the other: indifference.

Suffice it to cite two of the most famous statements ('All is pretty'; 'In the future everyone will be world-famous for 15 minutes')[69] and a few groups of works to illustrate this strategy of indifference, the blurring of differences and the levelling of values. When electric chairs, car accidents, lynchings, and suicides are as 'pretty' as Marilyn Monroe's face or the screen prints of scissors, money, or cows, this can only be understood as an erasure of differences and thus of meaning. It is no different with the 15 minutes of fame in which everyone will be able to bask in the future. Fame that everyone enjoys is not fame. The inflation of superstar status that Warhol pursues with his numerous films runs counter to the semantics of the star itself. What the films evoke through the fixed camera and the pseudo-documentary style is the impression of the artist's complete neutrality towards his subject. The fact that this artist, Warhol, produces his works in the form of a process organized by a division of labour and is often not even responsible for the choice of subject[70] completes this image of the disappearance not only of the individual behind the persona of the artist Warhol, but also of the obliteration of differences in value and aesthetic preference on the artist's part. The fact that both artist and individual disappear behind a mask of aloofness and disinterested friendliness takes away the heuristic value of even autobiographical notes such as those

68 Jane Daggett Dillenberger, *The Religious Art of Andy Warhol* (New York: Continuum, 1998).

69 *All Is Pretty*, poster by Moderna Museet, Stockholm, on the occasion of his exhibition from 10 February to 17 March 1968. The famous sentence about the 15 minutes of fame is no longer attributed to Warhol. See Rachel Nuwer, 'Andy Warhol Probably Never Said His Celebrated "Fifteen Minutes of Fame" Line' in *Smithsonian Magazine* (8 April 2014).

70 See Andy Warhol and Pat Hackett, *Popism* (London: Penguin, 2007 [1980]), p. 10.

about his vulnerability or the problems with which he could not come to terms. Warhol may have been convinced that his goal was to put an end to his emotional life. Although perhaps such an admission merely represents a new stage in the fictionalization of everything real, a further turn towards the pure play of pure performance.

> The acquisition of my tape recorder really finished whatever emotional life I might have had, but I was glad to see it go. Nothing was ever a problem again, because a problem just meant a good tape and when a problem transforms itself into a good tape it's not a problem any more. An interesting problem was an interesting tape. Everybody knew that and performed for the tape. You couldn't tell which problems were real and which problems were exaggerated for the tape. Better yet, the people telling you the problems couldn't decide any more if they were really having the problems or if they were just performing.

And referring to the assassination attempt carried out by Valerie Solanas on 3 June 1968, he writes:

> Before I was shot, I always thought that I was more half-there than all there—I always suspected that I was watching TV instead of living life. People sometimes say that the way things happen in the movies is unreal, but actually it's the way things happen to you in life that's unreal. The movies make emotions look so strong and real, whereas when things really do happen to you, it's like watching television—you don't feel anything.[71]

When Warhol realized at the beginning of his career that the difference between applied and free art played a role in the art world, he concealed his past as an illustrator. At the height of his career, he reversed the relationship: he now describes his art as business art, as the art that comes after art ('or whatever it's called'). In his art, he recycles remnants that often bear witness to the bad taste of the masses. By turning them into art

71 Andy Warhol, *The Philosophy of Andy Warhol: From A to B and Back Again* (New York: Harcourt Brace Jovanovich, 1975), pp. 13, 32.

('You're recycling work and you're recycling people')[72] he transforms these remnants into something of value. The equation of people with things can also be found in his dealings with superstars in his orbit and members of The Factory. The indifference with which he observes Edie Sedgwick's decline is only the best-known example among many.[73]

Warhol's *Philosophy* is full of passages about beauty, happiness, and money, and it is difficult to decide whether they are naive, tasteless, or perfidiously ambiguous. He naturally prefers some things to other things, some states to other states, thus making distinctions, but these usually lead to statements of grotesque banality. Entire pages are filled with agonizingly boring, meaningless stories about shopping and conversations on the phone, so that even this tedium and emptiness can be interpreted as strategically and semantically motivated statements. Warhol is fascinated by the idea of equality in a twisted way when he praises 'Studio 54', saying that democracy prevailed inside the club because there were no stars, because everyone was a star; or when he writes that the beauty of America is equality, and the greater the equality, the more American it is. This then leads him to the idea that only pictures of the same size should be produced, showing the same motif, so that no one could claim that the works in his possession were better than the works that someone else had in their collection. It is therefore logical that he dreams of an exhibition of his works entitled *Nothing Special*.[74]

At the same time, however, there are passages in which he describes himself as a specialist in doing the wrong things in the right place and the right things in the wrong place. In his perspective, he has built his entire

72 Warhol, *Philosophy*, p. 33.

73 See the corresponding passages in Bockris, *The Life and Death of Andy Warhol*. For these reasons, it is also difficult to understand Warhol's refusal of morality as a different or alternative form of morality, as Elizabeth Edwards does. See Elizabeth Edwards, 'The Banal Profound and the Profoundly Banal' in Dorota Glowacka and Stephen Boos (eds), *Between Ethics and Aesthetics: Crossing the Boundaries* (Albany, NY: State University of New York Press, 2002), pp. 255–74; here, p. 265. The distinction between kynism and cynicism, from which, however, no consequences are drawn.

74 Bockris, *The Life and Death of Andy Warhol*, p. 302; Warhol, *Philosophy*, pp. 36, 50, 49.

career on this ability.[75] He prefers this principle of reversal or inversion because something 'funny' always happens.

Of course, Warhol is criticized for the 'emptiness' of his art; from another perspective, however, he is celebrated as a sharp-eyed critic of American society who, as a kind of double agent, sees and depicts the broken world in a double focus. Susan Sontag, in turn, criticizes him as a symptom of capitalism: he is incapable of being outraged by anything, and in his fetishization of the pretty he reflects the obsession of consumer culture with easily marketable and quickly consumable goods,[76] yet such an observation is as accurate as it is banal if it is true that all art as a 'fait social'[77] reflects the society of its time.

But what if Warhol's art is neither empty nor critical? What if the absence of criticism does not mean a hedonistic affirmation of American consumerism, but is to be understood as self-enclosure and self-erasure? The all-round, unconditional, and permanent affirmation not only makes all objects disappear in their specificity, but also the judging subject in the white noise of equivalence. The indistinguishability of all parts of what is present and the absence of a discriminating judgement complement each other and produce not only an inaccessible world, but also a hermetic and at the same time ubiquitous persona that is hardly recognizable any more as a subject, but makes itself invisible in the mask of the Everyman ('nothing special') by being present everywhere. Insofar as the production of meaning presupposes the observance or production of differences,[78] the production of indifference is the assertion of the possibility of being able to produce nonsense or a sense as something absent. Warhol's self-description as 'machinery' reveals his intention to become free of intention. Insofar as values are tied to interests or arise from interests,[79] the attempt to become machine-like and disinterested presupposes the interest in being able to

75 Warhol, *Philosophy*, p. 55.

76 Bockris, *The Life and Death of Andy Warhol*, p. 317.

77 Theodor W. Adorno, *Ästhetische Theorie* (Frankfurt am Main: Suhrkamp, 1970), pp. 335, 401.

78 G. Spencer Brown, *Laws of Form* (New York: Julian Press, 1972), p. 3.

79 Ralph Barton Perry, *General Theory of Value* (London: Longmans, Green and Co., 1926), especially pp. 520–86.

formulate not only the absence of meaning, but also the absence of value. Even if this cannot succeed (as it is not possible to make no decision, just as it is not possible to break out of the compulsion to freedom), Warhol, assuming such an intention, nevertheless reaches an extreme point in the attempt to produce a work that exemplifies the absence of value rather than a counter-value or non-value.[80] Far from being just value-blind, Warhol produces something that both criticizes and affirms all the values that may apply in the society around him and thus turns his own work and its point of reference into a thing free of the idea of value, into a collection of things that can be found in the world as if they had been created without intention and thus without any interest. To align a creation with what is merely produced, and a work of art with objects reduces the level of the artwork's 'aboutness'[81] to a minimum and places it in the mass of all things that can be bought and used as commodities. It is possible to understand the fact that Warhol was seen as a cynic if one associates his approach with the concept of cynicism as formulated by Georg Simmel:

> Nothing can meet this mood [of cynicism] more effectively than the ability of money to reduce the highest as well as the lowest values equally to one form of value and thereby bring them, however different their types and measures, to the same fundamental level.

And:

> What for those paradoxical descendants of Socratic wisdom was a means or a secondary result, has here become the centre and has thus completely changed in its meaning. [ . . . ] The concept of the market price for values, which by their very nature reject any estimation other than that of their own categories and ideals, is the perfect objectification of what cynicism represents in subjective reflex.[82]

---

80 On exemplification, see Nelson Goodman, 'Kunst und Erkenntnis' in Dieter Henrich and Wolfgang Iser (eds), *Theorien der Kunst* (Frankfurt am Main: Suhrkamp, 1992), pp. 569–91; here, p. 580.

81 Arthur C. Danto, *Die Verklärung des Gewöhnlichen* (Frankfurt am Main: Suhrkamp, 1991 [1981]), p. 130.

82 Georg Simmel, *Philosophie des Geldes* (Berlin: Suhrkamp, 2001 [1900]), pp. 263–

The non-stop production that Warhol perfects in order to add another commodity to the world of commodities, but which the public believes transports a surplus of meaning that the soup can does not possess—this machinery that works without interruption—is the disinterested and value-levelling machinery of capitalist society, to which Warhol turns when he transforms a commodity into art because society wants it to be more and different from a mere commodity. He thus leaves the production of meaning and the practice of differentiation as well as the attribution of value to the public or a market in which products must possess markers of difference so that they can be used as distinguishing features.[83]

The term subversion in this context may well be a misnomer. It may be misleading, as it implies the reversal of relationships, the revaluation of values, the reorganization of constellations and hierarchies. In fact, Warhol succeeds in something different and possibly even more disturbing than subversion, which always requires perspectives, locations, and definitions. He succeeds in a form of erosion and attrition that is more far-reaching and disruptive than subversion could be. By designing a world of disinterest, of neutral voyeurism, of disengaged curiosity, of indifference and lack of value, and by holding it up to contemporary society (and indeed in a form of mimicry, of assimilation to the social, which lacks any degree of criticality, but rather reflects back what meets its surface with the smiling mask of complete conformity); by equating his creations to things and declaring everything to be interchangeable with everything, Warhol succeeds in something that may be the significance of his artistic strategy: Warhol is irrefutable. Not only does anyone who admits that he paints garbage and that his own pictures are bad confront every possible criticism with the affirmation of this criticism and thus set in motion a potentially endless process of affirmation of criticism and criticism of its affirmation.[84] Moreover, by equating his works with commodities and people with things, he produces an impenetrable world of factuality that lacks any other side,

---

64. Aristotle, *Nikomachische Ethik*, Franz Dirlmeier trans. and ed. (Stuttgart: Reclam, 1969), V, 1133a12–29, also understands money as a medium of equality, but without being able to draw the same conclusions as Simmel.

83 Pierre Bourdieu, *Die feinen Unterschiede*: *Kritik der gesellschaftlichen Urteilskraft* (Frankfurt am Main: Suhrkamp, 1982 [1979]).

84 Warhol, *Philosophy*, p. 48; Bockris, *The Life and Death of Andy Warhol*, p. 318.

whose inhabitants lack any possibility of a critical standpoint that attempts to transcend the merely factual.

It is this erasure of the notion of a world structured by meaning, which takes place in the process of self-closure and self-elimination (or, if you like, self-emptying), the levelling of all differences and the equalization of all values, that can be understood as Warhol's scandalous truth. Far removed from the interventionism of the kynical Beuys, but related to him in his practice of a life that is public in its inaccessibility and hidden in its emptiness, Warhol as *idiota* pursues the practice of a centripetally organized and monosemantic art. It is monosemantic insofar as it revolves around a single theme: the absence of meaning; it is centripetal insofar as it is not interested in transgressions and interrogations of the concept of art, quite unlike Beuys.[85] At the same time, Warhol opens a new chapter in the history of the relationship between society and outsiders. Not only does he succeed in producing an enormous body of work, which constitutes the erasure of meaning, with a persona behind whose mask hides a person who simultaneously shows everything and hides everything, but also in producing a new incarnation of the outsider who is in the midst of society and is an integral part of society insofar as he is an outsider. The figure of jurodivyj, which Richardson thoroughly misunderstands, plays an equally catalytic role here as that of the *idiot savant*, as which Warhol is touted as.[86] His role as outsider[87] corresponds with the logic of the production of the new as a valorisation of the profane, which responds to the profanization of the sacred.[88] In the economy of values in the twentieth century, the outsider functions as an ambassador of what is supposedly new, which this

85 Warhol's *Invisible Sculpture* from 1985 may be an exception, but it was itself merely an outdated provocation.

86 Henry Geldzahler, 'Andy Warhol: A Memoir' in Geldzahler, *Making It New* (New York: Harcourt Brace Jovanovich, 1994), p. 43. The twist in the whole story, however, is that Warhol asks back what an 'idiot savant' is. It is thus hard to decide whether he is illiterate enough not to know what 'idiot savant' means, or whether he assumes the role of the idiot in order to counter it with his knowledge of foreign languages, albeit in the form of a supposed misunderstanding or mishearing.

87 See Fred Lawrence Guiles, *Loner at the Ball: The Life of Andy Warhol* (Nashville: Turner Publishing, 2022 [1989]), pp. 5–68.

88 Boris Groys, *Über das Neue* (Frankfurt am Main: Fischer, 2002 [1992]).

economy needs. The new is its fuel. In this respect, not only is Warhol dependent on it, but the public reacting to him is also interested in him maintaining his status as an outsider. In the early 1980s, when interest in his works and his person died out and when the novelty wore off, the gallery owner Bruno Bischofberger encouraged him to collaborate with Jean-Michel Basquiat (1960–88), who in turn entered the art scene as an outsider, a sprayer, a black artist, an autodidact, and quickly achieved cult status. Warhol benefited briefly from the young artist's outsider image, even if the collaboration did not last long, as Basquiat, possibly worried that he would be perceived as nothing more than a mascot for the older artist, distanced himself after the poor reviews of their 1985 exhibition.[89] In any case, it is true that outsider status is necessary in order to be successful and that, conversely, earning millions does not detract from outsider status. Thus Basquiat (he died of an overdose on 12 August 1988) could still function as a martyr of the art scene and as a paradigmatic outsider in 1989, although he was presented by the most powerful gallery owners in the Western world (Gagosian, Boone, Bischofberger) during his lifetime and was already represented at documenta in 1982 and at the Whitney Biennial in 1983.[90]

Paradoxically, the outsider thus finds himself in the midst of society. It produces him because it needs him as its other and as a representation of the new. Only in rare cases is the history of his integration actually one of tolerance. Much more often, however, it is one of the production and consumption of a commodity in the attention economy, in which the quality of the new can be financialized. To a certain extent, it is enough simply to claim the position of outsider in order to set the process of capitalization and financialization in motion. The outsider, whether in the form of the shaman or kynic or in the form of the *idiot savant*, the silent oracle, the meaningless sphinx, has been driving not only the economy of values in the field of culture since the 1980s, but also the economy of the art sector with enormous amounts of circulating capital.

---

89 See Phoebe Hoban, *Basquiat: A Quick Killing in Art* (New York: Viking, 1998), p. 266.

90 Paolo Bianchi, 'Outsidertum am Beispiel Basquiat' in *Kunstforum International* 101 (June 1989): 96–103.

CHAPTER NINE

# Punk

## Precursors

A great moment in media history: in 1974, Lou Reed, with yellow hair and sunglasses, answers questions from Australian journalists who want to elicit scandalous statements from the 'Rock 'n' Roll Animal'[1] with questions about drug use and sexual transgressions. Reed, sipping his drink in between, answers with a deadpan expression.

> What do you think you are? —Average. —Is your anti-social behaviour part of your show-business gimmick? —Anti-social behaviour? —You seem to be a man of very few words. Why is this? —I have nothing to say. —Do you like to talk to press people? —No. —Do you shun publicity? —No. —You tend to keep to yourself? —No. —What messages do you try to get across? —I don't have one. —To put it bluntly, are you a homosexual or a transvestite? —Sometimes. —Which one? —I don't know. What's the difference? —What do you like most in life? —Everything. —Is there anything you like better than others? —No.

And unsurprisingly, when asked whether Warhol still means anything to him, he replies: 'Oh yes. He is everything'.

Lou Reed was the singer and guitarist of the Velvet Underground, the band that played a decisive role in Warhol's gaining credibility as an underground artist before he squandered it as a society artist. The Velvet Underground was formed around 1964 with Lou Reed, Sterling Morrison, Angus MacLise, and John Cale. Maureen Tucker replaced Angus MacLise on drums in 1965, and from 1966, for the first album with the famous banana cover, Nico was a member of the band. Nico had something of a

1 This was the title of Lou Reed's 1974 album, on which he attempted to recapture his earlier success after the failure of *Berlin* with a number of cover versions of songs by the Velvet Underground.

reputation as a superstar, having appeared in a supporting role in Fellini's *La Dolce Vita* and having a child with Alain Delon, and it was Andy Warhol who persuaded her to sing on some songs despite opposition, particularly from Lou Reed. John Cale had studied composition at Goldsmiths College in London and was awarded a scholarship in 1963 to further his studies at the Tanglewood Music Center in Lenox, Massachusetts. After leaving Lenox, he went to New York to work with La Monte Young. Along with Young, his wife Marian Zazeela, and his roommate Tony Conrad, who would later have a decisive influence on the development of structural film with *The Flicker* (1965), John Cale was part of the 'Dream Syndicate', a formation which, alongside the aforementioned Angus MacLise, also included Jon Hassell, who would later become known for his extravagant trumpet playing as a soloist, but also in collaboration with Brian Eno and Talking Heads. Maureen Tucker, one of the best and most original drummers in the history of rock music, had no remarkable background, nor does she ever seem to have been interested in the idea of fame. In fact, after the Velvet Underground broke up, she preferred to look after her children and, later, grandchildren again. Sterling Morrison turned to his academic interests after the Velvet Underground finally disbanded in 1971 (with the exception of a brief reunion in 1992) and taught at the University of Texas at Austin. He died unexpectedly in 1995.

Andy Warhol was looking for a band to provide the music for his *Exploding Plastic Inevitable* project, and in 1965 the director Barbara Rubin pointed him in the direction of the band, which was beginning to cause a sensation with its deafening music and dark lyrics. *Exploding Plastic Inevitable* was what was later known as multimedia: Warhol simultaneously projected films and slides onto the wall behind the stage on which the band performed, accompanied by Gerard Malanga, who performed whip dances with Edie Sedgwick or Ingrid Superstar.[2] The show provoked enthusiastic and angry reactions; visitors threw bottles at the band, and the singer Cher said that the whole event could only be topped by one thing: suicide.[3]

---

2 Ronald Nameth, *Andy Warhol's Exploding Plastic Inevitable*, UbuWeb Films (1966), https://ubu.com/film/nameth_velvet.html.

3 Bockris, *The Life and Death of Andy Warhol*, p. 189.

The Velvet Underground became one of the most important precursor bands to punk, which was to change the music world from 1976 onwards. The complexity of the song structure was reduced and the volume level increased. The lyrics of Lou Reed's songs vary on themes such as sadomasochism, drug addiction, and mental disorientation, which may be due to autobiographical facts, as Reed had to undergo treatment as a teenager in which electric shocks were used.[4] Much more important than biographical references, however, is the Velvet Underground's affiliation to the long history of the art of forgetting, the conscious and intentional strategy of replacing mastery with immediacy and directness. Anyone who reads the lyrics of 'Heroin' ('I feel like Jesus' son / And I guess, I just don't know') or 'Venus in Furs' ('I am tired, I am weary / I could sleep for a thousand years / A thousand dreams that would awake me / Different colours made of tears') autobiographically overlooks the fact that the band was part of an art project and that its career was largely due to Warhol's influence.

In their sophisticated aesthetic, the music and stage performance disguise the difference between actual and staged authenticity, actual or merely staged not-knowing. The reduction of the songs to a few chords and the ambitious lyrics, which refer to Baudelaire, Sacher-Masoch, and Rimbaud, are due to an academically informed practice of the scandal of truth-telling, which, if not with truth, has a lot to do with truthfulness. However, the sound produced by the Velvet Underground is not in the tradition of the street, but in the tradition of the academy, which, weary of itself, is oriented towards its supposed opposite. John Cale had a major influence on this sound; it owes much more to La Monte Young's drone music, especially *Day of Niagara* from 1965, than to any variety of rock 'n' roll, from which Lou Reed came and to which he returned after John Cale left the band. There could be no bigger contrast than that between 'Heroin' and 'Sister Ray' (from the second album *White Light / White Heat*, released in 1968),[5] on the one hand, and 'Candy Says' or 'Jesus' from the third album, the first recorded without John Cale, on the other. Lou Reed set

4 Victor Bockris, *Transformer: The Lou Reed Story* (New York: Simon & Schuster, 1994), pp. 14–15.

5 'Sister Ray' is covered by Suicide on *Half Alive* (1981), which contains recordings from 1974 to 1979. Joy Division also covered the song.

out to become a rock star and on *The Blue Mask* from 1982 he flirted with stately anthems ('The Day John F. Kennedy Died') and long love songs including overwhelming sobs ('Heavenly Arms') as well as violent fantasies ('The Gun') and feedback orgies ('The Blue Mask'). This is not to evoke the conflict between Cale and Reed once again.[6] Cale was also able to skilfully combine crowd-pleasing madness performances with noisy rock. But it should be emphasized that Reed's contributions to the Velvet Underground were, on the one hand, decisive for what the band is remembered for; on the other hand, this episode in his biography is an exception: he came from rock 'n' roll and returned to it, whereas Cale, coming from avant-garde music, eventually ended up with pop and rock via drone music. However, it must also be mentioned that Reed, with *Metal Machine Music*, produced an album unlike any other in 1975: four sides of a double LP with feedback, without any rhythmic structure, without any human voice, without any melody. *Metal Machine Music* is certainly one of the most extreme productions of contemporary music and, influenced by La Monte Young himself, was of great importance for the later-emerging noise and industrial scene.

Cale turned to more conventional songwriting and producing for other bands; he produced *The Marble Index* for Nico in 1969 and *Horses* for Patti Smith in 1975. As early as 1969, however, he had already turned his attention to a band whose singer would later be declared the 'Godfather of Punk'. I am talking about the Stooges with their singer Iggy Pop.[7] Iggy Pop grew up as James Osterberg in Ann Arbor, Michigan, and came to music as the drummer in a band called the Iguanas. After a brief spell as a member of the blues band the Prime Movers and a stint in Chicago, he and brothers Scott and Ron Asheton formed the Psychedelic Stooges with bassist Dave Alexander, but quickly changed their name to the Stooges. The name goes back to the television comedy *The Three Stooges*, which,

---

6 For *Songs for Drella* (1990), they joined forces once again in honour of Andy Warhol.

7 The details below are taken from Paul Trynka, *Iggy Pop: Open Up and Bleed* (London: Sphere, 2009), digital edn; Legs McNeil and Gillian McCain, *Please Kill Me: The Uncensored Oral History of Punk* (New York: Penguin, 1996); Jeff Gold, *Total Chaos: The Story of the Stooges, as Told by Iggy Pop* (New York: Third Man Books, 2020).

like Laurel and Hardy, was known for physical slapstick and a robust sense of humour. A comedy of the same title and similarly bad taste was released in 2012. The band's first gig was in Detroit in January 1968, followed by concerts as a supporting act for the MC5, Blood, Sweat and Tears, and Cream. By the time the band broke up, two more albums (*Fun House* and *Raw Power*) had been released alongside *The Stooges*; Pop then pursued a solo career, which brought him into contact with Lou Reed, whom he admired, and, more importantly, with David Bowie, when both lived in Berlin from 1976 to 1978. Pop and Bowie briefly shared a flat at Schöneberger Hauptstraße 155. Pop recorded *The Idiot* in Berlin, produced and partly co-written by Bowie. Bowie had produced Reed's 1972 album *Transformer* and played *White Light / White Heat* from the Velvet Underground's second album at his own concerts. The cover of *The Idiot* shows Pop in a nocturnal scene, in a pose reminiscent of a self-portrait by Egon Schiele.[8]

When James Osterberg shaved off his eyebrows before his first appearance with the Stooges in 1968, it was a reference to an acquaintance who had lost all his hair due to a nerve disease. His name was Jim Pop, and James Osterberg took his surname from then on. Pop's early performances established his fame as a personification of pre-punk: he threw up on stage, exposed his genitals, doused himself in alcohol, smeared peanut butter over his body, rolled in broken glass, and cut up his (always bare) chest. A photograph by James Fortune, later chosen as the cover image for *California Bleeding*, a live album by the Stooges, shows the bleeding Pop in the Whisky a Go Go in Hollywood in 1974. His drug addiction was in stark contrast to his athletic appearance, which he still maintains today.[9]

---

8 Allegedly, when Ian Curtis, the singer of Joy Division, hanged himself on 18 May 1980, *The Idiot* was on the turntable.

9 This importance of demonstrating physical fitness (at least on a visual level) correlates with the importance that the kynics attached to health. See Foucault, *Der Mut zur Wahrheit*, p. 363. Maybe also the title of his collection of lyrics, *'Til Wrong Feels Right* (New York, 2019), and the lyrics of songs like 'I Wanna Be Your Dog' (1969) or 'King of the Dogs' (2009) point not only in the direction of inversion, but of kynic inversion.

After Pop had seen how Jim Morrison, the singer of the Doors, insulted his audience,[10] he realized that performances were also possible in which negative or angry reactions from the audience not only served as publicity, but could also be integrated into the performance as a genuine component. Ultimately, the aim was to present concerts as the entirety of the interaction between audience and performers, which means nothing other than the dissolution of the separation between performer and spectator. An important means in this dissolution of the boundary between audience and performer, between stage and auditorium, was stage diving, which Pop practised like his role model Morrison and which was later integrated into shows by both punk musicians and established stadium-music greats such as Peter Gabriel ('Lay Your Hands on Me', 1982). Pop's ranting tirades were also ultimately an expression of the idea of the equal status of performer and listener or an ethic of equality, which in punk meant that every listener who made it onto the stage was accepted, while efforts by security to clear the stage of excited listeners were sometimes prevented by the members of the bands. Everyone is allowed to fight with everyone.

From 1976 onwards, however, something else began in England that was not limited to music, but referred to itself as a practice: punk. Like the music of the Velvet Underground, punk was not simply a derivative of rock 'n' roll, but a movement originating in British art schools that encompassed music, fashion, design, typography, music production and distribution, and thus also a new economic model of reaching out into society. Punk is generally considered to have been born with the release of the Sex Pistols' single 'Anarchy in the UK' on 26 November 1976. However, alongside the Velvet Underground and Iggy Pop, punk had its forerunners such as the Ramones, the New York Dolls, who were important for glam rock, and the Modern Lovers, whose song 'Pablo Picasso' was later covered by John Cale. He also produced their first album, which was recorded between 1971 and 1972 but not released until 1976.[11]

---

10 Jim Morrison not only insulted his audience, but also allegedly exhibited his genitals on stage. Revered as a shaman by his fans, he died in Paris on 3 July 1971, possibly from a heroin overdose or a drug cocktail, and it was Iggy Pop whom the public saw as his shamanistic successor, and who accepted this role, for example in a 1983 interview with Ron Young: https://www.youtube.com/watch?v=bzsts5h3Be0.

11 'Pablo Picasso' was also covered by Iggy Pop, David Bowie, Simple Minds and Jack White. The original line-up of the Modern Lovers included Jerry Harrison, who would

The literature on the Sex Pistols and their spiritus rector, Malcolm McLaren, fills shelves and need not be dealt with here. What is decisive is that the Sex Pistols, like the Velvet Underground, were an art product that originated in the academy and owed its enduring virulence to its anti-academic impulse, which was compatible with clearly formulated economic interests.[12] Punk was possibly also the protest of the street against an elitist public or against an economy from which its members had been excluded; but punk was also, and maybe even more often, an art practice aimed at revolt and provocation, at crossing boundaries and scandal and thus completely in line with the ideology of twentieth-century avant-garde art.[13]

Just as the Asheton brothers got their inspiration from attending a Who concert where they witnessed Pete Townshend smash his guitar—a performance that was in turn influenced by Gustav Metzger's Auto-destructive art, from which Townshend had taken ideas as an art student at Ealing Art College after Metzger had given a lecture there in December 1962[14]—punk owes its existence to the auto-subversive impetus of the avant-garde, which was directed against its own position. Since the beginning of the twentieth century, mainstream and outside can no longer be understood as oppositions, but as the two sides of a certain social situation, or, to put it another way, as the two sides of a distinction. There is no longer an outside that influences the mainstream, but rather a diversified whole whose details are seen by observers as ordinary or unusual, as conforming or non-conforming, as conventional or unconventional. If you

later become famous as a guitarist with 'Talking Heads. The single 'Roadrunner' from their first album was covered by the Sex Pistols in 1975.

12 Simon Reynolds, *Totally Wired: Postpunk Interviews and Overviews* (New York: Catapult, 2010), p. 377.

13 'My name is Malcolm McLaren. In my time I have brought you many things. Teddy Boy revivalism, zoot suits, sex clothes, bondage, whips, chains, the whole bloody lot [ . . . ]. But the most successful of all was an invention of mine they called [ . . . ] Punk Rock'. Malcolm McLaren, quoted in Paul Gorman, *The Life & Times of Malcolm McLaren* (London: Little, Brown, 2020).

14 See Kunsthalle Nürnberg (ed.), *Gustav Metzger: Ein Schnitt entlang der Zeit* (Nuremberg: Verlag für moderne Kunst, 1999), p. 12. After Metzger's death on 2 March 2017, Townshend in a series of obituaries pointed out the importance that Metzger had had for him. See also Pete Townshend, 'Gustav Metzger 1926–2017' (2 March 2017): https://www.thewho.com/petes-blog/gustav-metzger-1926-2017/.

follow the incredibly rapidly unfolding history of punk, it becomes clear how new orthodoxies and deviations, catholicisms and heresies were constantly being produced at an almost incomprehensible speed. Subversions of subversion and transmutations of revolt were formulated and practised in ever-new incarnations, the idiosyncrasies of which were comprehensible only to the initiated. The wrong leather jacket for the wrong concert, the wrong badge with the wrong haircut at the wrong time, gay or lesbian among straight people or the other way round—and you were already an outsider in a community that defined itself as opposition to society through its outsider-ness.

The thesis that it was the art world that needed punk, and that it was punk that needed the art world, can be illustrated by a simple vignette:

Brian Eno left Roxy Music in 1973, after which he devoted himself to solo projects and produced albums such as *Taking Tiger Mountain (By Strategy)* (1974) and *Before and After Science* (1977). *Taking Tiger Mountain* not only contains 'Third Uncle', a song that anticipates punk energy, but also a track like 'The True Wheel' with a two-note solo, for which the Buzzcocks would become famous three years later (1977) with 'Boredom' on *Spiral Scratch*. *Before and After Science* contains the song 'King's Lead Hat', which on the one hand operates with the simplicity familiar from the Velvet Underground, but whose title on the other is an anagram of Talking Heads. Brian Eno went on to produce Talking Heads, also an art-school product, from their first album in 1977 to *Remain in Light* from 1980. Eno's affinity to punk (and eventually to post-punk) is demonstrated by the LP *No New York*, which he produced in 1978, and on which, among others, groups such as the Contortions, Mars, and DNA, of which Arto Lindsay was a member, are represented. Eno's 'Kurt's Rejoinder' on *Before and After Science* features a recording of Kurt Schwitters' *Ursonate*. When Talking Heads recorded *Fear of Music* in 1979, they played a song that was completely out of place in the context of the album: *I Zimbra*, which paraphrases the text of Hugo Ball's 1916 poem 'Gadji beri bimba'. Needless to say, the madman and the psychotic play an important role in both 'Psycho Killer' from 1977 and 'Cross-Eyed and Painless' from 1980.

Another vignette concerns the recourse of parts of the punk and post-punk scene to Dadaist anti-cultural revolt figures who had become canonical. In the 1970s, the band Pere Ubu, which otherwise could not be classified as belonging to any particular style, was consistently and commercially unsuccessful for decades and was associated with Talking Heads and DNA in terms of personnel and artiness.[15] The only thing that remained stable was the presence of singer David Thomas.[16] Founded in 1975 in Cleveland, Ohio, the band initially performed cover versions of the Stooges, the Velvet Underground, and MC5 due to a lack of their own material. Alongside David Thomas, it was keyboardist Allen Ravenstine, in particular, who drove Pere Ubu towards experimental, sometimes poppy, sometimes noisy, sometimes weird, sometimes dark no-wave music. Pere Ubu's band name is a reference to the famous play of the same name by Alfred Jarry (1873–1907), which was written by the fifteen-year-old schoolboy in Rennes and premiered in Paris in 1896. In five acts, it tells the story of the Polish usurper 'Father' Ubu, who murders King Venceslas, takes his place, disempowers the nobility and at the same time harasses the people by increasing taxes at a horrendous rate. Finally, after the people rise up against him, Père Ubu and his mother leave for France.

The play was both a success with audiences and a scandal. One critic wrote:

> Basically, King Ubu is nothing but a tissue of scantiness, with the exorbitant faecal spews of a shallow mind. Ubu plots, kills the king, makes himself king, is in turn overthrown and flees by ship; he is dirty, uncouth, greedy, avaricious, gray, and cowardly. That is all.[17]

---

15 See Simon Reynolds, *Rip It Up and Start Again: Postpunk 1978–1984* (New York: Penguin, 2005), CHAP. 5.

16 He sadly passed away on 23 April 2025.

17 Paul Souday, quoted from Alfred Jarry, *König Ubu: Drama in fünf Aufzügen*, translated and edited by Ulrich Bossier (Ditzingen: Reclam, 1996), pp. 71–72. The success of the play was also Jarry's curse. He identified more and more with his artificial character, whose way of speaking he imitated and in whose name he signed letters. Jarry died on 1 November 1907 as a result of alcoholism and meningitis.

Alfred Jarry's second important work, *Gestes et opinions du docteur Faustroll*, was published posthumously in full in 1911. Its reception did not begin until after the Second World War and continued until the 1980s. The book, which obviously alludes to the literary tradition of Dr Faustus, propagates a parodistic science dedicated, for example, to problems such as measuring the surface of God. In 1948, the writers Raymond Queneau and Boris Vian founded the 'Collège de 'Pataphysique', dedicated to this caricature of science, to which Marcel Duchamp, Max Ernst, and Jean Dubuffet, among others, belonged from 1960 to 1965, probably through Queneau's mediation.[18]

## Punk, Industrial, and *Geniale Dilettanten*

The word 'punk' first appeared in English in the late sixteenth century. It describes, among other things, a prostitute, something worthless and lowly, the passive partner in a homosexual constellation, a stupid, naive, or foolish person or, for whatever reason, an untrained circus elephant.[19] It is therefore a word whose range of meanings goes far beyond what it has denoted since the 1970s—a certain form of aggressive, fast, loud music, produced and received by people with studded belts, mohawks, and safety pins in their ears and cheeks, who hang around in big cities in front of supermarkets and brazenly beg passers-by for money, provoke fights, get into brawls, and consume alcohol. The punk is the one who pushes an old woman down the stairs and shouts after her: 'Hey grandma, why are you walking so fast?' He is a malicious, antisocial being who resists integration into society with a repulsive appearance, shocking behaviour, and cynical humour. At the same time, punk is more than just the name of a particularly loud and fast variation of rock 'n' roll, it is more than just a form of music, a particular way of dressing or wearing your hair; rather, it is the name for

---

18 Alfred Jarry, *Œuvres complètes*, VOL. 1 (Paris, 1976), pp. 619–734. Ilse Pollack, *Pataphysik, Symbolismus und Anarchismus bei Jarry, Junge Wiener Romanistik* 6 (Hans Hinterhäuser ed.) (Vienna, Cologne and Graz: Böhlau, 1984), especially pp. 169–91. See the letter to Renato Barilli (15 February 1960) in Dubuffet, *Prospectus et tous les écrits suivants*, VOL. 2, p. 328.

19 Thomas Lau, *Die heiligen Narren: Punk 1976–1986* (Berlin and New York: De Gruyter, 1992), p. 9.

a way of life that, while also encompassing a certain taste in music or a certain form of fashion, also includes a certain way of living everyday life. This life is also a life in public: the punk hanging out in front of a store is something more than a sponger. He is also the personification, perceived as a nuisance, of an attitude in which the traditional values of post-industrial England or Germany (or other countries of the global North) are rejected. Neither interested in inversion nor working on the revaluation of values, punk, in its discursive, sub-proletarian malice and impertinence, represents the desire for a third that does not seek its goal in the formulation of an Other to the respective social situation, not in dialectical counter-positioning, but rather points, largely without theorization, to the possibility or necessity of a third that, in doing so, is not much more than something inconceivable, an emptiness, a void. And it remains so. This is the much-criticized apolitical nature of punk: it devises no concept and has no programme. There is no manifesto for the liberation of any class whatsoever, even if belonging to or being part of the proletariat, if that at all existed at the end of the 1970s, was part of what was considered punk. The disrespectful attitude towards the bourgeoisie and whoever cooperated with the art world and big business did not reveal any political orientation. The punks did fight with skinheads, but otherwise they threw the Marxist convictions of the left overboard and cultivated a strategy of non-distinction. The hippie was as despicable as the yuppie, the eco as disgusting as the bank employee: from a punk perspective, they were all united by the mistaken notion that society, as it was, only needed to be configured correctly for everything to change for the better. And that was precisely what punk was against. The famous slogan, 'No Future', is not a comfortable nihilistic attitude that indulges in negativism. Repeated ad nauseam, it is rooted in the context of a conception of time that is closely linked to the question of the perfectibility of the world and can, somewhat pretentiously but rightly, be described as late-period consciousness.[20] If time no longer played a role for St Francis, because the true world was redeemed and the one in which he lived was only its calcifying reflection, protruding into time, unwinding meaninglessly, then the world of punk is one that is irredeemably far removed from any perfectibility and whose survival is irrelevant.

20 Niehues-Pröbsting, *Der Kynismus*, p. 314.

The punk is lost to the world like the Poverello and his disciples or Daimonides' 'distinguished foreigner', but he lacks the certainty of transcendence that strengthened the Franciscans and the Russian jurodivyj in their actions.

Punk does not have a positive vision; in fact, it has no vision at all. Or it is missing the clarity of a faith that can also be formulated as theology and is only somewhat traceable, in its negative form, in the rage, the noise, the asocial behaviour, and in the anger and pain that one inflicts on oneself and others. Moreover, even if punk had no vision, its followers had an inkling of the hell they staged as pleasure-pain performances in public, with the ethos of despisers of worldly goods, as voluntary paupers and beggars, as homeless, and as misfits.

There was also punk in Germany before 1977. Big Balls & The Great White Idiot performed in Hamburg as early as 1975, followed by PVC in 1977 and a band called Dirty Needs a year later.[21] Role models were the Ramones, the Velvet Underground, and the Stooges (Big Balls & The Great White Idiot covered both *White Light / White Heat* by the Velvet Underground and 'Search and Destroy' by the Stooges on their 1977 LP *Big Balls*). The centre of West German punk was Düsseldorf with the Ratinger Hof. Hamburg and West Berlin, later Frankfurt, Limburg an der Lahn, and Munich also played a role, as did East Berlin in the GDR, then Leipzig, Dresden, and Halle with groups such as the art-student punk band Zwitschermaschine (Twittering Machine), named after a painting by Paul Klee from 1922, or Schleim-Keim (Slime-Germ), which formed in 1980 in Stotternheim near Erfurt.[22] In the West, bands such as S.Y.P.H., Charleys Girls, Mittagspause, DIN-A-Testbild, Liaisons Dangereuses, ZK, or Stukka Pilots, and others were formed in quick succession and disbanded again; there were a number of overlaps and double engagements.[23] Even before

21 Gerrit Meijer, 'Punk ist erledigt' in Jacek Slaski, *Gespräche mit Genialen Dilletanten* (Berlin: Merve, 2018), pp. 59–62; here, pp. 59–60.

22 On punk in the GDR, see Ronald Galenza and Heinz Havemeister (eds), *Wir wollen immer artig sein . . . Punk, New Wave, HipHop und Independent-Szene in der DDR von 1980 bis 1990* (Berlin: Schwarzkopf & Schwarzkopf, 1999). Florian Lipp, *Punk und New Wave im letzten Jahrzehnt der DDR* (Münster: Waxmann, 2021).

23 See Cyrus Shahan, *Punk Rock and German Crisis: Adaptation and Resistance after 1977* (New York: Springer, 2013), p. 12. See Diedrich Diederichsen, 'Genies und ihre

punk reached its full force in 1980, some of its protagonists, such as Peter Hein from Fehlfarben, had already expressed their displeasure at where punk was heading. The famous line 'It's too late for the old movements' from the 1980 Fehlfarben single 'Abenteuer & Freiheit' (Adventure & Freedom), which some thought could refer to the hippies, already pointed to punk. Many of the most important protagonists, such as Holger Hiller or Peter Hein, disappeared into smaller projects or left the country, while some multiplied their commitments and filled several roles at the same time. Gudrun Gut, co-founder of Einstürzende Neubauten and member of Mania D. and Malaria, for example, devoted herself to a variety of professions as a DJ, label manager, radio presenter, and festival organizer.

Punk was accompanied by a tremendous unleashing of creativity. New record labels were founded, new fashion was invented, fanzines were cobbled together, there was the wonderful format of the cassette compilation, magazines such as *Spex* in Germany were launched and survived into the 2000s.[24] It goes without saying that many of the labels and magazines went the way of everything secular in capitalism: they disappeared or were sooner or later integrated into the logic of the production of cognitive capital. This also corresponds to the regularity of the interaction between the mainstream and the outside: in the dialectical process of observing observation, society designs and produces the Other in communication about itself and integrates this supposed Other into the social and thus also economic process as the New.

A special role was played in Germany by the TV show *Hitparade*, whose programme was based on sales figures of German-language songs from the mid-1970s onwards. Although no German-language punk bands appeared in the *Hitparade*, bands from the Neue Deutsche Welle (NDW) soon did, which on the one hand increased its popularity and freed it from the mustiness of Schlager, but on the other hand accelerated the commercialization of post-punk and NDW. While bands such as Ideal or

---

Geräusche: Deutscher Punk und Neue Welle 1978–1982' in Mathilde Weh and Leonhard Emmerling (eds), *Geniale Dilletanten* (Ostfildern: Hatje Cantz, 2015), pp. 10–22.

24 *Spex* announced its own end on 15 December 2021 due to the coronavirus pandemic.

D.A.F. stayed away from the *Hitparade*, Trio, for example, used the TV show as a stage and presented their minimal music with children's guitars, cheap Casios, and Dadaist nonsense lyrics ('Da Da Da; Lass mich rein, lass mich raus'; Da Da Da, let me in, let me out), which in turn contributed to the flattening of NDW towards nonsensical fun culture with bands such as Hubert Kah and UKW, while provoking puffed-up pseudo-relevant songs such as '99 Luftballons' by Nena. The liaison between television, Schlager, and NDW ultimately led to the format of sing-alongs compatible with the mainstream such as 'Alles hat ein Ende, nur die Wurst hat zwei' (Everything has an end, only the sausage has two; Stephan Remmler, 1987), which finally suffocated punk in the drivel and booze of the carnival.

Punk had various derivatives and parallel phenomena. Bands such as NoMeansNo (from 1979), the Jesus and Mary Chain (from 1983), the Pixies (from 1986), or Fugazi (from 1987) developed punk further in the direction of hardcore, straight edge, or shoegaze, each genre in turn quickly splintering into a multitude of sub-genres before a new mainstream was established with grunge. For the present text, not all of these varieties and styles are equally interesting, but industrial and Geniale Dilletanten are.

Industrial formed almost at the same time as punk. An important band that can be described as the incubator of industrial music is Throbbing Gristle, but there are precursors such as Cabaret Voltaire, whose name refers to the Zurich cabaret and who also released songs such as 'The Dada Man', in which they prove themselves to be pioneers of *bruitisme* by means of electronic music. In 1970, the duo Suicide formed, producing a bizarre and dark mixture of the Velvet Underground and rockabilly with drum machines and cheap synthesizers on the one hand and Elvis Presley-inspired vocals on the other. Exotic phenomena such as Laibach from Yugoslavia or SPK from Australia complete the picture. SPK is named after the Socialist Patients' Collective, which was founded in 1970 at the Psychiatric Clinic of Heidelberg University, the clinic that houses the collection compiled by Prinzhorn and named after him. Motivated by the conviction that a pathogenic society itself needed healing before subjecting outsiders to sometimes drastic therapeutic measures, the therapy community was formed by patients and doctors under the leadership of the physician Wolfgang Huber. Jean-Paul Sartre contributed the foreword to their manifesto *Turn Illness into a Weapon*. Due to the suspicion that members of the collective were RAF supporters, houses were searched, and this resulted in shootings and arrests, leading to convictions and in some cases long prison sentences.[25]

SPK made an important contribution to the formation of industrial, but from 1986 onwards developed the pseudo-religious and speculative form of music of ostensibly Byzantine provenance, which is recorded by Graeme Revell, who alone is behind SPK. He had already performed with Tödliche Doris at SO 36 in Berlin in 1982. Four years later he released an album with interpretations of Adolf Wölfli's compositions.[26]

What distinguishes Throbbing Gristle from Laibach or SPK is their massive, deeply disturbing irreconcilability. As early as 1969, Genesis P-Orridge founded the artist collective COUM Transmissions, to which Cosey Fanni Tutti later belonged.[27] The scandalous and perfectly orchestrated exhibition *Prostitution* at the Institute of Contemporary Arts in London (1976) enabled them to establish and consolidate their reputation as highly provocative. The exhibition caused a scandal in the press and in Parliament and led to the loss of their government grant. In an article in the magazine *Studio International* (July–August 1976), P-Orridge and COUM member Peter Christopherson refer not only to de Sade and Aleister Crowley, but also to the Viennese actionists and Hugo Ball in an attempt to situate their work in a tradition.

After the *Prostitution* exhibition, P-Orridge and Fanni Tutti go on tour in the USA, where they perform five versions of *Cease to Exist* in Chicago, Los Angeles, and Santa Monica. *Cease to Exist* takes its title from

25 Christian Pross, with Sonja Schweitzer and Julia Wagner, *Wir wollten ins Verderben rennen: Die Geschichte des Sozialistischen Patientenkollektivs Heidelberg* (Cologne: Psychiatrie Verlag, 2016). See *Sozialistisches Patientenkollektiv: SPK—Aus der Krankheit eine Waffe machen. Eine Agitationsschrift des Sozialistischen Patientenkollektivs an der Universität Heidelberg, mit einem Vorwort von Jean-Paul Sartre*, 5th EDN (Heidelberg, 1987).

26 Bauhaus also referred to Wölfli with the cover of the LP *In the Flat Field* (1980), which shows a naked man with a paper trumpet.

27 Simon Ford, *The Wreckers of Civilisation* (London: Black Dog Press, 1999).

a song by Charles Manson. What they performed surpasses the actions of the Viennese actionists in terms of the extremes they go to.[28] On stage, the two inflict injuries on their genitals, vomit, urinate, and defecate on stage, and practise sexual intercourse in the mixture of blood, mucus, excrement, and vomit that spreads across the floor.

The post-Throbbing Gristle self-aggrandizement by P-Orridge and Fanni Tutti into a cult à la Charles Manson (Thee Temple ov Psychick Youth) implodes relatively quickly. P-Orridge and his partner Lady Jaye devote themselves to the creation of a non-binary, pandrogynous gender identity from 2000 onwards (he dies in 2020), while Cosey Fanni Tutti now makes harmless synth-pop with her partner Chris Carter.

What COUM Transmissions or Throbbing Gristle or Temple of Psychick Youth do is by no means appreciated by punk. The links to the art scene and the fact that many performances are clearly in the tradition of radical art experiments, which COUM Transmissions had reduced to sex, meet with a cultivated boredom within the art milieu on the one hand and an allergic reaction from punk on the other, whose supporters see their performative behaviour as nothing more than an attempt to pander to the establishment. The fact that most of the appearances and performances by COUM Transmissions or Throbbing Gristle take place in art contexts certainly justifies the assumption on the part of punk that P-Orridge and his comrades-in-arms are by no means taking the diametrically opposed position that they claim for themselves, but basically just want to use the medium of scandal to buy themselves an entry ticket into the art milieu.

Alongside industrial, the Geniale Dilletanten were the second, somewhat delayed parallel phenomenon that is important in the context of this book. Although inspired by music and fashion in the USA and Great Britain, and being internationally connected, it is limited to Germany—but interestingly to both parts of Germany. The scene is difficult to narrow down. Despite the fact that the musicians in Düsseldorf and Hamburg come from the art milieu, they get along well with the left-wing riot punks. The Berlin scenes are more clearly separated from each other, probably

---

28 Ford, *The Wreckers of Civilisation*, pp. 30ff.

also simply because the milieus are less dependent on each other due to the greater choice of possible meeting places.[29] In general, there has been a close intertwining of dilletantes and the art scene from the beginning to the present; the central figure at the beginning is Martin Kippenberger, who had already organized a dilletante action in 'Kippenbergers Büro / Kippenberger's office' in 1978 with Mania D. and Mittagspause, among others, which was followed a year later by a second one with Pisskrücke in Hamburg. Kippenberger played with A. R. Penck in various bands, as did Markus Oehlen (Mittagspause) and Werner Büttner (Männer in nassen Kleidern). Carmen Knoebel, the wife of Beuys' student Imi Knoebel, runs the 'Pure Freude' / 'Pure Joy' label in Düsseldorf, and the members of F.S.K. in Munich, who come from underground journalism, now represent important positions in the art and literature scene: Michaela Melián as an artist and professor who has won numerous prizes, Thomas Meinecke as an author at Suhrkamp, and Justin Hoffmann as an art critic and curator in Wolfsburg.

After Einstürzende Neubauten formed rather by chance in 1980, they were invited to the Paris Biennale and documenta just one year after the release of their first LP *Kollaps*.[30] In 1983, they refer to the works of the Gugging artist Oswald Tschirtner with *Drawings of Patient O. T.* This was followed by a series of publications such as *Halber Mensch* (Half Man) (1985) and *Haus der Lüge* (House of Lies) (1989). The band quickly became the epitome of radical and experimental German post-punk music, in part due to their collaboration with Peter Zadek and Heiner Müller, to which Bargeld's rolling Rs, his haunting whispers, and the cult of apocalypse, which is reflected in his cleverly constructed lyrics, certainly contributed. Like the music, which increasingly relies on sampling and keyboards instead of steel and jackhammers and consists of ever more finely organized

29 Diederichsen, 'Genies und ihre Geräusche' in Weh and Emmerling (eds), *Geniale Dilletanten*, pp. 10–22; here, p. 18.

30 On the back of the cover, Neubauten re-stage the famous shot on the back cover of Pink Floyd's double LP *Ummagumma*, released in 1969. The hostile relationship between punk and the dilletantes, on the one hand, and bands such as Yes, Genesis, Pink Floyd and other protagonists of laser-show stadium rock with double-necked guitars and keyboard fortresses, on the other, is well known.

sound architectures, the texts also develop into elegantly built structures of meaning that often work with mishearing ('Meta Meta Meter' in *Interimsliebenden* on *Tabula Rasa*, 1993) or the homophony of words, such as Geschoss (floor) and Geschoss (projectile) in *Haus der Lüge*. The song begins with the deaf, the blind, and the madman whose hands are in his lap. After the passage through the house, in whose attic God shoots himself, he returns to the basement and to the beginning: 'This is a cellar / Here I live / This here is dark / Moist and pleasant / This here is a womb'.

Bargeld (actually Christian Emmerich) takes his name from the Dadaist Johannes Theodor Baargeld (1892–1927), who published the pamphlet *die schammade* (*dilettanten erhebt euch*!) (the shammade [dilettants rise]) with Max Ernst in 1920. The fact that the dilettantism of the Geniale Dilletanten has its predecessor in Dadaism is not only suggested by this name change but in particular by the sense of the grotesque and absurd. This is addressed by the Neubauten in complete seriousness and the grand tragic gesture, but with irony, lightness, and, simultaneously, conceptual consistency by Wolfgang Müller, Nikolaus Utermöhlen, and Käthe Kruse of the Tödliche Doris. On 4 September 1981, Müller organized the 'Festival of Geniale Dilletanten' at the Tempodrom in Berlin, the subtitle of which was 'The Great Doom Show'. The play with apocalypse and doom, which characterizes punk and post-punk as well as the Dilletanten in equal measure, and which in retrospect has something of the coquettish and the pleasure of the romanticism of ruins about it, has its real background in the NATO Double-Track Decision of 12 December 1979 and the escalating rearmament, which is perceived as even more life-threatening in the city of Berlin, encircled by a wall, than in the rest of the Federal Republic, which is still suffering from the after-effects of the German Autumn of 1977 and the effects of terrorism on the one hand, dragnet investigations and the poisoned political atmosphere on the other. The fear of a nuclear emergency is real: 'It was a total end-of-time atmosphere [ . . . ]. I didn't seriously believe at the time that I would turn 18. [ . . . ] We were really convinced that the world was going to end'.[31]

31 Neubauten member Alexander Hacke, quoted from Weh and Emmerling, *Geniale Dilletanten*, p. 138.

In his text *Die wahren Dilletanten* (The True Dilettantes),[32] Wolfgang Müller refers to Johann Wolfgang von Goethe and his concept of dilettantism. Müller criticizes Goethe for judging dilettantism too negatively, overlooking the fact that in misreading and misspeaking, in misunderstanding and mis-linking, stuttering and omitting words, lies the possibility of finding and producing something new that cannot be made possible by intention. What Müller is referring to is a collection of notes from 1799, which Johann Wolfgang von Goethe and Friedrich Schiller used to prepare a text for the *Propylaea*, but which was never published. The concept of dilettantism has had a varied career since then. Most writers have followed the path of criticism of dilettantism laid out by the two friends and have predominantly seen the phenomenon as a symptom of laxity and decadence.[33] Schiller links dilettantism with sentimentalism, which he believes is a tendency to 'melt'. This melting in turn, as he illustrates with the example of concert-goers, obviously has a quite disconcerting effect:

> Everything that melts is preferred. [ . . . ] An expression of sensuality that goes as far as the animal then usually appears on all faces, the drunken eyes swim, the open mouth is all desire [ . . . ], in short, all the symptoms of intoxication appear. [ . . . ] All these stirrings, I say, are excluded from art by a noble and masculine taste, because they please only the senses, with which art has nothing to do.[34]

---

32 Wolfgang Müller, *Geniale Dilletanten* (Berlin: Merve, 1982), p. 9.

33 A history of the oscillation of the term can be found in Michael Wieler, *Dilettantismus—Wesen und Geschichte; am Beispiel von Heinrich und Thomas Mann* (Würzburg: Königshausen & Neumann, 1995). See also Julia Kerscher, *Autodidaktik, Artistik, Medienpraktik: Erscheinungsweisen des Dilettantismus bei Karl Philipp Moritz, Carl Einstein und Thomas Bernhard* (Göttingen: Vandenhoeck & Ruprecht, 2016), pp. 31–94. See also Hans Rudolf Vaget, *Dilettantismus und Meisterschaft* (Munich: Fink, 1971). See also Georg Stanitzek, 'Dilettantismus' in Klaus Weimar et al. (eds), *Reallexikon der deutschen Literaturwissenschaft*, VOL. 1 (Berlin and New York: De Gruyter, 2007), pp. 354–66. The members of the British 'Society of Dilettanti', which was founded in 1734, were not committed to their own pleasure, but to educating the population in the sense of classical education. See Lionel Cust, *History of the Society of Dilettanti* (London: Macmillan, 1898).

34 Friedrich Schiller, 'Über das Pathetische' in *Sämtliche Werke* (Gerhard Fricke and Herbert G. Göpfert eds), VOL. 5 (Munich: Hanser, 1989), pp. 512–37; here, p. 516.

As these and similar passages and the notes on dilettantism suggest, Schiller and Goethe are concerned with preventing art from being entirely subjective by drifting into the merely sentimental, irrational, and emotional. Instead, they demand the knowledge and application of rules:

> One may assume that art must also be learned and practised according to rules, even though these rules, like those of a craft, are not fully recognized and the laws of the so-called liberal arts are only intellectual and not civil.[35]

In the dilettante's case, perception immediately leads to the desire for production, a fact that distinguishes the dilettante from the genius: the latter avoids any form of imitation. In this sense, the (genius) artist's relationship to the dilettante is similar to that between craftsmanship and bungling. 'Because the dilettante only receives his vocation for self-production from the effects of the works of art on himself, he confuses these effects with the objective causes and motives [ . . . ]. Art gives itself laws and commands time. Dilettantism follows the tendency of the time'.[36] Schiller and Goethe concede, however, that where the subjective itself is important in the arts, for example in poetry, dance, or music, the dilettante can approach true art, even if he is unable to follow the objective rules.

What Goethe and Schiller clearly intend is to work against the 'subjective aberrations'[37] in the production and reception of art. In the knowledge that a canon can no longer be cemented,[38] they attempt to counter the 'wrong direction'[39] in which art is at risk of moving unless the bunglers and the incompetent are reined in. Although genius is a natural gift, it requires discipline and diligence as well as the acquisition of knowledge. Only knowledge and skills hone the talented person into a genius, the antithesis of which is the dilettante.

---

35 Quoted from *Goethes Werke*, VOL. 43 (Stuttgart and Tübingen: Cotta, 1833), pp. 256–85; here, pp. 256–57.

36 *Goethes Werke*, VOL. 43, p. 262.

37 *Goethes Werke*, VOL. 43, p. 277.

38 See Vaget, *Dilettantismus*, p. 214.

39 *Goethes Werke*, VOL. 43, p. 260.

The emergence of the aesthetics outlined by Goethe and Schiller is closely linked to the rise of a society based on merit rather than traditional privileges, transforming itself from stratification into the functionally diversified society of modernity. This is why Goethe and Schiller place so much emphasis on the element of work, the acquisition of skills, and study. The *sprezzatura* reserved for the aristocracy, the casual disposal of one's own time, which can be filled with dabbling at the piano or at the easel, belongs to the past with the emergence of bourgeois society, based on the division of labour and on establishing a strict economy of time.[40] In this respect, it is true that the problem of dilettantism marks a 'breaking point of modernity',[41] at which it is decided whether or not the rationality of the division of labour and methods of production is able to establish itself as a value.

There is therefore a close connection between the provocation of the punk, who can master but three chords on his guitar, and the ethos of the bourgeoisie and its time regime: the punk is not only uneducated, ugly, degenerate, and unkempt; he also tries to resist the administration of his world and the dictatorship of a society based on the economic maximization of utility and time. Dilettantes and punks counter the ethos of industriousness with the assertion that it is not the citizen, but they, the bunglers, who correspond to the image of the 'whole person' that Schiller speaks of, whereas the citizen ekes out a pseudo-existence as half a person.[42]

Moreover, the provocation of dilettantism and punk is that their ethos is not one of merit, but of gift. One has the ability to do something—be it music or fashion, design or art, literature or theatre—not because of the training of skills, but because this ability is given to every individual as part of their own humanity. One does not need to know anything, but always already knows how to do, whereby not knowing leads to not wanting to know, to make possible what Frieder Butzmann talks about: 'What we

40 See Uwe Wirth, 'Strategischer Dilettantismus' in *Neue Rundschau* (2017), pp. 7–25; here, p. 8.

41 Georg Stanitzek, 'Über Professionalität' in *Mitteilungen des Deutschen Germanistenverbandes* 43(4) (1996): 18–26; here, p. 19.

42 Wieler, *Dilettantismus*, p. 21. See Einstürzende Neubauten, *Halber Mensch* (1985) and the accompanying film by Sogo Ishii.

have in common is that we acted out of nothing, never wanted to imitate anyone and had no role models'.[43] Finding the point zero, the nothing, out of which the new emerges and which is encountered in the Dadaists as well as in Dubuffet and Baumeister, requires not knowing, or the art of forgetting. In this respect, the dilettantism of the Geniale Dilletanten is both the inversion of the values of a meritocratic society, whose main medium for granting recognition, sanctioning or punishment, and implementing regulations is money, as well as the classical concept of genius. Wolfgang Müller short-circuits the genius with its opposite in his combination of words: now genius is not someone who develops his talent through study and the acquisition of skills on the basis of rules and trust in the objectivity of motives, but someone who renounces rules and subverts them instead. Only then does he achieve—in another volte-face back to the concept of genius—an art 'for which no specific rule can be given'. Part of this genius is that it 'does not itself describe how it achieves its product, scientifically or otherwise', but that 'nature is the rule'.[44] The ingenious dilettante works like nature. He either does not owe his ability to theoretical knowledge, but to the permanent practice of the creative, or his theory is a practice of lived knowledge or knowledge as life practice. He simply knows how to carve wooden spoons.

In the context of the theory of pop, Diedrich Diederichsen calls this knowledge an 'existential knowing-better'.[45] What is to be protected here from attempts at appropriation and judgement by the academy is a knowledge 'from within', a knowledge that refuses to accept external prescriptions and therefore knows what it is about because it does what it knows. And it is important that this thinking is a public thinking that is aware of its own experimentation. Understood as a public exploration of uncharted territory, it is an experimentation with the question of how action and knowledge,

---

43 Frieder Butzmann, 'Gegen alles sein, und alles noch einmal von vorn anfangen' in Slaski, *Gespräche mit Genialen Dilletanten*, pp. 107–21; here, p. 118.

44 Immanuel Kant, *Kritik der Urteilskraft* (Stuttgart: Reclam, 1963 [1790]), §46, pp. 236–37.

45 Diedrich Diederichsen, *Der lange Weg nach Mitte: The Sound und die Stadt* (Cologne: Kiepenheuer & Witsch, 1999), p. 36.

practice and reflection can be brought into harmony with one another—and thus also an experiment with failure.

While the Einstürzende Neubauten, with their sometimes martial tabula rasa attitude, most clearly represent the anti-intellectualist attitude of the Geniale Dilletanten, bands such as Die Tödliche Doris and Der Plan represent a direction that can be understood as a highly reflective version of the art of forgetting and of dilettantism.

Der Plan was founded by the artists Frank Fenstermacher and Moritz Reichelt, who ran the small gallery 'Art Attack' in Wuppertal. Initially, Chrislo Haas and Robert Görl, who later co-founded D.A.F., were also involved with the band. In 1979, Kurt Dahlke, aka Pyrolator, replaced them. Most of the concerts took place in the gallery; on their label 'Ata Tak' they featured befriended bands such as D.A.F., Fehlfarben, and Die Tödliche Doris. The mixture of the dilettantism of the artist-musicians and the professionalism of Pyrolator, as well as the idiosyncratic costumes and masks with which they performed, became the band's trademark.

Der Plan took its inspiration from various sources. The cover of their album *The Whip of Life* is a shot of the three musicians in a room full of works of African tribal art, with the covers of *Sweet Revenge* (1978) by Amanda Lear (with a whip) or *The Ritual of the Savage* (1951) by Les Baxter on the floor. Also present are references to the cover of the second Beatles record *With the Beatles* (1963) and the cover of the first Residents record *Meet the Residents* from 1974. On this cover sleeve, the portraits of the four Beatles are transformed into slightly moronic figures, images of zombies, squinting and sticking out their tongues or hiding behind masks. The Residents are a band from San Francisco, most likely founded in the late 1960s, whose members consistently hide behind masks and in costumes, so that their identity is still unknown even after forty years. It is likely that today's musicians are no longer the same as the members of the original band. The cover of *The Whip of Life* picks up on the myth that the Beatles were hiding behind the masks of the band members in the 1960s and 1970s. In addition to Hugo Ball's shamanistic Dada suit, the stage costumes Der Plan used were probably inspired by the Residents' disguises in *Third Reich*, for example. This video is made in the style of an expressionist film. The musicians, performing as Ku Klux Klan Neanderthals, are slaughtered by an alien, while a tank driven by a skull curves through a backdrop with a swastika. Finally, after the animated swastika has been crushed by two schnitzel-like forms, Hitler makes an appearance.

In their works, Der Plan interweave a multitude of references. The Dadaist childishness of the music with the monotonous singsong, the corresponding lyrics, and the animated films between *Muppet Show* and persiflage of German auteur films undermines every expectation of good taste. As pioneers of electronic music, they distort singing voices to a Mickey Mouse pitch and rumble through their songs with a heavy sound, which, as on *Geri Reig* (1980), contain numerous references to mental illness and idiocy ('Gefährliche Clowns [Manisch Idiotisch]'; 'Ich bin Schizophren').

Die Tödliche Doris was also founded by two art students, Wolfgang Müller and Nikolaus Utermöhlen. After 1980, first Chris Dreier, then Dagmar Dimitroff became part of the band, before Käthe Kruse and Tabea Blumenschein joined them. The band always worked with a large number of guest musicians. Like Der Plan, Die Tödliche Doris is the opposite of punk and industrial, trimmed for authenticity, even though they performed with Einstürzende Neubauten with albums such as *Wassermusik* from 1982. It is more about reflection than it is about authenticity. In a highly involved manner, not only the origin of punk, but also their own production in a potentially endless loop of reflection, repeatedly becomes the subject of their own practice. This ranges from the painterly transfer of all the individual frames of the only 1.83-seconds-long film *Die Gesamtheit allen Lebens und alles darüberhinausgehende* on forty-four screens, to the enigmatic production of an *Invisible 5th LP*. The latter consists of the simultaneously produced, but subsequently released, LPs *Unser Debut* (1985) and *Sechs* (Six), which are played at the same time. The auto-destructive impulse of punk is addressed in the *Natural Disaster Concert* from 1984, in which Käthe Kruse demonstrates her fire-breathing skills by setting a microphone on fire, which subsequently picks up not only the dilettantish scratching of Wolfgang Müller on the violin and the screeching of Nikolaus Utermöhlen's accordion, but in particular the sound of its own burning, until it falls silently cauterized on the sandy floor after the cable has burnt through.

With the 1981 Super 8 film *The Life of Sid Vicious*, Die Tödliche Doris succeeds in creating an iconic work that distances itself from punk, but at the same time uses its provocative moments and reinforces them with a twist. Sid Vicious, bassist of the Sex Pistols, was arrested in October 1978 after his girlfriend, the model Nancy Spungen, was found murdered in the Chelsea Hotel in New York. This hotel had been memorialized by Andy Warhol and Leonard Cohen. Whether Vicious had stabbed her to death remains unclear to this day. The film by Die Tödliche Doris not only refers to this sad event, but also to Vicious' famous walk along the Champs-Élysées in 1978, which in turn recalls Brus' walk through Vienna. Under his leather jacket, Vicious wore a T-shirt with a swastika. The protagonists in the film are Dagmar Dimitroff's three-year-old son and an unidentified seven-year-old girl named Angie. The little boy runs through the streets of Berlin wearing a shirt with a swastika and beaming with happiness before he 'stabs' Angie, who is unusually made up for her age, with a plastic knife. The film was edited by Utermöhlen and dubbed by Wolfgang Müller.[46] In many ways, the film is both an over- and understatement of a provocation. The fact that Vicious marched across the Champs-Élysées as a revenant of the German Nazi occupiers was, of course, a provocation in the sense of punk. Restaging this well-documented performance with a child as the protagonist adds to the provocation both in intensity and as a shift in emphasis: using the child as the unconscious actor of a punk possibly guilty of murder is a scandal insofar as it violates the consensus on what a child can be made to do. Staging the murder of the young woman as the stupid act of an infantile idiot waving a knife around in a further infamy because it seems to absolve Vicious. But this Sid Vicious, who appears here as a child dabbling with a knife, was the demigod of the punk scene in the late 1970s. While all standards of bourgeois morality and aesthetics are consequently violated, the means of infantilization simultaneously exposes to ridicule the very aesthetics that are so keen to challenge those very bourgeois values and aesthetics, namely punk in the version of Malcolm McLaren and Vivienne Westwood.

---

46 *Die Tödliche Doris, Kino/Cinema* (Berlin: Martin Schmitz Verlag, 2004), p. 29.

Both the punk and the dilettantes can be linked to the spoon-carver in Cusanus' *Idiota* dialogues as well as to the proto-kynic Diogenes. Even though it may seem strange to use the word virtue in connection with punk, they all share the virtue of action, not of knowledge.[47] Punk vehemently endorses the claim made by the *idiota* and *illiteratus* that no book knowledge knows how to teach one to master an art. Its 'existential knowing-better' cannot be refuted by any knowledge that has been acquired. But punk lacks what characterizes kynism (and the Dilletantes): humour. Although punk also has an 'unusually evil gob', as Jacob Burckhardt writes about Diogenes,[48] it holds up a mirror to the members of the majority society with its form of truth-telling, a form of *parrhesia* that is free of any form of satire or irony. The self-irony of Iggy Pop, with which he relativizes his extravagances on stage, is lacking in a parallel figure such as GG Allin. He did not carry out his suicide, announced on stage on Halloween 1989, only because he was in prison, although he finally died of a heroin overdose in 1993. It is also lacking in most of his younger colleagues. The parallels between kynism and punk can be drawn with regard to praxiological criteria—like self-deprecation, voluntary outsiderism, demonstration of self-imposed poverty as a sign of inner independence, contempt for money—but the similarities end with the style and genre chosen to express these attitudes: punk and industrial have no feel for humour. Authenticity forbids distance from one's own actions, inner necessity permits no fun. Extreme expressivity and radical individualism leave no room for a playful approach to oneself.

The Geniale Dilletanten survive both punk and its demise, which they conjure up in their show at the Tempodrom. The future is already on the horizon in 1981: among the participants in the *Great Untergangszauber* (The Great Doom Show) is a young musician named Maximilian Lenz, who, as WestBam, was to become one of the founding figures of a new music in Germany. Techno was already on the scene when punk, in the 'comfort of [its] cynicism',[49] still believed that there is no future. That there

47 See Niehues-Pröbsting, *Der Kynismus*, p. 144.

48 Quoted from Niehues-Pröbsting, *Der Kynismus*, p. 321.

49 Friedrich Nietzsche, 'Vom Nutzen und Nachteil der Historie für das Leben' in *Kritische Studienausgabe*, 2nd EDN (KSA), VOL. 1, §9, p. 312.

is a future (even if one may have imagined it differently) is testified to not only by techno, but also by a punk rock band like Green Day, who released *American Idiot* in 2004 to protest against the policies of George W. Bush. The album sees itself as a concept album in the vein of *Quadrophenia* by the Who (1973). Insulting rednecks and the protest against an atmosphere of hysteria and paranoia make the album, with its single *Boulevard of Broken Dreams*, the band's most successful production. In 2009, the story of 'Jesus of Suburbia' was adapted for a musical that premiered in Berkeley before moving to Broadway in 2010. What Green Day produce is actually just stadium-ready plastic rock à la Nickelback or the Offspring, which comes across as punk with a decent tattoo and a bit of kohl around the eyes. It's good for a lot of things—for millions in sales, musical success on Broadway, and for protesting against Donald Trump's election: on the evening of 8 November 2016 the music channel VIVA plays the song 'American Idiot' in an endless loop. The game of dialectics knows no end.

In Germany, Rainald Goetz's novel *Irre* (1983) signals that the time of the idiot as a positive figure belongs to the past, just a few years after the *Great Untergangszauber*. The protagonist's hatred of Werner Schroeter's film *Tag der Idioten* (1981) stands not only for a generational shift, but also for a paradigm shift.[50] The projective casting of the idiot as a figure of resistance appears as idealized hippie stuff, which Goetz counters with the experience of the doctor, saturated with reality, despairing of his art of healing. And it seems as if the real experience of mental illness pushes both the image of the idiot and any positive conception of the mentally ill outsider, romanticizing the madman with anti-psychiatry rhetoric, into the background. *Irre* stands in line not with Heinar Kipphardt's novel *März* (1976),[51] but with Gottfried Benn's collection of poems *Morgue und andere Gedichte* from 1912.

---

50 Goetz was born in 1954, Schroeter in 1945—nine years make a generational difference in the field of art.

51 In it, Kipphardt adapted the biography of Gugging patient Ernst Herbeck (1920–91), whose poems were published by Leo Navratil. In addition to the novel, he also wrote a radio play, a play and a film.

Lars von Trier's *The Idiots* (1998), the second film in his Golden Heart trilogy after *Breaking the Waves* (1996) and before *Dancer in the Dark* (2000), finally takes up the motif of the idiot as a social outsider, but turns the narrative towards the story of a group's failure due to the implications of their own strategy and the striving for dominance by Stoffer, their 'leader'. The members of the group present themselves to the public as mentally handicapped, more or less kept in check by a female 'supervisor'. Pressure from Stoffer results in authoritarian patterns of behaviour and structures of a sect. Karen, who, as we learn, has lost her child, joins the group and adopts the maxim that one should give free rein to one's own idiocy when she returns to her family after a two-week absence. The last scene shows Karen making a fool of herself and leaving the family, abused by her husband. Lars von Trier has also done away with the idiot as a positive figure. Provocation by means of self-presentation as mentally handicapped is intertwined with peer pressure, authoritarian behaviour, and violence; in this milieu, Karen takes on the role of the outsider, who, however, does not take on the task of provocation, but of self-humiliation and behaves 'idiotically', not to tear down bourgeois facades, but to add the social contempt of her family to the pain of having lost her child. She figures as an outsider both in terms of her old bourgeois life and in terms of the group of 'idiots' who have degenerated into a sect. As in other films by Lars von Trier, it is the woman who is confronted with the task of taking on the role of the victim, who voluntarily accepts this role as the woman of sorrows.

These changes in the role of the figure of the idiot and the mentally ill are accompanied by the fragmentation of milieux, the dissolution of traditional class structures, the change from a hardware to a software economy, from a production to an information and financial economy, and the rapidly increasing diversification of society in the countries of the Global North. As already mentioned, there is a multitude of microstructures in the further differentiating matrix of the social, which offer a wide range of possibilities for self-realization and self-positioning, but which have lost the crucial ability to form a subculture in a shared network. Subcultures require stable relationships, an intact enemy image, and the long-term anchoring of their protagonists in the structures they wish to change. Where contexts begin to slip, the concept of subculture loses its meaning, and with it the figures fade that were useful as hollow forms of identification and surfaces to project onto. The crossing and mixing of identity markers that had previously been mutually exclusive, the migration of these markers through social strata, the permanent processes of melioration and pejoration, the revalidation and revaluation of functions and status, the continuous revaluation of values—all of this adds up to the image of a social complexity. In this context, being located in opposition to one element may imply that one is in agreement with other elements, although it does not mean that these do not enter into different relations of mutual exclusion or affirmation with other elements. It is not that societies have ever been non-complex; but now we know this and incorporate this knowledge into our own operations. Complexity is no longer the sole characteristic of society, but a strategic guiding category for dealing with one's own position in society.

CHAPTER TEN

# The Presence of the Idiot

Recapitulation: The path that led from Paul's *idiota* via the saloi of the East, via St Francis and Cusanus to Nietzsche and the modern forms of radical outsiderism is the path of an inversion of values. It is not power, wealth, and rank that triumph, but humility, poverty, and self-abasement. *Apatheia*, indifference to one's own bodily fate and to the course of all things worldly, is set against the worldly by way of an ethic of indifference, dispassion, and non-distinction. Faced with the question of whether this world is the creation of a flawed demiurge that must be rejected, or the work of a loving God in whose kingdom of grace humanity has lived since the death of Christ, which is why all efforts to attain grace are superfluous, the *idiota* opts for redemption. Even then, the world is not worth talking about.

While the rhetorician and the philosopher have to go through laborious study to acquire knowledge through the medium of books, the *idiota* possesses an implicit, existential knowledge of practice and empiricism: what neither nature nor the ancients know how to teach, he knows through intuition. The proof that what he knows is right lies in the fact that he can do what he does. The short path not only of virtue but also of knowledge is open to him. But this privilege is vehemently opposed by the monastic and clerical elite: it relegates the *idiota* to the fringes of the *illiterati* and lay brothers. Lack of book knowledge becomes a stigma, while the granting or denial of education is wielded like an instrument to maintain the class structure of preindustrial society. In the course of the development of a science of man that gradually frees itself from religious preconceptions, the *idiota* is then given the fool's cap and his participation in the 'wisdom of the streets' is declared void and irrelevant. What he knows and what he does is at best a distorted reflection of reality and by no means the enigmatic knowledge of a third way beyond the dialectic. While the jurodivyj in the Eastern Church leads his Janus-faced existence between charlatan and saint, Western medical science relegates the *idiota* to the problem of a taxonomy of the psychic, pushes him off to the asylum, and degrades him to nullity by means of psychiatric nomenclature. He celebrates his resurrection in Dostoyevsky's novel and in Nietzsche's *Ecce Homo* as the *alter ego* of the tortured saviour who, with *Zarathustra*, provides the following generation of expressionists with the formula for their humanitarian pathos. However, after the steel thunderstorm of the First World War at the latest, this only sounds hollow. The Dadaists were already aware of this in the midst of the war when they used the idiot as a projective stimulus for anarchic protest on the one hand and portrayed him as an animalistic, dull victim of even the bluntest perpetrator of violence on the other. Only briefly does he raise his lamenting head as the personification of proletarian resistance, when psychiatry ingratiates itself with politics in order to make itself indispensable as a central science in the service of the ideology of public health. More than the idiot, however, the madman, the lunatic, the schizophrenic attract the interest of avant-garde circles, and it is they who take on the more important role as the protagonists in the game between the majority of society and the outsider. The idiot, closed in on himself and unapproachable, only occasionally performs as a figure of identification in a society of unrest, whose constantly alert attention requires a permanent readjustment of focus and perspective. He then serves merely as a negative image, as a fool and a moron, a deflated shell, the epitome of dullness and stupidity. While he disappears, with the exception of the brief phase of punk, as a positively connoted figure representing protest and resistance, the pejorative meaning of the word gains the upper hand, in its inverted form. However, at the same time, his career as a public figure begins. In order to show what is meant by this, we have to go back before the Christian era and look for the origin of the word in Greek.

The word *idiot* is derived from the Greek ἰδιώτης (*idiōtēs*) or ἴδιος (*idios*). *Idios* refers to that which is peculiar to a thing or a person. *Idiōtēs*, on the other hand, refers to a person who holds a military office but does not participate in political life, a simple soldier without commanding authority.[1]

---

1 'Idiotes' in *Brill's New Pauly Online*. See also Josef Girshovich, *Weltbürgertum, Kosmopolitismus und der Leviathan* (Berlin: Berliner Wissenschaftsverlag, 2015), p. 28.

On the other hand, *idiotai* also refers to those speakers in the popular assembly who are not professional rhetors, but who participate in political discourse as amateurs, taking the podium as the occasion demands and presenting their views and concerns.[2] The *idiōtēs* thus represents, to some extent, the ideal of a democracy in the functioning of which all citizens participate. Governing the community does not require a complicated structure of representation; it is everyone's business. Greek democracy therefore knows neither parliament nor the separation of powers and, just as the distinction between private and public is of little importance to it, so too is the distinction between individual and society. The common good or the well-being of the community (*koinōnia*) is central to the Greek understanding of democracy,[3] and the slogan that the private is also the political, which made its career after 1968, may have sounded banal and self-evident to participants in the political life of the polis.[4] Leading one's life entirely as a private person seemed scandalous to the Greeks: 'We Athenians alone regard the man who keeps away from politics not so much as a person who refrains from mingling with the people, but rather as a decidedly useless person'.[5]

Hannah Arendt defined the *agora* as a space in which the political is realized as the coexistence of many different people.[6] The *isonomia* or indifference of the law towards all who participate in the production of this political is central. Only equals and the free may participate in its production. Those who do not renounce their right to exercise dominion in

---

2 Mogens Herman Hansen, *Die athenische Demokratie im Zeitalter des Demosthenes* (Berlin: De Gruyter, 1995), p. 149.

3 Kurt A. Raaflaub, Josiah Ober and Robert W. Wallace (eds), *Origins of Democracy in Ancient Greece* (Berkeley: University of California Press, 2007), p. 157.

4 Paul Cartledge, *Ancient Greek Political Thought in Practice* (Cambridge: Cambridge University Press, 2009), p. 18.

5 Pericles, as quoted in Matthew Landauer, 'The 'Idiōtēs' and the Tyrant: Two Faces of Unaccountability in Democratic Athens' in *Political Theory* 42(2) (2014): 139–66; here, p. 145.

6 Hannah Arendt, *Was ist Politik? Fragmente aus dem Nachlass* (Ursula Ludz ed.) (Munich: Piper, 2015), p. 9.

the *agora* deprive themselves of their freedom: 'By exercising dominion over others, they deprive themselves of the society of their equals in which they could have been free'.[7]

In Arendt's perspective, the political aims at the phenomenon of the participation of all in the production of the *sensus communis*[8] as the production of a shared reason, in which the wishes and needs of the individual as well as necessities and constraints are negotiated as facts that affect all members of society equally and which must be transformed into decisions of temporary validity.

In a functionally diversified society, the democratic ideal is realized in the form of representative democracy through the exercise of the active and passive right to vote and through the political or voluntary civic engagement of citizens. To a certain extent, it can be said that every member of society who exercises the rights granted to them by society or for which they fight within it, contributes to their own self-formation, even if they make use of the right not to participate. Just as there is no possibility of not making decisions, there is no possibility of not participating in society, even if this participation only consists of an ostentatious refusal to participate. Even those who reject participation in politics as the production of binding decisions are part of the political as the coexistence of the different. While it is possible to abstain from politics, it is impossible to withdraw from the political. There is no escape from the political.

7 Hannah Arendt, *On Revolution* (London: Penguin, 1990 [1965]), p. 31: 'By assuming the rule over others, he (the ruler, LE) had deprived himself of those peers in whose company he could have been free'. See Jakob Stefan Seitz, *Hannah Arendts Kritik der politisch-philosophischen Tradition* (Munich: Herbert Utz, 2002).

8 Kant, *Kritik der Urteilskraft*, §40, p. 214. See Gadamer, *Wahrheit und Methode*, p. 37, who links common sense with the concept of solidarity. See also Birgit Recki, *Ästhetik der Sitten* (Frankfurt am Main: Klostermann, 2001), p. 313: 'Here we must once again recall that Kant [ . . . ] presented aesthetic judgement as a *sensus communis* in order to know what the "capacity to be able to share oneself intimately and generally" is all about. General participation, obviously in the medium of moral feeling, which Kant calls emphatic at the end of the paragraph, and this general communication, which he understands as a performance of aesthetic feeling, thus form the *elements of a human culture*'. Emphasis in the original; translated LE.

Democratic politics is legitimized through procedures,[9] through the strict separation of powers and the autonomy of institutions that prepare, accompany, and correct the political process of making and implementing decisions. The functioning of these institutions, in an ideal world independent of the individuals running them, is guaranteed by their constitutionality and their orientation towards the law. Their autonomy makes it possible to balance the difference between law and morality, which reflects the difference between politics and the political. Institutions deal with the constantly recalibrated imbalance between the constituted and the constituent or, in other words, they process irritations that jeopardize the stability of a system as incursions from the environment or from subsystems. Through the procedural modalities of reflection, function, and performance, they keep the past present, orient themselves towards the functioning of the overall system, and develop instruments for solving possible future problems, the exact contours of which cannot yet be clearly defined.[10]

*

So, what about the participatory ideal of the *idiōtēs* in Greek democracy at the beginning of the twenty-first century? Is he a citizen who sporadically intervenes in the political opinion-forming process, who enters the public sphere and withdraws again as soon as he has put forward his concerns? Or is he the *idiota* of the third way, who has the 'wisdom of the street' and knowledge that extends far beyond the horizons of the *literati* and rhetors? Or has he simply transformed himself into the figure of the idiot, a pejorative figure of speech in contemporary usage?

Probably the latter. It seems as if the idiot has become the dominant figure of political practice, on both sides of the political divide: as the elected and the electorate, as governor and governed, ruler and ruled. In our context, at least two factors are relevant in this regard: the boom of social media and the explosive arrival of the category of creativity in the age of cognitive capitalism.

---

9 Niklas Luhmann, *Legitimation durch Verfahren* (Frankfurt am Main: Suhrkamp, 1983 [1969]).

10 Niklas Luhmann, *Systemtheorie der Gesellschaft* (Berlin: Suhrkamp, 2017), p. 808.

Until well into the last decades of the twentieth century, creativity was the privilege of those who were regarded as artists. It is a faculty to be found within the human being, enabling one to catch up with one's own possibilities and empowering one towards self-realization. Creativity helps the individual to express themselves as resistance to social pressure. It has a subversive function. However, the 'new spirit of capitalism'[11] makes for the mutation of creativity into a capitalist resource and into a commodity that participants in the social sphere have to offer on the proprietary markets.[12]

Anyone who wants to participate successfully in society must bow to the imperative of creativity. At the same time, creativity is now claimed by any start-up as a surplus value traditionally attributed to the arts. The guiding criterion of creativity now contributes to the development of a society that is diversified not only functionally, but also in terms of the everyday world into a multitude of parallel milieus without horizontal links. Today, creativity is neither subversive nor emancipatory, but rather singularizing, thus stabilizing the system, and for this reason oppressive.

Secondly, social media have triggered a historically unprecedented surge in participation in the political and social sphere, the effect of which is both the increasing agglomeration and aggregation of data as well as the increasing singularization of all individuals and the fragmentation of society.[13] The specific responsiveness of the algorithms, which, as we know, enables providers to make suggestions to users willing to buy on the basis of their previous purchases or to suggest new 'friends' and areas of interest based on previous online activities, has the effect that the opinions and views reflected back to them are primarily those that correspond to the search queries they have already made and the opinions and views they have expressed.[14] In these echo chambers, in which only one variation of

---

11 Luc Boltanski and Ève Chiapello, *Der neue Geist des Kapitalismus* (Cologne: Herbert von Halem, 2018 [1999]).

12 Michael Betancourt, *Kritik des digitalen Kapitalismus* (Darmstadt: Wissenschaftliche Buchgesellschaft, 2018 [2016]), pp. 34–35.

13 See Andreas Reckwitz, *Die Gesellschaft der Singularitäten* (Berlin: Suhrkamp, 2017), pp. 225ff.

the same thing bounces back, as if its infinitely refracted sound were the music of the entire world, the user finds his doubts confirmed, his beliefs supported, and his intentions vindicated. For a specific type of producer on the opinion market, called politicians, social media enable detailed market research and precise voter targeting and thus the aggregation of support on a scale unknown in the pre-digital age. In the case of the consumer, on the other hand, the procedural logic of the algorithms supports their social and political homophily, with the result that unwelcome positions and opinions contrary to their own views are suppressed. People live in the belief, produced and permanently confirmed by the feedback loop, that they share the same opinion as the majority of their fellow human beings and are therefore right.

At the same time, the boundaries between providers/producers and customers are becoming blurred. The promise of the platform economy lies in promising the *produser* equal participation in the opinion-forming process. Opinion markets are created that promote the emergence of structural populism, as they seem to enable unmediated, immediate participation of everyone in the political sphere.[15] The tendency to aggregate data corresponds to the tendency to isolate users. This is not just about the lonely first-person shooter or the nerd who, pale in the blue light of the screen, munches his chips while dabbling as a programmer or firing posts into the digital world; rather, it is about the tendency towards the individualization of behaviours, opinions, beliefs, and actions. This tendency goes hand in hand with the transformation of creativity and is reinforced by the digitality of communication, which no longer has to prove itself right by comparison with a common reason, but is considered correct and justified if it is in line with the feedback in the echo chamber. This isolation of subjects and the fragmentation of society into parallel milieus allows

14 For the following, I refer to Eli Pariser, *The Filter Bubble: What the Internet Is Hiding from You* (New York: Penguin, 2011). Natalie Jomini Stroud, 'Selective Exposure Theories', *Oxford Handbooks Online* (1 May 2014; updated 11 January 2018). Jan Philipp Rau and Sebastian Stier, 'Die Echokammer-Hypothese: Fragmentierung der Öffentlichkeit und politische Polarisierung durch digitale Medien?' in *Zeitschrift für Vergleichende Politikwissenschaft* 13(3) (2019): 399–417.

15 See Vogl, *Kapital und Ressentiment*, pp. 174, 176.

the framework for the game between individual and society, outsider and majority, to be constantly redefined and the game to be played again and again in new and different ways. On the matrix of the social, in a society that is diversified not only functionally and in the experience of daily life, but also communicatively, the subject chooses his or her position in the face of a multitude of possible, communicatively accessible contexts as required. Intersectionality was once a term that, even if meant only descriptively, certainly had moral-normative implications. It demanded that the subject both had an awareness of his or her own simultaneous integration into a multitude of environments and also took this fact into account when assessing the behaviour and statements of a counterpart. Today, however, intersectionality stands for the free availability of a cocktail of versions of oneself and options for action in a multitude of contexts. In this multitude, the user reconceptualizes himself and locates himself according to the advantage that a position grants him or her. This results in inversions of a new kind: members of the majority society profile themselves as victims of a minority that insists on its right to participate, while those who enjoy privileges choose the position of being unjustly persecuted by envious people when their justification is called into question. The agricultural industry, for instance, kept alive by billions of euros, stylizes itself as a community of victims of a fabulated eco-terrorism, white middle-class men complain about marginalization, vaccination campaigns turn into genocide,[16] universities mutate into safe spaces, and intellectual rigour becomes a trauma trigger. And because the individual voice is drowned out in the cacophony of millions of opinions in the digital space, everyone turns into a neglected quantity, a nullity. Thus, being overheard and overlooked, they raise their voice all the louder with the tremolo of the stigmatized by discrimination and declare themselves victims of the mainstream, the lying press, the establishment, or any other exclusionary mechanism, among whose multitude they can easily choose, while at the same time all expertise and all expert opinion is defamed as latently oppressive and as exclusionary and unjust for being classist. The various forms of social capital are paid into the social fund in different currencies

16 Cristian Stefanescu, "'Stoppt den Impf-Genozid!'", *DW* (18 May 2021).

according to need. Those who cannot pay in the capital form of money pay in education (middle-class intellectuals vs *nouveaux riches*); those who cannot pay in education pay in power (politicians vs intellectuals); those who cannot pay in power pay in identity (LGBTQI+ and BIPOC vs establishment); those who cannot pay in identity pay in social merits (citizens, skilled workers, house builders vs migrants, BIPOC and/or LGBTQI+). Today, the opposition of right and left no longer makes sense. Due to the micro-differentiation of society into different milieus, one or other form or position of disadvantage can always be identified, which, regardless of the relationship of the 'affected' to society, can be framed as an outsider position and whose form of discourse can be fed as a value currency into the clash of opinions and the scramble over the validity of claims.

*

The *idiota*'s claim to have privileged access to a form of 'third' knowledge was legitimized by the assumption of a realm of transcendence, whose laws and truths determined his actions and lent him legitimacy. His foreignness on earth resulted from his direct participation in a religious knowledge that remained equally incomprehensible to those who were attached to the world and to the *literati* who were merely striving for written knowledge. In the either complementary or antagonistic parallelism of the world and the hereafter, the behaviour of the *idiota* found a structure in which anchoring his depravity opened up the possibility of legitimizing his asocial behaviour both with regard to the profane sphere of bourgeois goings-on and with regard to the sacred sphere of institutionalized faith. The short path of virtue and knowledge, which was open to the *idiota*, was barred to both spheres of the earthly, the bourgeois-profane and the institutionalized-sacramental. However, as the 'wisdom of the street', it was open to the common man, the classless, who as a subaltern was still to be located below the categories of the proletarian.[17]

17 On subalternity, see Dipesh Chakrabarty, 'A Small History of Subaltern Studies' in *Habitations of Modernity* (Chicago: University of Chicago Press, 2002), pp. 3–19, and Chakrabarty, 'Subaltern Histories and Post-Enlightenment Rationalism' in *Habitations of Modernity*, pp. 20–37.

The collapse of a binding idea of the transcendent, its disintegration into a question of the design of one's own life, its inversion into a problem of this-worldly life design aimed at happiness, satisfaction, and spiritual fulfilment entails the disappearance of all negativity in the positive totality of reality. In the totality of this world, otherness is only a variation of what already exists; there are always alternatives, but no alterity. In this constellation, the figure of the *idiota* and thus a well-founded conception of the outsider loses its significance. From now on, the outsider is the product of a projective process by means of which society creates its own fictional counter-image. The medium of choice is art, whose task consists of spelling out, testing, modifying and, if necessary, rejecting counter-concepts to the seemingly blind operation of society, without fearing any major damage on this side of aesthetic difference. Accordingly, and in accordance with the logic of the production of an inverted transcendence, the folding of the otherworldly into the this-worldly and its subsequent unfolding as difference within society, artists act as the primary protagonists of these projective procedures. However, they are more than just art casters; rather, as the bearers of the fiction of alterity, they take on the task of designing the possibilities of otherness from the centre of social reality. Even if in the totality of all that exists, in the complete this-worldliness of maximally condensed communication, no gap remains for a nothingness that could serve as the source of an unthinkable Other, art, as a function of the social, keeps the utopia of an Other alive.

Following the collapse of the systems of transcendence in a society that sees itself as secular, the boundaries between the *idiota* and the common man on the one hand, and the bourgeois-profane and institutionalized sacred on the other, have collapsed, too. The post-religious and post-conventional society, which has agreed on its absolute this-worldliness, takes the outdated differentiations as internal differences and reformulates them as differences of class, status, and rank, or as different forms and degrees of successful or unsuccessful social integration. Just as the common man transforms himself into the plebs, the *idiota* transforms himself into the idiot, who now claims to have the privilege of the short path. Yet he does not walk this path in the light of a wisdom radiating from a beyond into the realm of the here and now, but in the spotlight of self-production, accompanied by the dull roar of the ever-threatening repetitive assertion of the universality of the particular. Just as the public sphere has become dark and opaque, the private sphere has been transformed into the visible, exhibited to the point of pornography.

Today's idiot has neither patience for the lengthy procedures of a representative democracy (or even a direct democracy like Switzerland's) nor a sense of the fact that sociality goes hand in hand with sublimation. If the *idiota*'s short path was a gift of grace, the demand for consideration of individual concerns as universally valid and the urge for immediate gratification, for immediate implementation of the respective concerns in social and political practice, are for the idiot a matter of pressure, if not of force. The idiot knows no difference between public and private. Whatever is of concern to him must be dealt with by the public with all the urgency it has for him. Any reference to procedures into which concerns and demands must first be fed before they can be processed in deliberations and transformed into decisions is merely a tactic of consolation, a gesture of disregard, a trick of a powerful clique that operates in secret networks ('the system') and whose invisible power can and must be opposed. The logic of aggregation corresponds to the logic of paranoia, to which every counter-argument infallibly coagulates into proof that a conspiratorial power is operating in the dark. It is everyone's right to resist this power. Since the constitutional state is merely a facade, recourse to constitutional procedures is pointless; a state of emergency prevails in perpetuity, and in this state civil disobedience and even violent resistance are legitimate.

At the same time, a sense of functional diversification is lost in a communicatively diversified society. The idiot, who, like the *idiōtēs* of Attic democracy, steps onto the political podium as a lay rhetor and represents his cause, claims authenticity and the virtue of honesty of the non-professional actor, for whom what he represents is a matter of the heart and not merely a means of political tactics. What distinguishes him from the representative of Greek citizenship, however, is the fact that the society in which he expresses these concerns is not a limited and communicatively accessible group of people who populate the *agora* with him, but rather a society that cannot be embraced and addressed in its entirety. It is at least potentially global due to digitality. Its complexity has reached such a degree that it can only be managed by diversifying tasks and functions, developing expertise and demarcating specialist areas. Whereas in the ideal case the *idiōtēs* was still able to oversee the totality of matters affecting the polis, today this is no longer possible. Not for the idiot, not for the expert, not for the scientist, not for the politician. But the idiot does not know this.

The idiot has lost the virtue of trust as well as the intellectual humility that required him to concede the possibility that he, like everyone else, does not have a direct understanding of the totality of all social, technical, scientific, ethical, and political contexts in a complex society. The idiot believes that he is allowed to demand and ask for everything that he wants and demands and for which he stands and fights, because there can be nothing in this world that he does not know, or because what he knows represents the world in its entirety. What he demands is everything that needs to be demanded, and what he demands has an urgency that has no equal.[18] Competing concerns must take a back seat. He alone represents the rights of those who need to make themselves heard in a state of emergency. Since the separation between private and public no longer exists, his struggle is the struggle of the individual for all. His particular is the universal, and what he fights for is the salvation of the whole world. What characterizes his world is the fact that it is built entirely according to his needs. His fight for all is a fight for those who are like him. Those who differ from him in their interests and concerns fall prey to ignorance and wilful oblivion as nullities.

The blurring of the boundary between public and private was prepared in the 1980s by the policies of neoliberalism, which set out to subordinate all areas of society to the primacy of economics.[19] What had been considered to be in the public interest—healthcare, education, pensions, infrastructure—was handed over to private interests, which restructured all

18 Its epitome is the single-issue voter who deliberately (or unintentionally) ignores the complexity of his world. For him, only one thing matters.

19 And neoliberalism itself emerged from the work of thinkers like F. A. von Hayek. See Friedrich August von Hayek, *The Constitution of Liberty* (Chicago: University of Chicago Press, 2011 [1960]). See also Foundational Economy Collective, *Foundational Economy: The Infrastructure of Everyday Life* (Manchester: Manchester University Press, 2019).

areas according to the criteria of economic profitability. While profits were privatized, losses were nationalized; what had been considered a matter for the public sector was now left to the arbitrariness of private investors, leading to a situation that has since been criticized as the commodification of public goods and a state of 'private wealth and public poverty'.[20] It is precisely in this scenario that the career of creativity must be placed: the disappearance of the socially integrated individual corresponds to its singularization as I Company Ltd., the overall social monopolization of profit corresponds to the diversity of products of creativity that economically prefigured subjects have to offer on the market.[21] Every waking minute is simultaneously self-realization and self-exploitation; assertion of individuality qua creativity corresponds to maximum self-alienation qua surrender of the self to the market.[22]

The homogenization of politics and society by the sometimes total, sometimes only partial application of the paradigm of economic profitability, to which all other possible categories of the social—solidarity, equality, social peace, justice, equal opportunities—are subordinated, produces fragmentation at the level of law, politics, and science and escalates individualization towards segmentation that is symptomatic of modernity.[23] Homogenization by means of the economization of the social weakens its antagonistic tendencies by producing fragmentation. The horizontal diversification it induces, as a surrogate for freedom of choice and decision, minimizes the possibilities for the development of a vertical integrative force that encompasses all areas of society.

For this reason, it is highly debatable whether the discourses of particularity that are pursued especially in the context of identity politics in

---

20 Philipp Staab, *Digitaler Kapitalismus: Markt und Herrschaft in der Ökonomie der Unknappheit* (Berlin: Suhrkamp, 2019), p. 267.

21 Staab, *Digitaler Kapitalismus*, pp. 226ff.

22 See Ulrich Bröckling, *Das unternehmerische Selbst: Soziologie einer Subjektivierungsform* (Frankfurt am Main: Suhrkamp, 2007), pp. 46ff. See Rainer Forst, 'Noumenale Entfremdung: Die Dialektik der Selbstbestimmung bei Rousseau, Kant und Marx' in Forst, *Die noumenale Republik*, pp. 39–76.

23 See Vogl, *Kapital und Ressentiment*, p. 128, where he speaks of 'informational monads'.

the wake of feminism and decolonization are emancipatory in character. The affirmation of particularity and identity as a focus on the *idios* not only leaves the paradigm of maximum profit untouched, which has long since become universal, but also harms competing paradigms such as the universality of equal rights for all people.[24] Nowhere is this clearer than in the usurpation of the nomenclature of emancipatory freedom projects of indigenous and formerly colonized populations since the Second World War by xenophobic and identitarian projects from the right (the only thing missing is the reference to the necessity of resistance against 'hegemonic power structures' in order to clothe right-wing uncivil politics in the garb of the perfect re-enactor of failed left-wing revolt projects). The 'identitarians' are the triumphant pallbearers of left-wing illusions. And the narcissistic focus on the microaggressions that supposedly befall the members of ever new, self-declared minorities and outsider communities clears the way for a general politics of *idios*, a politics of the collapse of particularity and universality, an inflation of the private, and the erasure of all meaningful concepts of the public sphere.

In Europe after the Second World War, it was probably Berlusconi who first thought he could govern Italy as if it were his private company. Thatcher's denial of social responsibility and Kohl's perversion of the concept of honour corresponded to Berlusconi's political strategy. In their politics, and subsequently in those of Bolsonaro, Trump, or Orbán, the lack of aptitude, education and expertise, sophistication and tact is the central category of a politics that presents itself as authentic. However, their idiocy is not one of obtuseness. It is rather a primitive but clever, uncultivated but devious, one-dimensional but cunning, radical, and exclusive monopolization of their own interests (and the interests of the associated cliques of claqueurs and beneficiaries) while largely ignoring other equally justified and legitimate interests. Insofar as values are based on interests, the politics of the idiots of our time is the inversion of any meaningful concept of 'value-based' politics, such as that advocated by moderate European politicians. The fact that a policy is 'value-based' does not constitute a value unless it is clear from which interests the values result.

24 See Omri Boehm, *Radikaler Universalismus* (Berlin: Propyläen, 2022).

When what is one's own is declared to be the measure of what is of general interest, when the *idios* is declared to be the decisive criterion for governing the polis, a value is established whose obtuseness is probably obvious to everyone, but whose validity cannot be disputed without difficulty if nothing more is at hand than the reference to other and competing values.

One such competing value is, for example, basing politics on rules, treaties, the constitution, and the law. But the success of paranoid and power-hungry, unscrupulous and narcissistically disturbed sociopaths such as Modi, Trump, Johnson, Erdoğan, Orbán, Kaczyński, Netanyahu, and some others[25] shows that modifying rules, regulations, procedures, and laws so that they primarily serve one's own interests is a tedious but not futile process. Thus, the reference to rule-based as well as value-based politics fails due to the fact that rules and values with which one does not agree cannot be delegitimized by opposing them with opposing rules and values that are located on the same communicative and procedural level. A third party is required. But this third party can today no longer be associated with the idea of the third way of the *idiota*, the short path of intuition and practice, the existentially and empirically saturated knowledge that 'it works'. It needs to be achieved by the laborious detour via the Other.

One can probably locate the beginning of this long detour in European thought at various points; I would like to let it begin where Kant establishes the landmark of respect. That, according to Kant, 'humanity itself [ . . . ] is dignity',[26] necessarily requires that the 'self-esteem of humanity [within us]'[27] must correspond to the appreciation of others. Disregarding the other is tantamount to disregarding what individuals regard as worthy of respect in themselves. The dehumanization of the other corresponds to the dehumanization of the self. By respecting the other, however, the individual assures himself of his own dignity, and only by respecting the other does he acquire the respect he deserves for himself and the other.

---

25 Putin and Netanyahu no longer belong in this list, since both have mutated into pure killers.

26 Immanuel Kant, *Die Metaphysik der Sitten* (Frankfurt am Main: Suhrkamp, 2014 [1797]), *Ethische Elementarlehre*, §38, p. 600.

27 Kant, *Kritik der Urteilskraft*, §6, p. 80; §54, p. 280.

Fichte and Hegel rework this category of respect into the category of recognition and place it in a central position in their respective moral and legal philosophies. Thus, Fichte writes: 'Neither can recognize the other unless both recognize each other: and neither can treat the other as a free being unless both treat each other as such'.[28] And Hegel: 'Each [consciousness] is the centre for the other, through which each mediates and unites with itself, and each is an immediate being for itself and the other, which at the same time is so for itself only through this mediation. They *recognize each other* as *mutually recognizing each other*'.[29] The recognition of the self is mediated by the recognition of the other through this self, just as the recognition of the self is mediated through the recognition of this self by the other. By means of the reciprocity of recognition, both recognize the freedom of the other. And in this reciprocity of respect and recognition lies the basis of morality.[30] The self that assures itself of its human dignity requires the other as a social subject. In this detour of culture, there is no subject that is a pure, non-socialized human being, or, to put it differently, it is only the socialized being who can be a human being.[31] It is this idea of 'individuation through socialization'[32] or of individuality as a state of sociality in the course of a politics of reciprocally practised recognition, from

---

28 Johann Gottlieb Fichte, *Grundlage des Naturrechts nach Principien der Wissenschaftslehre* (Leipzig: Gabler, 1796), p. 38.

29 Georg Wilhelm Friedrich Hegel, *Phänomenologie des Geistes*, Eva Moldenhauer and Karl Markus Michel eds, on the basis of the *Werke* of 1832–1845 (Frankfurt am Main: Suhrkamp, 1989 [1807]), p. 147. Emphasis in the original.

30 Niklas Luhmann, *Die Moral der Gesellschaft* (Frankfurt am Main: Suhrkamp, 2008), p. 104.

31 Karl Marx, 'Ökonomisch philosophische Manuskripte' (1844) in Karl Marx and Friedrich Engels, *Werke*, Ergänzungsband 1 (Berlin: Dietz, 1968), p. 538: 'Alone, even if I am scientifically etc. active [ . . . ], I am socially active, because I am active as a human being. Not only the material of my activity is given to me [ . . . ] as a social product, my own existence is social activity. [ . . . ] Above all, it must be avoided to fix "society" again as an abstraction in relation to the individual. The individual is the social being.'

32 Jürgen Habermas, 'Individuierung durch Vergesellschaftung' in *Nachmetaphysisches Denken* (Frankfurt am Main: Suhrkamp, 1988), pp. 153–86. See also, from an anthropological perspective, Gehlen, *Moral und Hypermoral*, p. 47. Like Habermas, Gehlen also refers to G. H. Mead, *Mind, Self and Society* (1934).

which the necessity of certain rules can be derived and on the basis of which the value of certain values (but not the value of having values) can be asserted. Because there is no shortage of values. Having values is as tacky as having an opinion. Values and opinions acquire their worth through the imputation of their semantics to the reason of others, ideally 'all of humanity'.[33] It is only in this process of reciprocal validation (or devaluation) of semantics that assertions of values and opinions, statements, and judgements gain (or lose) their value.

This imputation of one's own judgement to the reason of the other, in order to affirm or deny the validity of this judgement, is not a process that is merely justified by the normativity of what is called communicative reason. Rather, Kant's concept of the formation of a common sense of what could be reasonable and morally right, which was developed on the basis of aesthetic judgement, proves to be valid because it can be linked to the category of observation and allows far-reaching conclusions to be drawn from it.

Communication is based on observation and is itself the subject of observation. All communication is the communication of observers.[34] Observers observe how communication is observed by others and are in turn observed as to what communicative conclusions they draw from this and what observation of observation they feed into the next communication. Due to expectations (double contingency), this process of observations aggregating to observations of various degrees is virtually infinite, unless this process is interrupted by means of discursive, epistemic, political, physical, or any other kind of violence.

The sphere of principally accessible communication has reached a planetary scale—even when taking into account measures taken by regimes to censor and isolate. This increase in communication made possible by digitality, in which observations of observations circulate, results in the increasing polycontexturality of all thought, opinion, speech, and action.

---

33 Kant, *Kritik der Urteilskraft*, §8, p. 88.

34 Humberto R. Maturana, *Erkennen: Die Organisation und Verkörperung von Wirklichkeit. Ausgewählte Arbeiten zur biologischen Epistemologie* (Braunschweig and Wiesbaden: Vieweg, 1982), p. 34: 'Everything that is said is said by an observer.'

It enables the (relatively) free availability of a multitude of positions on the social matrix. However, if communication is not to give up its claim not only to truthfulness but also to truth,[35] it requires the consideration of this multitude of positions, in which communication takes place, in the process of communicating. If communication under the sign of polycontexturality wants to maintain its claim to truth, there is no shortcut open to denying the internal diversity, the inner 'mixedness' of each position. This internal mixedness alone requires not only the imputation of the statements of different subjects to the reason of the respective other, but also the internal comparison of arguments within the communicative subject itself before it expresses these arguments to a third party. This was once called reflection.

The category of first-, second-, and third-order observation and the resulting categories of polycontexturality and double contingency require a non-normative thinking that is aware of the fact that its truth is always only relational,[36] whereby it can remain undecided whether it is necessarily or unnecessarily so. Truth exists because there is the possibility of negation.[37] All positing of truth takes place within the horizon of its possible negation. If the communicative act excludes this possibility of negation of its propositional content, it obscures its intentional content on the one hand, and on the other hand it withdraws both forms of its content from

35 On the distinction between truth and truthfulness, see Jürgen Habermas, *Moralbewusstsein und kommunikatives Handeln* (Frankfurt am Main: Suhrkamp, 1983), pp. 68, 147ff. See also Habermas, *Theorie des kommunikativen Handelns*, VOL. 2 (Frankfurt am Main: Suhrkamp, 1987), pp. 183–84.

36 See Gadamer, *Wahrheit und Methode*, p. 416, where he emphasizes that only the *logos* as a principle of assignment, of relation, which 'places being in one respect', can be granted the capacity for truth.

37 Luhmann, *Systemtheorie*, pp. 489–90: 'Truth always exists if and insofar as communication partners agree that a reported selection is to be treated as experience on both sides, that is, is to be attributed to the world and not to be booked *à conto* decision'. Luhmann, *Systemtheorie*, p. 492: 'True or untrue, however, is only the information and the possibility of its reproduction. The contingency of states and events is the condition of the possibility of truth, because it is the condition of the possibility of selectivity. According to this view, truth is necessarily unnecessary. It only appears in a horizon of other possibilities.'

the access of second-degree observers, whose freedom would consist in checking this content for its usefulness for further communication. This freedom consists essentially in the right to dispose of other, differing interests and values and to be able to feed these into the communicative game as prima facie justified. Withdrawing a communicative act from further processing by asserting it as not only relational or functional, but as intrinsically true, represents an act of violence. Those who postulate the normative inviolability of their own assertion deprive other observers of their freedom to observe and process this observation and deny them what they concede to themselves. While they keep the world at their disposal as an object of observation, they withdraw their own communication, which is part of this world, from the judgement of others. This act of setting one's own propositional content as transhistorically and transculturally true and immunizing it against the processing based on observation through further communication is the basic form of immoral behaviour as self-exemption from a principle that is claimed by oneself and as a universalization of the particular.[38]

What the idiot wants today is a world of grandiose simplicity, of almost paradisiacal innocence, of pre-civilizational and pre-cultural plainness and beauty. His short-tempered, snap-to-the-moment mind, which treats the distant as the near and perceives in the other only what resembles its own, perishes on its way if the next stimulant, the next trigger, the next scandal does not immediately grant him gratification for his effort. And nothing frightens the idiot more today than the idea of *aporia*—the contradiction that cannot be resolved immediately in terms of time or space, intellectually or emotionally, and which demands reflection and a desire to understand it. *Aporias* as nodes of contradiction linked to systemic points require time. However, the idiot prefers a sword thrust that cuts the knot to patiently dealing with a possible solution. It is no wonder that Diogenes preferred to stay in the barrel.

---

38 Niklas Luhmann, 'Über Natur' in *Gesellschaftsstruktur und Semantik*, VOL. 4 (Frankfurt am Main: Suhrkamp, 2016 [1999]), p. 29: 'The prohibition of self-exemption [ . . . ] is the secret basic principle of morality.'

The stubbornness of the outsider and *idiota* in the face of a society homogenized by the pressure to conform meant asserting and defending the dignity of being human, equally inherent to every subject, regardless of social rank and status. In a post-traditional and post-conventional society that is diversified in terms of function, lived realities, and communication, however, asserting and insisting on the right of unmediatedness and immediacy, of independent, erratic authenticity and individuality, is not only a defence of an illusion, but also a defence of barbarism. If the *idiota*, the humblest of the humble, the lowliest of the lowly, asks for recognition of his individuality and dignity as a human being, the idiot denies this dignity to the other by granting validity to nothing but his own interests. In the inversion of the inversion, the idiot re-establishes the constellation of power against which the *idiota* had stood in the name of the ineffable dignity of the human. It is not the obstinacy of the human, which he recognizes in the other as in his mirror image, but the blind obstinacy of greed for power that drives him to substitute coercion, intimidation, and violence for the desire to create a *sensus communis*.

And yet another inversion of the inversion can be observed: The Attic polis was unfamiliar with the idea of human rights.[39] Human beings were those who were able and entitled to participate in the political process. Christian humanism and the Enlightenment turned this construction on its head: the human being as such is 'dignity'. However, it now seems as if the current boom of the idiot is an involuntary return to the Attic figure of the political, but today, as always when history repeats itself, in the form of a farce. As if one were only fully human when one can participate in the noisy general public, as if the silence around one meant social death and as if only the constant ambush of digital communication proved that one was still alive, the idiot subject stumbles, with his package of views, interests, and values, from the *agora* into the echo chambers of permanently and endlessly bouncing opinions. The socialized individual is no longer an individual who, mindful of his own dependence on the recognition of others, contributes to the fragile edifice of shared reason and thus to the,

39 Jacob Burckhardt, *Griechische Kulturgeschichte*, VOL. 1 (Stuttgart: Spemann, 1939), p. 78.

albeit utopian, yet conceivable design of universal freedom through mutual obligation. Rather, the idiot individual of today is the opaque slave of an economy of status and an economization of the self in his alienation, a digital troglodyte who cobbles together his own world in his echo chamber. Instead of Socratic *maieutics*, the art of midwifery as the art of dialogical conversation, which in Dubuffet's texts was declared the generative power of nothingness and mimetically repeated the miracle of world-becoming on a human scale, the idiot of the present practices the monological *creatio ex nihilo*, the post-Oedipal realization of the dream of a persona committed only to itself, free of any *aporia* in a world without alterity.

Dubuffet's dream of the creative power of nothingness was part of the tradition of modernity. Its belief in progress made a break with tradition seem to be an indispensable prerequisite for the creation of the new. This newness could not find its place in the 'horrible home' of the father; the place of the new was the 'blessed strangeness'.[40] Modernity was necessarily fatherless and, as it conceived of itself, ideally, as being without contexts. However, the figure of the up-and-comer, who supposedly owes everything he has and everything he possesses to his own abilities and skills, repeats the modernist myth of the fatherless creative genius as its distorting, grotesque inversion. Not all elements of the myth are included in the inversion. The national-chauvinist revisionism, embellished with a little pasted-on cultural tinsel and pseudo-knowledge, which, paired with dull machismo,[41] characterizes the idiotic policies of Höcke, Johnson, Putin, Bolsonaro, Orbán, Trump, Weidel, Le Pen, and Erdoğan, fills the empty shell of nation and people and identity with the fantasized charisma of a wonderful past, which only needs to be restored in order to repair the damage that modernity has caused. The idiot of the present is not interested in creating a future that could be built on the ruins of tradition. Rather, he always trudges backwards into his past. It forms the hollow cliché of a present without origin and without history. As he knows only about himself, the idiot's present resembles a past that only he knows. In the repetition of time ('Make . . . again') lies his power. Now time is both fulfilled and abolished.

40 Harnack, *Marcion*, p. 225.

41 Meloni and Le Pen add their feminine charm to this picture.

The *idiota*'s rejection of the world turns into the devaluation of the present as the eternal afterimage of a past that exists only as a phantasmatic one. The abolition of the world as the place of the many-different has succeeded. In the hypertrophic, bloated form of an abundance that leaves no space beyond the *idios*, the megalomania of the idiot manifests itself in his dream of self-creation qua his own power as today's form of evil.

# Acknowledgements

This book would not have been possible without the support of many friends and collaborators. First, I would like to thank my wife Catherine, who from time to time questioned the sanity of my disappearing into the world of idiocy; the publishers of the German edition, Federica Romanini and Ingo Vavra of Turia + Kant, who generously agreed to license the English edition. I owe a great deal to Naveen Kishore for his continuous support, to Bishan Samaddar for his meticulous work as an editor, and, of course, to Parnal Chirmuley, who, again, did a wonderful job as a translator, with so much patience and attention to detail and to the intricacies of language.

I am honoured by W. J. T. Mitchell's friendship, and cannot thank him enough for contributing such a thoughtful and insightful preface. My brother, Andreas Emmerling-Skala, has always willingly and patiently served as my sounding board for ideas and their value; for this book he again supported me by voicing his critical concerns. I would like to thank Shuddhabrata Sengupta for his encouragement to write this book in its early stages, and for his ongoing friendship. Jan Völker and Wolf Iro supported me with ideas and leads, Andreas Urs Sommer provided cues and encouragement, and, last but not least, Achim Wesjohann, without any hesitation, made available to me literature that would have been inaccessible to me otherwise. I am deeply indebted to all of them, and I guess that what these acknowledgements and the book demonstrate is the fact that the *idios* doesn't lead far; we are what we are by being with others, through others.

# Bibliography


Ackerknecht, Erwin H. *Kurze Geschichte der Psychiatrie*. Stuttgart: Enke, 1967.

Adorno, Theodor W. *Ästhetische Theorie*. Frankfurt am Main: Suhrkamp, 1970.

Adorno, Theodor W. *Minima Moralia*. Frankfurt am Main: Suhrkamp, 1989 [1951].

Agamben, Giorgio. *Die Zeit, die bleibt*. Frankfurt am Main: Suhrkamp, 2006 [2000].

Allen, Jim. *The Skin of Years*. Auckland: Clouds & Michael Lett, 2014.

Anz, Thomas, and Michael Stark (eds). *Expressionismus: Manifeste und Dokumente zur deutschen Literatur 1910–1920*. Stuttgart: Metzler, 1982.

Arendt, Hannah. *On Revolution*. London: Penguin, 1990 [1965].

Arendt, Hannah. *Was ist Politik? Fragmente aus dem Nachlass* (Ursula Ludz ed.). Munich: Piper, 2015.

Aristotle. *Metaphysik: Schriften zur ersten Philosophie* (Franz F. Schwarz trans. and ed.). Stuttgart: Reclam, 1970.

Aristotle. *Nikomachische Ethik* (Franz Dirlmeier trans. and ed.). Stuttgart: Reclam, 1969.

Bachtin, Michail M. *Literatur und Karneval: Zur Romantheorie und Lachkultur*. Frankfurt am Main: Fischer Taschenbuch Verlag, 1990.

Badenberg, Nana. 'Südsee-Insulaner als Kunsttrophäen: Mai 1914: Nolde in Neuguinea, Pechstein in Palau' in Alexander Honold and Klaus R. Scherpe (eds), *Mit Deutschland um die Welt: Eine Kulturgeschichte des Fremden in der Kolonialzeit*. Stuttgart: Metzler, 2004.

Baumeister, Willi. *Das Unbekannte in der Kunst*. Stuttgart: Curt E. Schwab, 1947.

Beck, Hans-Georg. *Das byzantinische Jahrtausend*. Munich: C. H. Beck, 1994.

Beda Venerabilis. *Liber primus homiliarum genuinarum* in *Opera Bedae Venerabilis presbyteri, Anglosaxonis: viri in divinis atque humanis literis exercitatissimi: omnia in octo tomos distincta, prout statim post praefationem suo elencho enumerantur: additum rerum et verborum indice copiosissimo*. Basel: per Ioannem Hervagium, 1563.

Bede the Venerable. *In Evangelium S. Lucae* in *Venerabilis Bedae Anglosaxonis Presbyteri Opera Omnia*, J.-P. Migne (series ed.), *Patrologiae Latina*, vol. 92. Paris: J.-P. Migne, 1862.

Beitin, Andreas, and Eckhart J. Gillen (eds). *Flashes of the Future*. Bonn: Bundeszentrale für politische Bildung, 2018.

Bertrand, Natasha, and Zachary Cohen. 'Hegseth did not inform the White House before he authorized pause on weapon shipments to Ukraine, sources say'. *CNN Politics*, 8 July 2025.

Bessen, Kathrin, Susanne Gaensheimer, Doris Krystof et al. (eds). *museum global: Mikrogeschichten einer ex-zentrischen Moderne*. Cologne: Wienand, 2018.

Betancourt, Michael. *Kritik des digitalen Kapitalismus*. Darmstadt: Wissenschaftliche Buchgesellschaft, 2018 [2016].

Billerbeck, Margarethe (ed.). *Die Kyniker in der modernen Forschung: Aufsätze mit Einführung und Bibliographie* (*Bochumer Studien zur Philosophie* 15). Amsterdam: B. R. Grüner, 1991.

Billerbeck, Margarethe. 'Stoizismus in der römischen Epik neronischer und flavischer Zeit' in Hildegard Temporini and Wolfgang Haase (eds), *Aufstieg und Niedergang der römischen Welt*, vol. 2. Berlin and New York: De Gruyter, 1986.

Binding, Karl, and Alfred Hoche. *Die Freigabe der Vernichtung lebensunwerten Lebens*. Leipzig: Felix Meiner, 1920.

Biser, Eugen. *Nietzsche: Zerstörer oder Erneuerer des Christentums?* Darmstadt: Wissenschaftliche Buchgesellschaft, 2002.

Bleuler, Eugen. *Dementia praecox oder Gruppe der Schizophrenien*. Leipzig and Vienna: Franz Deuticke, 1911.

Bluhm, Harald. 'Dostojewski- und Tolstoi-Rezeption auf dem "semantischen Sonderweg": Kultur und Zivilisation in deutschen Rezeptionsmustern Anfang des 20. Jahrhunderts'. *Politische Vierteljahresschrift* 40(2) (1999): 305–27.

Blumenberg, Hans. 'Ernst Cassirers gedenkend' in *Wirklichkeiten, in denen wir leben*. Stuttgart: Reclam, 1981.

Blumenberg, Hans. 'Nachahmung der Natur—Zur Vorgeschichte der Idee des schöpferischen Menschen' in *Wirklichkeiten, in denen wir leben*. Stuttgart: Reclam, 1981.

Blumenberg, Hans. *Die Legitimität der Neuzeit: Säkularisierung*. Frankfurt am Main: Suhrkamp, 2017 [1966].

Boehm, Omri. *Radikaler Universalismus*. Berlin: Propyläen, 2022.

Bogousslavsky, J., and O. Walusinski. 'Marcel Proust and Paul Sollier: The Involuntary Memory Connection'. *Schweizer Archiv für Neurologie und Psychiatrie* 160(4) (2009): 130–36.

Boime, Albert. 'Portraying Monomaniacs to Service the Alienist's Monomania: Géricault and Georget'. *Oxford Art Journal* 14(1) (1991): 79–91.

Boltanski, Luc, and Ève Chiapello. *Der neue Geist des Kapitalismus*. Cologne: Herbert von Halem, 2018 [1999].

Bonaventura. *Stimulus divini amoris*. Brixen, 1599.

BONIZO SUTRENSIS. *Liber ad amicum sive de persecutione ecclesiae. Patrologiae Latina*, VOL. 150. Paris: J.-P. Migne, 1854.

BOSTRÖM, Antonia. *Messerschmidt and Modernity*. Los Angeles: Getty Publications, 2012.

BOURDIEU, Pierre. *Die feinen Unterschiede: Kritik der gesellschaftlichen Urteilskraft*. Frankfurt am Main: Suhrkamp, 1982 [1979].

BRAUN, Wilhelm. 'Stichwort "Laie"' in Elisabeth Charlotte Welskopf (ed.), *Das Fortleben altgriechischer sozialer Typenbegriffe in der deutschen Sprache*, VOL. 5. Berlin and New York: De Gruyter, 1981.

BRENNECKE, Detlef. *Die Nietzsche-Bildnisse Edvard Munchs*. Berlin: Spitz, 2000.

BRÖCKLING, Ulrich. *Das unternehmerische Selbst: Soziologie einer Subjektivierungsform*. Frankfurt am Main: Suhrkamp, 2007.

BROWN, G. Spencer. *Laws of Form*. New York: Julian Press, 1972.

BÜCHER, Karl. *Arbeit und Rhythmus*. Leipzig and Berlin: Teubner, 1909.

BULTMANN, Rudolf. *Geschichte und Eschatologie*. Tübingen: Mohr [Paul Siebeck], 1964.

BURCKHARDT, Jacob. *Griechische Kulturgeschichte*, VOL. 1. Stuttgart: Spemann, 1939.

BUSCH, Gräfe et al. (eds). *Encyclopädisches Wörterbuch der medicinischen Wissenschaften*, VOL. 17. Berlin: Veit et Comp., 1838.

BUSCH, Werner. 'Goya und die Tradition des "capriccio"' in Max Imdahl (ed.), *Wie eindeutig ist ein Kunstwerk?*. Cologne: DuMont, 1986.

BUSCH, Werner. *Die notwendige Arabeske: Wirklichkeitsaneignung und Stilisierung in der Kunst des 19. Jahrhunderts*. Berlin: Mann, 1985.

BUSINE, Laurent, and Inge Jàdi. *La beauté insensée*. Heidelberg: Wunderhorn, 1996.

CAMUS, Albert. *Der Fremde*. Hamburg: Rowohlt, 1961 [1940].

CAMUS, Albert. *Der Mythos des Sisyphos*. Hamburg: Rowohlt, 2000 [1942].

CARTLEDGE, Paul. *Ancient Greek Political Thought in Practice*. Cambridge: Cambridge University Press, 2009.

CASTEL, Robert. *Die psychiatrische Ordnung: Das goldene Zeitalter des Irrenwesens*. Frankfurt am Main: Suhrkamp, 1979 [1976].

CHAKRABARTY, Dipesh. 'A Small History of Subaltern Studies' in *Habitations of Modernity*. Chicago: University of Chicago Press, 2002.

CHAKRABARTY, Dipesh. 'Subaltern Histories and Post-Enlightenment Rationalism' in *Habitations of Modernity*. Chicago: University of Chicago Press, 2002.

CHATEAUBRIAND. *Essai sur les révolutions*. Paris: Ladvocat, 1826.

CHATTOPADHYAYA, Debiprasad. *Lokayata: A Study in Ancient Indian Materialism*. Mumbai: People's Publishing House, 1959.

CHRYSOSTOM, John. 'Second homily on the incomprehensibility of God' in Philipp Mayer (ed.), *Des Johannes Chrysostomos ausgewählte Homilien*. Nuremberg: Stein, 1830.

CIORAN, E. M. 'Der böse Demiurg' in *Die verfehlte Schöpfung*. Frankfurt am Main: Suhrkamp, 1979.

CLARKE, W. K. Lowther. *The Lausiac History of Palladius*. New York: Macmillan, 1918.

CLARUS, Julius. Review of Guillaume Ferrus, *Mémoire sur le goître et le crétinisme*. *Schmidt's Jahrbücher der in- und ausländischen gesammten Medizin*, VOL. 69 (1851): 274–76.

CLÉMENT, C. *Géricault*. Paris: J. Claye, 1879.

CLEMENZ, Manfred. *Der Mythos Paul Klee*. Cologne, Weimar and Vienna: Böhlau, 2016.

COLLINS, R. Douglas. *Charles Meryon: A Life*. London: Garton & Co., 1999.

CRACRAFT, James. *The Church Reform of Peter the Great*. London: Macmillan, 1971.

D'SOUZA, Aruna. 'I think your work looks a lot like Dubuffet: Dubuffet and America, 1946–1962'. *Oxford Art Journal* 20(2) (1997): 61–73.

DAPENA-TRETTER, Antonia. 'Jean Dubuffet & Art Brut: The Creation of an Avant-Garde Identity'. *Platform* 11 (Autumn 2017): 12–33.

DAVEY, James George. 'On Moral Idiocy'. *Association Medical Journal* (September 1856): 783–86.

DEINHARDT, Heinrich, and Jan Daniel Georgens. *Die Heilpädagogik mit besonderer Berücksichtigung der Idiotie und der Idiotenanstalten*, VOL. 1. Leipzig: Fleischer, 1861.

DELACAMPAGNE, Christian. *Outsiders*. Paris: Mengès, 1989.

DETERING, Heinrich. *Der Antichrist und der Gekreuzigte: Friedrich Nietzsches letzte Texte*. Göttingen: Wallstein, 2010.

*Die Dreigefährtenlegende des Heiligen Franziskus: Die Brüder Leo, Rufin und Angelus erzählen vom Anfang seines Ordens* (Engelbert Grau and Sophronius Clasen eds). Werl [Westfalen]: Dietrich-Coelde-Verlag, 1972.

*Die Tödliche Doris, Kino/Cinema*. Berlin: Martin Schmitz Verlag, 2004.

DIEDERICHSEN, Diedrich. 'Genies und ihre Geräusche: Deutscher Punk und Neue Welle 1978–1982' in Mathilde Weh and Leonhard Emmerling (eds), *Geniale Dilletanten*. Ostfildern: Hatje Cantz, 2015.

DIEDERICHSEN, Diedrich. *Der lange Weg nach Mitte: The Sound und die Stadt*. Cologne: Kiepenheuer & Witsch, 1999.

DIEFENBACH, Natalia. *Die Vita der hl. Xenia von St. Petersburg* (*Journal für Religionskultur* 223). Frankfurt am Main: Goethe-Universität, 2016.

DILLENBERGER, Jane Daggett. *The Religious Art of Andy Warhol*. New York: Continuum, 1998.

DINZELBACHER, Peter. *Deutsche und niederländische Mystik des Mittelalters*. Berlin and Boston: De Gruyter, 2012.

DONIGER, Wendy. *Against Dharma: Dissent in the Ancient Indian Sciences of Sex and Politics*. New Haven and London: Yale University Press, 2018.

DREHER, Thomas. *Performance Art nach 1945: Aktionstheater und Intermedia*. Munich: Fink, 2001.

DREWS-SYLLA, Gesine. *Moskauer Aktionismus*. Munich: Fink, 2011.

DUBUFFET, Jean, and Claude Simon. *Correspondance, 1970–1984*. Paris: L'Échoppe, 1994.

DUBUFFET, Jean. 'Anmerkungen für die Schöngeister' in *Malerei in der Falle, Schriften Band I* (Andreas Franzke ed., Elke Kronjäger trans.). Bern and Berlin: Gachnang und Springer, 1991.

DUBUFFET, Jean. 'L'art brut préféré aux arts culturels' in *Prospectus et tous les écrits suivants*, VOL. 1 (Hubert Damisch ed.). Paris: Gallimard, 1967.

DUBUFFET, Jean. 'Tables paysagées, paysages du mental, pierres philosophiques' in *Prospectus et tous les écrits suivants*, VOL. 2 (Hubert Damisch ed.). Paris: Gallimard, 1967.

DUBUFFET, Jean. *Asphyxiante Culture*. Paris: Les Éditions de Minuit, 1986.

DUBUFFET, Jean. *Bâtons rompus*. Paris: Les Éditions de Minuit, 1986.

DUBUFFET, Jean. *Die Autorität des Vorhandenen: Autobiographisches, Schriften Band IV* (Andreas Franzke ed., Elke Kronjäger trans.). Bern and Berlin: Gachnang und Springer, 1994.

DUBUFFET, Jean. *Lettres à J.B.: Lettres à Jacques Berne (1946–1985)* (Jacques Berne ed.). Paris: Hermann, 1991.

DUBUFFET, Jean. *Prospectus et tous les écrits suivants* (Hubert Damisch ed.). VOLS 1–2. Paris. Gallimard, 1967; VOLS 3–4 Paris: Gallimard, 1995.

DUBUFFET, Jean. *Wider eine vergiftende Kultur, Schriften Band II* (Andreas Franzke ed., Elke Kronjäger trans.). Bern and Berlin: Gachnang und Springer, 1992.

DUCHESNE, E. (ed. and trans.). *Le Stoglav, ou les cent chapitres*. Paris: É. Champion, 1920.

EDWARDS, Elizabeth. 'The Banal Profound and the Profoundly Banal' in Dorota Glowacka and Stephen Boos (eds), *Between Ethics and Aesthetics: Crossing the Boundaries*. Albany, NY: State University of New York Press, 2002.

EINSTEIN, Carl. 'George Grosz' in *Bebuquin und die Dilettanten des Wunders*. Leipzig and Weimar: Reclam, 1989.

EINSTEIN, Carl. 'Rudolf Schlichter' in *Bebuquin und die Dilettanten des Wunders*. Leipzig and Weimar: Reclam, 1989.

ELIADE, Mircea. *Schamanismus und archaische Ekstasetechnik*. Frankfurt am Main: Suhrkamp, 1975 [1951].

ELLIS, W. C. *Traité de l'aliénation mentale, ou de la nature, des causes, des symptômes et du traitement de la folie*. Paris: Rouvier, 1840.

*Encyclopédie, ou dictionnaire raisonné des sciences, des arts et des métiers*, VOL. 8. Neufchâtel: Société typographique de Neuchâtel, 1765.

ENGELHARDT, Dietrich von. 'Der Kranke und seine Krankheit in der Literatur' in Heinrich Schipperges, Wilhelm Doerr and Hans Schaefer (eds), *Der Mensch in seiner Eigenwelt: Anthropologische Grundfragen einer theoretischen Pathologie*. Heidelberg: Springer, 1991.

ERASMUS, Desiderius. *Encomium moriae; sive, Declamatio in laudem stultitiae*. Tilburg: Tilburg University Press, 2019.

ERASMUS, Desiderius. *Lob der Torheit* (Heinrich Hersch trans.). Hamburg: Nikol, 2019.

ERMOLDUS NIGELLUS. *Carmen elegiacum de rebus gestis Ludovici Pii, ab anno 781 usque ad annum 826. Patrologiae Latina*, VOL. 105. Paris: J.-P. Migne, 1851.

ERMOLDUS NIGELLUS. *Lobgedicht auf Kaiser Ludwig, und Elegien an König Pippin* (Theodor Gottfried Martin Pfund trans.), Georg Heinrich Pertz, Jacob Grimm, Karl Lachmann, Leopold Ranke and Karl Ritter (eds), *Die Geschichtschreiber der deutschen Vorzeit in deutscher Bearbeitung*, VOL. 3. Berlin: Wilhelm Besser, 1856.

ESQUIROL, Jean Étienne. *Des maladies mentales*, VOL. 2. Brussels: Maloine, 1838.

ESQUIROL, Jean Étienne. *Rapport statistique sur la maison royale de Charenton pendant les années 1826, 1827 et 1828*. Paris, 1829.

'Fastnacht / Karneval' in Christoph Auffarth, Jutta Bernard and Hubert Mohr (eds), *Metzler Lexikon Religion*, VOL. 1. Stuttgart and Weimar: J. B. Metzler, 2005.

FEDOTOV, Georgi. *The Russian Religious Mind*, VOL. 1. Cambridge, MA: Harvard University Press, 1966 [1946].

FEILCHENFELDT, Walter Maria. *Vincent van Gogh & Paul Cassirer, Berlin: The Reception of van Gogh in Germany from 1901 to 1914* (*Cahier Vincent* 2). Zwolle: Waanders, 1988.

FELD, Helmut. *Franziskus von Assisi, der Zweite Christus*. Mainz: Philipp von Zabern, 1991.

FELD, Helmut. *Franziskus von Assisi*. Munich: C. H. Beck, 2013 [2001].

FETSCHER, Iring. *Rousseaus politische Philosophie*. Frankfurt am Main: Suhrkamp, 1988 [1960].

FICHTE, Johann Gottlieb. *Grundlage des Naturrechts nach Principien der Wissenschaftslehre*. Leipzig: Gabler, 1796.

FICINO, Marsilio. *Opera Omnia*. Lyon: Antonium Vincentium, 1557.

FILMER, Robert. *Patriarcha and Other Political Works* (Peter Laslett ed.). Oxford: Basil Blackwell, 1949.

FLECKNER, Uwe. *Carl Einstein und sein Jahrhundert*. Berlin: De Gruyter, 2006.

FLÖGEL, Karl Friedrich. *Geschichte des Grotesk-Komischen*. Leipzig: Werl, 1862.

FLORES, Dan. *Coyote America*. New York: Basic Books, 2016.

FONTENELLE, Bernard Le Bovier de. 'Réflexions sur la poétique' in *Œuvres complètes*, VOL. 3. Paris, 1790.

FORBES, John, and John Conolly (eds). *The British and Foreign Medical Review*, VOL. 1. London, 1836.

FORST, Rainer. 'Die Rechtfertigung des Fortschritts und der Fortschritt der Rechtfertigung' in *Die noumenale Republik*. Berlin: Suhrkamp, 2021.

FOSTER, Hal. 'Viennese Actionism' in Hal Foster, Rosalind Krauss et al. (eds), *Art Since 1900*. London: Thames & Hudson, 2004.

FOUCAULT, Michel. *Psychologie und Geisteskrankheit*. Frankfurt am Main: Suhrkamp, 1968 [1954].

FOUCAULT, Michel. *Wahnsinn und Gesellschaft*. Frankfurt am Main: Suhrkamp, 1973 [1961].

FOUNDATIONAL ECONOMY COLLECTIVE. *Foundational Economy: The Infrastructure of Everyday Life*. Manchester: Manchester University Press, 2019.

FRANCIS OF ASSISI. *Sämtliche Schriften: Lateinisch/Deutsch* (Dieter Berg ed.). Stuttgart: Reclam, 2014.

FRANZ, Norbert P. *Stalker: Protokoll des Films in der Original- und der deutschen Synchronfassung*. Potsdam: Universitätsverlag Potsdam, 2009.

FRIEDMAN, Ken (ed.). *The Fluxus Reader*. Chichester: Academy Editions, 1998.

FRIMMEL, Sandra. *Kunsturteile: Gerichtsprozesse gegen Kunst, Künstler und Kuratoren in Russland nach der Perestroika*. Cologne, Weimar and Vienna: Böhlau, 2015.

FULDA, Bernhard, and Aya Soika. *Max Pechstein: The Rise and Fall of Expressionism*. Berlin and Boston: De Gruyter, 2012.

GADAMER, Hans-Georg. *Wahrheit und Methode: Grundzüge einer philosophischen Hermeneutik*. Tübingen: Mohr Siebeck, 1999 [1960].

GALENZA, Ronald, and Heinz Havemeister (eds). *Wir wollen immer artig sein . . . Punk, New Wave, HipHop und Independent-Szene in der DDR von 1980 bis 1990*. Berlin: Schwarzkopf & Schwarzkopf, 1999.

GALLIANO, Luciana. *Japan Fluxus*. Lanham, MD: Lexington Books, 2019.

GEHLEN, Arnold. *Der Mensch: Seine Natur und seine Stellung in der Welt*. Frankfurt am Main: Klostermann, 2016 [1940].

GEHLEN, Arnold. *Moral und Hypermoral: Eine pluralistische Ethik*. Frankfurt am Main: Klostermann, 1969.

GELDZAHLER, Henry. 'Andy Warhol: A Memoir' in *Making It New*. New York: Harcourt Brace Jovanovich, 1994.

GERCKE, Hans, and Inge Jarchov (eds). *Die Prinzhornsammlung*. Königstein/Taunus: Athenäum, 1980.

GILL HOLLAND, J. (ed. and trans.). *Edvard Munch: We Are Flames Which Pour Out of the Earth: The Private Journals of Edvard Munch*. Madison: University of Wisconsin Press, 2005.

GIRAUD, Cédric. 'La réception des *Meditationes sive orationes* d'Anselme de Cantorbéry à l'âge de l'imprimé'. *Revue de l'histoire des religions* 230(4) (2013): 75–102.

GIRSHOVICH, Josef. *Weltbürgertum, Kosmopolitismus und der Leviathan*. Berlin: Berliner Wissenschaftsverlag, 2015.

GOETHE. *Goethes Werke*, VOL. 43. Stuttgart and Tübingen: Cotta, 1833.

GOODMAN, Nelson. 'Kunst und Erkenntnis' in Dieter Henrich and Wolfgang Iser (eds), *Theorien der Kunst*. Frankfurt am Main: Suhrkamp, 1992.

GORMAN, Paul. *The Life & Times of Malcolm McLaren*. London: Little, Brown, 2020.

GRABISCH, Joseph (ed.). *Unterredungen mit Epiktet*. Jena and Leipzig: Diederichs, 1905.

GRÄSSER, Erich. *Das Problem der Parusieverzögerung in den synoptischen Evangelien und in der Apostelgeschichte*. Berlin and New York: De Gruyter, 1977.

GREENBERG, Clement. 'Review of Exhibitions of Jean Dubuffet and Jackson Pollock'. *The Nation* 164(5) (1 February 1947): 137.

GROSZ, George. *Ein kleines Ja und ein großes Nein*. Hamburg: Rowohlt, 1955.

GRÖTZ, Thomas. 'Meine Herrschaften, Ihre eingerosteten Ohren klingen: Überlegungen zur Ursonate von Kurt Schwitters' in Gerhard Schaub (ed.), *Kurt Schwitters 'Bürger und Idiot': Beiträge zu Werk und Wirkung eines Gesamtkünstlers*. Berlin: Fannei & Walz, 1993.

GROYS, Boris. *Über das Neue*. Frankfurt am Main: Fischer, 2002 [1992].

GRUNDMANN, Herbert. *Religiöse Bewegungen im Mittelalter*. Darmstadt: Georg Olms, 1977 [1935].

GSTACH, Johannes. *Kretinismus und Blödsinn: Zur fachlich-wissenschaftlichen Entdeckung und Konstruktion von Phänomenen der geistig-mentalen Auffälligkeit zwischen 1780 und 1900 und deren Bedeutung für Fragen der Erziehung und Behandlung*. Bad Heilbrunn: Julius Klinkhardt, 2015.

GUALTERUS TARVANENSIS. *Vita Caroli Boni, comitis Flandriae. Patrologiae Latina*, VOL. 166. Paris: J.-P. Migne, 1854.

GUILES, Fred Lawrence. *Loner at the Ball: The Life of Andy Warhol*. Nashville: Turner Publishing, 2022 [1989].

HABERMAS, Jürgen. 'Individuierung durch Vergesellschaftung' in *Nachmetaphysisches Denken*. Frankfurt am Main: Suhrkamp, 1988.

HABERMAS, Jürgen. *Moralbewusstsein und kommunikatives Handeln*. Frankfurt am Main: Suhrkamp, 1983.

HABERMAS, Jürgen. *Theorie des kommunikativen Handelns*, VOL. 2. Frankfurt am Main: Suhrkamp, 1987.

HAHN, Johannes (ed.). *Spätantiker Staat und religiöser Konflikt*, *Millennium-Studien*, VOL. 34. Berlin and New York: De Gruyter, 2011.

HANSEN, Mogens Herman. *Die athenische Demokratie im Zeitalter des Demosthenes*. Berlin: De Gruyter, 1995.

HARDICK, Lothar. 'Franziskus, die Wende der mittelalterlichen Frömmigkeit'. *Wissenschaft und Weisheit* 13(3) (1950): 129–41.

HARNACK, Adolf von. *Marcion*: *Das Evangelium vom fremden Gott*. Leipzig: J. C. Hinrichs, 1924.

HAUPT, Herman. *Die religiösen Sekten in Franken vor der Reformation*. Würzburg: A. Stuber's Buch- und Kunsthandlung, 1882.

HAYEK, Friedrich August von. *The Constitution of Liberty*. Chicago: University of Chicago Press, 2011 [1960].

HEGEL, Georg Wilhelm Friedrich. *Phänomenologie des Geistes* (Eva Moldenhauer and Karl Markus Michel eds). Frankfurt am Main: Suhrkamp, 1989 [1807].

HEIDEGGER, Martin. 'Platons Lehre von der Wahrheit' in *Wegmarken*. Frankfurt am Main: Vittorio Klostermann, 1978 [1967].

HEIDEGGER, Martin. 'Vom Ursprung des Kunstwerks' (1935/36) in *Holzwege*, GA 5. Frankfurt am Main: Vittorio Klostermann, 1977.

HEIDEGGER, Martin. *Sein und Zeit*. GA 2. Frankfurt am Main: Vittorio Klostermann, 1977.

HEIDEGGER, Martin. *Vom Wesen der Wahrheit*. GA 34. Frankfurt am Main: Vittorio Klostermann, 1988.

HEYER, F. *Beiträge zur Lösung der Idiotenfrage*. Berlin: August Hirschwald, 1861.

HOBAN, Phoebe. *Basquiat*: *A Quick Killing in Art*. New York: Viking, 1998.

HOFFMANN, David Marc. 'Idiot' in Henning Ottmann (ed.), *Nietzsche-Handbuch*. Stuttgart: Metzler, 2011.

HOFFMANN, Eberhard. *Das Konverseninstitut des Cisterzienserordens in seinem Ursprung und seiner Organisation*. Freiburg: Universitäts-Buchhandlung Otto Gschwend, 1905.

HOFSTRA, Jan. *Leontius von Neapolis und Symeon der Heilige Narr*. Drachten: Karmel, 2008.

HUBACH, Hanns. *Matthias Grünewald: Der Aschaffenburger Maria-Schnee-Altar: Geschichte—Rekonstruktion—Ikonographie*. Mainz: Gesellschaft für Mittelrheinische Kirchengeschichte, 1996.

HUELSENBECK, Richard. 'DADA und Existentialismus' in Willy Verkauf (ed.), *Dada: Monographie einer Bewegung*. London: St Martin's Press, 1975.

HUELSENBECK, Richard. 'Einleitung' in *Dada Almanach*. Berlin: Erich Reiss, 1920.

HUELSENBECK, Richard. 'Was wollte der Expressionismus?' in *Dada Almanach*. Berlin: Erich Reiss, 1920.

HUELSENBECK, Richard. *Der Idiot*. 1916. Repr. in Karl Riha (ed.), *Dada Zürich: Texte, Manifeste, Dokumente*. Stuttgart: Reclam, 2015 [1992].

HUELSENBECK, Richard. *En avant Dada*. Hanover: Paul Steegemann, 1921.

HUNT, Priscilla, and Svitlana Kobets (eds). *Holy Foolishness in Russia: New Perspectives*. New York: Slavica Publishers, 2011.

HUSSERL, Edmund. 'Philosophie als strenge Wissenschaft' (1911) in *Vorträge und Aufsätze, Husserliana*, VOL. 25. Dordrecht: Kluwer Academic Publishers, 1987.

*I fioretti*, CHAP. 8 (Luigi Luzzatti ed.). Milan: Istituto Editoriale Italiano, 1917.

IRO, Wolf. *Tertium non datur: Ideologie und Soziologie in Isaak Babels Konarmija*. Frankfurt am Main: Peter Lang, 2001.

ISENBERG, Vincent. *Die Stigmatisierung des Franziskus von Assisi*. Bochum: Ruhr-Universität Bochum, 2019.

IVANOV, Sergey A. *Holy Fools in Byzantium and Beyond*. Oxford: Oxford University Press, 2006.

JÁDI, Inge, and Bettina Brand-Claussen (eds). *August Natterer: Die Beweiskraft der Bilder. Leben und Werk. Deutungen*. Heidelberg: Wunderhorn, 2001.

JANTZEN, Wolfgang. 'Die Entwicklung des Begriffs Imbezillität als Beispiel des gesellschaftlichen Umgangs mit Minderheiten: Ein Beitrag zur Ideengeschichte von Psychiatrie und Behindertenpädagogik'. Lecture delivered at the Arbeitstagung der Dozenten für Sonderpädagogik in deutschsprachigen Ländern, Essen, October 1980.

JANZARIK, Werner. 'Der bildnerische Ausdruck seelischen Krankseins als projektiver Stimulus' in Hans Gercke and Inge Jarchov (eds), *Die Prinzhornsammlung*. Königstein/Taunus: Athenäum, 1980.

JARRY, Alfred. *König Ubu: Drama in fünf Aufzügen* (Ulrich Bossier trans. and ed.). Ditzingen: Reclam, 1996.

JARRY, Alfred. *Œuvres complètes*, VOL. 1. Paris, 1976.

JASPERS, Karl. *Strindberg und Van Gogh*. Berlin: Springer, 1926.

JOANNES DE GARLANDIA. *Opus synonymorum. Patrologiae Latina*, VOL. 150. Paris: J.-P. Migne, 1854.

JONZE, Tim. '$5.2m for a duct-taped banana: Has the buyer of Maurizio Cattelan's artwork slipped up?'. *The Guardian*, 21 November 2024.

JULIAN, Emperor. *The Works of the Emperor Julian*, VOL. 2 (Wilmer Cave Wright trans.). London and New York: Heinemann and Macmillan, 1913.

KAFKA, Franz. 'Ein Hungerkünstler' in *Das Urteil und andere Erzählungen*. Hamburg: Fischer, 1954.

KANT, Immanuel. *Die Metaphysik der Sitten*. Frankfurt am Main: Suhrkamp, 2014 [1797].

KAUFMANN, Christian. 'Dada liest ethnologische Quellen: Vom Wissen um fremde Kunstwelten zum poetischen Verstehen' in Ralf Burmeister, Michaela Oberhofer and Esther Tisa Francini (eds), *dada Afrika*. Zurich: Scheidegger & Spiess, 2016.

KERSCHER, Julia. *Autodidaktik, Artistik, Medienpraktik: Erscheinungsweisen des Dilettantismus bei Karl Philipp Moritz, Carl Einstein und Thomas Bernhard*. Göttingen: Vandenhoeck & Ruprecht, 2016.

KIEFER, Klaus H., and Liliane Meffre (eds). *Carl Einstein, Briefwechsel 1904–1940*. Berlin: Metzler, 2020.

KLEIN, Peter K. 'Insanity and the Sublime: Aesthetics and Theories of Mental Illness in Goya's *Yard with Lunatics* and Related Works'. *Journal of the Warburg and Courtauld Institutes* 61 (1998): 198–252.

KOMJAKOV, A. S. (Chomjakov). *L'église latine et le Protestantisme au point de vue de l'Église d'Orient*. Lausanne and Vevey: B. Benda, 1872.

KRAEPELIN, Emil. *Psychiatrie: Ein Lehrbuch für Studierende und Ärzte*, VOL. 4. Leipzig: Johann Ambrosius Barth, 1915.

KRAFFT-EBING, Heinrich. *Lehrbuch der Psychiatrie auf klinischer Grundlage*. Stuttgart: Ferdinand Enke, 1890.

KRIEGER, Gerhard. 'Conceptus Absolutus: Zu einer Parallele zwischen Wilhelm von Ockham, Johannes Buridan und Nicolaus Cusanus' in João Maria André, Gerhard Krieger and Harald Schwaetzer (eds), *Intellektus und Imaginatio: Aspekte geistiger und sinnlicher Erkenntnis bei Nicolaus Cusanus*. Amsterdam: Grüner, 2006.

KRIS, Ernst, and Otto Kurz. *Die Legende vom Künstler*. Frankfurt am Main: Suhrkamp, 1980 [1934].

KRUEGER, Derek. *Symeon the Holy Fool: Leontius's Life and the Late Antique City*. Berkeley: University of California Press, 1996.

KUES, Nikolaus von. *Idiota de mente / Der Laie über den Geist* (Renate Steiger ed.). *Schriften des Nikolaus von Kues in deutscher Übersetzung*, Heft 21; lateinisch-deutsche Parallelausgabe. Hamburg: Meiner, 1995.

KUNSTHALLE NÜRNBERG (ed.). *Gustav Metzger: Ein Schnitt entlang der Zeit*. Nuremberg: Verlag für moderne Kunst, 1999.

LACH, Friedhelm (ed.). *Kurt Schwitters: Das literarische Werk*, VOL. 5, *Manifeste und kritische Prosa*. Cologne: DuMont, 1981.

LACHMANN, Renate. 'Der Narr in Christo und seine Verstellungspraxis' in Peter von Moos (ed.), *Unverwechselbarkeit: Persönliche Identität und Identifikation in der vormodernen Gesellschaft*. Cologne: Vandenhoeck & Ruprecht, 2004.

LANDAUER, Matthew. 'The "Idiōtēs" and the Tyrant: Two Faces of Unaccountability in Democratic Athens'. *Political Theory* 42(2) (2014): 139–66.

LAU, Thomas. *Die heiligen Narren: Punk 1976–1986*. Berlin and New York: De Gruyter, 1992.

LEINKAUF, Thomas. 'Der Begriff des Schönen im 15. und 16. Jahrhundert' in Heinrich F. Plett (ed.), *Renaissance-Poetik / Renaissance Poetics*. Berlin and New York: De Gruyter, 1994.

LEONTIUS OF NEAPOLIS. 'Vita S. Symeonis Sali confessoris' in *Hesychii Hierosolymitani presbyteri, Olympiodori Alexandrini, Leontii Neapoleos in Cypro episcopi, opera omnia, Patrologia Graeca*, VOL. 93. Paris: J.-P. Migne, 1865.

LÉVI-STRAUSS, Claude. *La pensée sauvage*. Paris: Plon, 1962.

LÉVI-STRAUSS, Claude. *Le cru et le cuit* (*Mythologiques*, VOL. 1). Paris: Plon, 1964.

LEWIS, Flora. 'An Outraged Artist Battles With Renault'. *New York Times*, 6 May 1977.

LICHACEV, Dmitrij S., and Aleksandr M. Pancenko. *Die Lachwelt des alten Russland*. Munich: Fink, 1991.

LIPP, Florian. *Punk und New Wave im letzten Jahrzehnt der DDR*. Münster: Waxmann, 2021.

LITTLE, Allan. 'How Trump is using the "Madman Theory" to try to change the world (and it's working)'. *BBC News*, 6 July 2025.

LOCKE, John. *An Essay concerning Human Understanding*. Philadelphia, 1854 [1690].

LOERS, Veit. 'Als die Bilder laufen lernten: Zur Ästhetik des frühen Wiener Aktionismus' in Dieter Schwarz and Veit Loers (eds), *Von der Aktionsmalerei zum Aktionismus: Wien 1960–1965*. Klagenfurt: Ritter, 1988.

LOICK, Daniel. *Der Missbrauch des Eigentums*. Berlin: August, 2016.

LOMMATZSCH, Erhard. *Gautier de Coincy als Satiriker*. Halle: Niemeyer, 1913.

LUCK, Georg. *Die Weisheit der Hunde: Texte der antiken Kyniker in deutscher Übersetzung mit Erläuterungen*. Stuttgart: Alfred Kröner, 1997.

LUDWIG, Claudia. *Sonderformen byzantinischer Hagiographie und ihr literarisches Vorbild: Untersuchungen zu den Viten des Äsop, des Philaretos, des Symeon Salos und des Andreas Salos* (*Berliner Byzantinistische Studien* 3). Frankfurt am Main: Peter Lang, 1997.

LUHMANN, Niklas. 'Funktion und Kausalität' in *Soziologische Aufklärung I*. Opladen: Westdeutscher Verlag, 1991 [1970].

LUHMANN, Niklas. 'Über Natur' in *Gesellschaftsstruktur und Semantik*, VOL. 4. Frankfurt am Main: Suhrkamp, 2016 [1999].

LUHMANN, Niklas. *Die Moral der Gesellschaft*. Frankfurt am Main: Suhrkamp, 2008.

LUHMANN, Niklas. *Legitimation durch Verfahren*. Frankfurt am Main: Suhrkamp, 1983 [1969].

'Mäeutik' in Christian Schäfer (ed.), *Platon-Lexikon: Begriffswörterbuch zu Platon und der platonischen Tradition*. Darmstadt: Wissenschaftliche Buchgesellschaft, 2013.

MAISSEN, Thomas. *Von der Legende zum Modell: Das Interesse für die französische Vergangenheit während der italienischen Renaissance*. Basel: Helbing und Lichtenhahn, 1994.

MALSON, Lucien. *Wolf Children and the Problem of Human Nature: With the Complete Text of The Wild Boy of Aveyron by Jean-Marc-Gaspard Itard*. New York: Monthly Review Press, 1972.

MARC, Charles Chrétien Henry. *Die Geisteskrankheiten in Beziehung zur Rechtspflege* (Karl Wilhelm Ideler trans.). Berlin: Voß, 1844.

MARSILIUS OF PADUA. *Defensor pacis*. Hanover: Hahnsche Buchhandlung, 1932 [1324].

MARX, Karl, and Friedrich Engels. 'Manifest der Kommunistischen Partei' in *Werke*, VOL. 4. Berlin: Dietz, 1959.

MARX, Karl. 'Ökonomisch-philosophische Manuskripte' (1844) in *Marx-Engels-Werke*, VOL. 40. Berlin: Karl Dietz, 2012.

MASOLINI, Serena. 'Crossing Lines between the Mediterranean, the Ecclesia Specularis, and the Self: Notes on a Recent Book on Opicino de Canistris'. *Mediterranea: International Journal for the Transfer of Knowledge* 4 (2019): 255–66.

MATEJOVSKI, Dirk. *Das Motiv des Wahnsinns in der mittelalterlichen Dichtung*. Frankfurt am Main: Suhrkamp, 1996.

MATURANA, Humberto R. *Erkennen: Die Organisation und Verkörperung von Wirklichkeit. Ausgewählte Arbeiten zur biologischen Epistemologie*. Braunschweig and Wiesbaden: Vieweg, 1982.

MAY, Gerhard. *Creatio ex Nihilo: The Doctrine of 'Creation out of Nothing' in Early Christian Thought* (A. S. Worrall trans.). London and New York: Bloomsbury, 2004 [1978].

MCGRADE, Arthur Stephen. *The Political Thought of William of Ockham: Personal and Institutional Principles, Cambridge Studies in Medieval Life and Thought*, 3rd SER., VOL. 7. Cambridge: Cambridge University Press, 1974.

MCNEIL, Legs, and Gillian McCain. *Please Kill Me: The Uncensored Oral History of Punk*. New York: Penguin, 1996.

MEIER-GRAEFE, Julius. *Vincent van Gogh*. Munich: Piper, 1910 [1904].

MEIJER, Gerrit. 'Punk ist erledigt' in Jacek Slaski, *Gespräche mit Genialen Dilletanten.* Berlin: Merve, 2018.

MEINDL, Matthias. *Reiner Aktivismus? Politisierung von Literatur und Kunst im postsowjetischen Russland.* Cologne and Weimar: Böhlau, 2018.

MENDELSSOHN, Moses. 'Rhapsodie, oder die Zusätze zu den Briefen über die Empfindungen' in *Ästhetische Schriften* (Anne Pollok ed.). Hamburg: Meiner, 2006.

MENNEKES, Friedhelm. *Christus Denken / Thinking Christ.* Cologne: Katholisches Bildungswerk, 1996.

METZLER, Irina. 'Intellectual disability in the European Middle Ages' in Michael Rembis, Catherine J. Kudlick and Kim E. Nielsen (eds), *The Oxford Handbook of Disability History.* Oxford: Oxford University Press, 2018.

METZLER, Irina. *Fools and Idiots? Intellectual Disability in the Middle Ages.* Manchester: Manchester University Press, 2016.

MICHAUD, Dominique Allan. *Gaston Chaissac: Puzzle pour un homme seul.* Paris: Gallimard, 1974.

MICHELS, Georg B. *At War with the Church: Religious Dissent in Seventeenth-Century Russia.* Stanford, CA: Stanford University Press, 1999.

MILLER, Margaret. 'Géricault's Paintings of the Insane'. *Journal of the Warburg and Courtauld Institutes* 4 (1941–42): 151–63.

MIRABEAU, Victor de Riquetti, marquis de. *L'ami des hommes, ou Traité de la population,* VOL. 1. Avignon, 1758 [1756].

MOELLER VAN DEN BRUCK, Arthur. 'Tschandala-Nietzsche' in *Die moderne Literatur.* Berlin and Leipzig: Schuster & Loeffler, 1902.

MOELLER, Magdalena M. (ed.). *40 Jahre Brücke-Museum Berlin: Dokumente der Künstlergruppe Brücke.* Munich: Hirmer, 2007.

MOELLER, Magdalena M. *Wege des Expressionismus.* Munich: Hirmer, 1985.

MOREAU DE TOURS. *La psychologie morbide dans ses rapports avec la philosophie de l'histoire, ou De l'influence des névropathies sur le dynamisme intellectuel.* Paris: Victor Masson, 1859.

MOREHEAD, Allison. 'The Musée de la folie'. *Journal of the History of Collections* 23(1) (2011): 101–26.

MOREL, P. Gall (ed.). *Offenbarungen der Schwester Mechthild von Magdeburg oder Das fliessende Licht der Gottheit.* Darmstadt: Wissenschaftliche Buchgesellschaft, 1980.

MORGENTHALER, Walter. *Ein Geisteskranker als Künstler.* Bern, 1921; Berlin: Medusa, 1985.

MOSER, Dietz-Rüdiger. *Fastnacht—Fasching—Karneval: Das Fest der 'verkehrten Welt'.* Graz: Edition Kaleidoskop, 1986.

MOSER, J. M. (ed.). *Lucius Annaeus Seneca des Philosophen Werke*, VOL. 5: *Von den Wohltaten*. Stuttgart: Metzler, 1829.

MÜHL, Otto. 'Die Materialaktion' in Dieter Schwarz and Veit Loers (eds), *Von der Aktionsmalerei zum Aktionismus: Wien 1960–1965*. Klagenfurt: Ritter, 1988.

MÜNCH, Christian. 'Narrenfreiheit um Gottes Willen: Vom Freiheitsstreben der "jurodiwye" in Russland'. *Geist und Leben: Zeitschrift für christliche Spiritualität* 92(1) (2019): 45–54.

MÜNCH, Christian. *In Christo närrisches Russland: Zur Deutung und Bedeutung des jurodstvo im kulturellen und sozialen Kontext des Zarenreiches*. Göttingen: Vandenhoeck & Ruprecht, 2017.

'Nadeschda Tolokonnikowa: Pussy Riot bei Videodreh durch russische Polizei gestoppt'. *Die Zeit*, 10 February 2020.

NAKAMURA, David. '"Maybe I have a natural ability": Trump plays medical expert on coronavirus by second-guessing the professionals'. *The Washington Post*, 6 March 2020.

NASSE, Friedrich. 'Ueber die Benennung und vorläufige Eintheilung des psychischen Krankseyns' in *Zeitschrift für psychische Aerzte*. Leipzig, 1818.

NEMES, Balázs J., and Elke Senne (eds). *Mechthild von Magdeburg, Lux Divinitatis: Das liecht der gotheit. Der lateinisch-frühneuhochdeutsche Überlieferungszweig des 'Fließenden Lichts der Gottheit'*. Berlin and Boston: De Gruyter, 2019.

NIEHUES-PRÖBSTING, Heinrich. 'Der "kurze Weg": Nietzsches "Cynismus"'. *Archiv für Begriffsgeschichte* 24(1) (1980): 103–22.

NIEHUES-PRÖBSTING, Heinrich. *Der Kynismus des Diogenes und der Begriff des Zynismus*. Frankfurt am Main: Suhrkamp, 2016 [1979].

NIETZSCHE, Friedrich. 'Über Wahrheit und Lüge im außermoralischen Sinn' in *Kritische Studienausgabe*, 2nd EDN (KSA), VOL. 1 (Giorgio Colli and Mazzino Montinari eds). Munich: Deutscher Taschenbuch Verlag, 1988.

NIETZSCHE, Friedrich. 'Vom Nutzen und Nachteil der Historie für das Leben' in *Kritische Studienausgabe*, 2nd EDN (KSA), VOL. 1 (Giorgio Colli and Mazzino Montinari eds). Munich: Deutscher Taschenbuch Verlag, 1988.

NIETZSCHE, Friedrich. *Also sprach Zarathustra* in *Kritische Studienausgabe*, 2nd EDN (KSA), VOL. 4 (Giorgio Colli and Mazzino Montinari eds). Munich: Deutscher Taschenbuch Verlag, 1988.

NIETZSCHE, Friedrich. *Der Antichrist* in *Kritische Studienausgabe*, 2nd EDN (KSA), VOL. 6 (Giorgio Colli and Mazzino Montinari eds). Berlin: De Gruyter, 1988.

NIETZSCHE, Friedrich. *Götzen-Dämmerung* in *Kritische Studienausgabe*, 2nd EDN (KSA), VOL. 6 (Giorgio Colli and Mazzino Montinari eds). Munich: Deutscher Taschenbuch Verlag, 1988.

NIETZSCHE, Friedrich. *Jenseits von Gut und Böse* in *Kritische Studienausgabe*, 2nd EDN (KSA), VOL. 5 (Giorgio Colli and Mazzino Montinari eds). Berlin: De Gruyter, 1988.

NIETZSCHE, Friedrich. *Nachgelassene Fragmente 1887–1889* in *Kritische Studienausgabe*, 2nd EDN (KSA), VOL. 13 (Giorgio Colli and Mazzino Montinari eds). Berlin: De Gruyter, 1988.

NITSCH, Hermann. *Orgien Mysterien Theater*. Salzburg: Residenz, 1990.

NOLDE, Emil. *Mein Leben*. Cologne: DuMont, 1996 [1976].

NUWER, Rachel. 'Andy Warhol Probably Never Said His Celebrated "Fifteen Minutes of Fame" Line'. *Smithsonian Magazine*, 8 April 2014.

OCKHAM, William of. *Opus nonaginta dierum* (1332–34) in H. S. Offler (ed.), *Opera politica*, VOLS 1–2. Manchester: Manchester University Press, 1940–63.

OFFERMANN, Ulrich. *Christus—Wahrheit des Denkens: Eine Untersuchung zur Schrift 'De docta ignorantia' des Nikolaus von Kues, Beiträge zur Geschichte und Theologie des Mittelalters*, VOL. 33. Münster: Aschendorff, 1991.

OSBORN, Max. *Max Pechstein*. Berlin: Propyläen, 1922.

OTTO, Beatrice K. *Fools Are Everywhere: The Court Jester around the World*. Chicago, IL: University of Chicago Press, 2001.

OTTOVORDEMGENTSCHENFELDE, Natalia. *Jurodstvo: Eine Studie zur Phänomenologie und Typologie des Narren in Christo; Jurodivyj in der postmodernen russischen Kunst: Venedikt Erofeev 'Die Reise nach Petuški', Aktionismus Aleksandr Breners und Oleg Kuliks*. Frankfurt am Main: Peter Lang, 2004.

OVERBECK, Franz. *Über die Christlichkeit unserer heutigen Theologie: Streit- und Friedensschrift*. Leipzig: E. W. Fritzsch, 1873.

PANOFSKY, Erwin. *Hercules am Scheidewege*. Leipzig: Teubner, 1930.

PAREL, Anthony. 'Aquinas' Theory of Property' in Anthony Parel and Thomas Flanagan (eds), *Theories of Property from Aristotle to the Present*. Ontario: Wilfred Laurier University Press, 1979.

PARISER, Eli. *The Filter Bubble: What the Internet Is Hiding from You*. New York: Penguin, 2011.

PASCAL, Pierre. *Avvakum et les débuts du raskol*. Paris and The Hague: Mouton, 1969 [1938].

PEIRY, Lucienne. *Art Brut: The Origins of Outsider Art*. New York: Rizzoli, 2006.

PERRY, Ralph Barton. *General Theory of Value*. London: Longmans, Green and Co., 1926.

PINEL, Philippe. *Traité médico-philosophique sur l'aliénation mentale*. Paris: Brosson, 1809 [1801].

Pinthus, Kurt. *Menschheitsdämmerung: Symphonie jüngster Dichtung*. Berlin: Rowohlt, 1919.

Piron, Sylvain. *Dialectique du monstre: Enquête sur Opicino de Canistris*. Brussels: Zones sensibles, 2015.

Plato. *Ion* (Friedrich Daniel Ernst Schleiermacher trans.). Berlin: Akademie Verlag, 1984.

Poskett, James. *Materials of the Mind: Phrenology, Race, and the Global History of Science, 1815–1920*. Chicago, IL: University of Chicago Press, 2019.

Pösl, Friedrich. *Leben und goldene Sprüche des seligen Aegidius von Assisi, Laienbruders und dritten Jüngers des hl. Franciscus: Nach den Bollandisten bearbeitet von Friedrich Pösl*. Passau: Ambrosi, 1847.

Prideaux, Sue. *Edvard Munch: Behind the Scream*. New Haven and London: Yale University Press, 2005.

Prinzhorn, Hans. *Bildnerei der Geisteskranken*. Heidelberg: Springer, 1922.

Pross, Christian, with Sonja Schweitzer and Julia Wagner. *Wir wollten ins Verderben rennen: Die Geschichte des Sozialistischen Patientenkollektivs Heidelberg*. Cologne: Psychiatrie Verlag, 2016.

Raaflaub, Kurt A., Josiah Ober and Robert W. Wallace (eds). *Origins of Democracy in Ancient Greece*. Berkeley: University of California Press, 2007.

Rancière, Jacques. *Der Hass der Demokratie*. Berlin: Matthes & Seitz, 2011.

Rasch, Johannes. *Neu Kalendar*. Rorschach am Bodensee: Leonhart Straub, 1590.

Raschzok, Klaus. 'Joseph Beuys (1921–1986) und die Figur des Schamanen im künstlerischen Werk' in Haringke Fugmann (ed.), *Schamanismus als Herausforderung*. Norderstedt: Books on Demand, 2015.

Rau, Jan Philipp, and Sebastian Stier. 'Die Echokammer-Hypothese: Fragmentierung der Öffentlichkeit und politische Polarisierung durch digitale Medien?' *Zeitschrift für Vergleichende Politikwissenschaft* 13(3) (2019): 399–417.

Recki, Birgit. *Ästhetik der Sitten*. Frankfurt am Main: Klostermann, 2001.

Reckwitz, Andreas. *Die Gesellschaft der Singularitäten*. Berlin: Suhrkamp, 2017.

Reinartz, Burkhard. 'Joseph Beuys und die Religion: Auferstehen muss der Mensch schon selbst'. *Deutschlandfunk*, 25 December 2019.

Reynolds, Joshua. *Discourses on Art* (Edward Gilpin Johnson ed.). Chicago: A. C. McClurg, 1891.

Reynolds, Simon. *Rip It Up and Start Again: Postpunk 1978–1984*. New York: Penguin, 2005.

Reynolds, Simon. *Totally Wired: Postpunk Interviews and Overviews*. New York: Catapult, 2010.

Richter, Hans. *Dada: Kunst und Anti-Kunst*. Cologne: DuMont, 1964.

RIHA, Karl (ed.). *Dada Zürich: Texte, Manifeste, Dokumente.* Stuttgart: Reclam, 2015 [1992].

RIHA, Karl (ed.). *Johannes Baader, Oberdada: Vierzehn Briefe Christi und andere Druckschriften.* Frankfurt am Main: Peter Lang, 1988.

RÖSKE, Thomas. 'Außerhalb der Kontinuität historischer Prozesse: Wilhelm Fraenger und Hans Prinzhorn blicken auf Kunst von Außenseitern' in Susanne Himmelheber and Karl-Ludwig Hoffmann (eds), *Neue Kunst—lebendige Wissenschaft: Wilhelm Fraenger und sein Heidelberger Kreis 1910–1937.* Heidelberg: Kulturamt der Stadt Heidelberg, 2004.

RÖSKE, Thomas. 'Hans Prinzhorn—ein "Sinnender" in der Weimarer Republik' in Thomas Fuchs et al. (eds), *Wahn, Welt, Bild: Die Prinzhorn-Sammlung. Beiträge zur Museumsöffnung, Heidelberger Jahrbücher* 46 (2002).

RÖSKE, Thomas. 'Inspiration, unerreichtes Vorbild' in Thomas Röske (ed.), *Surrealism and Madness.* Heidelberg: Wunderhorn, 2009.

ROUSSEAU, Jean-Jacques. *Abhandlung von dem Ursprung der Ungleichheit unter den Menschen* (Ursula Goldmann ed.). Weimar: Böhlaus Nachfolger, 2000 [1765].

ROUX, Guy, and Muriel Laharie. *Art et Folie au Moyen Âge: Aventures et Énigmes d'Opicinus de Canistris (1296–1351?).* Paris: Le Léopard d'Or, 1997.

RUBIN, William S. 'Primitivism' in *20th Century Art: Affinity of the Tribal and the Modern,* VOL. 1. New York: Museum of Modern Art, 1984.

RUBIN, William S. *Dada and Surrealist Art.* New York: Harry N. Abrams, 1969.

RUCH, Martin. *Franz Karl Bühler.* Offenburg: Museum im Ritterhaus, 1993.

RUDOLPH, Kurt. *Die Gnosis: Wesen und Geschichte einer spätantiken Religion.* Göttingen: Vandenhoeck & Ruprecht, 1994.

RUH, Kurt. 'Beginenmystik: Hadewjich, Mechthild von Magdeburg, Margarete Porete' in *Kleine Schriften,* VOL. 2. Berlin and New York: De Gruyter, 1984.

RUH, Kurt. 'Zur Grundlegung einer Geschichte der franziskanischen Mystik' in *Kleine Schriften,* VOL. 2. Berlin and New York: De Gruyter, 1984.

RYBKA, Heinrich. *Elias von Cortona.* Leipzig: Naumann, 1874.

SABATIER, Paul (ed.). *Actus Beati Francisci et Sociorum Eius.* Paris: Librairie Fischbacher, 1902.

SABBATINI, Marco. 'The Pathos of Holy Foolishness in the Leningrad Underground' in Priscilla Hunt and Svitlana Kobets (eds), *Holy Foolishness in Russia: New Perspectives.* New York: Slavica Publishers, 2011.

SAEGERT, C. W. *Ueber die Heilung des Blödsinns auf intellectuellem Wege.* Berlin: Self-published, 1846.

SAGERT, Dietrich. 'Tarkowskijs Gottesnarren'. *forum* 259 (September 2006).

Sailer, Johann Michael (ed.). *Das Buch von der Nachfolgung Christi*. Sulzbach: Seidel, 1845.

Salomon, Richard G. *Opicinus de Canistris: Weltbild und Bekenntnisse eines Avignonesischen Klerikers des 14. Jahrhunderts*. 2 vols. London: Warburg Institute, 1936; repr. Lichtenstein: Kraus Reprint, 1969.

Sander, Jochen. *Hugo van der Goes: Stilentwicklung und Chronologie*. Mainz: von Zabern, 1992.

Saward, John. *Perfect Fools*. New York: Oxford University Press, 1980.

Scaliger, Julius Caesar. *Poetices libri septem*. Critical edition by August Buck. Stuttgart: Friedrich Frommann, 1964.

Schaffer, Karl. 'Beiträge zur Nosographie und Histopathologie der amaurotisch-paralytischen Idiotieformen'. *Archiv für Psychiatrie* 42 (1906): 127–60.

Schäffler, August. 'Böhm, Hans' in *Allgemeine Deutsche Biographie*, vol. 3. Leipzig: Duncker & Humblot, 1876.

Schaub, Gerhard (ed.). *Kurt Schwitters 'Bürger und Idiot': Beiträge zu Werk und Wirkung eines Gesamtkünstlers*. Berlin: Fannei & Walz, 1993.

Scheidegger, Gabriele. *Endzeit: Russland am Ende des 17. Jahrhunderts*. Bern: Peter Lang, 1999.

Scheler, Max. *Die Stellung des Menschen im Kosmos*. Munich: Nymphenburger Verlagshandlung, 1947.

Schellmann, Jörg. *Joseph Beuys: The Multiples*. Munich: Schellmann, 1992.

Schiller, Friedrich. 'Über das Pathetische' in *Sämtliche Werke*, vol. 5 (Gerhard Fricke and Herbert G. Göpfert eds). Munich: Hanser, 1989.

Schlageter, Johannes. 'Rundbrief des Bruders Elias zum Tod des St. Franziskus' in Dieter Berg, Leonhard Lehmann and Johannes-Baptist Freyer (eds), *Franziskus-Quellen: Die Schriften des heiligen Franziskus, Lebensbeschreibungen, Chroniken und Zeugnisse über ihn und seinen Orden*. Kevelaer: Butzon & Bercker, 2009.

Schmidt, Gunnar. *Klavierzerstörungen in Kunst und Popkultur*. Berlin: Reimer, 2013.

Schmuhl, Hans-Walter. *Rassenhygiene, Nationalsozialismus, Euthanasie: Von der Verhütung zur Vernichtung 'lebensunwerten' Lebens, 1890–1945*. Göttingen: Vandenhoeck & Ruprecht, 1987.

Schneede, Marina, and Uwe M. Schneede. *Vor der Zeit: Carl Fredrik Hill und Ernst Josephson*. Berlin: Fröhlich & Kaufmann, 1984.

Schneid, Rebecca. 'Trump Speaks Out After Using Term Widely Considered to Be Antisemitic: "Never Heard That"'. *TIME*, 5 July 2025.

Schneider, Ulrich Johannes. 'Foucault und die Aufklärung'. *Das Achtzehnte Jahrhundert* 23(1) (1999): 13–25.

SCHREINER, Karl. 'Zisterziensisches Mönchtum und soziale Umwelt: Wirtschaftlicher und sozialer Strukturwandel in hoch- und spätmittelalterlichen Zisterzienserkonventen' in Kaspar Elm (ed.), *Die Zisterzienser: Ordensleben zwischen Ideal und Wirklichkeit, Ergänzungsband*. Cologne: Rheinland-Verlag, 1982.

SCHULZ, Hans. *Deutsches Wörterbuch*. Strasbourg: Institut für Deutsche Sprache, 1901.

SCHWARZ, Dieter, and Veit Loers (eds). *Von der Aktionsmalerei zum Aktionismus: Wien 1960–1965*. Klagenfurt: Ritter, 1988.

SCHWEBEL, Horst. *Glaubwürdig: Fünf Gespräche über heutige Kunst und Religion*. Munich: Kaiser, 1979.

SÉGUIN, Édouard. *Die Idiotie und ihre Behandlung nach physiologischer Methode* (S. Krenberger trans.). Vienna: Graeser, 1912.

SHAHAN, Cyrus. *Punk Rock and German Crisis: Adaptation and Resistance after 1977*. New York: Springer, 2013.

SHTYRKOV, Sergei. 'The Unmerry Widow: The Blessed Kseniia of Petersburg in Hagiography and Hymnography' in Priscilla Hunt and Svitlana Kobets (eds), *Holy Foolishness in Russia: New Perspectives*. New York: Slavica Publishers, 2011.

SIMMEL, Georg. *Philosophie des Geldes*. Berlin: Suhrkamp, 2001 [1900].

SIMON, Marie. 'Stichwort "Idiot"' in Elisabeth Charlotte Welskopf (ed.), *Das Fortleben altgriechischer sozialer Typenbegriffe in der deutschen Sprache*, VOL. 5. Berlin and New York: De Gruyter, 1981.

SLOTERDIJK, Peter. *Kritik der zynischen Vernunft*, VOL. 1. Frankfurt am Main: Suhrkamp, 1983.

SOLLIER, Paul. *Psychologie de l'idiot et de l'imbécile*. Paris: Germer Baillière et Cie, 1891.

SOMMER, Andreas Urs. 'Ex oriente lux? Zur vermeintlichen "Ostorientierung" in Nietzsches *Antichrist*'. *Nietzsche-Studien* 28 (1999): 194–214.

SOMMER, Andreas Urs. *Kommentar zu Nietzsches Der Antichrist, Ecce Homo, Dionysos-Dithyramben, Nietzsche contra Wagner*. Berlin and Boston: De Gruyter, 2013.

SOMMER, Andreas Urs. *Nietzsche und die Folgen*. Stuttgart: Metzler, 2017.

*Sozialistisches Patientenkollektiv: SPK—Aus der Krankheit eine Waffe machen. Eine Agitationsschrift des Sozialistischen Patientenkollektivs an der Universität Heidelberg, mit einem Vorwort von Jean-Paul Sartre*. 5th EDN. Heidelberg, 1987.

SPEYER, Wolfgang. *Büchervernichtung und Zensur des Geistes bei Heiden, Juden und Christen*. Stuttgart: Hiersemann, 1981.

SPIES, Werner. 'Art Brut avant 1967'. *Revue de l'Art* 1–2 (1967): 123–26.

SPIES, Werner. 'Genie und Irrsinn: Zur Ausstellung "Art Brut" in Paris'. *Frankfurter Allgemeine Zeitung*, 16 May 1967.

Spies, Werner. *Max Ernst: Collagen. Inventar und Widerspruch.* Cologne: DuMont, 1975.

Staab, Philipp. *Digitaler Kapitalismus: Markt und Herrschaft in der Ökonomie der Unknappheit.* Berlin: Suhrkamp, 2019.

Stanitzek, Georg. 'Dilettantismus' in Klaus Weimar et al. (eds), *Reallexikon der deutschen Literaturwissenschaft*, vol. 1. Berlin and New York: De Gruyter, 2007.

Stanitzek, Georg. 'Über Professionalität'. *Mitteilungen des Deutschen Germanistenverbandes* 43(4) (1996): 18–26.

Stefanescu, Cristian. '"Stoppt den Impf-Genozid!"'. *DW*, 18 May 2021.

Steppich, Christoph J. *Numine afflatur: Die Inspiration des Dichters in der Renaissance.* Wiesbaden: Harrassowitz, 2002.

Stock, Brian. *The Implications of Literacy: Written Language and Models of Interpretation in the Eleventh and Twelfth Centuries.* Princeton, NJ: Princeton University Press, 1983.

Strauss, David Levi. *Between Dog & Wolf: Essays on Art and Politics.* Brooklyn, NY: Autonomedia, 1999 [1990].

Strecker, Christian. *Die liminale Theologie des Paulus: Zugänge zur paulinischen Theologie aus kulturanthropologischer Perspektive.* Göttingen: Vandenhoeck & Ruprecht, 1999.

Strik, W. K. 'Die psychische Erkrankung Vincent van Goghs'. *Der Nervenarzt* 68 (1997): 401–09.

Stroud, Natalie Jomini. 'Selective Exposure Theories'. *Oxford Handbooks Online*, 1 May 2014; updated 11 January 2018.

Stuckey, Charles F. *Andy Warhol: Heaven and Hell Are Just One Breath Away! Late Paintings and Related Works, 1984–1986.* New York: Rizzoli, 1992.

Stuffmann, Margret et al. (eds). *Eugène Delacroix: Spiegelungen: Tasso im Irrenhaus.* Munich: Hirmer, 2008.

Sudhalter, Adrian. *Johannes Baader and the Demise of Wilhelmine Culture: Architecture, Dada and Social Critique, 1875–1920.* New York: New York University Press, 2005.

Susman, Margarete. 'Expressionism'. *Die Masken: Blätter des Düsseldorfer Schauspielhauses* 14 (1918/19): 93–96.

Tarkovskij, Andrej. *Die versiegelte Zeit.* Leipzig and Weimar: Gustav Kiepenheuer, 1989.

Tarkovskij, Andrej. *Opfer* (with images by Sven Nykvist). Munich: Schirmer/Mosel, 1987.

Tertullian. *Apologeticum* in Franciscus Ochler (ed.), *Septimi Florentis Tertulliani.* Halle: Halae Saxonibus, 1849.

TERTULLIAN. *Septimi Florentis Tertulliani*, VOL. 1. E. F. Leopold (ed.). Leipzig: Tauchnitz, 1839.

TERZIĆ, Zoran. *Idiocracy: Denken und Handeln im Zeitalter des Idioten.* Zurich: Diaphanes, 2020.

*The Laws of Manu* (Max Müller ed., G. Bühler trans.), *The Sacred Books of the East*, VOL. 25. Oxford: Oxford University Press, 1886.

THÉVOZ, Michel. *L'art brut.* Geneva: Skira, 1975.

THOMAS OF CELANO. *Vita prima S. Francisci Assisiensis.* Ed. a patribus Collegii S. Bonaventurae. *Analecta Franciscana*, X. Quaracchi, 1926.

THOMAS OF CELANO. *Vita Secunda S. Francisci Assisiensis* in *Legendae S. Francisci Assisiensis saeculis XIII et XIV conscriptae ad codicum fidem recensitae a patribus collegii, Analecta Franciscana* 10. Quaracchi: Typographia Collegii S. Bonaventurae, 1927.

TIERNEY, Brian. *The Idea of Natural Rights.* Grand Rapids, MI: Eerdmans, 2001.

TIMM, Werner. *Edvard Munch: Graphik.* Berlin: Henschelverlag, 1974.

TÖTEBERG, Michael (ed.). *Rainer Werner Fassbinder*, VOL. 2. Reinbek: Rowohlt, 2002.

TRYNKA, Paul. *Iggy Pop: Open Up and Bleed.* London: Sphere, 2009.

TZARA, Tristan. 'Negerlieder' in Richard Huelsenbeck (ed.), *Dada Almanach.* Berlin: Erich Reiss, 1920.

TZARA, Tristan. 'Toto-Vaca' in Richard Huelsenbeck (ed.), *Dada Almanach.* Berlin: Erich Reiss, 1920.

UEBINGER, Johann. 'Der Begriff docta ignorantia in seiner geschichtlichen Entwicklung'. *Archiv für Geschichte der Philosophie* 7(1) (1895).

VAGET, Hans Rudolf. *Dilettantismus und Meisterschaft.* Munich: Fink, 1971.

VANHAGENDOREN, Koen. 'Individuelles religiöses Erleben auf dem Hintergrund stoischer Vorgaben? Aspekte von Epiktets Gottesbild'. *Hermes* 132(4) (2004): 495–510.

VERSPOHL, Franz-Joachim. 'Avantgarde und soziales Bewußtsein: Das Beispiel Joseph Beuys'. *Marburger Jahrbuch für Kunstwissenschaft* 22 (1989): 241–46.

VIETTA, Silvio, and Hans-Georg Kemper. *Expressionismus.* Munich: Fink, 1983.

VIETTA, Silvio. *Die literarische Moderne: Eine problemgeschichtliche Darstellung der deutschsprachigen Literatur von Hölderlin bis Thomas Bernhard.* Stuttgart: Metzler, 1992.

*Vita s. Norberti Auctore Canonico Praemonstratensi Coaevo. Patrologiae Latina*, VOL. 170. Paris: J.-P. Migne, 1854.

VOGL, Joseph. *Capital and Ressentiment: A Short Theory of the Present* (Neil Solomon trans.). Cambridge: Polity, 2023.

VOGL, Joseph. *Kapital und Ressentiment: Eine kurze Theorie der Gegenwart*. Munich: C. H. Beck, 2021.

VOISIN, Félix. *Des causes morales et physiques des maladies mentales et de quelques autres affections nerveuses, telles que l'hystérie, la nymphomanie et le satyriasis*. Paris: J.-B. Baillière, 1826.

VOLMAT, Robert. *L'art psychopathologique*. Paris: Presses Universitaires de France, 1956.

WARHOL, Andy, and Pat Hackett. *Popism*. London: Penguin, 2007 [1980].

WARHOL, Andy. *The Philosophy of Andy Warhol: From A to B and Back Again*. New York: Harcourt Brace Jovanovich, 1975.

WASMUTH, Jennifer. 'Östliche Orthodoxien: Die Verbreitung des 'Sobornost'-Konzepts in den östlichen Kirchen' in *Europäische Geschichte Online* (*EGO*), 16 April 2012.

WEH, Mathilde, and Leonhard Emmerling (eds). *Geniale Dilletanten*. Ostfildern: Hatje Cantz, 2015.

WEIGAND, Rudolf. 'Die Rechtslehre der Scholastik bei den Dekretisten und Dekretalisten' in Rudolf Weigand (ed.), *Ius canonicum*, VOL. 16. Pamplona: Ediciones Universidad de Navarra, 1976.

WESJOHANN, Achim. 'Individualitätsbewußtsein in frühen franziskanischen Quellen? Eine Suche nach Indizien' in Gert Melville and Markus Schürer (eds), *Das Eigene und das Ganze: Zum Individuellen im mittelalterlichen Religiosentum*. Münster: LIT Verlag, 2002.

WESJOHANN, Achim. 'Simplicitas als franziskanisches Ideal und der Prozeß der Institutionalisierung des Minoritenordens' in Gert Melville and Jörg Oberste (eds), *Die Bettelorden im Aufbau: Beiträge zu Institutionalisierungsprozessen im mittelalterlichen Religiosentum*. Münster: LIT Verlag, 1999.

WESJOHANN, Achim. *Mendikantische Gründungserzählungen im 13. und 14. Jahrhundert*. Berlin: LIT, 2012.

WHITTINGTON, Karl. *Body-Worlds: Opicinus de Canistris and the Medieval Cartographic Imagination*. Turnhout: Pontifical Institute of Mediaeval Studies, Department of Publications, 2014.

WICKHAM, Parnel. 'Conceptions of Idiocy in Colonial Massachusetts'. *Journal of Social History* 35(4) (Summer 2002): 935–54.

WIELER, Michael. *Dilettantismus—Wesen und Geschichte; am Beispiel von Heinrich und Thomas Mann*. Würzburg: Königshausen & Neumann, 1995.

WILCKE, Hans-Alwin. *Das Problem eines messianischen Zwischenreichs bei Paulus*. Zurich and Stuttgart: Zwingli, 1967.

WILMES, Daniela. *Wettbewerb um die Moderne*. Berlin: De Gruyter, 2012.

WILSON, Sarah. 'From the Asylum to the Museum: Marginal Art in Paris and New York, 1938–1968' in *Parallel Visions: Modern Artists and Outsider Art*. Los Angeles: Los Angeles County Museum of Art, 1992.

WINCKELMANN, Johann Joachim. *Gedanken über die Nachahmung der griechischen Werke in der Malerey und Bildhauerkunst*. 2nd EDN. Dresden and Leipzig: Walther, 1756.

WINKLER, Gerhard (ed.). *Bernhard von Clairvaux: Sämtliche Werke lateinisch / deutsch*, VOL. 2. Innsbruck: Tyrolia, 1992.

WIRTH, Uwe. 'Strategischer Dilettantismus'. *Neue Rundschau* (2017): 7–25.

WITTKOWER, Margot, and Rudolf Wittkower. *Künstler: Außenseiter der Gesellschaft*. Stuttgart: Klett-Cotta, 1989 [1963].

WODZIŃSKI, Cezary. *Saint Idiot*. Paris: Difference, 2012.

WOODYARD, Kerith M. 'Pussy Riot and the Holy Foolishness of Punk'. *Rock Music Studies* 1(3) (2014): 268–86.

WUNDERLI, Richard. *Peasant Fires: The Drummer of Niklashausen*. Bloomington, IN: Indiana University Press, 1992.

ZEHNDER, Christian. 'Erneuertes Gestern? Zum Verhältnis von Selbstopferung und Rückkehr bei Andrej Tarkovskij' in Norbert P. Franz, *Tarkovskij Klassiker: Beiträge zum Ersten Internationalen Tarkovskij-Symposium an der Universität Potsdam*, VOL. 2. Potsdam: Universitätsverlag Potsdam, 2016.

ŽIŽEK, Slavoj. 'The Thing from Inner Space' in *Angelaki* 4(3) (1999): 221–31.